Criminal Justice and Law

Enforcement Books

of

WEST PUBLISHING COMPANY

St. Paul, Minnesota 55102

November, 1976

CONSTITUTIONAL LAW

Maddex's Cases and Comments on Constitutional Law by James L. Maddex, Professor of Criminal Justice, Georgia State University, 816 pages, 1974. Maddex's 1976 Supplement.

CORRECTIONS

Burns' Corrections—Organization and Administration by Henry Burns, Jr., Professor of Corrections, The Pennsylvania State University, 578 pages, 1975.

Kerper and Kerper's Legal Rights of the Convicted by Hazel B. Kerper, Late Professor of Sociology and Criminal Law, Sam Houston State University and Janeen Kerper, Attorney, San Diego, Calif., 677 pages, 1974.

Killinger and Cromwell's Selected Readings on Corrections in the Community by George G. Killinger, Director of the Institute of Contemporary Corrections, Sam Houston State University and Paul F. Cromwell, Jr., Member, Texas Board of Pardons and Paroles, 579 pages, 1974.

Killinger and Cromwell's Readings on Penology—The Evolution of Corrections in America by George G. Killinger and Paul F. Cromwell, Jr., 426 pages, 1973.

Killinger, Cromwell and Cromwell's Selected Readings on Issues in Corrections and Administration by George G. Killinger, Paul F. Cromwell, Jr. and Bonnie J. Cromwell, San Antonio College, 644 pages, 1976.

Killinger, Kerper and Cromwell's Probation and Parole in the Criminal Justice System by George G. Killinger, Hazel B. Kerper and Paul F. Cromwell, Jr., 374 pages, 1976.

Krantz' The Law of Corrections and Prisoners' Rights in a Nutshell by Sheldon Krantz, Professor of Law and Director, Center for Criminal Justice, Boston University, 353 pages, 1976.

Model Rules and Regulations on Prisoners' Rights and Responsibilities, 212 pages, 1973.

Rubin's Law of Criminal Correction, 2nd Edition (Student Edition) by Sol Rubin, Counsel Emeritus, Council on Crime and Delinquency, 873 pages, 1973.

Rubin's 1977 Supplement.

CORRECTIONS—Continued

Smith & Berlin's Introduction to Probation and Parole by Alexander B. Smith, Professor of Sociology, John Jay College of Criminal Justice and Louis Berlin, Chief, Training Branch, New York City Dept. of Probation, 250 pages, 1975.

CRIMINAL JUSTICE SYSTEM

Kerper's Introduction to the Criminal Justice System by Hazel B. Kerper, 558 pages, 1972.

CRIMINAL LAW

Dix and Sharlot's Cases and Materials on Basic Criminal Law by George E. Dix, Professor of Law, University of Texas and M. Michael Sharlot, Professor of Law, University of Texas, 649 pages, 1974.

Ferguson's Readings on Concepts of Criminal Law by Robert W. Ferguson, Administration of Justice Dept. Director, Saddleback College, 560 pages, 1975.

Gardner and Manian's Principles, Cases and Readings on Criminal Law by Thomas J. Gardner, Professor of Criminal Justice, Milwaukee Area Technical College and Victor Manian, Milwaukee County Judge, 782 pages, 1975.

Heymann and Kenety—The Murder Trial of Wilbur Jackson: A Homicide in the Family by Philip Heymann, Professor of Law, Harvard University and William Kenety, Instructor, Catholic University Law School, 340 pages, 1975.

Loewy's Criminal Law in a Nutshell by Arnold H. Loewy, Professor of Law, University of North Carolina, 302 pages, 1975.

CRIMINAL PROCEDURE

Davis' Police Discretion by Kenneth Culp Davis, Professor of Law, University of Chicago, 176 pages, 1975.

Dowling's Teaching Materials on Criminal Procedure by Jerry L. Dowling, Professor of Criminal Justice, Sam Houston State University, 544 pages, 1976.

Ferdico's Criminal Procedure for the Law Enforcement Officer by John N. Ferdico, Assistant Attorney General, State of Maine, 372 pages, 1975.

Israel and LaFave's Criminal Procedure in a Nutshell, 2nd Edition by Jerold H. Israel and Wayne R. LaFave, 372 pages, 1975.

Johnson's Cases, Materials and Text on The Elements of Criminal Due Process by Phillip E. Johnson, Professor of Law, University of California, Berkeley, 324 pages, 1975.

Kamisar, LaFave and Israel's Cases, Comments and Questions on Basic Criminal Procedure, 4th Edition by Yale Kamisar, Professor of Law, University of Michigan, Wayne R. LaFave, Professor of Law, University of Illinois and Jerold H. Israel, Professor of Law, University of Michigan, 790 pages, 1974. Supplement Annually.

Uviller's the Processes of Criminal Justice—Adjudication by H. Richard Uviller, Professor of Law, Columbia University, 991 pages, 1975.

Uviller's the Processes of Criminal Justice-Investigation by H. Richard Uviller, 744 pages, 1974.

CRIMINAL JUSTICE BOOKS

EVIDENCE

Klein's Law of Evidence for Police by Irving J. Klein, Professor of Law and Police Science, John Jay College of Criminal Justice, 416 pages, 1973.

Rothstein's Evidence in a Nutshell by Paul F. Rothstein, Professor of Law, Georgetown Law Center, 406 pages, 1970.

INTRODUCTION TO LAW ENFORCEMENT

More's The American Police—Text and Readings by Harry W. More, Jr., Professor of Administration of Justice, California State University at San Jose, 278 pages, 1976.

Police Tactics in Hazardous Situations by the San Diego, California Police Department, 228 pages, 1976.

Schwartz and Goldstein's Law Enforcement Handbook for Police by Louis B. Schwartz, Professor of Law, University of Pennsylvania and Stephen R. Goldstein, Professor of Law, University of Pennsylvania, 333 pages, 1970.

Sutor's Police Operations—Tactical Approaches to Crimes in Progress by Captain Andrew Sutor, Philadelphia, Pennsylvania Police Department, 329 pages, 1976.

INVESTIGATION

Markle's Criminal Investigation and Presentation of Evidence by Arnold Markle, The State's Attorney, New Haven County, Connecticut, 344 pages, 1976.

JUVENILE JUSTICE

Faust and Brantingham's Juvenile Justice Philosophy: Readings, Cases and Comments by Frederic L. Faust, Professor of Criminology, Florida State University and Paul J. Brantingham, Professor of Criminology, Florida State University, 600 pages, 1974.

Fox's Law of Juvenile Courts in a Nutshell by Sanford J. Fox, Professor of Law, Boston College, 286 pages, 1971.

Johnson's Introduction to the Juvenile Justice System by Thomas A. Johnson, Professor of Criminal Justice, University of Kentucky, 492 pages, 1975.

Senna and Siegel's Cases and Comments on Juvenile Law by Joseph J. Senna, Professor of Criminal Justice, Northeastern University and Larry J. Siegel, Professor of Criminal Justice, Northeastern University, about 600 pages, 1976.

MANAGEMENT AND SUPERVISION

More's Criminal Justice Management: Text and Readings, by Harry W. More, Jr., about 350 pages, 1977.

Wadman, Paxman and Bentley's Law Enforcement Supervision—A Case Study Approach by Robert C. Wadman, Rio Hondo Community College, Monroe J. Paxman, Brigham Young University and Marion T. Bentley, Utah State University, 224 pages, 1975.

POLICE–COMMUNITY RELATIONS

Cromwell and Keefer's Readings on Police-Community Relations by Paul F. Cromwell, Jr., and George Keefer, Former F.B.I. Agent, 368 pages, 1973.

CRIMINAL JUSTICE BOOKS

PSYCHOLOGY

Parker and Meier's Interpersonal Psychology for Law Enforcement and Corrections by L. Craig Parker, Jr., Criminal Justice Dept. Director, University of New Haven and Robert D. Meier, Professor of Criminal Justice, University of New Haven, 290 pages, 1975.

VICE CONTROL

Ferguson's the Nature of Vice Control in the Administration of Justice by Robert W. Ferguson, 509 pages, 1974.

Uelman and Haddox' Cases, Text and Materials on Drug Abuse Law by Gerald F. Uelman, Professor of Law, Loyola University, Los Angeles and Victor G. Haddox, Professor of Criminology, California State University at Long Beach and Clinical Professor of Psychiatry, Law and Behavioral Sciences, University of Southern California School of Medicine, 564 pages, 1974.

POLICE ADMINISTRATION
AND
MANAGEMENT

By

SAM S. SOURYAL

Professor of Criminal Justice and Police Administration
Institute of Contemporary Corrections
and the Behavioral Sciences

Sam Houston State University

CRIMINAL JUSTICE SERIES

ST. PAUL, MINN.
WEST PUBLISHING CO.
1977

Library of Congress Cataloging in Publication Data

Souryal, Sam, 1930–
  Police administration and management.
  Includes index.
  1. Police administration. 2. Police administration—United States.
I. Title.
HV7935.S68   352'.2   77–5751

ISBN 0–8299–0141–8

Souryal Police Adm. & Man.Cr.Js.

DEDICATION

The mind is the gift of God. Developing it, however, and shaping it over the years is the responsibility of the fortunate man who is gifted with wise friends.

This book is dedicated to two groups:

To those friends who helped shape my mind over the years;

N. C. Wilson
M. T. Ramsi
A. S. Goneid

And to those who graciously put up with it the way it is over the years;

M. F. Souryal
T. O. Souryal
L. S. Souryal

The assistance by David and Audrey Price will forever be remembered.

*

ACKNOWLEDGMENT

I am indebted to Dr. Elliott T. Bowers, President of Sam Houston State University, for his most inspiring leadership which offered me the true academic luxury of freedom, security, pride, and above all, peace of mind.

I am also indebted to Dr. George G. Killinger, Director of the Institute of Contemporary Corrections and the Behavioral Sciences, for his executive talent, his keen understanding of faculty needs, and his personal concern for the enrichment of Criminal Justice research.

I am finally indebted to a group of friends, acquaintances, and staff members at the Institute without whose encouragement and help this book would have never been completed. Dr. Ralph Pease diligently read the whole manuscript and corrected me on many parts of the text. Drs. Rolando del Carmen and Jerry Dowling provided me with many valuable opinions and thoughts. Bonnie Barker assiduously typed the many drafts that made the final copy of this book and never complained.

My appreciation, furthermore, must be expressed for the invaluable help I received from the Institute's most industrious research assistants; Lois Seal, Mary Beck, Jessie Ferguson, and Dianne Key.

I certainly wish each and every one of these individuals a most successful and gratifying future.

*

PREFACE

Academic endeavors have been traditionally divided between students of theory, students of research, and students of administration. Theoreticians philosophize over events, researchers test their validity and reliability, and administrators cope with them.

While each group tends to exaggerate the importance of its endeavor, theory and research separately or in a joint effort cannot directly deal with the problem. Administration can. Throughout human history man survived, conquered his immediate environment, and fared considerably well without a pressing need for theory or research. Man subdued other creatures, won wars against enemies, ruled, and established a stable society primarily by administering brute force and coping with situations as they arbitrarily arose.

This should not, however, be interpreted to mean that theory and research have a useless function. Nothing could be more naive than entertaining such a proposition since the successful handling of any project or operation must necessarily be based on a wise theory tested in advance. But, it also follows that without the need for an administrative act such a "wise theory tested in advance" will have no chance of being considered or applied and thus proving or disproving its usefulness.

Administration, the actual handling of situations and coping with events, must, therefore, be seen as the most significant mover of human life. Through administrative action roads are built, patients are healed, criminals are locked up, lands are cultivated, and goods are produced. While theory and research obviously guide administrative thought and refine management techniques, the obligation to improve the quality of administration in today's complex society is clearly paramount.

In the area of the police, the need to upgrade the quality of administration is even more crucial. Being the most potent institution in charge of regulating social order, maintaining domestic tranquility, and preserving the rights of "the people to be secure in their persons, houses, papers, and effects," adds an awesome responsibility on those entrusted with managing police organizations. Furthermore, the fact that police personnel are charged with making some most sensitive decisions involving the life and death of innocent citizens, without much time to apply a rational theory or a tested hypothesis, clearly signifies the need for professionally trained police administrators. Moreover, it must be stressed that failure to upgrade police practices and management techniques would not only undermine police efficiency and effectiveness but also have an adverse multiplying effect on all human activities, the pursuit of which hinges on safety, privacy, stability, and freedom.

In the first three chapters this book attempts to explain the basic administrative framework of our society in terms of the concept and practice of state, government, and bureaucracy. The location of police organizations is described and related to its immediate environment, the criminal justice system. A historical survey of police administrative thought follows in the discussion of ancient philosophies, medieval applications, and modern practices, with a special elaboration of the British police system.

In chapter four, a discussion of police bureaucracies in America is presented and analyzed.

In chapter five, police administration is further discussed in terms of its two interdependent components: a) police organization, and b) police management. The dynamics of the organizational component is further discussed including the interrelations which control the bureaucratic structure of police administration. This entails a discussion of such elements as hierarchy, authority, power, span of control, delegation of authority, communication, and the trinity.

In chapter six, the need for the other component, management, is discussed followed by a presentation of some administrative models which mold current managerial thought. This includes the major works by Max Weber and his traditional cohorts, Frederick Taylor and his Scientific Management approach, Elton Mayo and his Human Relationists, and finally the modern work by the Behavioralists and their Systems Approach.

In chapter seven, the managerial side of police administration is presented with emphasis on the practical aspects of values, goals, and innovations. A thorough discussion of some managerial problems recently cited in task force reports is presented and a number of innovative police projects are discussed.

The next four chapters are entirely devoted to the study of the major elements of police management:

Police Management of Planning
Police Management of Decision-Making
Police Management of Communications
Police Leadership Management

PREFACE

The last part of the book examines the results of effective police management. It presents an in-depth study of:

Police Professionalism
Suppression of Police Corruption
Increasing Police Productivity Through Organizational Development

A comprehensive index is located at the end of the book to help students' research and facilitate the use of the book.

SAM S. SOURYAL

Huntsville, Texas
April, 1977

*

TABLE OF CONTENTS

TABLE OF CONTENTS

PART THREE.   THE ADMINISTRATION OF POLICE BUREAUCRACIES

PART FOUR.   ELEMENTS OF POLICE MANAGEMENT

TABLE OF CONTENTS

TABLE OF CONTENTS

†

POLICE ADMINISTRATION AND MANAGEMENT

PART ONE

FRAMEWORK OF POLICE ADMINISTRATION

CHAPTER ONE

STATE, GOVERNMENT, AND BUREAUCRACY

Historical Overview

In the beginning, it was God. All creatures were made by Him. And since man has always failed to understand creation and the intriguing secrets of the universe, man has always feared God, revered Him, and honored His commandments. Throughout history man considered God as a "source of being" and as an "absolute sovereign" accountable to none. Such a symbol of ultimate power, man thought, had complete control over the universe. Without the blessings of God, the heavens and earth would crumble and mankind would be destroyed. This view is still held firmly today by a multitude of people around the world who call unexplained phenomena "an act of God".

In subsequent stages of man's socialization, the concept of God as "source of being", "symbol of ultimate power", and "accountable to none" never really left man's mind. He built temples and shrines to perpetuate God's sovereignty and to publicly pay tribute to God's unlimited power. Whether the sovereign then was the God whom we in western societies today worship or some other image (i.e. sun, fire, wind, man, etc.) makes little difference to the study of sovereignty. One pattern, however, seems to have always prevailed: man has continuously chosen submission to godly symbols. Man accepted the theory of an absolute sovereign because it made up for his lack of knowledge and provided him with a real, and in many cases imaginary, sense of security, unity, direction, and satisfaction.

As man congregated and increased in sociality, his knowledge also increased considerably. He discovered more "facts" of life: how to perceive and conceive, to organize and plan, to protect and control, and to cope with his environment. In time, such increase of knowledge and power stimulated man to reconsider his conception of sovereignty in light of these three realizations:

    a.   He discovered his own potential for shaping his own life and destiny.

    b.   He realized the remoteness of an abstract sovereign "somewhere there in the clouds", and the sovereign's inability to directly straighten out man's daily troubles.

    c.   He consequently discovered the need for a "tangible" sovereign capable of providing man's sacred needs from "within" as well as his materialistic needs from "without".

In man's tribal age the concept of sovereignty developed along the lines of a dualistic "sacred-secular" image. Not only did chieftains preside visibly over the tribe representing the power, the kingdom, and the glory of sacred sovereigns, but they also held absolute secular powers over the welfare of their followers. Chieftains not only made the laws, they also enforced the laws and interpreted their applicability. Their authority over their followers was autocratic and they were accountable to no one. Chieftains, elders, and princes viewed their functions as dualistic in nature. Their mission was to fulfill God's purposes by wordly powers. Ancient Egyptian history is replete with cases of rulers who were really believed to have been conceived by Gods and who reigned as half Gods and half humans.[1] Also among the early Jewish communities it was common to have "chief priests and the elders of the people" responsible for defending the faith against acts of blasphemy, sedition, or rebellion.[2]

During the feudal period in medieval Europe, between the ninth and the thirteenth centuries, the concept of "Lord Sovereign and Master" widely flourished. Bishop Stubbs described the nature of sovereignty that prevailed by saying "the Lord judges, as well as defends, his vassal; the vassal does suit as well as service to his Lord." The Bishop further added that in societies where feudal rule had reached its utmost growth the political, financial, judicial and every branch of public administration was "regulated by the same conditions." [3]

During the later part of the medieval age in Europe the dual concept of sovereignty apparently reached its climax. Between the thirteenth and the seventeenth centuries, the sovereignty of the church rapidly emerged as the unifier of the human race. The Pope claimed and received the deference of his subjects. He made kings and re-

1. Aziz S. Atiya, *History of Eastern Christianity*, (Notre Dame, Indiana: University of Notre Dame Press), 1968, p. 20.

2. *Bible*, Matthew 27:47.

3. *Constitutional History of England*, Vol. I, p. 274.

moved them. He mobilized armies and sent them out to fight and win religious wars. Thousands of followers, as well as enemies, were killed by "unsacred swords" for a "sacred cause". The head of the church not only concerned himself with sacred law, but he also made secular prohibitions, and in so doing he controlled the destinies of most European principalities and feudal communities. The Pope was viewed—probably until the flamboyant King Henry VIII rebelled and publicly broke away for marital reasons—as "God's Shadow on Earth". Civil authorities which existed were insignificant as well as ineffective. Sir Humphrey Waldock makes the reference that "even in England the idea of the omnicompetence of the civil power would have been unthinkable." [4]

The age of reformation signaled a significant change of thought in Europe. The question of sovereignty was foremost. Reformation in one of its most important aspects was in fact a rebellion by the loosely-knit principalities against the increasing power of the church. The reformists, abhorred by the disarray of the European states following the great Thirty Years War, declared their determination to replace church sovereignty (the city of God) with civil sovereignty (the nation-state). This new order, while giving the death-blow to the lingering domination of Christendom, gave birth to a new concept of civil sovereignty by nation states. The Peace of Westphalia, which in 1648 brought to an end the Thirty Years War of religion in Papal Europe, marked the acceptance of the new political order of state sovereignty.[5]

CIVIL SOVEREIGNTY

Out of the new order of nation states which developed from the ideas of the Reformation there arose a new version of civil sovereignty. It was based on the concept of nationalism rather than on religious, economic, or historical factors. In contrast to the religiously dominated medieval state, the nation-state, under civil sovereignty, seemed likely to become the final goal of political unity. This idea of a nation-state was strongly supported by Machiavelli's *The Prince* written in 1513, which gave to the world a relentless analysis of the art of government based on the conception of the state as an entirely self-sufficing and amoral entity.

Constitutional Sovereignty

Jean Bodin, the famous French constitutionalist, wrote in 1576 in his *De Republica* that a state without *summa potestas* (ultimate pow-

4. Sir Humphrey Waldock, J. L. Brier-   5. *Ibid.*
    ly, *The Law of Nations*, VI edition,
    (New York: Oxford University Press),
    1963, p. 4.

er) would be like a "ship without a keel." He defined a state as a multitude of families and the possessions that they have in common ruled by a supreme power and by reason. Bodin was convinced that a confusion of uncoordinated independent authorities would be fatal to a state, and that there must be one final source—and not more than one—from which laws proceed. The essential manifestation of civil sovereignty is the state's power to make the laws and to enforce them within its territory.[6]

Bodin, in his analysis of sovereignty, contended that although civil sovereignty represented the possession of ultimate power, like sacred sovereignties, it must be bound by the divine law and the laws of nature and reason common to all nations. Such laws originally stemmed from the previous image of a godly sovereign. Today they are the laws of the constitution or constitutional law. Although Bodin believed in a strong monarchy in France—"strong enough to curb the subversive influences of feudal rivalries and religious intolerance",[7] he envisioned the French sovereignty in his time as neither arbitrary nor irresponsible. Sovereignty, he insisted, must be derived from, and defined by, the *leges imperii* or the laws of the government.

Totalitarian Sovereignty

Hobbes who wrote his *Leviathan* in 1651, believed like Bodin that sovereignty was the essential principle of civil order. He argued that men, in their association, need for security "a common power to keep them in awe and to direct their activities to the common benefit".[8] The person or body in whom this power resides, is the sovereign. Hobbes argued that laws never make the sovereign, and that Law is merely what he commands. Moreover, since the power that is the strongest clearly cannot be limited by anything outside itself, it follows that sovereignty must be absolute and illimitable. Hobbes contended that sovereign power must be "as great as possibly men can be imagined to make it".[9] This theory is what today underlines and characterizes totalitarian rule.

Popular Sovereignty

With the coming of constitutionalism, or limited government, John Locke—and after him Jean Jacques Rousseau—propounded the theory that, after all, the sovereign—whoever he is and however he acquired power—is a fallible human who cannot be trusted with "ultimate power" over all his followers. With the rapidly emerging concepts of freedom, human rights, and equality, Locke espoused the theory that the people as a whole were the sovereign. This view later

---

6. *Ibid.*, pp. 8 and 9.   8. *Leviathan*, Chapter XVII.

7. *Ibid.*   9. *Ibid.*, p. 13.

evolved in the doctrine of Democracy which was used to justify the
American and the French Revolutions and which has influenced the
human quality of life considerabily. As a protest against arbitrary
government and a demand that governments should serve the interests of the governed as well as the governors, the doctrine of popular
sovereignty has had beneficial results. But as a scientific doctrine, it
caused confusion and chaos. Popular sovereignty tried to combine
two contradictory ideas: that of absolute power somewhere in the
state and that of the responsibility of every individual citizen for his
share of power which he holds. While it is possible to locate a sovereign in Bodin's ideal as well as in Hobbes' ideal, it seemed extremely
difficult in democracy to develop a functional power as long as it is
divided between a multitude of unskilled, part-time, power-holders.
Another question raised regarding popular sovereignty is the inability
of such multitudes of power-holders to act except by a majority rule.
Majorities, the argument goes, are, after all, only parts of wholes, and
in pursuance of Locke's initial doctrine of "the people as a whole"
ought not be made all-powerful.

THE STATE

Overview

As mentioned earlier, man's concept of a sovereign God seemed
never to have left his mind. In Western societies where the doctrines
of democracy flourished, individuals and groups realized the need for
a functional personification of sovereignty. The concept of independent states provided the most appropriate framework for democratic
sovereignty.

States emerged primarily out of the collapse of the feudal order
in Europe. At the same time, they developed as a means to break
away from the orthodox, intangible, metaphysical, and unrealistic supremacy of the church. As man grew in knowledge, and as social relations grew in size as well as complexity, communities realized the
need for more effective sovereignty operating from within rather
than from without. Societies, stimulated by the maverick ideas of
freedom, equality, and human dignity, turned to a system of civil sovereignty embedded in the secular concept of state. Groups as well as
individuals also realized the need to sacrifice some of their personal
freedoms in favor of a central, strong, power entrusted to the state
system. The role of the new creation was seen in terms of protector,
regulator, and arbitrator. In an environment consistently threatened
with a breakdown in communal relations, the state system appeared
as the most rational agency capable of achieving man's basic objectives of survival, stability, and progress.

Man, however, whether a member of a democratic society or a
communist society, could not forget his natural fallibility or totally

abandon his sense of submission to a sovereign God. It is therefore most interesting to note the striking resemblance between modern state systems created by man and those originally established by God:

(A) Church systems always maintained a "book" of scriptures and doctrines, whether it was a Bible, Koran, catechism, Torah, etc. The state adopts a "constitution" to embody state doctrines and principles. Constitutions, in a political sense, are given reverence similar to that given to church "books" by worshipers.

(B) Church systems always maintained a set of flags under which "Christian soldiers" united and marched. The state also uses flags to capture the enthusiasm of its citizens and rally their loyalty.

(C) Church systems maintained songs and musical compositions to stimulate the devotion of its followers. The state adopts national anthems and "hymns of the Republic" to be played as frequently as needed as a reminder of national unity and patriotism.

(D) Church systems had "holidays" specified on particular dates when the worshipers celebrated the birthday of the sovereign or other religious occasions. The modern state celebrates "days of independence" and other glorious days of state achievement.

(E) Church systems, since their inception, have developed a hierarchy of ranks, titles, and positions charged with prescribed duties and responsibilities. So has the state in terms of its government echelons, ranks, and levels of seniority.

(F) Church systems required members to pay tithes and offerings to sustain the system. So citizens of the state have to pay taxes. Failure to pay church dues caused the members to lose religious rights; failure to do the same in the state system may cause the citizen to forfeit his civil rights.

Definitions

The concept of state can be viewed and defined from different points of view.

- From a sociological point of view, a state is "a man-made agency of social control consisting of institutions designed to enhance man's social relations".

- From a political point of view, a state is "a concept describing the ultimate source of power that presides over a prescribed territory and exerts control through effective government".

- From a legal point of view, a state is "the concept of a supreme institution equipped with highest authority for the resolution of conflicts and the imposition of sanctions within a specified jurisdiction".

Modern states are sovereign states. They possess the supreme decision-making and decision-enforcing authority over their citizens. They are regarded as the "highest" institution within modern societies. No other institution, whether it be social, economic, or military, can rival the supremacy of the state. In democratic societies, however, states are neither absolutely free from restraint nor do they enjoy absolute freedom of action. State conduct is both conditioned by the prescriptions of international law in her dealings with other states and by consent of the majority of the people forming its population.

In a moral sense, the state in democratic societies is restrained by natural law (*jus naturale*). This consists of universal laws governing human relations in accordance with "moral" standards derived from divine laws. Although it is understood that states "may not cheat, lie, or steal", in contemporary realpolitik no state has managed to get by with less than a fairly long list of crimes more condemnable than "cheating, lying, or stealing". The extent of this, of course, depends on the the nature of the state in question and the kind and intensity of stress its leaders are confronted with at the time.

STATES AND POLICE SYSTEMS

As will become evident in following chapters, the system and conduct of the police are closely related to the character of the state they serve. If one observed an American policeman, a Russian policeman, a French policeman, and an Israeli policeman, one would be surprised as to the many similarities they share. They are all just about the same height, wear similar uniforms, carry similar guns, drive similar fast and marked vehicles, and talk with a similarly high degree of authoritativeness. This, however, does not imply that these policemen would behave alike if faced with the same situation. Sharp differences would be easily and clearly discerned in their basic ideology and mentality. American police organizations, for example, fundamentally differ from Russian police organizations, not only in terms of procedures but also in inherent philosophies. Doctrines such as dignity of man, rule of law, and presumption of innocence are uncommon and unrecognized in the Russian state system. On the other hand, policies like police detention, domestic passports, or surveillance of foreigners are totally alien to the American police.

The purpose of the police in America is to serve society, the embodiment of sovereignty, and protect the individual. The purpose of the Russian police, on the other hand, is to serve the Communist party, the real sovereign, and protect the state. Therefore, while American police tend to apply humanistic police procedures compatible with the democratic concepts of the rule of law, individualism, constitutionalism and civil rights, the Russian counterparts strongly follow a set of repressive procedures espousing the state doctrines of class struggle, centralism, dictatorship of the workers, and elitism of the ruling party. The nature and character of the state in any country provides the socio-political environment of the police and colors their basic mentality, occupational culture, and performance. Members of a society get the police "they deserve". Democratic societies get democratic police, repressive societies get repressive police, militant societies get militant police and benevolent societies get benevolent police.

In the next part, a brief analysis of the most common ideologies adopted by contemporary states will be presented.

TYPES OF STATES

There are four major types of states: democratic, communist, fascist, and socialist.

I. Democratic States

The democratic ideology is constructed around the liberal values of individual freedom, equality, human dignity and brotherhood, constitutionalism, the rule of law and a democratic political process.

Although numerous political philosophers since Aristotle have contributed to the ideology of democracy, the foundations for modern democratic states were fashioned by eighteenth and nineteenth century liberals, who helped to transform them from a theoretical formulation into a working system of government. Major contributors to democratic theory during this period included John Locke, Jean Jacques Rousseau, Thomas Jefferson, Thomas Paine, James Mill, John Stuart Mill and Alexis de Tocqueville. The twentieth century has seen the further transformation of democratic doctrines from their earlier legal forms and principles to a full-blown ideology that postulates the concepts for the "best" society, one noted for individual freedom, social justice, and human dignity.

Democratic theory today encompasses a loose-knit congeries of theories, concepts, and practices, diversely interpreted and pragmatically applied, which reject dogma and accept the belief that the social good can be objectively and scientifically determined. It presupposes that the individual can make social policy judgments and that a free society provides the "best" environment for constructing social institutions and ordering human relations.

Political democracy, as applied in the United States of America, the United Kingdom, west European states and other societies fashioned after this type of system, emphasizes the following major doctrines: [10]

(1) Individualism.

(2) Popular Sovereignty.

(3) Accountability.

(4) Rule of Law.

(5) Constitutionalism.

(6) Majority Rule.

(7) Civil Rights.

Individualism. This concept, underlying democratic state systems, holds that the chief purpose of the state is to foster the well-being of the individual and to permit each person to realize his full capabilities. The doctrine of individualism presumes that the state has an obligation to respect and to protect each person's rights and to safeguard them from deprivation by other individuals or groups.

Popular Sovereignty. This is the basic concept that the people are the ultimate source of all legitimate political authority. The doctrine holds that the people possess supreme authority and that they grant the state and delegate powers to public officials through a social contract or a constitution. The doctrine also implies that the officials created by the state remain accountable to the people who retain the supreme authority.

Accountability. This is a fundamental tenet of the previous doctrine which establishes the ultimate responsibilities of all public officials to the people. Accountability is maintained through elections, constitutional controls, judicial decisions, public opinion surveys and polls, the activities of political parties, public meetings, freedom of speech and press.

Rule of Law. This is a fundamental principle of democratic systems that proclaims the supremacy of law and thus limits public officials in the exercise of their powers. The concept of the rule of law, which basically states that "everybody is subject to the law and no-

10. The discussion of these concepts is based on the presentations and analyses of political systems by William Ebenstein, Jack Plano, and Roy Olton. For more detailed information on the subject see, William Ebenstein, *Today's Isms*, (Englewood Cliffs, N.J.: Prentice-Hall, Inc.), 1970; also see *Great Political Thinkers*, by the same author, (New York: Holt, Rinehart & Winston), 1969; Jack C. Plano and Roy Olton, *The International Relations Dictionary*, (New York: Holt, Rinehart, and Winston, Inc.), 1969; Friedrich Hayek, *The Road to Serfdom*, (Chicago: University of Chicago Press), 1960.

body is above the law", protects the rights of individuals from arbitrary interference by public officials and provides a rule for "governing the governors".

Constitutionalism. This is a concept which simply means "limited government". According to this concept, states must abide with the "basic law of the land" which serves as the mandate given by the people to the state. This concept limits the authority of the "statesmen" to those powers and functions authorized by the people. Public officials violating such mandates would be sanctioned for operating *ultra vires* or without authority.

Majority Rule. This is the principle that decisions in democratic systems should be made by the greater number of citizens in any political unit. If the majority does not rule, power must then be exercised by an elite group selected on other bases, such as wealth, status, or ability. Thus, the system may take the form of absolutism or authoritarian control. Although under the rule the majority possess the right and the power to govern, democratic theory also demands that minority rights be protected and that the minority be permitted to criticize and offer alternatives to the policies of the majority and seek, through the electoral process, to become the majority.

Civil Liberties. These are guarantees built into democratic states through constitutional provisions. Such guarantees provide that individual freedom will not be arbitrarily curtailed. Civil liberties which are usually incorporated in a bill of rights enumerate specific limitations on the authority of public officials. Major rights include freedom of assembly, association, press, religion, speech, and property as well as due process and fair trial for the accused. Increasingly, in the modern era, democratic states have also assumed a positive role in offering protection for the civil rights of individuals and groups in such areas as racial or sexual discrimination, school busing, or the right to register and vote.

II.   Communist States

Communist states champion a communist ideology. Though communist theories today vary considerably from one state to another, the fundamentals of them all (Marxism, Leninism, Stalinism, Maoism, Titoism, Castroism) are basically the same. Communism is an ideology fostered by a revolutionary movement that calls for the elimination of capitalist institutions and the establishment of a collectivist society in which land and capital are socially owned and in which class conflict and the coercive power of the state (idealistically) no longer exist.

Although ancient political philosophies had developed theories embracing diverse forms of communism, "modern" communist doc-

trines were first postulated in the nineteenth century by socialist reformers such as Francois Fourier, Robert Owen, and Claude Saint-Si-
mon.   Dismissing this group along with church communalists as
"Utopians", Karl Marx and Friedrich Engels fashioned a doctrine of
"scientific socialism" that has become the basis of the contemporary
ideology of communism.

The most important contributors to the contemporary ideology
of communism developed by Karl Marx have been Vladimir Lenin, Joseph Stalin, Leon Trotsky, Mao Tse-tung, and Josip Broz Tito, with
Lenin's contributions recognized by communist leaders as the most
formidable.   Marxism-Leninism espouses a philosophy of history that
provides for an inevitable progression from capitalism to socialism as
a result of contradicting economic interests.   This will, according to
communist ideology, produce intensifying class warfare and imperial
and colonial rivalry culminating in the overthrow of the bourgeoisie
by a proletarian revolution.   A socialist program carried out under a
"dictatorship of the proletariat" (working class) will then end class
warfare, eliminate wars, abolish the state, and move the society into
the final, classless, stateless stage of "pure communism".   Needless to
say, that stage of "pure communism" has not been reached yet by
any communist system.   All communist states today are still laboring
their way up, with a reported few a little ahead of the rest.

Communism practiced by contemporary communist states like
the Union of the Soviet Socialist Republics, the People's Republic of
China, the People's Republic of Germany, the People's Republic of
Vietnam, and other self-proclaimed communist states vary, yet all
emphasize the following major doctrines:[11]

(1) Class Struggle.

(2) Democratic Centralism.

(3) Dialectical Materialism.

(4) Dictatorship of the Proletariat.

(5) Historical Inevitability.

(6) Economic Interpretation of History.

(7) New Communist Man.

Class Struggle. The communist doctrines assume that there are
only two social classes in capitalist society, with contradictory interests, and that each will become implacably hostile toward the other.
This will produce the inevitable conflict between the bourgeoisie and
the proletariat.   The only solution, communist theoreticians believe,
will be the victory of the latter.

11.   Jack Plano and Roy Olton, *Ibid.*,
pp. 90–95.

Democratic Centralism. This is the only sanctioned method for making and implementing decisions within communist states. The concept calls for democratic participation through free discussion and deliberation by all communist party members in the development of party policies. Once the decision has been made, however, further dissent and debate are no longer tolerated, and well-disciplined party members are expected to lend their full support to the executing of policies by the centrally directed party organization.

Dialectical Materialism. The dialectical concept was basically developed by Friedrich Hegel to mean a process by which each idea (thesis) produces a contradictory idea (antithesis), leading to a conflict out of which a new higher idea (synthesis) emerges. Karl Marx adapted the dialectical method to his materialistic outlook. Marx used it to describe the process in which the dominant economic classes in each society engage in struggle and produce new economic systems, with the process culminating ultimately in the creation of a pure, classless, stateless society of communism.

Dictatorship of the Proletariat. This is the movement that immediately follows a proletariat revolution. Such a dictatorship is required in communist theory for the realization of the goals of communism. During this period, communist power becomes consolidated, the bourgeoisie are eliminated as a class, and socialism is established. The dictators during this period are the workers who will take over the machinery of the state and use it to reorganize society, convert the means of production from private ownership to public ownership, and provide for the transformation of society into the final stage of pure communism.

Historical Inevitability. This is a philosophy of history by which Marx posited the preordained necessity and scientific certainty for the replacement of capitalism by socialism. Historical inevitability, according to Marx, results from the contradictions embedded in society's mode of production which under capitalism and preceding primitive, slave, and feudal patterns, has pitted the servile class against the exploiting class, producing an automatic movement from one stage to the next. To an orthodox Marxist, free will and individual initiative are insignificant in the broad sweep of the historical development of mankind.

Economic Interpretation of History. It is the assumption that the basic economic system or "mode of production", of a society determines its political, moral, legal, cultural, and religious superstructure and further provides the motivative force that guides the development of society from lower to higher stages. Marx's "materialistic conception of history" starts with the proposition that man's basic activity relates to the production and acquisition of his means of subsistence. The system for the organization, ownership, and operation of these productive forces and for the distribution of food and material wealth produced by them determines the nature of society while class conflict produces the inner motivative power for the society's evolution. The three factors of production identified by Marx as most related to social change and historical development are labor, raw materials, and the instruments of production.

New Communist Man. This is the belief that an evolution of human nature can be produced by changing man's social environment. The concept of the "new communist man" assumes that man's true nature—kindly, cooperative, and gregarious—has been warped by the competitive, hostility-prone, and conflict-ridden social environment of capitalist society. When private property is abolished and capitalist institutions are replaced by socialist design, according to communist theoreticians, man's potential virtue will prevail. This doctrine gives Marxism a religious basis since it postulates that man will, in effect, be reborn and recast in an earlier, uncorrupted form guided by a new and higher set of moral values. This will occur, according to the communist theory, in the final historical stages of pure communism, when man will live in a classless, stateless, cooperative society free from arbitrary restraint and coercive power.

III.   Fascist States

The ideology of fascism is one of the extreme right-wing which fosters an authoritarian society based on rule by an elite headed by a supreme leader or dictator. Fascists usually win power in a state through a coup d'état or during a turbulent revolutionary period when real or imaginary fears of communism lead large numbers of people to accept a radical transformation of democratic institutions to meet the problem of government instability.[12]

Fiscism is often based on an exaggerated adulation of a nation, rejecting individualism and democratic concepts of limited government in favor of a system in which a disciplined people give their full loyalty to an organic, monolithic state. Dissent is eliminated and unity is fostered by terroristic use of secret police, by extensive propaganda programs, by the curtailment of civil liberties, and by a single party monopolization of power. An aura of xenophobia and militarism often pervades a fascist state. Under fascism, private ownership of land and capital is retained, in contradiction with communism, but all private businesses and organizations are regimented and regulated by the state in pursuit of national objectives.

Modern fascism emerged out of the social, economic, and political crises of the interwar period of the 1920's and 1930's. The prototype

---

12.   *Ibid.*, p. 102.

of a fascist state was forged by Benito Mussolini in Italy in the years following his coming to power in 1922 in the wake of an anticommunist reaction to the Bolshevik Revolution in Russia. Fascist regimes were established subsequently by Adolf Hitler and the Nazi party in Germany, by Francisco Franco and the Falangist party in Spain, by Juan Peron and his Peronista party in Argentina, and in several eastern European countries during the 1930's and 1940's. Although fascism as an ideology came into general disrepute following the defeat of the Axis Powers during World War II, neo-fascism has made gains in many of the new developing countries of the world where military juntas have seized power following the breakdown of fledgling democratic institutions.

Fascism, as an ideology, contemptuously rejects the democratic political processes based on freedom, fair elections, and accountability. Its most active hostility is, however, directed against communism and left-wing socialists. Fascist states, like communist states, vary slightly in the application of fascism, but fundamentally emphasize the following basic doctrines: [13]

(1) Anti-communism.

(2) Elitism.

(3) Statism.

(4) Militarism.

(5) Totalitarianism.

Anti-communism. This is the belief and widely applied propaganda technique of fascism which holds that only a united, totalitarian state headed by a supreme leader (dictator) can defeat the threat posed by the conspiratorial tactics of "world communism". The anti-communism of fascism exploits the fear of communism prevalent in all classes in the state, using it both to win and to retain power.

Elitism. This is the principle that state power should be exercised by a hierarchically structured single party, highly centralized and nationalistically inspired, headed by a supreme leader or small group of oligarchs. Fascist elitism rejects democratic processes, constitutional limitations on state power, and pluralism in favor of an organic state in which every group and individual plays the role assigned by the governing elite. Opposition to rule by the elite party (i.e. Fascist party in Italy, the Nazi party in Germany) is not tolerated, and the power of the state is used to destroy all resistance to the regime.

Statism. It is the concept that sovereignty is vested not in the people but in the national state, and that all individuals or groups ex-

13. *Ibid.*, pp. 102–105.

ist only to enhance the power, the prestige, and the well-being of the state. The fascist concept of statism repudiates individualism and exalts the nation as an organic body headed by the supreme leader and nurtured by unity, force, and discipline. Under this doctrine, the state creates *worthy* individuals who realize their destiny only by contributing to the glory of the state. Nationalism, militarism, and —in some fascist states—racism have been used to inculcate values that exist and assumed importance because the state decrees it. The entire ideology of fascism is dominated by dogmas which subject and immerse the individual to the mystical entity of the state.

Militarism. It is the emphasis placed by fascist regimes on military organization and discipline in order to strengthen the single national party and to provide order and security for the state. Under fascism, militaristic values are inculcated in the young at school and in youth organizations. Military heroes are revered, and spectacular ceremonies and parades extolling the virtues of the soldier are used to cultivate an honored role for the military (as the defenders of the nation) and to encourage acceptance of a well-disciplined social order. Adolf Hitler and Benito Mussolini, for example, donned uniforms and became the commanders-in-chief of their nations' forces, thus dominating the military rather than permitting it to dominate them. It is believed such militaristic patterns of fascist states compensate for the mass frustration stemming from the failure of democracies to produce the promised bounty of economic development.

Totalitarianism. This is a fundamental concept of fascism, which has outgrown the mother ideology and probably gained ideological significance comparable to that of fascism itself. Totalitarianism today has been used to connote authoritarian control by the state over individuals and organizations so that all activity is harmonized with the policies and goals of the regime. Not only does totalitarianism seek the imposition of autocratic control over the people of the state, it also strives at effecting some major changes in the peoples' way of thinking, social behavior, and selection of future destiny. Totalitarian tactics include utilizing secret police and terroristic operations, eliminating dissent, denying civil rights, and carrying on an all-pervasive propaganda program through state-controlled media of communication. For fascists, totalitarianism is aimed at uniting the people in a highly integrated nation where the public interest always predominates over private interests. Of the fascist states, Germany achieved the highest level of totalitarian control during the 1930's and 1940's. That single fascist party, inspired by the ideology of totalitarianism, was able to effect serious politico-military dislocations throughout the world, the effects of which will take several centuries to be erased from the human memory.

IV. Socialist States

Contemporary socialist ideologies are ambivalent, controversial, and in many cases, guised. While socialism is viewed by "puritan" democrats as a system of advanced democracy, ardent communists consider it as the "A, B, C's to communism". A socialist ideology may therefore appear to be a middle ground policy which provokes little anger from either camp. In fact, an implicit amount of socialism is always tolerated and quietly incorporated by all contemporary governments, whether they admit it or not.

Socialism is an ideology that rejects individualism, private ownership, and private profit. It favors a system based on economic collectivism, governmental, societal, or industrial-group ownership of the means of production and distribution of goods, and social responsibility.[14]

As mentioned earlier, the doctrines of socialism have varied from those which espouse democratic values to those that call for forms of absolutism and dictatorship. Advocates of socialism have included utopians, Christians and other religious groups, political parties, esoteric sects and societies, welfare proponents, and anarchists. In terms of normative strategy, however, contemporary socialist ideology falls into either of two categories: democratic socialists, who strive to use the political machinery of the state to achieve "true" democracy in terms of extensive welfare programs, suppression of monopoly, economic abundance, and equitable distribution of goods; or Marxian Socialists, who believe that such benevolent achievements can only be accomplished through violence and the destruction of existing capitalist institutions. Socialists are also divided, in terms of objectives, between those who wish to establish a centrally organized system utilizing the power of the state, and the syndicalists, who aim for a decentralized system with groups of workers owning and controlling the means of production.

In the twentieth century, systems of democratic socialist states have been established in some of the most advanced industrial nations, such as Great Britain, Sweden and New Zealand. Such systems emphasize the need and usefulness of extensive state welfare programs and governmental ownership of basic industries and services. On the other hand, several systems of Marxian socialist states have erupted among the developing nations such as in Cuba and Chile and in some parts of the Middle East. Although socialism is often attacked in democratic countries as a system that stifles initiative and encourages inefficiency, many of its supporters today view it as a viable alternative to both capitalism and communism.

14. *Ibid.*, p. 111.

The fundamental doctrines of socialism may be described as:

(1) State Ownership.

(2) State Regulation and Planned Economy.

(3) The Welfare State.

State Ownership. This is an ideology often referred to as "nationalization" or the takeover of the means of production, basic industries, and sensitive services by the state or one of its prescribed public corporations. Through such a practice, socialism aims at achieving the "most good for the most people". One familiar line of reasoning insists that whoever owns or controls a commodity, such as steel, or a service, such as transportation, will wield power over his fellowmen since everybody needs it. Therefore, such power should be a function of public authority. Another argument contends that certain industries (coal, for example) are essential to the functioning of all the rest, so that if it is desirable to plan and coordinate the economy as a whole, ownership of a few "key" concerns facilitates the regulation of the remainder.

Although the concept of state ownership is not novel even among democratic states, the element of novelty, today, consists only in determining whether this or that specific enterprise should be under public or private auspices. Some state-owned undertakings (police forces, post offices, national parks) are long established and therefore universally accepted. Some, such as the generation of electric power, gave rise to classic controversy in the United States two decades ago, but are now less vehemently contested. Others, like the British government's acquisition of the iron and steel industry and nationalization of health services in the 1950's, continue to be centers of controversy.

State Regulation. This entails, instead of state ownership of an enterprise, regulating those who own it privately. Certain regulatory activities by the state, for example, are of such long standing or satisfy such universal demands that they are accepted without question. Rules for safeguarding public health and sanitation fall into this category, as do provisions to ensure the supply of pure food and drugs. Only a generation ago the regulation of railroads and public utilities, in America, by public agencies that fix their rates and prescribe their service, occasioned fierce battles in some states like Wisconsin and California, and also in the halls of Congress. The latest version of state regulation practices in the United States involved the famous wage and price freezes which still provide heavy ammunition today for the ideological war between labor, management and government.

The traditional case in favor of state regulation represents the relationship of the state to the economic process as that of an "effective" umpire or arbitrator laying down and enforcing the rules of a contest in which private individuals and groups are engaged. When the latter are left purely to their own devices, abuses are bound to occur. Monopolies can fleece the public, the weak can be forced to the wall, and the drive for individual gain can imperil the fabric of the democratic society.

Socialism, therefore, as a system in which the state regulates but private persons own and operate, is often extolled for combining the best of both worlds. While private ownership touts efficiency because of the profit motive and the competitive stimulas (except in case of monopoly), state surveillance ensures that service to the public interest will be considered along with profit. State regulated economy is pictured by the leaders of socialism as a "middle way" lying between the aberrations of communism on the left and laissez faire capitalism on the right.

The Welfare State. Besides altering the socio-economic culture by operating businesses of its own and regulating those of others, socialist states intervene directly as an agency of social welfare. Under this heading belong the activities of the state in the areas of education, health, housing, and social security—to mention only a few of the principal areas. The ideological reason advanced in favor of such a role by the state is the undeniable—and eternal—coexistence, within any society, of the community of the rich and that of the poor. Through their wealth, the rich can provide for the medication of their bodies and the education of their minds. They can reside in homes that are spacious and gracious. The poor can do none of these things. To the rich neither unemployment nor age presents a financial crisis since the revenue from the capital they accumulate does not cease to flow. To the poor the expectation of loss of earnings through age or unemployment is an ever-haunting dread. Those to whom the price of private education, private medicine, private housing, and private insurance is prohibitive can obtain such services from one source only, namely, a public agency sponsored by the state.

Irrespective of label, however, socialist welfare states which claim to reduce the gap between the "haves" and the "have nots" by utilizing unequitable programs have entailed the expenditure of large sums of money that can only be obtained by levying more taxes on those who possess a surplus beyond their needs. Thus financed, socialist states obviously exercise a redistribution of national incomes by subordinating private wealth to general welfare and the rules of ethics to those of economics.

CONSTITUTION AND GOVERNMENT

Regardless of their types, states are primarily considered as "symbolic" entities. They represent national sovereignty, legal order, and overwhelming power. A state, consequently, draws the loyalty of the society as a whole which surpasses sectional loyalties to any part of it. The concept of state, therefore, remains a "state of mind" shared by its population by which they can regulate the power relationships within their society and achieve common human objects. While all national duties are carried out in the name of the state, the latter by itself does not possess the practical means for achieving the desired ends. Merely symbolizing "great" doctrines, the state cannot meet man's needs or solve his daily problems. Great doctrines have to be operationalized in a code of procedures, referred to as the constitution, and implemented by an effective forum called government.

CONSTITUTION

Since, as mentioned earlier, the state is a "symbolic" entity, its authority—if it is to be meaningful—must be vested in a "real" instrument of control in the hands of selected public officials capable of carrying it out. But since man cannot totally trust men, and since public officials are "only humans"—unique, fallible, and unpredictable —advanced societies could not rest assured without a legal contract to prohibit abuse of power and to hold public officials accountable before the tribunal of the state. The constitution, therefore, was designed as a set of legal, political, moral, and organizational standards which regulate the behavior of government. It prescribes the basic organs of government and defines their functions, structures, authorities, and powers. The constitution stipulates government relationships with the state it represents and the public it serves. In the United States the Constitution stands at the center of government and represents the chief symbol of state sovereignty. It is the supreme law of the land to be honored, revered, and obeyed at all times.

In an attempt to solve the chronic, age-old problem of making government responsive and responsible (that is, of giving it the authority to serve effectively, but limiting its power to dominate), the distinctive feature of western systems of government is the special role of the Constitution. Whereas the English revolution of the seventeenth century left the parliament supreme, the American revolution resulted in the supremacy of the Constitution. This paramount position of the Constitution was ensured by several measures. Its drafting was undertaken by a special convention of delegates presided over by accepted leaders. The adoption of the finished product was referred to the states, debated, voted on and approved by the representatives of the people. Ever since it went into effect, the Constitution has possessed the unique status that its founders intended it to have. The preamble announces unequivocally that "We the people . . . do ordain and establish this Constitution", thereby affirming that the government is founded upon popular will. While it is the people who created the Constitution, it is the Constitution that created the government and restrains its institutions. All such institutions—the Congress, President, and Supreme Court—as well as the State institutions and their officials—are subordinate to the Constitution of the United States, to laws that conform to it, and to treaties made under its authority. All these together comprise "the supreme law of the land".[15]

Besides being asserted, the supremacy of the Constitution must be enforced. This is accomplished, in the first place, by the requirement that all government officials—federal, state, and local, elected and appointed—take an oath or affirmation to support the Constitution. Secondly, it is accomplished by the provision of judicial procedures and penalties, including impeachment, in case an official betrays the people's trust. Thirdly, it is guaranteed by the institution of a special system, distinct from the ordinary process of legislation, for amending its written text. Further, for good measure, there is still a fourth method—the judicial review of legislation. Under it, any statute enacted by the legislature and approved by the chief executive, or repassed over his veto, may be challenged on the ground of unconstitutionality. A case will then be heard in the courts, where it is the judiciary who determines whether the contested statute is to be obeyed as law or disregarded as null and void.[16]

The Constitution is the instrument of government; its language has had to be given life and meaning by the historical events that have occurred since 1789. Congress animates the Constitution every

---

15. Leslie Lipson, *The Great Issues of Politics*, (Englewood Cliffs, New Jersey: Prentice-Hall, Inc.), 1954, p. 233.

16. The doctrine of judicial review was established in the case of *Marbury v. Madison* (1 Branch 137, 1803). Chief Justice Marshall in that case used a relatively minor incident as an opportunity for proclaiming the momentous power of judicial disallowance of legislation enacted by a coordinate branch of the same government. His words deserve to be quoted:

It is a proposition too plain to be contested, that the constitution controls any legislative Act repugnant to it; or, that the legislature may alter the constitution by an ordinary Act. Between these alternatives there is no middle ground. The constitution is either a superior paramount law, unchangeable by ordinary means, or it is on a level with ordinary legislative Acts, and, like other Acts, is alterable when the former part of the alternative be true, then a legislative Act contrary to the constitution is not law; if the latter part be true, then written constitutions are absurd attempts, on the part of the people, to limit a power in its own nature illimitable. Certainly all those who have framed written constitutions contemplate them as forming the fundamental and paramount law of the nation, and consequently the theory of every such government must be that an Act of the legislature repugnant to the constitution is void . . . It is emphatically the province and duty of the judicial department to say what the law is. Those who apply the rule to particular cases must of necessity expound and interpret that rule. If two laws conflict with each other, the courts must decide on the operation of each.

time it passes a law or holds a hearing. The President construes the Constitution whenever he makes a decision, issues an executive order, or signs a bill into law. The Constitution of the United States must be viewed as the body of practice built up during the decades of American history. It is manifested in the historic crises the nation has met—Lincoln facing the disintegration of the Union, Franklin D. Roosevelt seeking to restore the national economy, or Nixon confronted with the national uproar over Watergate.

Constitutions may range in complexity and content from the rigid document of the German Weimar Republic to the flexible Constitution of the United States. An extremely rigid, detailed constitution is usually symptomatic of a minimal degree of consensus regarding the ends and means of government. In a consensual society like the United States, the Constitution was confined to some basic principles and adapted to changing conditions by means of statutory and judicial interpretations rather than by formal amendment. In communist and fascist systems, which in many cases publicize some extremely democratic-sounding constitutions, the application of such a "basic law of the land" is bent and misinterpreted in order to provide legitimacy for the regime and to perpetuate the rule of a few rather than the public will.

Whether written as in the United States, or unwritten as for example in the United Kingdom, a constitution has four main functions: [17]

(1) It must provide the structure of the governmental system, the organs and institutions of public authority.

(2) It must authorize the powers that the government is to possess and allocate them among the various branches and organs.

(3) It must state the scope of governmental authority and the limitation on governmental power.

(4) It must provide for some means other than violent revolution by which the constitutional design can be adapted to future necessities.

GOVERNMENT

Though the terms state and government are usually used interchangeably, they are not synonyms. States are symbolic but governments are real. In almost every case the state comes first and then a government is created; the reverse is extremely rare. States are also permanent entities (except when they are abolished forcefully by a foreign power or voluntarily by means of merger with another state). Governments, on the other hand, are designed to be transi-

17. *Ibid.*, p. 3.

tional in accordance with a constitutional system of succession. Moreover, while it is not uncommon to have more than one government in a state (i.e., federal, state, and local) it is almost unheard of today to have a government serving more than one state.

The institution of government in a nation-state system is the most powerful instrument for socio-political control yet devised by man. It takes precedence over other institutions such as family or church. Organized societies operating under a state system appreciate the role of government, which exercises a rule-making power and enjoys the monopoly of force necessary to insure ultimate compliance. Without such powers anarchy can not be prevented and organized societies would not be able to survive.

A government can be defined as both a system and a process: as a system, government "is a body of political institutions entrusted with discharging state sovereignty by regulating man's social interaction and enhancing his goals of survival, stability, and progress"; as a process, government "is a set of sequential decisions that seek the organization and coordination of man's relations with one another and with the agencies that regulate these relations".

The nature of government can be further explained in terms of four major characteristics:

(1) The use and monopoly of force.

(2) Officials and the public.

(3) Force and consent.

(4) Authority and power.

The Use and Monopoly of Force

Since the state originates from the need for common protection, order, and justice, it must then operate a government equipped with the amount of force that can insure the attainment of those goals. Protection against attacks from outside cannot be provided unless the government can repel force with force. Likewise, order and justice for the people call for the establishment of agencies, like police, national guard, courts, and prisons capable of applying coercion to the disorderly and the lawless. The tribunals that are expected to settle disputes must be able to enforce their decisions; otherwise nobody will have assurance that the rules he obeys will be observed by his fellows. The national monopoly on the use of force, it must be also added, stems from the fear that any other force organized from within might be able to usurp the legitimate power of government.

Officials and the Public

It is characteristic of the state to entrust its decision-making capability by which laws are made, enforced, and litigated, to certain persons who are recognized by the society as acting on their behalf. In this sense, a distinction can be drawn between the governors and the governed, and a vastly different social significance may attach to the selfsame action, according to the persons who perform it and the methods they employ.

Force and Consent

All governments in the world use force, but all are also founded on some measure of consent. People expect certain results from their government, and they are willing that their officials have the means of bringing those results to fruition. They, therefore, give their consent to the general body of law which prescribes the order they desire, and, along with the law, they approve coercive enforcement against those who would infringe it. Force may be sufficient for protection, but to create order and justice, considerable consent and support are needed.[18]

Authority and Power

The authority of government is its right to act and control. It is the prerogative of government which all accept as legitimate. Its exercise is therefore sanctioned by all those who approve the particular governmental decision and is tolerated by those who disapprove. Power, on the other hand, is the ability to achieve results through concentrated action. It is the product of the mobilization of force and consent. Confronted with power, the citizen has a choice: to support or to oppose. Confronted with authority, on the other hand,

18. The nature of this relationship has been very well explained by A. D. Lindsay, *The Modern Democratic State*, (New York: Oxford University Press), 1947, Vol. 1, p. 206. Lindsay stated the following:

Many people think that the state's use of force gives the lie to the doctrine that government can rest on consent, yet it is also clear that without some sort of consent the government's force would not exist. This puzzles more people than should be so confounded. Men have been accustomed so much to think of the law as restraining other people than their respectable selves that they easily think of the state's force as necessary to enable some people to restrain others . . . . But a little consideration will show us that we need and desire the power of the state to restrain ourselves. Con-

sider a simple example from traffic control. Most of us think there ought to be law regulating traffic, compelling us to light our lamps at a certain time and so on. Such rules have our consent and approval. Yet most of us, if we are honest, know that we are likely to break those laws on occasion and that we are often restrained from breaking them by the sanctions of the law. Most laws are like that. They will work and can be enforced because people want usually to keep them. The state can have and use organized force because most people usually want common rules and most people want those rules to be universally observed; there must be force because there are rules which have little value unless everyone keeps them, and force is needed to fill the gap between most people usually and all people always obeying.

it is his duty to obey. While resistance to power may be lawful, resistance to authority is always unlawful. Legal-rational governments must possess both authority and power and use them harmoniously. Authority alone would be meaningless, and power alone could be tyranny.[19]

THE DESIGN OF THE AMERICAN GOVERNMENT

Prior to the development of the American government, the doctrine of separation of powers had evolved in long, slow sequence. Its origin can be traced to Aristotle, if not indeed to earlier writers. In the *Politics,* Aristotle presented a design of government founded on three "parts", or branches of government: the deliberative, executive, and judicial. Based on Aristotle's criteria, the Puritan revolution in seventeenth century England offered a philosophical inquiry into the fundamentals of free government. John Locke in his *Treatise* distinguished between three powers that existed in every commonwealth. He called these powers the legislative, the executive, and the federative. The shape of constitutional government, was further articulated by Montesquieu who envisioned civilized governments primarily designed—similar to Locke's conception—in terms of separation of powers. In his insistence that these powers must be entrusted respectively to different personnel, Locke went considerably beyond his predecessors by saying:

> In every government there are three sorts of power: the legislative . . . by virtue (of which) the prince or magistrate enacts temporary or perpetual laws, and amends or abrogates those that have been already enacted; executive (by which) . . . he established the public security and provides against invasion; by the third (which) we shall call the judiciary power . . . there is no liberty if the judiciary power be not separated from the legislative and executive.[20]

The doctrine of separation of powers, however, was not explicitly stated in the American Constitution; rather, it was implied. The threefold division of powers has grown, in the American experience of government, to refer to a pattern of distribution oriented towards the cooperation between branches rather than the isolation of each. This naturally called for a system of checks and balances. The function of legislation was assigned to the Congress, but the President in charge of the Executive branch can check its powers by participating

19. Leslie Lipson, *op. cit.*, pp. 68–69.

20. John Locke, *Spirit of the Laws*, XI, 6, ed. Franz Neuman, trans. Thomas Nugent (New York: Hafner Publishing Co., Inc.), 1949, pp. 151–152.

in recommending bills, by summoning the Congress to special sessions or by vetoing bills. The judicial branch is in charge of the courts and can check the congress. Congress can also check the President's powers by overriding his vetos as well as restricting the executive budget. On the other hand, congress can check the judiciary by limiting the jurisdiction of the Supreme Court and by the process of confirming the appointment of its members. Furthermore, the President can check the judiciary by his appointive power over Supreme Court justices and by intervening in the business of federal courts through his power of pardon for all offenses except treason. State and local governments in the United States follow by and large the federal system of government. Though governmental functions at these levels are more or less amalgamated by virtue of their smallness and locality, their basic patterns reflect the doctrines of distribution of power and ample checks and balances.

Governments, as creations of the state, espouse the same ideology of that state. Therefore democratic states foster democratic governments, communist states communist governments, fascist states fascist governments, etc. One may ask why this is necessarily so. The answer naturally lies in the fact that states, as well as governments, are products of the power relationships within a society. Powerful segments, whether they are a democratic majority, a royal family, a predominant party, or a military junta, shape the state ideology and constantly oversee its implementation through a compatible system of government.

Regardless of type, all governments in modern states make and enforce law, provide services for their citizens, and administer justice. Maintaining a responsive government, however, is determined by the way governments are formed, controlled and overseen. Unrestrained governments may experience "canceric" trends and produce despotic rule. Militarily controlled governments produce martial law types of rule, while constitutionally controlled governments produce democratic rule and practices.

CONSTITUTIONAL GOVERNMENT

A distinction must be made between "constitution" and "constitutionalism" or the state of a "constitutional government". As mentioned earlier, a constitution is a basic design of the structure and power of the government and the rights and duties of its citizens. In this sense every civilized state with an established form of government has a constitution. To say that a state possesses a constitution, however, does not say much about its democratic or dictatorial character.

Constitutionalism, on the other hand, is a term that does have definite implications. It is bound up with the democratic theory and the notion of the rule of law. It embraces the practice of "limited government" letting private groups and individuals pursue their interests without much government intervention. Government officials must, therefore, be restricted in their exercise of power and public servants must conduct themselves according to a set of fair and equitable procedures. The major limitations of constitutionalism are incorporated in the fundamental laws of the land (constitution, legislation, court decisions, and legal traditions), whether written or unwritten, and are given formal or tacit approval by the people of the state.

In the United States, the Constitution prohibits the officials of the executive branch of government from exercising certain powers which infringe on the peoples' liberties and freedoms or which are in violation of the Bill of Rights. By democratic tradition, the judicial branch of government exercises a strong power of judicial review over the laws and governmental actions that exceed constitutional limitations. Such laws and actions can be struck down as unconstitutional by the courts, thus buttressing the principle of limited government.

The principle of constitutionalism as applied in the United States provides the basic attributes which distinguish a democratic system from those based on absolutism. Besides the fact that public officials are inherently restricted from acting *ultra vires*, or beyond authority, the individual can sue such public official in the court of law for damage incurred by public action. In no other system can the principle of constitutionalism be so spectacularly demonstrated as in the American traumatic cases of Watergate, 1972–1973. A President was called "unnamed conspirator" by a grand jury, and top public officials in the White House and Department of Justice were indicted, convicted, and jailed for violating the privacy of some individuals and political groups. Without constitutional government, the rights of individuals would be overshadowed by an artificial web of entangled lines of authority and power, private and public, consent and force, domestic and foreign, legal and illegal, therefore debasing man's society to one of crude jungle existence.

BUREAUCRACY AND ADMINISTRATION

The terms state, government, and bureaucracy are often used interchangeably. Analytically, however, they mean three different entities. The state is primarily symbolic and is possessed with sovereignty. Government is dynamic and is possessed with authority. Bureaucracy is operational and is possessed with the power to administer common affairs. Figure 1 shows this telescopic relationship between the three entities.

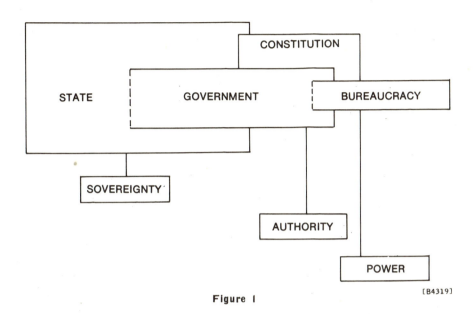

Figure I

[B4319]

The Telescopic System

Man, in the material reality of social life, does not live by state doctrines alone. Neither can the authoritative decisions by government solve his complex problems. What man, in essence, is seeking is the actual satisfaction of his daily needs and resolution of problems whether they are protection oriented, justice oriented, or economic oriented.

Government, as explained earlier, is a political entity. It is mostly motivated by the interests of its incumbents and reinforced by their desire for power. With this in mind, the goals of government may not necessarily coincide with those of the governed, especially in the case of non-constitutional governments. As long as "men are not angels, and angels do not run government", as James Madison stated in the 51 Federalist paper, people will always have considerable worries about the conduct of government, its capability, accountability and responsiveness.

Politicians in government (senators, representatives, and elected officials and judges) are just a fraction compared to the population of a state. They also, thanks to the democratic principles of freedom and equality, enjoy a great amount of diversity. Their abilities are unique, their education and training are unique, and their motives are certainly hard to determine. Their attitudes naturally vary from one to another, so does their bias from one issue to another. Consequently, their submission to political pressures and their vulnerability to corruption are unpredictable.

The public, on the other hand, seeks standard application of state protection, equitable enforcement of laws, and fair interpretation of justice. Citizens expect "fair" government practices under the ideal principles of rule of law, equality, and due process of law. Democratic societies, in particular, expect their governments to be ones of "laws not of men", thus, predictable, legalistic, fair, and accountable. Industrialized communities, furthermore, require a system of government characterized by efficiency, effectiveness, and economy. If all such expectations are to be achieved, government practices and decisions have to be institutionalized, formalized and established on a fairly stable basis. To maintain such a state of public responsiveness, governments have had to create specialized organizations and agencies responsible solely for the appropriate dispensation of government services. This multitude of public organizations and agencies constitutes the bureaucracy.

Bureaucracy is the long arm of government. It implements operational and tactical decisions. It is capable of reaching out and physically tackling the problems. It is tangible and constantly visible as reflected by the armies of soldiers, policemen, teachers, doctors, diplomats, and judges, just to name a few. Only government bureaucracies can effectively fight wars, combat crime, educate students, treat patients, conduct foreign policy, or settle disputes among adversary groups and individuals.

BUREAUCRACY

The term "bureaucracy" was originally coined by Max Weber, the German sociologist, around the turn of the century to denote the "power of the office". "Bureau" is the French word for office, and "cracy" is the anglicized word for the Greek, "karatia" which meant value, or power. Amitai Etzioni used "complex organization" to refer to Weber's notion of office power. Peter Blau called it "formal organization". The essence of bureaucracy is "a system of government organization of experts officially authorized by the legislative branch to administer public affairs by means of standard operating procedures".[21]

21. Though the term bureaucracy can apply to any formalized organization, complex organization, or big organization governed by rules and procedures (like the church, General Motors, the United Nations), the term will be used throughout this text to refer to government organizations unless so stated.

Although the term bureaucracy was never mentioned in the Constitution, its legitimacy stemmed from the President's constitutional power to "take care that the laws be faithfully executed".[22]   Bureaucracy, today, is assuming more and more power at the expense of the legislative and judicial branches.   It even becomes rather doubtful today to describe the American bureaucracy as a part of the executive branch of government controlled by the President.   Because of its growth in size and power it became ordinarily referred to by political scientists as the "fourth headless branch of government".

The purpose of bureaucracy is to translate political decisions made in federal and state congresses and in city halls, into physical actions experienced by the layman on the street.   Noting the diversity of human grievances and expectations, contemporary bureaucracy certainly has an overwhelming power over the welfare and destiny of the citizenry.   Bureaucracies, therefore, must be staffed by a special group of public officials who are well selected, trained and controlled.

In democratic societies, especially in the American system, the behavior of public officials—bureaucrats—has to be legal, rational, and predictable.   Decisions made by public officials on public affairs, cannot be left to spontaneity or the desires and whims of whoever is in charge at the time.   Bureaucratic behavior, therefore, must be regulated by sets of standards and rules previously approved by the people or their representatives.   The personal preference of individual bureaucrats must be held in abeyance, as much as realistically possible, in favor of standardized measures and procedures.

Philosophies on bureaucracy range from the extreme classical concepts where discretion is prohibited to the extreme modern concepts where standards are almost nonexistent.   The classic theory contends that bureaucrats are "half machine-half man".   They are considered like machines on the job and men (not totally without restrictions) off the job.   In their public capacity, they are assigned to narrow tasks, forced to comply with routine, and constantly check their decisions with a tall hierarchy of overseers.   The modern theory, on the other hand, emphasizes broad tasks, self control, and vast areas of personal discretion.   A lengthy discussion of these models and others will be later introduced in Chapter Six.

To sum up this discussion, it is important to return to the telescopic relationship between the state, government and bureaucracy.   While three of them could be compressed within the realm of a "political system", each, when spread, has distinguishable functions which stem from its particular nature and capability; the state is ideological, government political, and bureaucracy administrative.

22. The Constitution, Section 3, Article 2.

Each component, while conceptually separate, is strongly linked to the other. The state creates and shapes government, which, in turn, creates and controls bureaucracy. While each affects, and is affected by, the other, as in the trinity, they can only be analyzed separately.

ADMINISTRATION

The business of bureaucracy is administration. Congress, state and local legislatures, which hold the authority to make laws, delegate the power to enforce these laws to bureaucracies to administer. Without administration, laws stay on the books and bewildered societies return to disorder and jungle life.

Administration is "getting the job done". It is the final step in the process of legitimate social control. Only through the administrative process can statutory ideals be transformed into effective action. Constitutional amendments, legislative decisions or legal edicts cannot by themselves physically effect change; administration can. Most legislatures in the United States meet only for several months of every year. They lack the technical know-how and expertise essential to the regulation of social conditions. Economic and social problems require the attention of specialized experts who have the time and facilities to remain continuously informed and equipped to respond promptly. It would be almost impossible for legislatures to fix intelligently the rates of public utilities, to fight fires, to combat crime, to maintain bridges, or to handle epidemics. A police agency, for example, must be able in a timely fashion to insure domestic tranquility, regulate traffic, and investigate crime without having to wait for legislative clearance. Without the functions of administration, modern organization, and advanced management, contemporary societies would not only become dysfunctional but would certainly collapse.

Administration can be perceived as both a system and a process. As a system, administration refers to fields of bureaucratic practices such as Police Administration, Business Administration, Hospital Administration, and Correctional Administration, to mention just a few. In a slightly different terminology we also refer to the Administration of Justice, the Administration of Criminal Justice, or the Administration of Law Enforcement. All such uses of the term refer to a "system" usually "consisting of several components working together in equilibrium toward the achievement of common goals". Administrative systems, as such, have stated goals, formulated standards, criteria for decisions, as well as adequate staff, methods, and—above all —ample funds. Detailed discussion of these elements will follow subsequently in Chapter Six.

As a process, administration refers to the internal ways and means by which the job is efficiently and effectively done. The process relates to the areas of decision-making, communication, planning, leadership, and the coordination of efforts toward the achievement of the prescribed goals. Ordway Tead described the process of administration as "the comprehensive effort to direct, guide, and integrate human striving which are focused toward some specific ends or aims".[23]

While the system of administration is primarily concerned with the organization of public agencies in a harmonic and cohesive pattern, the process of administration focuses on the management of resources and the integration of men, methods, monies and machines. Its chief goal is the achievement of rational cooperation among workers within a set up administrative system.

Police administration, the basic concern of this book, is thus the study of public organization and management in the field of the police. Legislative bodies in America can make the laws of social control, courts can interpret them and supervise their application, but only through police administration can they be executed and transferred into actions that touch the daily endeavors of each American citizen.

23. Dwight Waldo, *Ideas and Issues in Public Administration*, (New York: McGraw-Hill Book Company), 1953, p. 25.

CHAPTER TWO

SYSTEMS OF SOCIAL ORDER AND LEGITIMATE CONTROL

Overview

James Madison observed in the 51 Federalist Paper that "if men were angels, or angels were to govern men", we would have no need for government and no worries about the conduct of men. But since neither condition prevails, there is a need, Madison admitted, for social precautions and legitimate control.

If men were angels, as Madison said, societies would not need the political institution of government, the executive institution of bureaucracy, the military institution of defense, the social institutions of family, school and church or the criminal justice institutions of police, courts and corrections. All such institutions were developed to "civilize" and control the behavior of men, whom God created "a little lower than angels".[1]

Although human knowledge cannot, in this reference, postulate about the nature and behavior of angels, it is quite acceptable from reading our religious heritages to suppose that angels exist in a highly stable, communal, and sin-free manner.[2]

But since men are not angels, then what are they? What constitutes their behavior? Can man live in an earthly utopia—a term coined by Sir Thomas More to designate an ideal social order on man's earth?

Answers to these questions have bewildered the scholars since the early days of man on earth. History of mankind has also shown how vicious human behavior can be. When, for instance, the total population of mankind was reportedly four individuals only, one of them murdered another (the case of Cain v. Abel) and thereby disposed of one-quarter of the human population in one blow. Today, with the serious threat of geothermal warfare among powerful nations, the possibility of exterminating the whole of mankind by the push of a button is certainly obvious.

If man were to live in a true utopia, he would have to live all by himself with neither spouse nor children, neighbors nor community, in a form of individual order. This, of course, would lead to the end of the human race. However, if man met, talked or interacted with other men, his individual order would certainly be challenged by others in his new social group. With social interaction, a pattern of so-

---

1. The Book of Psalms, No. 8.

2. Note the exception in the case of Lucifer v. God, Book of Genesis.

cial order must emerge so as to accommodate the individual desires and whims of the members of the group. Such an accommodative order must be a balance between individual needs and group needs, between individuality and conformity. Such a balance must be maintained if the "common good" is to prevail.

Man's individuality stems from his lack of supreme knowledge. Some know more and some know less. And since no two men are exactly alike, each and every man must then be considered unique. Each individual possesses an undetermined amount of biological, cultural, and environmental residue. Because of his uniqueness, man behaves in a manner obsessed with self, motivated by interest, and prejudiced by the possession of power.

Man's conformity also lies in his lack of supreme knowledge. Since no man can grasp all knowledge, he therefore needs the cooperation of those who know what he can't know. In order to secure such a desired cooperation, individuals realize the necessity for sacrificing portions of their "selves", interests, and powers. Without such sacrifices, families, tribes, clans and later societies would not have developed, and man's gregariousness and capacity for joint activity would not have been possible.

Social order is a *system of people, relationships, and customs operating smoothly to accomplish the work of a society.* It can be defined as the *totality of normative social relations that characterize a society.* It always seeks the maintenance of a balance between individuality and conformity within a given society. If this balance is tilted in favor of individuality, social permissiveness and anarchy may result. If it is tilted toward conformity, social formalization and domination may result. The problem of maintaining and enforcing just the right balance has been man's dilemma since ancient history. Ironically, the critical questions raised by Socrates, Plato, and Aristotle with regard to freedom, equality, law and legal rights are just about the same raised today by Erich Fromm, Emile Durkheim, Howard S. Becker or Hazel Kerper.

THE SYSTEM AND PROCESS OF SOCIAL ORDER

Social order is both a system and a process. As a system, social order consists of a set of institutions, relationships, customs, and laws which operate among the members of society and help them achieve the goals of societal living. In this reference, sophistication of a society hinges primarily upon the sophistication of its institutions and the way they function. Foremost among these functions are division of labor and flexible coordination.

Division of Labor

Division of labor is the allocation of various tasks. In advanced group structures, different participants have to do different tasks, and their respective activities are integrated into a gratifying end product or service.   In the institution of criminal justice, the policeman does not have to prosecute the suspect he arrests nor does the judge have to implement the incarceration sentence of a convicted defendant.   Such group activities within the criminal justice system involve some expected behavior and the experiences of a number of people each with a somewhat different contribution to make.

Division of labor by social institutions produces a society organized by positions and roles.   Positions are functional occupations needed to keep the society operative and are held by officials who are ranked according to the importance of their contribution to society. The physician, the lawyer, the policeman, the teacher, the carpenter, are examples of positions held within the formal division of labor.

Roles, on the other hand, are prescribed patterns of behavior expected of persons in given situations by virtue of their positions. Roles also represent reciprocal claims and obligations expected of various position holders.   The role of the judge, for instance, is expected to reflect fairness, patience and legal expertise as well as firmness.

Only institutions are capable of creating sets of positions and roles.   Institutions also formulate laws which govern the hierarchy of positions, jurisdictions, authorities, and powers, and establish the expectations of role acquisition, playing, and displacement.

Flexible Coordination

Flexible coordination is that high degree of adaptability which members of a society have to exercise to meet the peculiarities and changes that occur in each society.   Through flexible coordination, institutions manage to bridge the gap between individual behavior by "free man" and regimented assignments by "soldiers".   Flexible coordination is necessary for the development and progress of dynamic groups.   A dynamic group may be regarded as a *collectivity of persons who are capable of consistent, coordinated action, directed toward common objectives, the achievement of which will bring gratification to all participants.*[3]

As a process, social order is the development, maintenance, and maturation of social control, which is the instrument of social order. It institutionalizes normative social relations among individuals and groups through the instruments of sanctions and rewards.   The consistent reinforcement of these instruments can suppress social deviance and produce social order.

3.   Tamotsu Shibutani, *Society and Personality; An Interactionist Approach to Social Psychology,* (Englewood   Cliffs, New Jersey: Prentice-Hall, Inc.), 1961, p. 33.

The process of social order—through its arm of social control agencies—can be attained by either peaceful or forceful means, which can be accomplished by public organizations or private organizations. Peaceful means are usually pursued by private organizations such as the Society for the Prevention of Cruelty to Children, the Family Services Association, Alcoholics Anonymous, Legal Aid Societies, Organizations for Parent Education and a multitude of other religiously affiliated organizations. Forceful means, on the other hand, are always the function of public, or government, agencies. Such agencies would fall within the realm of several executive departments. Other than the criminal justice system, which is closely associated with the Department of Justice, such forceful means are also handled by agencies of social welfare such as Vocational Rehabilitation, Children Welfare Services, Veterans' services, and Social Security.

PEACEFUL MEANS OF SOCIAL CONTROL

The major means of peaceful social control are:

A.   Socialization.

B.   Group experience.

Socialization

Socialization is the process whereby culture is transmitted from one generation to another. Through socialization the younger generations learn to internalize the norms of their seniors and adopt the common patterns of society. As a result of socialization, individuals develop a distinct sense of "self" amalgamated with society and expressed in terms of approval, belonging, and support. Institutions of socialization are the family, school, church, and later—through political participation—political parties and government.

Group Experience

Group experience is the realization of distinctive behavior patterns which continue throughout life. Without group experience, human personality does not develop and modal behavior may never be forthcoming. Modal personality represents a series of personality traits which are most common among the members of a group or groups in a society. Modal behavior does not describe "goodness" or "sinfulness" of behavior. It merely describes personality traits, a great many of which are shared by the members of that group. Group persuasion in the neighborhood, in the military, in social gatherings, as well as in business and athletic encounters, shape the modal behavior of individuals and groups. When individual behavior extends beyond what the group considers modal, or normal, then that person is considered "deviant". If such "deviance" is not corrected by further socialization processes or group experience, forceful means by criminal justice institutions may be called in to maintain the social order.

FORCEFUL MEANS OF SOCIAL CONTROL

Forceful means of social control are means administered by the state on behalf of the people. They are devised by the system of government and conducted by the appropriate bureaucracy.

Forceful means do not "always" have to be violent. Policemen may effectively maintain law and order with the threat of the use of force; public prosecutors do not have to prosecute all cases; trial judges, likewise, do not have to incarcerate all convicted defendants.

Forceful means of social control, unlike peaceful means are invoked by formal organizations such as the police, prosecutors, courts, and correctional institutions. They ordinarily are not party to the social conflict and have no private interest in settling it one way or another, if at all. Such agencies are necessarily public agencies performing under the auspices of the state to maintain social order.

Agencies of forceful social control today are modern bureaucracies, equipped, trained, and instructed by the state so as to be capable of exerting physical force should force be needed. They are organized to augment their capability and are provided with adequate management techniques to enhance their effectiveness. Such agencies include the police, national guard and federal troops, as well as probation and parole officers and officials of correctional institutions. Foremost among such agencies are the police. Due to their size, their constant authority over the public, their continuous training and readiness, and their hardly restrained right to use guns, police organizations enjoy a special status among agencies of forceful social control.

LEGITIMATE CONTROL

Legitimacy is generally seen as the ruler's right to rule when that right is recognized by the ruled. In our system of government, this can be stated by saying that only the assent of a popular majority, the will of the people, in a given constituency or electoral district, can make government practices legitimate.

Max Weber offered his celebrated threefold division of legitimacy. He suggested that political systems, and their bureaucratic institutions, may fall within the boundaries of traditional, charismatic, or rational-legal patterns of legitimacy. The first term relates to systems of government and bureaucratic practices exercised by a polity of a few and based on unquestionable beliefs gradually developed by tradition. Authority and power exerted by tribal chieftains, monarchs, and religious groups are prime examples of traditional legitimacy. Charismatic legitimacy is based solely on the leader's capacity to elicit from his populace deference, devotion, and awe toward himself as the source of authority. Examples of charismatic legitimacy cannot be clearer than in the cases of Adolf Hitler, Benito Mussolini, Fidel Castro and Gamal Abdel-Nasser. Societies under those leaders have accepted governmental policies and methods of control (many of which appear illegitimate and even criminal by American standards) out of love and obedience to the so-called "national saviour."

The last pattern of legitimacy, suggested by Weber, is the rational-legal. It designates the political constellation in which, as mentioned earlier, a ruler is believed by those he rules to have the right to do so. Such recognition is based on the rules of reason, human equality, and individual obligation to participate directly or indirectly in the system of government that rules him. Rational-legal legitimacy is founded upon firm beliefs in the fallability and dispensability of rulers and, therefore, on the supremacy of the rule of law as prescribed by a binding constitution.

Legitimacy of social control institutions and practices in the U.S. requires that such institutions and practices be in compliance with the letter and spirit of the Constitution. As a matter of fact, the term legitimate in America today may be considered as synonymous to constitutional. Institutions of social control cannot be sanctioned except with the approval of the governed—symbolized by the approval of their representatives in Congress. Forceful control measures in particular are closely monitored and examined by legislative bodies, judicial forums, the mass media, and the public at large. The Supreme Court, as well as the highest court within a state, can prohibit and commute "illegal" control measures if they are found in violation of the Constitution. Repealing the Prohibition Act in 1933, the Internal Security Act in 1964, or the No-knock practice by the police in 1974 are examples of rational-legal legitimacy.

Not only can legislative bodies and judicial forums in this country prohibit illegal social control measures, they can also discipline institutions of social control. Police bureaucracies have been prohibited from flagrantly arresting people on the street without a warrant by the magistrate or a demonstrable probable cause. Even upon arrest, policemen cannot interrogate or detain suspects without clearly informing them of their constitutional rights. Subsequent steps toward prosecuting the individual cannot proceed in the absence of qualified counsel. Even if indicted, a suspect before a trial court cannot be forced to take the stand, to incriminate himself or be denied the opportunity to confront the witnesses against him. If convicted and incarcerated, correctional institutions have to comply with constitutional rights of the convicted and treat them humanely, equally and fairly.

Forceful institutions of social control are public agencies operated by the state. They constitute bureaucracies which vary in size and power according to the nature and ideology of the state. Although citizens in the United States may complain of the size and power of the police, the courts, or even the correctional institutions, such institutions cannot be compared with their gigantic counterparts in Nazi Germany before the war or the Soviet Union today. Another example which entails the legitimacy of social control in different countries would be the issue of the armament of the American policemen as compared to their "bare-handed" British counterparts. To the average Englishman, carrying a gun by the regular patrolman (or constable in England) constitutes—in itself—illegitimate control. Communist and fascist governments tend, by and large, to expand the area of legitimate control by its agencies while democratic systems tend to reduce it or at least impose stringent checks and balances by which public scrutiny over it can be constantly maintained.

Illegitimate agencies of forceful control, on the other hand, are nongovernmental organizations. Mostly terrorist or criminal in nature, they may be popular among large populaces. Examples of such organizations are the Ku Klux Klan, the Weathermen or the Simbionese Liberation Army in the U.S.; the IRA in Northern Ireland; the PLO in Middle Eastern countries; and the Mao Mao movement in some African countries. Such illegitimate forceful groups normally develop in unstable societies or among those experiencing "legitimacy gaps" in order to provide individuals and communities a type of "artificial legitimacy" they are yearning for in the absence of authentic state legitimacy.

THE CRIMINAL JUSTICE SYSTEM

The Systems Approach

The system theory of administration has gained a lot of recognition lately. The systems approach seems to be the most rational framework for analysis and problem solving. It emphasizes the study of hierarchical systems and the examination of their relationships. It treats all administrative functions as necessarily related in a systematic fashion. The system containing such relationships is, in turn, a part of a bigger system. The latter would in turn be viewed as part of an even bigger system. The police system, for example, is a part of the Criminal Justice System which is part of the Social System within which people interact.

The systems approach provides a viable methodology by which conceptual models of administration can be conceived, examined, and evaluated. The systems methodology is particularly concerned with the flow of inputs and outputs among related components and the influences incurred by environmental pressures over the system.

While a detailed discussion of the system approach will follow in Chapter Six, it is necessary to describe at this stage the general notion of systems.

All systems are related in a hierarchy of super-systems and sub-systems. The United States as a whole is a super-system. It relies on four fundamental systems, namely the political, criminal justice, defense, and the socio-economic system. The United States may also be seen as a system within a global environment which in turn may be considered a super-super-system. The latter naturally includes the Russian super-system, the British super-system, the Chinese super-system, as well as the one hundred and thirty-six super-systems represented in the United Nations. If, conceptually speaking, we can assume that there are other civilizations on other planets, we must then think in terms of super-super-super-system in an interplanetary interaction. The system theory therefore technically treats each state as a domestic super-system, an international system, and probably as an interplanetary sub-system.

The domestic super-system of state, as mentioned earlier, consists of the four fundamental systems of politics, criminal justice, defense, and socio-economy. Each of these systems has sub-systems. The political system, for instance, encompasses a legislative sub-system, an executive sub-system, a judicial sub-system, an electoral sub-system, etc. The criminal justice system in most states encompasses a police sub-system, a prosecution sub-system, a legal sub-system, a correctional sub-system, and a rehabilitation sub-system.

Sub-systems, however, are not the smallest units of the system theory. The police sub-system in America, for example, consists of federal sub-sub-systems, state sub-sub-systems, and thousands of local sub-sub-systems. By the same token, organizing a local police department into a patrol division, a detective division, or a traffic division must understandably produce virtually millions of sub-sub-sub-systems.

THE AMERICAN SYSTEM OF CRIMINAL JUSTICE

The main system of legitimate forceful control in America is the criminal justice system. The Preamble to the Constitution refers to the criminal justice system as second only to the political system. According to the order of systems implied in the Preamble, reference is made to the criminal justice system even ahead of those of defenses, general welfare, or securance of liberty.

The Preamble states the following:

We the people of the United States, in order to form a more perfect union, establish justice, insure domestic tranquility, provide for the common defense, promote the general welfare, and secure the blessings of liberty to ourselves and our posterity, do ordain and establish this Constitution for the United States of America.

As clearly understood from the wording of the Preamble, the basic goals of the new nation were survival, stability and progress. Towards the achievement of these goals, the following systems were implied in the Preamble text:

	Reference	System	Goal
A.	"in order to form a more perfect union"	political	survival
B.	"establish justice, insure domestic tranquility"	criminal justice	stability
C.	"provide for the common defense"	defense	survival—stability
D.	"promote the general welfare and secure the blessings of liberty"	socio-economic	stability—progress

The criminal justice system *is a set of components working together—in equilibrium—towards the achievement of the common goals of justice and domestic tranquility.* The components are police agencies, prosecutorial agencies, courts, correctional agencies and rehabilitative agencies.

The criminal justice system in America is real and active. Needless to say that while the average observer may not be able to conceptualize the system in operation, the products of the system are clearly visible. Offenders are arrested, charges are pressed, indictments are handed down, court sessions are convened, verdicts and convictions are reached, incarcerated criminals are kept behind bars and, freed convicts are directed toward the assumption of a new law-abiding behavior. These processes are sequentially performed by the components of the system. Each process is handled by a sub-system closely related to the mother system.

The criminal justice system in America is a legal system. It originally stemmed from the court system and branched out to encompass peace keeping, law enforcement, provision of services, and other responsibilities. In the early years of this Republic the whole system of criminal justice was entrusted to trial judges to handle. Today, because of the tremendous increase in population, the complexity of social living, the apparent breakdown of other agencies of social control, and the rapid change in social ideologies, the role of trial judges has become much more specialized. Achievement of domestic tranquility today by a competent sub-system of police and equally competent sub-systems of incarceration and rehabilitation of offenders has probably matched in significance the role of the trial judge.

The legal nature of the criminal justice system, however, should not be overlooked or shaken. After all, the process of rendering justice or insuring domestic tranquility cannot exist bereft of legal control by the courts. Whether the system is operated totally or in part by trial judges, all sub-systems must comply with the legal aspects of justice. The values of fundamental fairness, propriety, equal protection, rule of law, and presumption of innocence must be established principles for the policeman, prison warden, and probation or parole officer just as they are to the judge behind the bench.

The criminal justice system in America is primarily a government operation. The sub-systems are staffed by public officials, are financed by tax-payers' funds and are organized along bureaucratic lines. The system and its sub-systems are governed and related to each other, as well as to the public, by voluminous sets of laws and rules. Authorities and powers within the system or its sub-systems are enumerated in a multitude of procedures and mechanics designed so as to achieve the system's effectiveness, efficiency, and neutrality. As a result, evaluation of the system and attempts to increase its capacity, speed, and workability are continuous, have become more scientific and have received much more support from the public and their government representatives.

The criminal justice system in America—like most government systems—is not a unitary system. Besides being divided in its five basic sub-systems (police, prosecution, courts, correction and rehabilitation), the system is also stratified along federal, state, and local lines with the Federal Department of Justice exerting nominal leadership over the multitude of agencies within the system. In order to amplify and to give the reader a glimpse of how decentralized the system actually is, the following breakdown is presented:[4]

Police Agencies:

There are at least 10 federal units not including the independent agencies,
50 state units,
35,000 local units, and
a sheriff's department in every county.

4. Committee for Economic Development, *Reducing Crime and Assuring Justice*, (New York), 1972, pp. 81–83.

Prosecution Agencies:

There are at least 93 federal prosecution units,
50 state attorney general's units,
a district attorney in every city or town, and about
3,000 county attorney units in all.

Courts:

There are the U.S. Supreme Court,
11 U.S. Courts of Appeals,
91 Federal District Courts,
50 State Supreme Courts, or equivalent, and a large number
   of intermediate Courts of Appeals, circuit courts, and
   courts of original jurisdiction.

There are also uncounted numbers of lower courts, mainly
   with original county jurisdiction, magistrates' courts,
   justices of the peace, special courts on traffic, domestic
   relations, juvenile offenders, etc.

Corrections:

There are six federal penitentiaries and 23 federal institutions,
   hundreds of youth camps, training centers, and state
   prisons, uncounted numbers of county and city jails.

Rehabilitation:

There are uncounted numbers of federal, state and local agencies of probation, as well as parole and psychological
   and mental services.

Because of the extremely decentralized nature of the American
system, it has recently come under serious attack.   Advocating
the famous theory of the "nonsystem" of criminal justice, James Campbell and his associates noted "the mosaic of discontent which pervades
the criminal [justice] process".   Public officials and institutions within
the system "see their special mission being undercut by the cross-pur-
poses, frailties or malfunctions of others".   Campbell proceeds by
saying that officials in the criminal justice sub-systems find "their
perception of justice varying or in conflict".   This conflict, explains
Campbell, is "intensified by the fact that each part of the criminal
justice process is overloaded and undermanned, and most of its personnel underpaid and inadequately trained".[5]

Whether the present system of criminal justice in America truly
qualifies as a system depends primarily on the use of the term "sys-

[5]. All quotations in this paragraph are   *Order Reconsidered*, (New York: Ban-
gleaned from James Campbell, Joseph   tam Books), 1970, pp. 261–268.
R. Sahid, and David Stand, *Law and*

tem". Most people tend to use the term in a casual manner to mean either an organization or a process. As an organization the term is used to refer to an "establishment", "incorporation", or a "closely related entity" performing some particular functions. Hence the terms political system, economic system, social system, or military system. As a process, the term is used to indicate the "way of doing things" or the "mechanics". The modern usage of the term, however, tends to combine both uses within some basic features:

     a.   complexity of relations;

     b.   interdependence;

     c.   utilization of science or technology;

     d.   common goals;

     e.   coordinating leadership;

     f.   planning and research;

     g.   advanced body of knowledge;

     h.   measurability of product;

     i.   formalization of procedures;

     j.   interaction with the environment;

     k.   the flow of feedback.

Critics of the present criminal justice system view the current structure as severely fragmented and consisting of thousands of independent units seeking their private goals and interests, bereft of effective leadership, planning, research, or formalized standards, and plagued with ignorance, conflict, and the lack of innovation. Critics argue that police agencies, for example, especially in intermediate-size and small towns or cities, are politically oriented, corruption stricken, unabashed, and, of course, unprofessional. Such police units, and critics argue they are the majority in the nation, care little, if any, as to the rule of law or presumption of innocence; civil rights or community relations; and certainly not to the sociological concepts of parolling prisoners or rehabilitating offenders. Furthermore, critics believe that most police agencies apply the little technology they have as a means of manipulating false appearances and fabricating statistics.

Police agencies, for example, seem hardly integrated in the criminal justice system. Seeing themselves as the only group which sacrifices itself for the system, policemen disapprove of the DA's dismissing charges against suspects, judges handing down lenient sentences for political reasons, prisons being run as comfortable hotels for criminals, or of probation and parole officers returning criminals back to the streets as fast as they are cleared off.

The example of police role and sentiment within the system is only an example of how other components may see themselves vis-a-vis other components. In the final analysis, critics argue, one can easily realize the amount of doubt, distrust, conflict and even sabotage within the present system. Components, the critics insist, do not speak "the same language", do not seek the same goals, do not approve of the same procedures, and seldom communicate intelligently or attempt to restore the "system spirit".

Proponents of the current system of criminal justice seem much more optimistic. Though they admit some shortcomings of the system, they argue that it works—at least in most cases. Their argument may be summarized in the following:

a. The rising rate of crime in America is not indicative of the breaking-down of the criminal justice system but of the socio-political and economic systems which have caused serious dislocations in the behavior of modern society.

b. The system is coming more and more under the control of the Supreme Court, legislative bodies and public scrutiny as evidenced by the numerous exclusionary rulings by the highest court, and by the avalanche of laws passed lately to streamline court procedures and sustain individual privacy.

c. There is an increase in communication between components of the system as evidenced by the annual plans, numerous conferences, and public meetings among representatives of sub-systems.

d. There has been an increase of public funds appropriated for the war against crime, as evidenced by the billions of dollars recently designated by the Department of Justice (LEAA) to promote criminal justice projects at the federal, state and local levels.

e. Education projects for policemen, prosecution officials, judges, correctional officers, and rehabilitation agents have been expanded.

f. There is greater application of technology in the system, as evidenced by the introduction of better communications systems, data collection and retrieval, and sophisticated crime lab techniques in police operations as well as computerizing court procedures, and upgrading correctional facilities.

g. There are indicators of a subsequent decline in crime rate, at least in some parts of the country, in regard to certain types of crimes.

THE POLICE SUB-SYSTEM

What distinguishes police practices in free societies from those exercised in communist or fascist societies is basically the relationship between the system of criminal justice and the sub-system of police. In the latter societies, police agencies simply operate on the assumption that they are, in fact, the criminal justice system. They interpret their role as the agency in charge of the whole system; therefore, it is their duty to control the populace, punish violators, defend the regime, and suppress individual liberties as they see necessary or fit under the circumstances. Constitutional scrutiny, judicial review, or popular checks are not taken seriously, and police powers become both limitless and checkless. In communist and fascist societies, police agencies grow into big, complex organizations so secretive and powerful that the average legislator may fail to identify the structure or the persons who run them. In some cases such a legislator might be seriously discouraged from asking detailed questions about police "organs" and "schemes"; otherwise he himself would become a "parasite" liable to be processed by the police "sewage disposal system", "thrown in the jug", "receive a tenner", or just be "finished off".[6]

In free societies, police agencies are, and must always remain, a sub-system—a component of the criminal justice system. Police administration and practices must stem from the criminal justice system—the legitimate agency in charge of "establishing justice and insuring domestic tranquility". Police goals are stipulated and developed to blend harmoniously with and to reinforce the strategic goals of the system. Police roles and functions are fashioned and controlled by the system in order to perpetuate democratic values and principles. Police authorities are limited, enumerated, and publicly scrutinized. Police powers are checked by legislative bodies, judicial review, internal investigations, mass media, and public scrutiny. In other words, police agencies must remain responsible and responsive to the system, subservient to it at all times and never its master.

Police agencies, on the other hand, cannot be truly treated as an equal component. By virtue of their extremely large size, their vulnerable front-line position against crime, and their special need to carry arms and utilize technological gear, police agencies in America have developed a privileged status in the criminal justice system. While other components may look with envy or resentment at that status, the police component can justifiably argue and defend their

6. For a thorough analysis of police practices in U.S.S.R., see Aleksandr I. Solzhenitsyn, *The Gulag Archipelago,* (New York: Harper and Row), 1973, Chapters 1, 2, and 3.

"superior" status. The police subsystem rivals all other components in terms of being:

1 —The largest component.

2 —The uniformed component.

3 —The armed component.

4 —The discretionary component.

5 —The specialist component.

A brief discussion of these features will follow.

The Largest Component

Police agencies are by far the largest component in the administration of criminal justice in the country. They are spread out all over the nation and permeate even the smallest communities in existence. Other components, such as prosecutors, courts, prisons and agencies of social rehabilitation are limited to cities, towns, and county seats. Police agencies in the U.S. employ, according to some latest estimates, about 500,000 persons.[7] The rest of all the agencies combined within the system can hardly match that number. Police funds follow the increase in police size. The total cost of administration of justice today is divided in a manner that gives police agencies more than 60% of the total funding.[8] The other components are sharing the 40% remaining amount in different portions. Correctional and rehabilitative institutions receive about 20%, prosecution and defense agencies 6%, and courts about 14%.[9]

The Uniformed Component

Policemen in America are all, with the exception of a very few insignificant number, clothed in uniform. They mostly use marked cars which produce loud and sometimes frightening siren sounds as well as dazzling, colored, flashing lights. Not only does such appearance reinforce the visibility of policemen, it also instills public fear of the police. The uniformed appearance of policemen naturally inhibits the public's ability to engage in a free conversation with them, to apply equal reasoning, or to display serious resentment toward their power. In the criminal justice system only policemen are in uniform (with the probable exception of prison officials within some correctional institutions). Public inhibitions referred to earlier do not usually exist in dealings with non-police authorities. There appear to be more safe-guards in talking with a district attorney or a

---

7.   Alan R. Coffey and Edward Eldefonso, *Process and Impact of Justice*, (Beverly Hills, California: Glencoe Press), 1974, p. 72.

8.   Committee for Economic Development, *Reducing Crime and Assuring Justice*, (New York), 1972, p. 84.

9.   *Ibid.*

judge than with a policeman. If such inhibitions occur, they are not usually as drastic or with far reaching results as they can be in the case of police officials.

The Armed Component

All policemen in America are armed while serving on the job. Each policeman carries at least one gun. They enjoy the legal monopoly over the use of force within their jurisdictions, and such legality, in case force is used, is mainly defined and determined by them. Not only do policemen today have the advantage of being legally armed agents, they have the advantage of legally overdefending themselves against armed or unarmed citizens. Policemen today, at least in large cities, are issued protective helmets, bullet-proof vests, mace and similar gear. This gives the police, in fact or by impression, an "aggressive" image which no other component of the criminal justice agency can match.

The Discretionary Component

The police sub-system is the most powerful component in the system in terms of its discretionary powers. Police officers initiate, in almost all cases, the criminal justice process. They can start a long chain of pre-trial procedures at almost any time. All they need to do is to stop a "suspicious" person or vehicle and ask a few intelligent questions. Arnold Trebach described this discretionary power by policemen with reference to "stop-and-frisk" by saying that, "No petty indignity or minor intrusion this—which may now be employed by any policeman in the U.S. suddenly in the throes of reasonable suspicion".[10] Justice William O. Douglas added to Trebach's remark, in the same reference, saying that:

> To give the police greater power than a magistrate is to take a long step down the totalitarian path .   .   .   . If the individual is no longer to be sovereign .   .   .   . If the police can pick him up whenever they do not like the cut of his jib . . . we enter a new regime.[11]

Once a policeman makes a wrong decision to stop, arrest, detain, search or seize, his decision unfortunately sticks for quite some time. The procedures needed to undo what the policeman initially did are too complicated, long, and frustrating. Such procedures may require the efforts of several other criminal justice agencies. A complete eradication of the long-term results of the policeman's wrong decision

10. Jack D. Douglas, ed., *Crime and Justice in American Society*, (New York: The Bobbs-Merrill Company), 1971, p. 59.

11. *Ibid.*

may never take place.   A policeman's decision to intervene usually causes ample damage to the individual even under the famous principle of "presumption of innocence."

Another aspect of the discretionary power by the policeman as compared to officials of other criminal justice agencies is the fact that he is generally the only agent authorized to go to the public, rather than have the public come to him.   The policeman carries his discretion along with him to the street, to public places, even to peoples' homes and businesses.   He associates with the public at all times and technically can trace people anywhere they go.   The prosecutor, the judge, the correctional official (except probation and parole officers checking on their clients) cannot exercise their discretion so comprehensively, for they have to wait for "cases" to be brought before them in their official capacity.   As a result, prosecutors and judges seldom encounter the public outside the boundaries of their offices, and their discretion is therefore much less comprehensive.

A third aspect of the policeman's discretionary power, and probably his most effective tool, is his discretion *not* to initiate the criminal justice process.   While policemen can single-handedly ignore or pretend not to witness a crime in progress or fail to respond to a citizen's complaint, prosecutors and judges cannot.   The initial contact between a policeman and a violation of the law is either audio-visual or verbal.   The contact at this stage can be easily overlooked by the policeman without much implication.   Unless the contact is later reported authoritatively by someone, the policeman can easily invoke a "never saw" or a "never heard of it" privilege.   Such power "not to initiate" the criminal justice process does not exist as easily with a prosecutor or a judge.   The latter deal with written documents, and their dispositions have to be substantiated by legal evidence in accordance with the law.

The Specialist Component

The police sub-system is the most technical component in the criminal justice system.   They possess and run sophisticated machines such as computers, spectrometers, fluoroscopes, high-powered microscopes, radar guns, digicombs, etc.   Without such technological devices, the occurrence of some crimes cannot be established, and without the existence of crime the existence and growth of prosecution, courts, prisons and institutions of social rehabilitation can be hardly justified.   The technological devices operated by the police sub-system illustrate, in a sense, the specialization of police agencies. Such technological devices, moreover, require a wide range of technical and scientific skills, and the police, in fact or by impression, have created a corps of specialists, quasi-scientists, and technicians.

The police sub-system also constructs and utilizes official statistics such as crime rate, crime index, clearance ratio, recidivism rate, etc. Utilization of such sophisticated data reflect an air of legitimacy on the total system. Members of other components of criminal justice explicitly, or implicitly, feel grateful to the technical role of the police since without such technical aid they could be voted out of existence.

The police sub-system is the largest, uniformed, armed, discretionary, and specialized component, and therefore, it may be hard to treat it like the other components. But failure to control and stabilize such a powerful element could be "a long step down the totalitarian path", to quote Supreme Court Justice Douglas. Without upgrading the police organizations and strengthening their management, such a powerful sub-system may go astray and eventually dominate the whole criminal justice system. Unless, therefore, the police sub-system is so organized and managed along lines of modern administration, professionalism, and democracy, the whole system of criminal justice might deteriorate into a notorious era of the police state.

Police administration seeks the organization and management of police agencies within the framework of the criminal justice system. Police administration is a field of cooperation among police officials towards the achievement of police goals in an efficient, effective, economical and an impartial manner. Police organization provides the appropriate structure of police hierarchy, tasks, functions, lines of communication, supervision, and control so as to achieve the stated goals. Police management, on the other hand, emphasizes the intellectual inputs by police managers, supervisors, and decision-makers. It provides the ways and means for appropriate leadership, planning, coordinating, budgeting, and formulating of policy decisions relating to the harmonious operation of police organizations within the legitimate boundaries of an effective criminal justice system.

PART TWO

POLICE BUREAUCRACIES IN AMERICA

CHAPTER THREE

HISTORICAL DEVELOPMENT OF POLICE ADMINISTRATIVE THOUGHT

Overview

The contemporary term "police administration" denotes the study of police organizations and management in a "scientific" manner. It attempts to examine the structure, roles, functions, and environments of police agencies as well as the behavior, decisions and action-patterns of those who operate them. The study capitalizes on the systematic analysis of police bureaucracies by breaking them down into manageable areas of inquiry related to the achievement of prescribed goals. This is naturally followed by the development of some "sensible" generalizations which efficiently, effectively, and economically govern the conduct of such organizations in the future.

Although the concepts of police administration could be traced to ancient human history, the term itself is fairly contemporary. It developed as an off-shoot of those studies in public administration which grew initially out of the works of Max Weber, Frederick Taylor, and Henri Fayol around the turn of the century. With later contributions by Woodrow Wilson, James D. Mooney, Paul Appleby, Luther H. Gulick, Dwight Waldo, Arthur F. Bentley, Marshall E. Dimock, John Pfiffner and several other students of government, the "scientific" conduct of public affairs finally evolved into the present discipline of Public Administration. Further studies in Public Administration followed more and more specialized approaches and branched out in substantive as well as in applicative dimensions. The former entailed Studies in Organization Theories, Personnel Administration, and Financial Administration, as well as Management Techniques and Technology. The latter evolved to include areas of application such as School Administration, Hospital Administration, Church Administration, City Administration, as well as, of course, Police Administration, Jail Administration, Correctional Administration and other emerging areas of Criminal Justice.

Forerunners to the present term of "police administration" are numerous. They include Police Science, Law and Order, Crime Prevention, Public Security, Law Enforcement, and even such vague terms as Peace Maintenance and Justice. Such terms, however, have failed to perpetuate themselves as an established discipline because they failed to demonstrate comprehension, completeness, independability, and, above all, compatibility with the modern aura of science and research. The term Police Administration seemed especially functional and appropriate during the last three decades during which the monumental writings by August Vollmer and O. W. Wilson appeared.[1]

The basic concepts of police administration, however, are by no means novel. Throughout human history there was always a dire need for social control which had to be handled by selected experts. No community ever survived which did not experience some sort of organized police control exerted through one or another pattern of police administration. Although as mentioned earlier, the term was not in use or even known fifty years ago, the essence of police administration always prevailed and police "administrators" in one form or another dominated the processes of social control.

The following stages may help illustrate the historical development and emergence of police administration systems and techniques:

1 —The Divine Model of Policing.

2 —The Ancient Societies and Kin Policing.

3 —The Greco-Roman Police Organizations.

4 —The Medieval Attempts at Improvement.

5 —The English Foundation.

THE DIVINE MODEL OF POLICING

The process of "establishing justice and ensuring domestic tranquility" can be traced as far back as the beginning of man in the Garden of Eden. As narrated in the Holy Scriptures, God appears to have been the original policeman. His "force" included a hierarchy of angels at different ranks and a codified system of punishment and rewards. God made and declared to the human community, at the time of Adam and Eve, a set of rules which governed their tiny com-

1. August Vollmer (1876–1955) and Orlando W. Wilson (1900–1972) were probably the greatest pioneers of police administration in the United States, and their impact on the field has been institutional. Though the latter was a student of the former, their works and publications must be seen as an integrated block of progressive police thinking unmatched by any follower or group of followers. Contributions by Vollmer included *Crime and the State Police*, 1935; and *The Criminal*, in 1949. Publications by Wilson included *Police Administration* published in 1957. For a comprehensive biography and discussion of the works of August Vollmer and Orlando W. Wilson see: Edward Eldefonso, Alan Coffey and Richard Grace, *Principles of Law Enforcement*, (New York: John Wiley and Sons), 1974, pp. 75–84.

munity. God, as the chief police executive, also provided Adam and Eve with a "constitution" declaring their rights and duties as well as limitations on their freedoms. For protection against environmental harms and threats to their survival, the tiny community had to abide by and conform to God's code of rules. When the community deviated from God-given laws, the chief police executive is reported to have reacted by investigating their crime, by taking action against the defendants and by executing his sentence. The Scriptures here say:[2]

God to Adam: "Where art thou?"

Adam: "I heard your voice in the Garden. I was afraid, and I hid myself."

God: "Who told thee that thou art naked? Hast thou eaten of the tree whereof I commanded thee that thou shouldest not eat?" (Leading questions which probably wouldn't be admitted in court by today's legal standards)

Adam: "The woman whom thou gavest to be with me, she gave me of the tree and I did eat." (a statement of admission)

God to Eve: "What is this that thou hast done?" (an interrogation)

Eve: "The Serpent beguiled me and I did eat."

God to Serpent: "Because thou hast done this, thou art cursed above all cattle and above every beast of the field." (a guilty verdict)

God to Woman: "I will greatly multiply thy sorrow and thy conception; in sorrow thou shalt bring forth children; and thy desire shall be to your husband and he shall rule over thee." (sentence)

God to Adam: "Because thou hast harkened unto the voice of thy wife .   .   .   cursed is the ground for thy sake; in sorrow shalt thou eat of it all the days of your life." (sentence)

In the famous murder case of Cain and Abel, God again investigated the crime, interrogated Cain and banished him: [3]

God to Cain: "Where is Abel thy brother? Why art thou wroth? Why is thy countenance fallen?" (interrogation that assumed unestablished facts)

Cain: "I know not. Am I my brother's keeper?" (a statement of defense)

God: "And now art thou cursed from the earth .   .   . a fugitive and a vagabond shalt thou be in the earth." (punishment)

2. Genesis, Chapters 9–17.   3. Genesis, Chapter 4.

The Divine model of policing certainly entailed divine ways and means which are beyond human understanding in today's secular society.   Throughout Judeo-Christian history, however, scriptural evidence shows that special police powers were delegated to spiritual leaders. "Scribes", "elders" and "chief priests" had exclusive police powers. They gathered intelligence, issued arrest warrants, ordered the use of force against agitators and trouble-makers, indicted defendants, and quite often returned (juristic) verdicts.

The police function performed by scribes, elders and chief priests was mainly a part of their religious mandate. Their charge was to protect the spiritual community by removing the heretics of the faith. Their authority—the right to act—stemmed from the sovereignty of God and their powers derived from the letter and spirit of the scriptures, social customs, and probably spiritual revelation. The powers of the scribes, elders, and chief priests seemed to be unlimited and in many cases final. They not only interpreted divine laws, but also zealously defended their mandate to maintain "God's Peace". The religious leaders controlled a paramilitary organization of "Captains of the Temple", and "officers" equipped with "swords and staves". Such organizations were authorized to carry out arrests against deviants and social activists and were instructed to "take them to the high priest's house".[4] Jesus Christ was known to have been arrested in the Garden of Gethsemane by "the chief priests and Captains of the Temple and the elders which were come to him".[5] The Book of Acts also indicates that Apostle Paul bore letters from the high priest and elders granting him the right "to arrest, bind and commit to prison both men and women".[6]

THE ANCIENT SOCIETIES AND KIN POLICING

There is ample historical evidence to indicate that some forms of police administration were not unfamiliar to early tribal people. Of course, people at that time did not employ police forces as we understand it today, but for all general purposes they were involved in some primitive systems of police administration. Archaeological findings, such as cave drawings and early tablets, give evidence that early human tribesmen were concerned with protection and the enforcement of tribal codes. Although emphasis was on tribe survival, the concept of protection from marauders and each other certainly led to the creation of a primitive police administration.[7]

4. Luke, 22:52–54.

5. *Ibid.*, also read the story of John the Baptist.

6. Acts 22:4.

7. Vern L. Folley, *American Law Enforcement*, (Boston: Holbrook Press, Inc.), 1973, p. 25.

Ancient African tribes looked at their chiefs for protection and the preservation of a patriarchal social order since the tribe consisted primarily of several warring clans and sects. The elders were responsible for maintaining peace among all dissenting groups. The chieftain—usually the fittest and shrewdest among the elders—was responsible for keeping the tribe's peace, cohesion and justice. He was basically in charge of making the tribe's laws, interpreting them and executing them. Though most tribal societies were characterized by a traditional, static, and unspecialized order, a charismatic leader usually managed to single-handedly control the peace-keeping process. His leadership and prestige hinged heavily on the shrewd management of his roles as regulator, stabilizer, and dispenser of justice.

"Kin policing" relates to the collective role of the tribe, clan or family in assuming the responsibility for obtaining justice. Such community policing was mostly fluid and lacked firm structures since formalized laws were undeveloped and mostly unknown. Such laws, in fact, were not popular until written records became commonplace. Tribal laws consisted of informal codes of conduct in conformity with customs, beliefs, and superstitions prevalent in the unscrupulous types of tribal life at these times.

The philosophy of tribal justice during ancient history was mainly based on the theories of retaliation and tribute. The former—referred to as *lex talionis:* an eye for an eye and a tooth for a tooth—related to the basic human drive of killing the killer and maiming the maimer. The latter, a more reconciliatory concept, provided for an opportunity for the killer or the maimer to save himself by paying a certain price usually in terms of a valuable tribal commodity, i.e., animals, property, or some particular rights. The authority to approve the payment of tribute rather than to require retaliation was vested in the chieftain by virtue of his wisdom, experience and power. In more serious crimes, punishments were naturally more serious and crude in nature. They included branding, flaying, impalement (usually executed publicly) or banishment.

Further development in police administration techniques in ancient societies corresponded with the degree of social sophistication the societies achieved. Although it should be emphasized that such developments included little reform by contemporary criteria, some ancient Egyptian communities, for instance, achieved higher levels of order than others. Also, although archaeologists and anthropologists certainly brought little information to bear on the ancient and prehistoric system of law enforcement and police administration, the following brief survey may be of particular significance.

With the rise of kings and potentates in the Middle East, the Sumerian rulers "Lipitishar and Pshnauan standardized what would constitute a crime and the expected social response to their occurrence".[8] Some hundred years later, around 2100 B.C., the Babylonian King Hammurabi attempted the first codification of customs in his famous Code of Hammurabi. The code dealt with the responsibilities of the individual to the group, private dealings between individuals, and emphasized penalties of the retributive type rather than *lex talionis*. Hammurabi, therefore, is probably the first known leader accredited with the establishment of a type of police organization. His code inscribed on stone of black diorite was found by modern archaeologists and is still legible.[9] The code prescribed and proscribed rules of conduct and provided specific methods of punishments for the violators. Policemen were organized in a "messengers" system and assigned to the tasks of carrying out the commands of the law.[10]

Nineveh, the ancient center of the Assyrian empire, is said to have had a system of courts with standing judges who dealt with "infamous crimes" such as murder, theft, and adultery. Around 1500 B.C., the Egyptians are reported to have had an expanded system of judges and courts and even sophisticated laws which included serious crimes as well as bribery and corruption. About 1400 B.C., King Amenhotob of Egypt is reported to have developed a specialized marine patrol to cruise the Nile River and check the custom houses on the northern coast near the delta.[11]

In the sixth century B.C., Persia, under Cyrus the Great, established a road patrol (a forerunner of traffic police) and a postal system which was operated as a police function. Under Darius, the empire was administratively divided into several provinces with "satrapes", protectors, responsible for insuring domestic tranquility, conducting public affairs and collecting taxes.

In the technological areas of police administration, especially in criminal investigation and crime detection, the ancient societies reportedly discovered some methods which later became the basis of modern techniques still in use. Erasistratus, a famous Greek philosopher who lived around 300 B.C., introduced the practice of testing the pulse of suspects as a means of telling guilt or innocence. In theory, this practice constitutes the essence of polygraph testing today. Ancient Chinese are known to have used a crude "endocrinal test" to tell guilt or innocence of suspects. They used to force suspects to

8. Edward Eldefonso, Alan Coffey and Richard Grace, *Principles of Law Enforcement*, (New York: John Wiley and Sons), 1968, p. 60.

9. Thomas F. Adams, *Law Enforcement*, (Englewood Cliffs, New Jersey: Prentice-Hall, Inc.), 1973, p. 55.

10. A. C. Germann, Frank D. Day, and Robert Gallati, *Introduction to Law Enforcement and Criminal Justice*, (Springfield, Illinois: Charles C. Thomas Publishers), 1970, p. 39.

11. *Ibid.*, p. 40.

chew, and later spit, an amount of rice flour. If the sample was "dry" upon spitting, the suspect was assumed guilty. If the sample was moist, then the suspect was considered innocent.

Ancient Indian communities are known to have used superstition for the examination of suspects and the determination of guilt. One most common superstition was the "Holy Donkey" story. The suspect would be put in a dark room all by himself except for a live donkey. The suspect would be instructed that he is in the presence of a holy animal which could tell guilt from innocence. The suspect would also be instructed that to prove his innocence, he had to pull the donkey's tail. If the suspect was innocent of the charges against him, the animal would remain quiet when its tail was pulled. If the animal brayed that would indicate that the suspect was guilty. Of course, a "guilty" suspect would refrain from pulling the donkey's tail lest it would bray and declare his guilt. When the suspect returns from the dark room, his hands would be examined by a group of elders who would then be able to find out whether the suspect actually pulled the tail. The tail would have been treated with a special dye before the experiment had begun.

Ancient African tribes and some nomad Arab tribes used similar tests like that of the Holy Donkey. The Africans had a large jug, full of boiling water, kept in a room. The suspect would be instructed to walk in by himself and dip his hands and arms in the jug. If his hands bloated, he would be guilty. If his hands did not, his innocence would be automatically assumed. The "guilty" suspect of course would not dip his hands while left alone and unwatched. Observing unbloated hands later by the elders would establish the suspect's guilt; naturally, all hands dipped in boiling water must bloat! The Arab tribes applied almost the same technique using a heated "pan" to be licked.

Ancient tribes used torture also as a means of telling guilt from innocence. Needless to say such tribes and communities were far from being "civilized", let alone democratic. The use of torture by the rulers was not only tolerated by the followers but also expected. "Barbaric" leaders were common and brutal practices were effective in maintaining law and order. Among the common techniques were those of chaining suspects, pulling their fingernails, filling their bodies with water, forcing them to wrestle until death with gladiators, and throwing them into animal dens.

It was not until the nineteenth century that Mosso, Lombroso and Galton developed scientific methods to substitute for torture as a means of distinguishing guilt from innocence. Such contributions by these humanitarian scientists lead to contemporary criminal investigation techniques common in civilized nations today. In the United

States and Great Britain, as well as most of the Western World, modern criminal investigation practices are commonplace. They are based on technological testing coupled with humanitarian and legal considerations. The supremacy of law and judicial procedures later evolved and civil rights became the main auspices under which determination of guilt is made.

By way of summation, police administration as performed by ancient tribes and societies was clearly primitive in nature, informal in organization, limited in purpose, and charismatic in its method of management. The organizational component of police administration was clearly undeveloped. Police structures in terms of hierarchies, specialized tasks, and defined roles and functions were totally lacking. Distinction between police, priesthood, and politics was extremely hard to ascertain. The management component—the personal abilities of leaders to run police operations, on the other hand, was considerably more effective and public safety then was more secure than it is today. Codes of customary conduct were adhered to religiously. Punishments were executed without delay and an aura of confidence in social order prevailed. The apparent lack of development in police administration during ancient history must be seen in terms of the general conditions at the time. Lack of formal writing media and communication techniques coupled with the slowness of social change and tools of discovery seem to have contributed strongly to the primitiveness of the field of police administration at the time.

THE GRECO–ROMAN POLICE ORGANIZATION

The early Greek cities witnessed some considerable developments from tribal (kin) policing to community (city) policing. The Greek system, and ultimately the Roman system, were quite influential in the processes of modernizing and solidifying law enforcement. Due to their administrative skills, as demonstrated by their advanced civilian and military organizations, Greco-Roman improvements in the areas of police, law, justice, and punishment were extremely impressive by all standards of the time.

Greek Philosophies and Practices

Plato, the greatest Greek master, presented one of the most valuable contributions to the democratic theory of government and social control. In his early dialogue entitled *Politeia,* as well as in his later dialogue *The Laws,* Plato struggled with notions of the city, *polis* (interpreted today as state), constitutions, social order, justice and the supremacy of laws. Plato argued that law and the laws, *nomas and nomoi,* were essential for the structuring of the *polis.* He emphasized that a "good" order of the *polis* could be secured only by the making of basic laws. In turn, laws, *nomoi,* were seen by Plato as "a participation in the idea of justice   .   .   .   and through it in the idea of good".[12] In Plato's later dialogue, *The Laws*, he established the foundation of the rule of law for civilizations to come. He wrote that "legislation and the establishment of a political order are the most perfect means in the world to achieve virtue" (*Laws*, 708). Plato later asserts that a government is merely the servant of the laws. Only a state in which "law is the ruler over the rulers" (*Laws*, 715) —that is to say, only a state in which the government is subject to the laws—can be expected to reap all the good which the "gods" hold ready for genuine communities, namely, the true happiness and satisfaction of the citizens. Plato, who was also involved in many other discussions, examined in length the notions of justice and punishment. The latter, he explained, had not only a retributive impact but rehabilitative impact as well. The aim of punishment, he wrote, is to make criminals "better". He regarded punishment of criminals as an instrument of reform and progress both for the individual criminal as well as for the society as a whole.

Solon, the famous law-giver of Athens (638–559 B.C.), was less philosophical than Plato though more pragmatic. Since he was the ruler of Athens, Solon had to adapt Plato's philosophy to realistic grounds. He applied democracy by divising a national assembly of freemen which was empowered to pass laws of the *Empire*. Solon also instituted courts in which juries were chosen from the citizenry and formal procedures of litigation were strictly adhered to. When Solon was once asked to name the essential ingredient of the ideal community, his answer, which should be memorized by every law enforcement professional was, "When those who have not been injured become as indignant as those who have!" [13]

Erasistratus, who was the ruler of Athens (300 B.C.), established a guard system responsible for three tasks: (1) safeguarding public utilities, (2) safeguarding traffic on highways, and (3) guarding the person and residences of the ruler. In today's police organizations this would look like a state police system with comprehensive jurisdiction of public safety, highway patrol, and protection of the person and mansion of the governor.

In Sparta, Athens' rival sister which has long symbolized Greek military prowess, there developed a unique system of police. The force was, as would be expected, authoritarian and militaristic in structure and management. The police force was commanded by a commission called *ephori* consisting of five members (*ephors*) who controlled such divisions as investigation, prosecution, trial, jury, and

12. Carl J. Friedrich, *The Philosophy of Law in Historical Perspective*, (Chicago: The University of Chicago Press), 1963, p. 17.

13. Germann, Day and Gallati, *op. cit.*, p. 40.

execution of sentences. The *ephori* system had almost limitless powers and no checks were put on their authority except in terms of their loyalty to the ruler and their influence on one another. It is no wonder, then, that the Spartan police system won the label of the first "secret police" system in the world.[14]

Roman Philosophies and Practices

The Roman Empire was definitely indebted to the Greek culture and civilization for its glory. Rome, "the mistress of the world", was capable and willing to carry the torch of enlightenment to the known corners of the world. With the population of Rome divided into Romans, aliens, and slaves, the literature by Roman philosophers and rulers developed further legalistic sophistication. Every jurist today may marvel at the great innovations in the legal theory attributed to Justinian.

The Justinian Code or *corpus juris civilis*, divided laws into three basic categories: (1) *jus naturale,* natural law, which is what nature teaches all living beings, (2) *jus gentium,* law of gentiles, which was instituted by man, supposedly to govern non-Roman citizens in conquered lands, and (3) *jus civile,* civil law, which dealt with non-criminal matters. The basic premises of the *corpus juris civilis* probably became the world's most famous and influential law book. It contributed to the concepts of fair trial, proof of guilt, and opportunity of the accused to meet his accuser. The law has been incorporated in the laws of most nations today including the Bill of Rights in the Constitution of the United States of America. Cicero, the famous Roman philosopher, wrote in his *De legibus* that "all men form one great community, that all men are equal, and that, however man may be defined, such definition must fit all men, and therefore all men share with one another the same basic law".[15]

In the area of administration, Roman philosophies of law and justice were to be maintained by the military legions of the rulers. Governors of Roman provinces, as well as of occupied lands, utilized *Quaestores* (inquirers) to preside on criminal courts. *Quaestores* were to rely on a military force set aside by Augustus, the emperor of Rome in 27 B.C., called the Praetorian Guard. Smaller units of the Praetorian Guard were called Urban Cohorts and were assigned to policing particular districts mostly where slaves and unruly citizens lived. A cohort unit was comprised of about 600 men and three such units were assigned to serve the *Quaestores* in charge of the city of Rome.[16] The method of arrest applied by the cohort units was mostly peaceful and rather ceremonial. It is reported that such offi-

14. *Ibid.*

15. Carl J. Friedrich, *op. cit.*, p. 30.

16. Vern L. Folley, *op. cit.*, p. 28.

cers used to go to the house of the suspect with an arrest warrant issued by the *Quaestor* and blow a trumpet as an indication of arrest.[17]

The inequity inherent in the Roman class system, however, engendered a considerable amount of resentment and hatred among the masses. Because of the wide gulf in the distribution of economic goods, most noncitizens had a loathsome existence. Slaves did most of the work, leaving citizens to live in almost complete idleness and subsisting on public doles of grain.[18] During the older age of the republic, gangs of thugs were reported to have terrorized the populace of Rome and fought pitched street battles which the authorities were unable to prevent. Organized crime also became prevalent as demonstrated by the career of two notorious ring-leaders, Clodius and Milo (57–53 B.C.), who were so powerful that Roman politicians kowtowed to them and sought their support at election time.[19]

The crime rate in Rome, especially for some time before its fall in 395 A.D., was reportedly high. Archeological digs of ancient Roman cities invariably uncover buildings in which the windows on the first floor and those accessible from the streets were barred. The prevalence of this type of anti-burglary device is compelling testimony of the high incidence of house theft to which the Romans were subjected.[20]

The Vigiles Organization

Emperor Augustus, apparently extremely disturbed by the absence of law and order and public security in the streets of Rome, ordered the reorganization of his police forces. The military legions of Rome had failed in maintaining public order in the capital city. The "vigiles" of Rome were, consequently, created as non-military units of several thousand men. They were assigned the combined function of keeping the peace and fighting the numerous fires in the city "made of wood and brick".[21] The vigiles were organized in units assigned to geographical precincts and, therefore, were referred to as the first municipal police force.

The Roman vigil wore an armor breast plate and a steel helmet. He was armed with a broad sword and a truncheon-type device called a festus. This weapon symbolized the twin aspects of his mission. The festus could be used as a night stick showing his police authority,

17. Germann, Day, and Gallati, *op. cit.*, p. 40.

18. George G. Killinger and Paul E. Cromwell, Jr., *Issues in Law Enforcement*, (Boston: Holbrook Press, Inc.), 1975, p. 5.

19. *Ibid.*

20. *Ibid.*, p. 6.

21. *Ibid.*, p. 4.

but also had a hook at one end useful in breaking wood in searching for embers and other tasks associated with fire fighting. Some commentators, noting their fire-fighting responsibility along with their police duty, have referred to them as the first instance of "integrated police-fire services". Tradition has it that the crest of today's firemen's helmet is traceable to the style of the steel cap which the vigiles wore.[22]

The organization of the vigiles, eventually numbering approximately nine thousand men, called for a system of seven subdivisions, each consisting of two sections. The vigiles of each subdivision had a headquarters or a police headquarters located in a central place near the boundary of the two sections and headed by a senior officer. Within each section there was a police substation called "excubitorem" under the command of a junior officer called "Praefectus Vigilum".[23]

Each excubitorem had jail-like cells for the detention of prisoners arrested for arraignment. The vigil assigned to the administration of the jail was called "karcerarius", hence the English word "incarceration". The karcerarius was a specialized officer responsible and trained for the custody of all suspects undergoing interrogation.

Another function of the vigiles was to interrogate suspects and occasionally put excessive pressure on them to secure confessions. Augustus, extremely disturbed about the lack of law and order in Rome, seemed to have been determined to suppress crime by all means. Management policies which originally emphasized the use of civilized and peaceful means were replaced by a policy of suppression and violence. The vigiles, like most municipal forces today, developed an image of brutality and repression which probably overshadowed that of the military legions which preceded them. They were viewed as the instrument of the establishment which was oppressive to the vast majority of Romans. Graffiti from the excavated ruins of the excubitorem of the seventh section indicates that vigiles experienced moments that were "serious, complaining, and melancholy." [24] The citizenry, somewhat derisively, referred to them as "spartoli", or buckets, which sounds quite similar to present day terms of "pigs" and "fuzz."

A third known function of the vigiles was criminal investigation. A specialized segment of the force was dressed in plainclothes and assigned to the gathering of information, penetrating organized crime rings, and tracing fugitives and runaway slaves. This segment of the

22. *Ibid.*, p. 7.   24. *Ibid.*, p. 10.

23. *Ibid.*, p. 8.

vigiles force was called "sebaciarii" and is considered the forerunner of present detective divisions. Their assignment—like today's detective work—was reported by roman historians as "dangerous and of a temporary nature".[25]

THE MEDIEVAL ATTEMPTS AT IMPROVEMENT

The Roman empire disintegrated in 395 A.D. With the sudden collapse of such an enormous and stabilizing power, Europe was left in a state of anarchy with warring nations engaging in brutal conflicts and plunder. For the next several centuries a curtain of feudal darkness fell over Europe. Maintenance of order as an organized function of the state almost disappeared except for sporadic showings in some developing communities. Not until law and order was restored in France and England as an essential protection against the widespreading ills of the industrial revolution around 1760, were features of police organization and management seriously put back together and their examination made historically possible. The Peelian reforms ultimately followed in 1829, ushering in a revolution in police administration and alerting the world to the fastest advancement in police administration ever experienced. For the remainder of this historical discussion, the era of medieval societies will be used to denote the period in European history between the fall of the Roman empire and the beginning of the industrial revolution around 1760.

The French Contributions

France, which enjoyed feudal governments under hundreds of kings and princes for centuries, experienced a relatively orderly period under Charles the Great, or Charlemagne, the most famous of medieval rulers, living around 771. Under Charlemagne, France is attributed to have presented three main improvements to the administration of law enforcement and criminal justice. The first was the geographical distribution of the land into manageable areas known as *Contes,* or counties, each under the control of a count responsible for the administration of police functions and the dispensation of justice. For the counts to manage their territories fairly, a set of standards and rules were issued by Charles the Great called *Les Capitulaires de Charlemagne,* or the laws of Charlemagne. These laws established the ways and means for handling crime and criminals, weights and measures, tolls and sales, as well as emergency procedures for famine, pestilence, etc.

The second improvement introduced by the French, and refined by Charlemagne, had a much more far-reaching impact on the administration of justice than probably all other French contributions put

25.   *Ibid.*, p. 9.

together. French kings developed the earliest seeds of the jury system which "became flesh and liveth amongst us" today as a main principle in the administration of justice. Leading persons were placed under oath and asked to render their opinion on conflicting matters. Twelve people (probably after the twelve disciples of Christ) were sworn in, and were known as *jurata* (those sworn), hence today's term "jury". Their opinion was usually handed to the king or count in terms of a *veredictum* (true saying), hence the term "verdict". Such leading persons were originally charged with the examination of issues relating to royal disputes, taxation, public order, and later to criminal allegations.

The third improvement provided by the French developed around 875 A.D. after the death of Charlemagne. The Marshals of France were made particularly responsible for the maintenance of public security. To facilitate the organization and management of such a function, a body of armed men known as *marechaussee* was established to enforce laws of public safety. The gendarmerie, men under arms, who police France in a rather authoritarian system today are the modern version of the marechaussee system.

The English Contributions

The development of police organization and management in the United States was directly influenced by the ideas, philosophies, and practices evolved in England before and during the Peelian era. One reason for that is the fact that the colonies were mostly controlled by English governors who applied the English laws and methods of social control. Another reason can be inferred from the fact that quite a few of the early settlers came from Great Britain and were already pregnant with current English doctrines on freedom, equality and rights of the individual. Liberal ideas derived from the *Magna Carta,* 1215, the Statute of Winchester, 1285, and the Glorious Revolution of 1688, were still fresh in their minds and the establishment of government and police systems in accordance with such philosophies seemed irresistible. The Peelian reforms of 1829 were later welcomed and viewed as a model of modern progress which the young nation felt compelled to incorporate as a part of its national inheritance.

Anglo-Saxon Practices

Anglo-Saxon England between 700 and 1066 consisted of a large number of *tuns* (towns) and villages hardly related by any means of a political system or organization for local justice or even defense. The systems of social control and justice were local in nature and primitive in character. Each community was responsible for its own self-discipline and dispensation of justice. Conflicts were resolved by tribal practices based on tradition and often superstitious beliefs. The most common means of settling disputes were:[26]

a. Trial by ordeal: As a method of determining guilt, it subjected the suspect to one or more survival tests such as boiling hot water or crossing hot beds of coal. If the suspect survived, he would be declared innocent.

b. Trial by combat: As a method of determining guilt, it required that contestants fight each other in a duel fashion; the survivor was acknowledged innocent.

c. Compurgation: As a means of determining guilt, it required that both parties to a conflict take a serious oath as to his innocence; the one who undertook the more serious oath was considered innocent.

Punishments in Anglo-Saxon England were severe. Although capital punishment was not often a part of the local judicial practice, branding as a method of deterrence, as well as of the identification of criminals, was commonplace. Restitution to the victim, to his family, or to his *tun* was common. Penalties were enforced by the community in a tribal fashion. If the offender escaped to another *tun*, he was to be returned or the other *tun* would be required to pay elaborate fines. The Anglo-Saxon practices, though they undoubtedly reflected an underdeveloped administration of justice, can at least be credited for their institutionalization of the concepts of fines, restitution, and extradition.

This concept of community policing later had to be upgraded to cope with the increasing instability within the *tuns* and villages, as well as with the increasing frequency of attacks by raiding tribes. King Alfred required all male persons, unless exempted by virtue of his high social position or the accumulation of property, to enroll in a group of ten families known as a *tithing*. They were made responsible for maintaining the peace and shared the duty of protecting the community. Each member of the *tithing* was responsible for the good behavior of his neighbor, and the *tithing* was responsible for the conduct of its members. A *tithingman*, or a headborough, was elected from the group and was given the responsibility of raising the hue and cry and meting out punishment. The hue and cry was a process whereby every able-bodied male had to join in the common chase for offenders. This activity is still on some police manuals today and obviously was the origin of the current concept of citizen's arrest.[27]

Ten *tithings* were called a *hundred* and a constable was assigned to supervise it and maintain its "armies". Several *hundreds* formed

26. Germann, Day, and Gallati, *op. cit.*,   27. *Ibid.*, p. 43.
      p. 42.

a *shire,* a geographical area equivalent to a county. The headman of the shire was a *royal reeve,* who exercised judicial and administrative powers in the *shire,* hence the term *"shire reeve",* or sheriff. In addition to his role as the head of the hundred court, the sheriff had a general responsibility to the King for conserving order and the maintenance of "the King's peace". He was authorized to hold the *posse comitatus* (power of the county) by which he could mobilize the whole available civil force of the shire in case of emergency.

The Norman Contributions

The Normans who conquered England in 1066 under William the Conqueror were not particularly keen about effecting any police reforms in the realm. They were primarily concerned with stabilizing their conquest in England and maintaining their French possessions across the Channel. King William reportedly kept the tithing-hundred-shire system during his reign. He reinforced its strength by giving the *shire-reeve* a military rank (since the country was under martial law) while he maintained its powerful civil position.

Later, however, the organization of *tithings, hundreds,* and *shires* was taken over by the Normans, modified, and systematized under the description of the frankpledge system (the term is derived from *fri-borg* which meant full security). A picture of this system at work is contained in the laws of Edgar, passed at the end of the tenth century, which ordained that enrollment in a *tithing* was compulsory: ".   .   .   every freeman be brought into a hundred and into a tithing   .   .   .   as soon as he is twelve years old".[28] The sheriffs were also stripped of their judicial powers and directed to focus on their police functions. To fill the gap, King William selected his own judges who traveled about the realm and became the forerunners of the circuit judge system of modern times.

The frankpledge later developed into a most repressive system. T. A. Critchley, in his comprehensive study of the history of police in England and Wales, states that the Norman sheriffs were "men of great power and little scruple   .   .   .   they extorted the payments of fines at the least opportunity or none".[29] Sheriffs were also reported to have behaved with a degree of barbarity uncommon even in that period. The Anglo-Saxon Chronicle recorded pitifully:

A.D. 1124. This same year after St. Andrew's Mass and before Christmas, held Ralph Basset and the King's thanes a 'gewitenemote' in Leicestershire   .   .   .   and there hanged more thieves than ever were known before; that is,

28. T. A. Critchley, *A History of Police in England and Wales,* (Letchworth, Hertfordshire, 1967), p. 3.

29. *Ibid.*

in a little while, four and forty men altogether; and despoiled six men of their eyes and mutilated them.   Many true men said that there were several who suffered very unjustly   .   .   .   first they are bereaved of their property and then they are slain.[30]

The Norman reign was not all notably repressive, however, for King Henry I, son of William the Conqueror, was more concerned with legalistic matters than the actual enforcement of the law.   He was a conciliatory ruler with philosophical abilities.   King Henry issued the *Leges Henrici,* laws of Henry, for which he earned the title of "law giver".   The laws reemphasized the supremacy of the state as responsible for maintaining the King's peace.   They divided crimes into "felonies", and "misdemeanors".   Felonies were serious law violations, such as murder, arson, false coinage and crimes of violence.   Misdemeanors, or bad behavior, included all less serious crimes.

King Henry II constructed county juries which the Normans had originally brought over from France.   Juries of twelve men were assigned to cases of individuals accused of committing crimes.   In later developments, rules of evidence were constructed, rights to challenge jurymen were installed and improved methods for impaneling the jury were inaugurated.

King John, who took the throne in 1199, added—though involuntarily—to the conciliatory mood of Norman kings by issuing the Magna Carta, the Great Charter, in 1215.   The king pledged in writing to observe the rights of the vassals.   Towns were not to be oppressed.   Merchants were not to be deprived of their goods for small offenses, nor the farmer of his "wagon and implements".   There is no more notable clause in the Charter than that of Article 39, which states that:

> No freeman may be taken or imprisoned or disseized or outlawed or banished or in any way destroyed   .   .   .   except by the lawful judgment of his peers, or by the law of the land.   We will not make men justiciaries, constables, sheriffs, of bailiffs, unless they understand the law of the land, and are well disposed to observe it.[31]

The Magna Carta is perhaps the most famous document in the history of government.   Special attention was given to the document by 18th century philosophers and by advocates of a democratic system.   Our founding fathers, in particular, insisted that a Bill of Rights including the concepts of the Magna Carta be incorporated in the Constitution.   The first ten amendments were thus added to the

30. *Ibid.*   31. Germann, Day, and Gallati, *op. cit.,*
                                            p. 49.

Constitution in 1791 and contained the basic freedoms of the American people as well as the basic restrictions on the powers of criminal justice and police organizations in the United States.

The Constable Organization

The Norman organization of police Constables seemed very similar to the Vigiles organization under the Romans. Both were formed as civilian organizations, in contrast to their military predecessors, and both were primarily created, organized, and utilized as "police forces".

The constable system in England was established, as was its distant successor the Metropolitan Police of 1829, as a reform measure forced upon the society at the time due to strong pressures. In the case of the constable system, the following conditions were most pressing:

(a) Revulsion from the barbaric practices by the sheriff and his men who had raised a great deal of public anguish and hostility.

(b) The assimilation of the Norman tribes and the vanquished Anglo-Saxons, which fostered an era of general relaxation and stabilized communal relations.

(c) The conciliatory tendency by the Norman kings who, after cementing the foundations of their reign in England, focused on winning the vassals to their side in order to fight the French.

(d) The monumental impact of the Magna Carta.

The early Norman constable system bore no relationship to the Saxon *tithingman,* although, of course, there was no complete break with the past.[32] The first statutory mention of the title "constable" was in 1252. The term originated from the French word, *comes stabli,* or Master of the Horse. The Normans, however, upgraded the office and elevated its status to one equal to that of mayor. The constable represented the fusion of popular and royal government more completely than any other local government official. He assisted the lord of the manor in regulating all the affairs of the community.

By the end of the thirteenth century, the constable had acquired three distinct characteristics. First, as the annually elected repre-

---

32. Nevertheless, a century or so after the conquest, we find a more lowly race of persons designated by the title "constable" taking over the tithingman duties. From the marriage of Saxon tithingmen and Norman constables, and with the assimilation of Norman and Saxon titles and offices, the verbal jungle thins out and the English constable of the Middle Ages seems to have emerged as the direct lineal descendant of the ancient tithingman. See T. A. Critchley, *op. cit.*

sentative of the manor or parish, he was its executive agent. His office embodied the principle of collective responsibility established by the Saxon *tithingman,* and in addition he made his presentments at the manorial court. Second, he was also an officer recognized by the Crown as having a particular responsibility for the keeping of the King's peace by hue and cry and other means. Third, his designation as "constable" gave his office a royal flavor which marked him substantially above most other local officers. By means of comparison, the office of the early English constable was analogous to the present office of the Sheriff in rural America today: he is elected by the populace though his authority is designated by the state as its top representative in charge of law and order as well as various local affairs.

In 1285, the office of the constable was further enhanced by the declaration of the Statute of Winchester. The statute was the only public measure of any consequence enacted to regulate police administration throughout the realm between the Norman Conquest and the famous Metropolitan Police Act of 1829. Thus, for nearly 600 years it laid down the basic principles of police administration in England.

The statute provided for some basic principles of police administration, which today are taken for granted by all modern police forces in the world:

1. The installment of a system of watch and ward: watch by night and ward by day. Town watchmen were selected to serve under the directon of the constable. A watch of up to sixteen men, depending on the size of the town, was to be stationed at every gate of a walled town between sunset and sunrise. This gave rise to the present concepts in police organization of day and night shifts, organizational hierarchy, span of control, as well as the general role of the police as a preventive and deterrent force. Arrested persons were detained in jail-type locations and handed over to the constable in the morning to be presented with the charges to court.

2. The constable had the authority to "deputize" unpaid part-time personnel to supplement the sworn force and to serve as a reserve force if needed.

3. The constables, their deputies, and watchmen, as well as the public at large were required to "bear arms". Every male between the ages of fiteen and sixty was to keep in his house "harness to keep the peace". Those of a superior rank (watchmen, constables and their deputies) were to maintain a "hauberke and helme of iron, a sword, a knife and a horse".[33] Poor people were to have available bows and arrows. Two high constables were to be appointed by the hundred court to make a half-yearly inspection of arms. The Second

---

33. T. A. Critchley, *op. cit.,* p. 6.

Amendment in the Constitution of the United States seems to have perpetuated this custom by stipulating that "the right of the people to keep and bear arms shall not be infringed".

4.   The system of hue and cry was revived as an inherent practice of the constable system; "and such as keep the watch shall follow with hue and cry, with all the towns near".[34]   This measure clearly explains the modern practices in the U.S. today regarding the duty of "citizen's arrest" and the police obligation to cooperate with neighboring forces.   The latter led to further needs for police coordination, communication and planning.

5.   The constable had a duty to present the offender and evidence to the court of jurisdiction.   This stipulation clearly implies an end to an era of communal justice by the public and establishes a clear separation between the law enforcement component and the court component in modern criminal justice systems.   A tint of the "system theory" can be inferred from that stipulation.

6.   The statute made no mention of frankpledge which leads us to assume that compulsory enrollment of the population in *tithing* as surety for each other had by this date become obsolete.

The organization of constables was even more elaborate by today's bureaucratic standards.   In carrying out his duties, the constable was supervised by a high constable who represented and acted as the executive agent of the hundred.   High constables, unlike the constable, were appointed by the hundred court (like county courts of today).   Administrative functions of the high constable included the following:

1.   Instruct the constables as to the nature of their office and the manner of operating it (training function).

2.   Supervise the constables in his *hundred* and receive their reports concerning the King's peace (supervisory function).

3.   To present any constable he considered to be negligent to the *hundred* court (disciplinarian function).

4.   To stimulate the constables to greater activity (leadership).

In the eighteenth century, with the advent of the early stages of the Industrial Revolution, it was apparent that local government officials were inadequate in coping with the problems of new roads and houses, public transportation, and urbanization.   High constables were therefore assigned additional quasi-judicial duties which included the inspection of weights, measures, roads and bridges.   Another duty was later added and since then has become a major function of constables and sheriffs everywhere: the collection of taxes.

34.   *Ibid.*

The Statute of Winchester must be seen as a major document in the study of police roles. The provisions presented by the statute creating the constable system have clearly established the three main types of today's police roles: the preventative role based on the watch and ward system, the deterrent role based on hue and cry, and the judicial role based on the constable's presentments before the court. Thus 1285, the year of the Statute, may be conveniently regarded as marking the end of the "first" police system in England, which pivoted largely around the *tithingman*, community responsibility, unrestrained police powers, and crude and cruel punishment.

Degradation of the Constable System

The office of the constable, the backbone of the English system of police administration for centuries, gradually began to decline with the emergence of the office of the justice of the peace around the fifteenth century. Like the American sheriff today, the English constable during the fifteenth and sixteenth centuries struggled hard to maintain his authority and to capitalize on his past achievements. Critchley reports that during that period the constable was still (at least in many areas) preeminent among the four principal officers of the parish who were annually elected: "constable, churchwarden, surveyor of highways, and overseer of the poor".[35] An unidentified author, who wrote a book on Degrees of People of England in 1586, suggested that at that time constables were chosen from among "the fourth and last sort of people [who] are daily labourers, poor husbandmen . . . tailors, shoemakers, carpenters who are to be ruled and not to rule others".[36] Around that time, the author made the inference that the constable system was commonly regarded as appropriate, "only to the old, idiotic, or infirm".[37]

The reasons for this degradation of the constable system in sixteenth century England, much like those of today's sheriff system in America, can be described as follows:

a. There was a reluctance of the wealthier merchants, tradesmen and farmers to serve their turn in undertaking the onerous and unpaid duties of the office.

b. There was the practice of many constables to pay deputies to act in their place. The deputies in turn paid others to do the job for them, hence the degradation of the office of the constable itself.

c. There was corruption in executing the duties of the office which was supposed to be done "truly without malice, affection or partiality".[38]

---

35. *Ibid.*, p. 10.

36. *Ibid.*

37. *Ibid.*, p. 11.

38. *Ibid.*, p. 11.

d. There was a lowering of selection requirements, especially in terms of knowledge and physical abilities.[39]

A lengthy examination of these reasons will follow when the discussion of the sheriff system in America is presented.

Deterioration and Reform

The degradation of the constable system of administration was not the only cause for the deterioration of the Winchester scheme of policing and the subsequent feverish search for a substitute. Two other factors strongly contributed to its eventual collapse and ultimately the emergence of the Metropolitan Police Organization in 1829.

The second cause for the collapse was the corruption which spread among the justices of the peace themselves and touched more closely the history of criminal law, local government and justice than that of the police. The seeds of the decline in the standards of integrity of many magistrates can be seen in the disaffection from the Crown, of a number of notable and reputable families who sided with the revolution of 1688 and who for generations had filled the offices of justice. The term employed to describe their successors' performance was the "justice of mean degree". Tradesmen, shopkeepers and often needy adventurers looked to the law, as to all else, for profit. The notorious "trading justice" of the first half of the eighteenth century emerged as the product of a system which aimed at making the administration of justice self-supporting by exacting a fee for every act performed. Magistrates were rewarded in proportion to the number of persons they convicted and evidently had little incentive to resist the corruption of the times. Ingenious criminals were able to exploit this state of affairs in such a way as to enjoy virtual immunity from prosecution.

The third cause of the collapse of the constable system was the rather sudden change in social and economic conditions in England as a result of the industrial revolution around 1760. The constable system demonstrated sheer inability to cope with the transformation. With England's population doubling from 6 to 12 million during the course of the eighteenth century, crime grew to alarming proportions.[40] The cities began to develop great slum areas. The men, women, and children became virtual slaves of the factory. Highwaymen infested the roads, footpads lurked about the urban areas, and bank robberies rose astronomically, numbering in the hundreds per year in large cities such as London, Liverpool, and Manchester. Women and children, under the circumstances, were report-

39. *Ibid.*   40. T. A. Critchley, *op. cit.*, p. 21.

edly starving and turning to crime in great numbers. One estimate indicates that at least 25,000 prostitutes were active in London alone. Children were trained as thieves, and for the first time juvenile delinquency became a sore problem.[41]

The deterioration of the constable system and the magistrate system along with the acute and sudden changes in the social and economic environments in England during the eighteenth century—led to the total ineffectiveness of the justice system and particularly to its law enforcement capability. National outcry for police reorganization became commonplace. Numerous bills were presented to Parliament for police improvement. Jeremy Bentham, the world famous philosopher, and other scholars, politicians, clergymen, and community leaders pressed their demands for immediate reform. The urgency of the situation was expressed by the Webbs (Sidney and his wife Beatrice, the famous nineteenth century economists and socialists) and described as "despair of conveying any adequate picture of the lawless violence, the barbarous licentiousness, and the almost unlimited opportunities for pilfering and robbery offered by the unpoliced London streets".[42]

It was natural under the circumstances of this unrestrained "criminal stampede" and the ineffective police forces, that the judicial sub-system would grow in power to avert the total collapse of social control. Punishments became increasingly severe, and at one time, there were 160 crimes punishable by death. Even stealing a loaf of bread was a hanging offense. In one month, over forty persons per day were executed. The severity of penalty, however, did not reduce crime and the common expression indicated that while "pick-pockets were being hanged, other pick-pockets were operating the crowds attending the executions".[43]

The first realistic attempt to deal with the reorganization of the English police occurred around 1770 by the announcement of the John Fielding Report. Sir John had been assigned by the Parliament "to inquire into burglaries and robberies in Westminster and London and whether it is a growing evil".[44] The report released by the Fielding committee was extremely helpful to the inception of the Peelian Reforms in 1829. It was the first document to discuss the need for police reorganization along modern administrative lines. The report also referred to major administrative problems of inefficiency, ineffectiveness, lack of defined jurisdictions, lack of appropriate planning

41. Germann, Day, and Gallati, *op. cit.*, p. 53.

42. S. and B. Webb, *English Local Government*, 1906, Vol. 1, pp. 463–473.

43. Germann, Day and Gallati, *op. cit.*, p. 54.

44. Killinger and Cromwell, *op. cit.*, p. 14.

and problems of personnel administration and motivation. A brief quotation from the report clearly refers to those problems:

> The watch is insufficient; their duty too hard, and pay too small .   .   .   . That as they are paid monthly, they borrow money of a usurer once a week .   .   .   . That the watch in Westminster is in every Parish under the direction of a separate commission: that Commissioners of the respective Parishes appoint the beats of their watchmen without conferring together, which leaves the frontiers of each Parish in a confused state, for that where one side of a street lies in one Parish, and the other side in another Parish, the Watchmen of one side cannot lend any assistance to persons on the other side.[45]

England, during the early nineteenth century, was moreover plagued by many problems other than the collapse of law and order —the war in America was going badly, Napoleon was riding high in Europe, and Roman Catholic groups in England and Wales were revolting against religious discrimination. Riots became commonplace and the burden on an antiquated constable system already crumbling increased. A hard winter in 1810 and the failure of the harvest in 1812 added to the misery. The Catholic Gordon riots and the anti-machine Luddite riots by unemployed subjects (1812) forced the government to realize once again the dire need for an effective civil agency capable of maintaining law and order.

More controversies and more riots erupted in 1820 over the trial of Queen Caroline whose husband, King George IV, sought to divorce her and marry one of his mistresses. Rioters fought against police forces in Kensington and Tottenham Court and military troops were called to restore public order. The Parliament got deeply concerned over the imminent state of anarchy and a government reshuffle was obviously essential. Sir Robert Peel, former Secretary for Ireland, was assigned to the Home Office (the English counterpart to the Department of Justice) in 1823. Immediate police reorganization was the stated—and the real—goal of Sir Robert.

Peel, an energetic and farsighted man, concerned himself with the organization of a modern, efficient, and prestigious police force. He was not the first to advocate police reform. Jeremy Bentham, Sir Patrick Colquhoun, Sir Samuel Romilly, and Sir James Macintosh preceded him, fighting a valiant and largely unsuccessful battle "until a member of the government was found ready to up their work".[46] Beside his basic concern for police reorganization, Sir Robert Peel

45. *Ibid.*

46. A. A. Ramsay, *Sir Robert Peel,* (London), 1928, pp. 49–50.

had to design a workable plan for the administration of criminal justice. In 1823 he consolidated into one statute 130 laws of theft and larceny. The death penalty was abolished for more than one hundred offenses. The benefits whereby clergy could escape punishment for some felonies were abolished. The number of judges operating in London and other cities and towns was increased. When he finally left office in 1830, he had reformed and consolidated "practically the whole of the Criminal Law of England".[47]

The monumental aspect of reform rendered by Sir Robert Peel which has gained him world-wide prestige and the title of "father of modern police organization" was his creation of the MET, London Metropolitan Police.

The Creation and Development of the London Metropolitan Police

In 1829, the Parliament approved Robert Peel's proposal and enacted "A Bill for Improving the Police In and Near the Metropolis". The bill incorporated the chief principles of modern police organization in terms of a hierarchy of authority, well-defined tasks, unity of command, delegation of power, supervision and control, discipline and morale, standards of performance, evaluation and reporting, among others.

The bill passed both houses and received the royal assent on June 19, 1829. Formal operation began on September 29 of the same year with 1,000 men in six divisions. To avoid any suspicion that they were a military force, members of the MET wore blue suits of civilian cut and top hats. They were, as they are today, unarmed except for a truncheon or a short nightstick. Their only distinguishing marks as policemen were the brass buttons bearing the word "Police" on their suits.[48] By the end of 1830, the first major reorganization was complete. The Metropolitan area, about 786 square miles (excluding the City of London Force which remains in charge of only 1 ¾ square miles in the center of London) was divided into 17 divisions. Each division had a superintendent in command assisted by an appropriate number of inspectors and sergeants while the rest were called PC's or Police Constable. Each division was further divided into eight sections, and each section into eight beats. Each PC wore a number on his shoulder for faster identification as well as the alphabet letter of his division.[49] The "Bobbies" or "Peelers", after Robert or Peel, worked in shifts and rotated around the clock with two-thirds of the force on night duty and one-third on day duty.

47. *Ibid.*, p. 68.

48. Killinger and Cromwell, *op. cit.*, p. 34.

49. Divisional letters run from "A" to "Z", omitting "I", "O" and "U". Policemen attached to Scotland Yard wear "CO", and members of the Traffic Department "TO".

The administration of the MET was charged to two commissioners appointed by the Crown upon the recommendation of the Home Office. The headquarters of the force was located at "Scotland Yard", in Whitehall Place. The name, Scotland Yard, which Englishmen like to think that everyone in the world, even if he knows nothing else, has at least heard of, predated the establishment of the force. The name grew from the location which opened on a courtyard long used as a residence by the Kings of Scotland. The office today only refers to the headquarters of the London Metropolitan Police. Recruitment of members of the force was made according to very high standards. Robert Peel reported to have been personally involved in interviewing all the candidates. It was extremely important that the moral character of the police be above suspicion. Sir Robert, therefore, wrote the following to his commissioners and superintendents on December 10, 1829:

> . . . all nomination for employment in the police, as well as promotions, . . . should depend exclusively upon the character, qualifications, and services of the person selected.[50]

The Metropolitan Police Instruction Book of 1871 emphasized that promotion of constables depended almost entirely on good conduct. The book stated:

> The rates of pay of the different classes and the allowances to constables are as follows: Fourth class, in which all constables are placed on entering the service, 20s (English Shilling) per week. In rotation by seniority, men are advanced from the 4th to the 3rd class with pay of 22s., . . . to the 2nd class, with pay of 24s., . . . to 1st class with pay of 26s., but all advancement in class is dependent on good conduct.[51]

From its inception, the civilian character of the police was stressed. Concepts of public service, self-control, and the importance of gaining the public's trust were especially emphasized. *Police Orders* for October 17, 1829, mentioned that because "some instances of rudeness on the part of the Police toward persons asking . . . civil questions had been reported", the Commissioners must call on all superintendents "to warn and instruct their men".[52] *Police Orders* in other references, consistently illustrated the basic theme of the preventive and protective nature of the police. Peel's philosophy

50. *Ibid.*, p. 35.

51. Metropolitan Police, *Instruction Book*, (London: Printed by G. E. Eyre and William Spottiswoode), 1871, pp. 17–18.

52. Killinger and Cromwell, *op. cit.*, p. 37.

clearly described the role of the police by saying: "It should be understood from the outset, that the principle object to be attained is the prevention of crime".[53]

The Peelian reforms were chiefly administrative in nature. They introduced major organizational principles as well as managerial techniques. Together, they were presented in twelve major principles often referred to as the "twelve commandments" of modern police administration. The following analysis will list each principle and indicate its administrative context and value:

1. The police must be stable, efficient, and organized along military lines.

The new administration clearly stressed the need for a structured organization, tightly knitted and well stratified along formal positions and ranks. Stability referred to the existence of clear lines of authority and responsibility. Efficiency referred to the ability of the organization to economically produce worthwhile services in return for the appropriations it expends. Reference to military lines, though it may confuse some students into mistaking the civilian PC for a sort of soldier, merely stressed the elements of discipline, control, obedience and hierarchical accountability.

2. The police must be under government control.

This principle emphasizes the public function of the police and its role in public service. It ended all previous voluntary systems: tithingmen-hundred-shire, feudal arrangements, and, most of all, the crown's unlimited power. While this principle is taken for granted by today's administrative thought, it was certainly a major departure from those traditional practices that had survived for many centuries.

Governmental control also stresses the funding of police organizations through public funds and the right of the Home Office (counterpart of Department of Justice in the U.S.) to oversee police policies and standards. The principle, furthermore, established the rule of civilian control over the police and the latter's commitment to uphold and enforce the laws of the land as determined by the governmental authority.

3. The absence of crime will best prove the efficiency of police.

Though this principle may be questionable from the criminological point of view, which holds that total absence of crime is impossible, the principle is administratively sound. It emphasizes the need for goal identification (fighting crime) and relates it directly to police effectiveness. Although absence of crime appears to be the "stated" goal of most police forces today, minimizing the occurrence of

53. *Ibid.*, p. 37.

crime through increased police efficiency seems to be the real police goal. Such a goal is not only possible but attainable.

4. The distribution of crime news is essential.

This is basically a "managerial" principle which seeks the achievement of the police goal of absence of crime. The principle serves several managerial purposes: a) distribution of crime news would help the legislators, police administrators, and other leaders of the criminal justice system to evaluate the performance of their units and upgrade current policies; b) distribution of crime news may demonstrate the high level of police effectiveness and thus deter the would-be criminals by increasing the chances of their being apprehended and promptly charged; c) distribution of crime news, especially when favorable to the police, would enhance the morale of police agencies and expand their base of public support. Should, on the other hand, the distribution of crime news indicate major police deficiencies such as poor training, inadequate leadership, lack of coordination, etc., this advanced knowledge would be most helpful to the processes of reorganization and correction.

5. The deployment of police strength, both by time and area, is essential.

This principle established two fundamental bases of modern police organization: the geographical distribution (the beat system) and the chronological distribution (the shift system). Without these organizational patterns, the comprehensive and uninterrupted provision of police services would be most difficult to maintain, if at all possible. Modern improvements in patrol administration through the use of tactical units and fluid patrol systems necessarily followed that basic organizational principle of distribution by time and area.

6. No quality is more indispensable to a policeman than a perfect command of temper. A quiet, determined manner has more effect than violent action.

This principle established the basis of modern police personnel administration. It originated the policies of police recruitment, selection, training, and conduct. The principle also relates to the democratic ideals of modern administration: concepts of fairness, legality, morality and compassion. It clearly condemns all aspects of police malpractice, brutality, or corrupton, and calls attention to the need for friendly police-community relations and programs.

7. Good appearance commands respect.

This principle brought to the fore the basic notions and subsequent studies of police image and public attitudes towards the police. Though the principle was stated in such a general manner so as to avoid any clear reference to police uniforms which today reflect a militaristic image, the salient of the principle remains obvious: in well-organized forces, a "good" police appearance reflects a professional image which in turn generates a favorable attitude by the public. Such a relationship enhances police-community relations and stimulates cooperation between the police and the public.

8.   The selection and training of proper persons are at the root of efficiency.

The emphasis in this principle is on personnel management. It reiterated the need to establish prescribed standards for selecting police recruits and for their training. It also emphasizes the fact that modern policing, like other specialized occupations, requires a special caliber of individuals with particular physical, educational, and psychological attributes. Furthermore, it stresses the need for continuous police training in order to maintain a high standard of aptitude and readiness. The principle clearly associates appropriate selection and training with an increase in police efficiency.

9.   Public security demands that every police officer be given a number.

Though the principle of a police number appears to be outdated, the original concept of an identification device is still held in personnel management. Carrying a number (or a name tag as is the custom today thanks to the technological advancement in the plastic industry) in addition to the division's letter (or the department's shoulder patch) is considered as necessary today as it was then. Besides their use for identification purposes, carrying a name tag and the department's shoulder patch enhances the officer's sense of identity as well as that of his division. Wearing shoulder patches also reinforces the officer's sense of belonging to his unit and signifies unity and group cohesion. Moreover, name tags and shoulder patches may stimulate interdepartmental competition among units and stimulate excellence of service.

10.   Police headquarters should be centrally located and easily accessible to the people.

This principle is at the heart of all contemporary police organizations. The idea that there should be multiple police locations serves the goal of functional decentralization, equitable division of labor, and efficiency in delivering police services. Furthermore, the concept facilitates the function of police supervision by assigning certain administrators to certain stations spread out over a large territory. Also as a necessary measure, Sir Robert Peel insisted that police stations and sub-stations be visibly marked and located in easily accessible locations. Selection of ideal locations must take into account the minimization of travel time to and from these locations, public convenience, and from a strictly police point of view, the minimization of response time intervals—the minimum time needed for policemen to arrive at crime scenes in response to crime reports.

11. Policemen must be hired on a probationary basis before permanent assignment.

This principle was monumental in establishing a basic concept in contemporary police personnel management: probationary appointments. The concept was designed for the protection of both the officer and the department. It made it easier for disenchanted police rookies to resign before finally committing their life-long career to a profession they have difficulty coping with. It also protected the organization from "getting stuck" with inept or poorly motivated officers. The concept, in fact, provided for a reasonable "face-saving device", so to speak. The officer may not realize the type of commitment he is making upon recruitment. Neither can the organization determine what kind of officer it will end up with after the initial selection of recruits. Contemporary police hiring regulations formulated under Civil Service laws almost without exception stipulate a probationary period, ranging usually between six months to two years.

12. Police crime records are necessary to the best distribution of police strength.

Police crime records were seldom kept, let alone reported, prior to the Peelian reforms. This principle referred to the need to keep a written record for each crime committed, its perpetrator, a synopsis of the procedures taken, and the final decision as to the outcome of the case. In order to substantiate police efficiency, stimulate comparative analysis and performance evaluation, a written record for each crime had to be accurately kept. The significance of the principle lies in the subsequent use of the record. Analysis of such records would help monitor the increase and decrease in crime rate, identify high-crime and low-crime areas, determine the extent of public support, and evaluate police effectiveness. Such analyses would consequently offer an extremely significant input in the decision making process. It would help evaluate police productivity, justify—or fail to justify—police expenditures, and compare the strength of the law enforcement component in relation to other criminal justice agencies. In today's police administration, such data are mostly computerized, easily retrieved, vastly exchanged, and continuously updated.

The Organization of the London Metropolitan Police

The London Metropolitan Police is housed today in a two-towered office headquarters known as the New Scotland Yard and in about 185 police stations spread over the thirty mile diameter of the MET. This area contains a fifth of England's population, a third of its real estate, and a quarter of its policemen.[54] The "Yard" houses the offices of the Commissioner and the Receiver, who is an independent officer serving as the financial watchdog of the MET on behalf of the Home Office.

The Commissioner position in England is unique. His office is apolitical and strictly administrative. He is appointed by the Queen upon the recommendation of the Home Secretary and may be relieved only by the Queen. He does not publicly associate with either political party. He is "not the servant of anyone, save of the law itself . . . no minister of the Crown can tell him that he must or must not keep observations on these places or those".[55] The responsibility for law enforcement lies solely with him. He is answerable to the law and to the law alone and does not even report to the Parliament. It is left to the Home Secretary, however, to explain the deeds or misdeeds of the Metropolitan Police to the Parliament.

The Commissioner is the chief executive of the force and is responsible only to the Home Office for the general operation of the agency. Although the latter has no formal power over the Commissioner, on the practical level, the Home Secretary controls the major long-term decisions of the Force. He advises the Crown on the appointment of the Deputy and Assistant Commissioners. He appoints Deputy Assistant Commissioners on the Commissioner's nomination, and approves the Commissioner's appointments to Commander.[56]

The Commissioner commands and directs all the operations of the force and is responsible for maintaining its effectiveness and high morale. He is aided by a Deputy Commissioner who besides assisting the Commissioner is responsible for other duties: granting licenses for public houses, buses and taxies, and granting permits for gun possession and street collections.

To aid the Commissioner and his Deputy, the organizational structure calls for four Assistant Commissioners to supervise the following seven departments: [57]

54. It is often mistakenly thought that Scotland Yard is the Headquarters of all Britain's police. This is, of course, not so. Scotland Yard is the headquarters of London Metropolitan Police only. It does, however, house certain central services, of which the best known is perhaps the Murder Squad, a team of experienced detectives who are available to provincial or colonial forces. Perhaps for this reason, "The Yard" has become synonymous in ordinary speech with the CID generally, although each police force in England and Wales has its own Criminal Investigation Department.

55. Peter Laurie, *Scotland Yard*, (London: The Bodley Head), 1970, p. 24.

56. *Ibid.*, p. 25.

57. All the information provided in this section has been gleaned from Peter Laurie, *op. cit.*, pp. 19–26.

'A' department which deals with the operations of the Uniformed Branch. Its concern is broadly in keeping order on the streets and in public places. 'A' provides communication, police dogs, mounted police, and all patrol units. Its women police look after juveniles and their families, and represent them before the courts. There is also a police-community relations unit, a riot-control unit, and others to handle situations of strikes, elections and disasters.

'B' department is in charge of traffic, or as it is described ". . . in charge of all machinery moving in the streets". It provides traffic patrols, supervises stopping places for buses and cabs, inspects traffic signals and supervises road works.

'C' department is responsible for Criminal Investigation. It supervises and coordinates divisional CID units throughout the MET. The department houses the Criminal Records Office (CRO), maintains the central crime lab, and directs the specialized criminal investigation squads.

'D' department deals with the human resources of the Uniformed Branch. It handles recruitment, training, appointments of policemen, dismissal and other personnel questions.

'E' department deals with the administration of civilian workers in the force. It also handles other odd functions such as accommodation addresses, amusements, registration of animals, child adoption, car passes, criminal injuries compensation, and the like.

'F' department deals with the financial administration of the force. It supervises the Budgetary Planning and Cost Accounting offices.

'G' department deals with the legal matters within the force. It examines all contracts, supplies, and claims and also operates the statistical bureau and the map room.

The organization of the MET further down the line provides for: [58]

17 Deputy Assistant Commissioners who carry the main administrative burden in the major seven departments referred to above.

39 Commanders, twenty-three of whom command operational divisions; the rest have jobs of equivalent responsibility at the Yard.

163 Chief Superintendents in charge of sub-divisions, the basic unit of policing.

158 Chief Inspectors.

663 Inspectors. This is the highest rank in work shifts. A Duty Inspector is assigned to run each police station at all times.

---

58. These figures were reported as the true figures and cited in Peter Laurie, *Ibid.*, pp. 26-27.

401 Station Sergeants whose basic job is to accept charges from arresting officers.

2,120 Sergeants in charge of supervising the PC's.

13,318 Police Constables to serve on beat service and traffic control.

The criminal Investigation Department consists of about 3,100 detectives and supervisors. The WPC's (Women Police Constables) total about 553 constables assigned to the equal duties like their male counterparts. The highest ranking WPC is a Commander and is assisted by 4 Chief Superintendents, 3 Superintendents, and 6 Chief Inspectors.[59]

Police candidates can join the MET between the ages of 19 and 30 from civilian life, or up to forty if they have served in the Armed Forces or the Merchant Navy. The candidate has to pass an educational examination, but may be exempted if he holds four "O" levels (equivalent to GED). Physically, recruits must be five feet eight (or taller) which is the median height for British men. As part of the screening process, the local police make discreet inquiries of employers and teachers of candidates' reliability, honesty, and sobriety. A search is made in Criminal Records, though a minor conviction at an early age would not rule a man out. Vision has to be reasonably good, though people who need glasses are not automatically excluded, as long as they don't squint and are not color blind. The principal medical reasons for rejection are bad teeth, defects of flat-feet, and diseases of the skin. Candidates must, of course, be British or Commonwealth subjects.

There are two sources for recruitment in the MET: 1) the police cadets, and 2) the general public. The former provides about one-third of the Force's intake while the latter provides the rest.

Police cadets are a unique breed. They are young adults who attend resident training at the Metropolitan Police school in-lieu of regular high schools. There, they spend half their time on academic subjects, the rest on physical sports, quasi-military discipline and the introduction to police work. They are considered to be an excellent source of man-power usually dedicated, fit, and already half-trained for the job.

Police recruits, whether from the cadet corps or the public at large, attend basic training at the Metropolitan Police School at Henden. Courses last for 13 weeks and include instruction in criminal law, criminal procedures, criminal investigation, pathology, methods of interrogation, and other subjects. The passing grade in the final examination is usually a stiff eighty-five per cent. The Metropolitan

59. *Ibid.*

Police School also conducts several specialized courses which include a Driving course, a CID course, a Dog and a Mounted course, as well as a Telecommunications course.

The National Police College at Bramshill is the most advanced training center in the MET. It serves as a combination of university and military-style education, modeled perhaps after the Army's Staff College. Housed in a beautiful, seventeenth-century brick mansion near Reading, the college provides courses at three levels:

(a) The Senior Command Course is designed to produce men capable of promotion to leadership positions from those at the Superintendent level.

(b) The Intermediate Command Course is designed to prepare officers for middle management positions.

(c) The Inspectors' Course is designed to train regular policemen and prepare them for the level of first line supervision.

A detailed discussion of the Bramshill model of police training will be further discussed in Chapter Eleven.

CHAPTER FOUR

AMERICAN POLICE ORGANIZATION

Historical Overview

With the arrival of the early settlers in America, a European system of policing was transplanted into the colonies. Considering the ethnic roots of the early American immigrants, it is not surprising to see the dominant influence of the English system, especially along the Atlantic coast of the "new world". The traditional constable-sheriff system was in full operation in the mother country, and it was only natural to see it rapidly introduced and adopted in the colonies. In the northern, more urban, and industrial areas, the constable system was incorporated to maintain law and order especially in big cities, while in the South the sheriff system took control over the vast, crude, undelineated countryside counties.

Around the mid-seventeenth century, a "night watch" was formed in Boston. In New York, a "rattle" watch was introduced by Peter Stuyvesant and consisted of an eight-man patrol who carried large rattles around their waists, thus producing enough noise to warn potential offenders of their presence. This probably was the forerunner of modern sirens mounted on top of squad cars.

In the 1700's Philadelphia used a watch and ward society, not unlike the earlier one in England. These were not true police departments but mostly volunteer groups. Members were conscripted as a part of their civic duty and, if they found it inconvenient to serve, were permitted to hire another man to take their place.[1] Members of such voluntary groups surprisingly had to work nightwatch only; it was perhaps assumed that no one would dare commit a crime during the hours of daylight! A single town constable normally was in charge of the operation of keeping peace during the day even in big cities like Boston, New York City, and Philadelphia.[2]

However, an increase in traditional crime confronted the American public during the early stages of the industrial revolution. The young nation had to face some hard economic difficulties during the nineteenth century. In 1837 Boston, for instance, witnessed a serious panic over unemployment followed by a major street riot. To the surprise of the participants, bayonet-wielding militiamen backed up by field cannons were brought in to restore order. The confrontation left many citizens seriously injured. Boston leaders, shocked by the

---

1. J. Norman Swaton and Loren Morgan, *Administration of Justice*, (New York: D. Van Nostrand Company), 1975, pp. 19–20.

2. George Killinger and Paul Cromwell, Jr., *Issues in Law Enforcement*, (Boston: Holbrook Press, Inc.), 1975, p. 42.

offensive way in which the militia had dealt with their countrymen, demanded and established a police force working around the clock and trained for "police" purposes. New York City followed suit in 1844 and instituted the second formal police force in the nation. Similar forces were later created in Chicago in 1851, in New Orleans and Cincinnati in 1852, and in Baltimore and Newark in 1857.[3]

From an administrative perspective, the organization and management of these police agencies—by modern standards—were primitive and crude, to say the least. America, like most nations at the time, was heavily immersed in the dark era of the spoils system; "to the victor goes the spoils". The basic elements of organization had not yet been developed and the principles of hierarchy, control and discipline were not seriously considered as necessary. Goals of objectivity, efficiency, and productivity sounded too academic to be considered practical. Separation between the roles of the police and politics was inconceivable especially to policemen and politicians. Peelian reforms were yet to be heard of. Allegiance was primarily to the political machine and was based on charisma, fear, and corruption. Loyalty was not to the police agency but rather to the interests of the ethnic group or the political party in control of the force. Education of policemen was probably viewed as a foolish myth, and training as a needless waste of effort. Morale among policemen consequently was low and corruption reportedly high.

During the formative years of police administration in the United States, the predominant ideology which distrusted the federal government was more obvious than it is today. Such strong and deeprooted fears successfully blocked the occasional tendencies toward the formation of a national police authority. State police forces developed gradually around the mid-nineteenth century primarily for military and economic purposes, and federal police units later slipped into formation in the early twentieth century for reasons of national exigencies.

Fear of concentration of power in police agencies had its vivid mark on the development of police organization and management thought during those formative years. Most police chiefs were elected, serving for short terms of two to four years, therefore sacrificing the concept of efficiency for local political expediency. Many officers held to their civilian occupations while in the police service, thus exposing public security to serious conflicts of interest. Untrained policemen had almost unlimited powers which, when compounded with the lack of formulated standards of performance, led to a situation close to total inefficiency and lack of control. Police powers until the early part of this century chiefly stemmed from those of the local po-

---

3. *Ibid.*, p. 43.

litical machine. The mayor, in most cases, assisted by his loyal lieutenants in the town or city, ran police activities at whim. Disciplined and judicially sanctioned police powers had quite a way to develop and mature into professionalism, a goal generally unfulfilled even in today's time.

In the mid-1800's, in an attempt to upgrade police administration and curtail the influence of political hegemony over police forces, police boards were established. Chiefs of police were appointed by these boards which attempted to maintain an overseeing authority over the police in lieu of the traditional blanket political power. These boards were composed of judges, mayors and private citizens, and police chiefs served at their pleasure. The board system which continues until the present clearly failed to put an end to widespread and unabated political influence. Also, since board members themselves were the product of political patronage, their administrative abilities and concern for seriously maintaining viable police organizations were understandably not beyond criticism.

Germann, Day, and Gallati recount that:

Efforts to reduce the effects of political manipulation continued. Police boards or commissions began to appear in cities, in order to disengage policing from the hands of ward politicians. In 1857, the state of New York experimented with a state board, but it proved to be unsuccessful. Such experimentation took place in other states, and there are still several cities in the U.S. where the head of the police department or commission is appointed by the Governor of the state.[4]

In 1881, a serious crime was committed which indirectly contributed abundantly to the development of police administrative thought in America. President James Garfield was assassinated by a frustrated job seeker and a wave of public revulsion followed, leading to the passage in 1883 of the Pendleton Act and the creation of the Civil Service Commission to control the unstable federal administration. As a result, the spoils era began to dwindle and the new commission started to "chase gross political interference from governmental operations".[5] Slowly, civil service processes were introduced "throughout state and local governments",[6] and police agencies covered by civil service grew to include the vast majority of law enforcement organizations across the nation today.

4. A. C. Germann, Frank Day, and Robert Gallati, *Introduction of Law Enforcement and Criminal Justice*, (Springfield, Illinois: Charles C. Thomas, Publisher), Sixteenth Printing, 1972, p. 60.

5. *Ibid.*

6. *Ibid.*

While civil service has not totally removed the problems of police administration, it certainly supplied the impetus to the elimination of political interference in policing, thus clearing the way for the application of proper organizational methods and effective police management techniques.

The next step in the evolution of police administration in America was state control of the local agencies. This system was a reaction to the politically corrupt local agencies and the theory was that the new system would be free from local partisanship and that the citizens throughout the state would be assured of adequate and uniform law enforcement. After all, it was argued, that criminal laws were promulgated for the entire state and the state could best determine how those laws should be enforced. While in theory the "streamlining function" of state police systems sounds plausible, in many states it was rejected for its imposition on the local hegemony of local agencies and its failure to provide proportionate fiscal support and uniform standards for police performance.[7]

Development of State Police Organizations

The emergence of state police agencies must be basically attributed to pragmatic reasons of a regional nature. Those reasons varied from one state to another according to their geographical, social and economic needs. Other reasons were general in nature and mainly developed in response to significant changes in life style of the American society.

Examples of these initial organizations and of the pragmatic needs which caused their creation include:

(a) The Texas Rangers which was organized in 1835 to deal with cattle rustlers, rebellious Indian tribes, and the marauding Indians who trespassed from across the Mexican-American border.

(b) The Massachusetts State Police which was established in 1865 for the suppression of vice in the emerging metropolitan centers of the state.

(c) The Pennsylvania State Police which came to being in 1905 as a strikebreaking force against the increasing militant labor groups around the coal mines which threatened the economic stability of the state.

The other group of reasons included a) the increase in population and therefore in the number of police departments and the subsequent need for adequate communication and coordination; b) the

7. Thomas F. Adams, *Law Enforcement* (Englewood Cliffs, N.J.: Prentice-Hall Inc.), 1973, p. 64.

invention of the automobile and the need for specialized police units to control traffic on the expanding network of highways, turnpikes, and interstate systems; c) the rapid growth in police technology and the need for regional technological centers, crime labs, and research facilities; and d) the emergence of a national efficiency-oriented approach which focused on the needs for police training programs, effective supervision, and reliable means of evaluation by a highly qualified central agency.

By the end of World War II, all the states except Alaska and Hawaii, had developed a state police force. Though some state police agencies are restricted to enforcement of vehicular laws and protection of life and property on the highways (e. g., California, Michigan), others have been given general law enforcement authority (e. g., Texas and New York). The latter often include some semi-independent bureaus assigned to such functions as criminal investigation, intelligence, narcotics, organized crime, record keeping, planning and research, and others.[8]

Federal Police Organizations

American democracy in all its tenets and ideals has consistently resisted authoritarian control. A main corollary of authoritarianism is centralization of police authority. Throughout modern American history, public stands to preserve local and state rights have never really relented, and the struggle between hard-core proponents of state rights and advocates of a strong federal government will never be laid to rest.

Since the term "police" or "law enforcement" was never mentioned in the Constitution nor referred to in the rights delegated to the federal government, the function of policing is considered a bona fide local function. However, since no government, as mentioned in Chapter One, can survive without a strong arm of bureaucracy, the federal government had to have, and to exercise, its own authority in order to insure that laws "are faithfully executed".

The present authority for federal police agencies is derived from the judicial interpretations of the stated powers in Article I, Section 8, Clause 18 of the Constitution, which deals with common defense, commerce, and promotion of the general welfare of the people. Such interpretations by the Supreme Court and subsequent legislative enactments by Congress provide the basis for federal police authority and legally justify their present existence in different sizes, shapes and forms.[9]

8. Germann, Day and Gallati, *op. cit.*, p. 61.

9. An early statement of the Supreme Court's position on police power was

The federal government, in order to be effective, presupposes that federal laws are to be enforced directly by federal agencies. The enactment of the federal criminal code, for example, necessitated the designation of a set of specialized bureaus or units empowered with a special authority to enforce these laws within a national jurisdiction. Almost, without exception, every federal law enacted led to the creation of a new federal enforcement agency unless the responsibility for its enactment could be reasonably assigned to an existing agency already in operation.

In 1789, with the enactment of anti-smuggling laws, a Revenue Cutter Service with special federal powers was created. In 1829, in order to prevent mail fraud, the Post Office Inspection System was established. In 1861, the United States Secret Service was created for the investigation of crimes against the United States and especially those of counterfeiting American currency. In 1868, the Internal Revenue Service was furnished with a special force of detectives for the investigation of tax evasion, and in 1886 the Border Patrol was created under the Customs Service to enforce immigration laws.

In 1908, President Theodore Roosevelt initiated an investigative force in the Department of Justice to combat land thieves and other federal violators. This investigative arm was later reorganized in 1934 as the Federal Bureau of Investigation. The Bureau was authorized to enforce several new laws including the National Kidnapping Act, the Banking Act, the Racketeering Act, and the Interstate Compact Act. As the Bureau grew in efficiency and integrity, new federal laws were further assigned to it for enforcement. In time, the Bureau grew to become America's watchdog for "all seasons". During the WWII era, it combatted espionage, sabotage, and subversion; during the cold war era it fought the threat of Communism; and today it is deeply involved in curbing civil disorders, organized crime, and international terrorism.

The emergence of federal police agencies in America has always reflected the tempo of the times. A careful examination of their roles indicates the major areas of government growth and change of values in the nation as a whole. Unlike local or state police agencies which are chiefly concerned with local and regional criminal and civil affairs, federal agencies are comprehensive in scope, reflect the national character of the country, and indicate future trends in constitutional, social, economic, and international concerns of the union as a whole.

given by Justice Harlan in the case of *Mugler v. Kansas* (1887) where the constitutionality of a state prohibition act was being challenged. Other decisions were handed down in the cases of *Powell v. Pennsylvania* (1888), *Jacobson v. Massachusetts* (1905), *Buck v. Bell* (1927), and *Sproles v. Binford* (1932).

THE MACRO AND MICRO VIEW OF POLICE
ORGANIZATIONS

To a foreigner or a tourist visiting the United States for the first time, the American organization of law enforcement must seem most confusing. As he drives along an interstate highway (especially in the eastern states), the visitor may notice law enforcement officers dressed in uniforms of different color and design, driving different-type vehicles, and displaying various shapes of decals, chest badges and shoulder flashes. If stopped by a policeman, for one reason or another, the visitor may realize that he is subject to different kinds of authority, criminal codes, and ordinances. He might find himself dealing with a federal agent, a state trooper, a municipal patrolman, a deputy sheriff, a constable, a marshal, an auxiliary policeman, a game warden, or one of the other enforcement agents.

This apparently "confusing" mosaic of police organizatons in the United States can hardly be seen as a product of a systematic administrative design. Contemporary organization of police agencies seems to have been developed by an invisible hand that blindly followed the historical evolution of the young nation. The end result clearly manifests the contradictions between democracy and efficiency, national government and state rights, legal heritage and social movements, in addition to the practical effects of individualism, faith and haste.

Theories of police organization may be viewed in two major perspectives: a macro-perspective and a micro-perspective. The former refers to the overall plan for the distribution and assignment of police resources within the country in pursuance of a set of national goals. The macro-perspective treats the country as a one chunk of territory, the problem of crime as a national integrated question and attempts to consolidate law enforcement agencies in a well-built force. This perspective, furthermore, aims at the creation of a national set of goals, a national leadership, a national masterplan for the organization of units and assignment of tasks, a national system of communication and reporting, a national plan for directing and coordinating police services and, above all, a national police budget. A macro-organization of police agencies would be hierarchical in nature, militaristic in character, and comprehensive in scope.

The micro-perspective of police administration, on the other hand, refers to the organization and management of independent local police agencies. It treats each agency as a separate entity and addresses itself to questions of authority within the department—such as delegation of functions, efficiency, effectiveness, and productivity —in as much as they reflect local expectations and enhance police relations with the local publics. Micro-organization is personalized in nature, limited in scope, and localized in jurisdiction. Organizational theories, in this perspective, vary from one agency to another and enjoy a significant latitude in application.

A macro-organization of police agencies similar to those in communist, fascist, and some socialist nations, needless to say, does not exist in the United States. There is no pyramidal shape that encompasses all police agencies. There is no uniting line of command. There is no central police authority empowered to direct lower police agencies. Federal units do not have the authority to command state units; neither do the latter have command over local units. National policies regarding police qualifications, training, planning, budgeting, and even reporting of crime statistics, are generally considered as guidelines with no mandatory effect. While macro-organization in other countries may be commended for its effectiveness and possibly for its efficiency and economy, such an organization of police forces clearly smacks with totalitarianism, unrestrained power, secrecy, and failure to conform to the constitutional character of the democratic system in the United States.

The fact that macro-organization of police agencies in America does not exist, however, should not obscure the latest trend toward standardizing efficient practices and consolidating duplicate functions. The Department of Justice, especially after the creation of the Law Enforcement Assistance Administration in 1968, has consistently and diligently embarked on increasing the effectiveness of the "whole" police system in America. Through devising national educational standards, consolidating communication systems, integrating record-keeping functions, and recommending more functional methods of organization and control, the Department has motivated substantial national reforms.

The micro-organization of police agencies in America is rapidly growing with strong tendencies toward functional integration and scientific reform. Innovative plans to improve police efficiency are commonplace and serous attempts at implementation are undertaken by quite a few departments. Model projects like Beat Commander in Detroit, Team Policing in Dayton, Ohio, Basic Car approach in Los Angeles, Police Generalists in Lakewood, Colorado, or Police Specialists in Cincinnati, to mention just a few, are attracting national attention. A detailed examination of several of these reform plans will follow in future discussions.

THE STRATIFIED BUREAUCRACY AND THE SYSTEM THEORY

As a compromise between the macro-organization view and the micro-organization view, the appropriate classification of present police organizations in America is perhaps a *stratified coalition* of federal, state, and local agencies working "harmoniously" in a compatible manner. While harmony clearly does not require regimentation, centralization or uniformity, the stratified bureaucracy seems most functional in pursuing common goals by means and methods compatible with local communities. The stratified bureaucracy is characterized with extensive decentralization at the bottom, considerable influence at the top, and voluntary compliance and readiness to cooperate in between. The conventional tools of organization, namely, men, money, machines and methods, would be locally procured, but partially subsidized by a higher level, and utilized independently in accordance with local environments, traditions, and national standards of expectations.

Thomas Adams, a notable police writer, however, criticizes this stratified bureaucracy and argues that it does not function as a system. He argues that while the average observer may assume that the American police constitutes a system, it is in fact "a facade", and what the observer is seeing is a set of separate, independent, and self-interested agencies. Adams states:

> . . . a police system—if one were to exist—in the United States would be a rank ordering of all the local police agencies in sequence, according to their relative importance; then higher up the scale would be placed the many state agencies, and finally a rank ordering up through all of the federal agencies to a single head or committee. Such a system does not exist in the United States.[10]

The "non-system" criticism of law enforcement agencies in America was also reiterated by Campbell, Sahid, and Stang in their rebuttal to the published *Report by the President's Commission on Law Enforcement and the Administration of Justice*.[11] The same criticism was later echoed and articulated in almost all studies done on the police or criminal justice agencies.

While a detailed analysis of the system approach was previously discussed in chapter two and will be touched on in later chapters, a brief clarification of this subject at this juncture is certainly in order.

A system is simply a set of components,, working together, in equilibrium (balance) toward the achievement of common goals. An ideal police system, therefore, assumes that all police agencies at the three levels of government would serve as integral components cooperating in a balanced relationship and striving towards the fulfillment of the same goals. Ideally, this association would presuppose the existence of a common leadership, a common national

10. Thomas Adams, *Law Enforcement*, (Englewood Cliffs, New Jersey: Prentice-Hall, Inc.), 1973, p. 69.

11. James S. Campbell, Joseph R. Sahid, and David P. Stang, *Law and Order Reconsidered*, (New York: The New York Times), 1970.

plan, a common medium of communication, and most importantly, a common understanding and belief in the same goals.   In order for such an ideal to become a reality, the system theory must also assume the existence of common standards for selecting personnel, a common level of education and training for everyone, and—to extend the discussion one step further—a common pay scale for all those who occupy analogous positions.

Idealism, in this case, however, is far detached from the objective reality of the American tradition.   Insistence on achieving this "ideal type" of technical organization may not only be too costly, but may also turn out to be unsatisfactory, if not goal-defeating.   By implementing the absolute notion of the system theory, independent police forces may have to fall into a regimented formation of "troops" centrally controlled, and masterminded by an "elitist" leadership.

Agencies of the Stratified Bureaucracy

There are approximately 40,000 separate police agencies in the United States today.   The exact number is hard to determine because of the frequent emergence of new forces and the absorption of others in consolidation plans.   The largest number of police agencies today are those in townships, boroughs, and villages, estimated at 33,200.   The next largest are municipal agencies, with about 3,700 agencies.   County agencies are next with 3,050.   State agencies follow with about 200 units and federal agencies trail with about 50 agencies.   Figure 2, below, illustrates the break-down of the stratified bureaucracy of law enforcement to its major groupings.

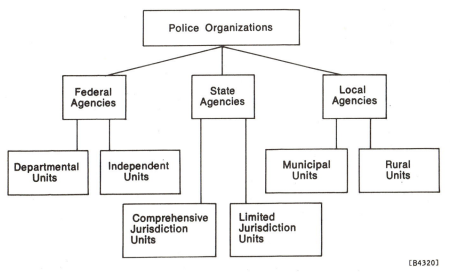

[B4320]

Fig. 2. Structure of the Stratified Police Bureaucracy

ORGANIZATION OF FEDERAL AGENCIES

Federal agencies were created by acts of Congress, as mentioned in the historical review, following the passage of federal laws and the need for special enforcement by federal agents. The need for federal agencies stemmed from the statutory restriction of local agencies to carry out police functions beyond their jurisdictional boundaries. For adequate enforcement of federal laws, federal agencies are granted national jurisdiction to cross state lines and to cooperate with the police of foreign governments in an extraterritorial capacity. Federal police agencies, like most bureaucratic organizations, have the tendency to slowly develop in little "empires". Once established they often manage to convince their supporters in Congress that only they are capable of performing the specific functions required by legislation and that any other arrangement would be catastrophic.[12]

Among the web of about 50 federal police agencies (divided between departmental and independent agencies) and operating mostly out of the nation's capital, it is necessary to realize that they share no rank order, no unity of command, and only vaguely pursue a common goal. Each operates within its own sphere of legislative authority and is required to report only to the "mother" department or administration to which it is responsible.[13]

Departmental v. Independent (Regulatory) Units

Federal police agencies, as mentioned earlier, have been created for the purpose of investigating and enforcing specific laws and to cope with specific problems which extend beyond the jurisdictional boundaries of state and local forces. Some such agencies are integral parts of the Executive branch, e.g., the Departments of Justice, Treasury, Transportation, Labor, Commerce, etc. The rest belong to Independent Agencies affiliated with the Executive Branch, e.g., Interstate Commerce Commission (ICC), Federal Communications Commission (FCC), The Civil Aeronautics Board (CAB), The Tennessee Valley Authority (TVA), and the like.

(A) Departmental Police Organizations. The purpose of this study is not to examine and analyze every federal police organization located within the eleven departments of the federal government. It is rather to cite the most important ones, briefly to explain their general functions, and later to conclude with the general characteristics of their organizational structure.

12. Thomas Adams, *op. cit.*, p. 70.   13. *Ibid.*, p. 86.

Department of the Treasury

The United States Secret Service: It was created in 1860 to guard the American mint and currency. Its services were later extended to protect the person of the President of the United States and members of his immediate family. Still later this protection was extended to the President-elect, the Vice-President, members of the cabinet and their immediate families as well as presidential candidates. Centralized in Washington, D.C., the agency provides for flexible protection service all over the nation as well as overseas when the persons under protection are on travel. Two main units of the Secret Service are especially important: the White House Police Force which protects the executive mansion and grounds, and the Treasury Guard Force which protects the main treasury vaults. The organization, a moderate-sized agency of about 1,200 special agents, is also charged with the responsibility of investigating counterfeiting activity, stolen government checks and bonds, and forged government securities.[14]

The Internal Revenue Service: The organization was created in 1862 and has two main police forces: the Intelligence Unit and the Bureau of Alcohol, Tobacco and Firearms. The Intelligence Unit is charged with the investigation of tax cases where criminal fraud is suspected and with the development of an indictable case. With the increasing involvement of organized crime in legitimate business operations, the IRS special agents, operating out of several regional offices across the Union, have intensified their efforts to counter its rapid growth.

The Bureau of Alcohol, Tobacco and Firearms: With 1,500 special agents the organization has the primary responsibility for the tax law enforcement relative to alcoholic beverage production and certain weapons. The enforcement agents of this unit enforce the National Firearms Act, which regulates the possession of automatic weapons and defines certain firearms that are illegal for private ownership.[15]

The Bureau of Customs: It was created in 1927 and today consists of a total of 7,000 persons divided in three basic branches. Custom inspectors, about 3,000 uniformed agents stationed at the ports of entry of the United States and enforce federal laws relative to illegal contraband. Custom patrol officers, who constitute the second branch of about 3,000 persons and operate between ports of entry in the manner of the border patrol. Their primary assignment is the prevention of illegal entry by undesirable aliens. The third branch,

14. Germann, Day and Gallati, *op. cit.*,   15. Thomas F. Adams, *op. cit.*, p. 87.
   p. 169.

of about 1,000 persons, are customs investigators who perform investigatory duties and prepare cases for both illegal contraband and aliens. The three branches cooperate, under the supervision of the Secretary of Treasury, in the enforcement of U.S. customs laws.[16]

Department of Justice

The Federal Bureau of Investigation: It is the largest and probably the most famous and prestigious federal police agency. The FBI, contrary to its popularized image, is not a national police force. It has broad investigative jurisdiction encompassing all federal law violations but limits its scope to about 170 laws, including all federal statutes not specifically assigned to other agencies. Among the primary crimes which the FBI directs its attention to are espionage, sabotage, treason, kidnapping, extortion, bank robbery, frauds against the government, interstate transportation of stolen vehicles or stolen property, thefts of government property, and the killing of federal officers. Among the other legislative acts enforced by the FBI are the Federal Reserve Bank Act, the Fugitive Felon Act, the Atomic Energy Act, the National Bankruptcy Act, the White Slave Act, and others.

With a force of about 8,500 special agents, the Bureau is the fact-finding arm of the Department of Justice. The agents assigned to 59 regional offices are strictly controlled by regional supervisors (Special Agents in Charge) who report directly to the Bureau's administration in the Washington D.C. headquarters. All information collected at the local levels is promptly received, analyzed, and evaluated by the top management of the steep pyramid-shaped organization.

In addition to the investigative functions of the organization, the FBI provides assistance to local law enforcement agencies through training of its officers and maintaining a criminal laboratory that is available for assistance in local investigative matters. Since 1930 the FBI has been the central clearing house for the most complete files on fingerprints and arrest files. The Bureau also serves all state and local enforcement agencies by maintaining criminal statistics and by disseminating the information on a regular basis in its Uniform Crime Reports.

The Immigration and Naturalization Service: It was created in 1891, and transferred to the Department of Justice in 1940. With its approximate 1,700 officers, the organization administers the immigration and naturalization laws relating to the admission, exclusion, and deportation of aliens as well as the naturalization of legal aliens present in the United States.

---

16. J. Norman Swaton and Loren Morgan, *op. cit.*, p. 147.

The Border Patrol is the enforcement arm of the organization. Patrol officers are assigned at and near the American ports of entry. Moreover, patrol inspectors travel along river beds or patrol vast desert stretches to prevent illegal entry of aliens. After making arrests, officers present their cases to the Department of Justice for prosecution which may produce deportation or punishment of the violators.

Drug Enforcement Administration: Formerly called Bureau of Narcotics and Dangerous Drugs, DEA was created in 1968 by transfer from the Department of the Treasury. DEA is responsible for enforcing the federal laws regulating the production, sale, and transportation of "controlled substances" (narcotics and drugs as defined in the U.S. Criminal code). Tasks in DEA are divided in two sections: the criminal section and the compliance section. The former uses about 2,200 special agents charged with the investigation, detection, and prevention of violations of the federal narcotic and marihuana laws, the Opium Poppy Control Act of 1942, and the Drug Abuse Control Amendments of 1965. The latter, the Compliance Section, uses some 300 investigators who mainly supervise the manufacturing of drugs in the United States for legal purposes, the licensing of such firms, and the auditing of the sale and distribution of these products. Operating under the jurisdiction of the Attorney General, DEA personnel are located in regional and local offices and report directly to their home base in Washington, D.C.

United States Marshals: They consist of nearly 100 persons (one for each federal judicial district) and are appointed by the President to four-year terms of office throughout the United States and the territories. Assisted by about 2,000 deputies, the force is the main arm of the federal judicial system. Operating under the authority of the United States Attorney General, the marshals and their deputies attend the federal courts, keep order in the court, handle federal prisoners, serve orders of the court, and assist if necessary in the implementation of its decisions.[17]

Department of Agriculture

The Forest Service: It administers more than fifty regulatory laws designed to protect the farmer and the consuming public as well as to administer national forests. The service is charged with the administration of over 150 national forests comprising about 180,000 acres. Its responsibility is to improve them, protect them from fire, insects and disease, and to manage and control livestock grazing and watersheds.[18]

---

17. *Ibid.*, p. 144.   18. Germann, Day, and Gallati, *op. cit.*, p. 173.

Department of the Interior

The United States Fish and Wildlife Service: The service has two bureaus: the Bureau of Commercial Fisheries, responsible for preventing the destruction and depletion of the nation's fishery resources, and the Bureau of Sports and Wildlife, which is responsible for insuring the conservation of the nation's wild birds, mammals, and sport fish.

The National Park Service: It is charged with the conservation of national parks, monuments, and similar reservations. Park officers enforce all federal laws relative to the prevention of fires, stream pollution, and injury to natural historic or prehistoric features.[19]

Department of Health, Education, and Welfare

The Food and Drug Administration: It was created in 1930 and is responsible for the enforcement of the Federal Food, Drug, and Cosmetic Act, the Tea Importation Act, the Import Milk Act, and the Caustic Poison Act, among others. Its activities are directed mainly toward promoting purity, standard potency, and truthful and informative labeling of essential commodities covered by the provisions of these acts.[20]

Department of Transportation

The United States Coast Guard: The Guard is considered a paramilitary police force during peace time but is automatically claimed by the Navy when war breaks out. Established in 1790, the Guard presents a united service made up of the old Revenue Cutter Service, the Lifesaving Service, the Lighthouse Service, and the Bureau of Marine Inspection and Navigation. The Guard carries out an effective port security program and enforces federal laws on the high seas or waters subject to the jurisdiction of the United States.

The Federal Aviation Administration: It promulgates and enforces safety regulations by inspecting, certifying, rating, and supervising the activities of airmen. It also enforces the regulations relating to the manufacture, registration, safety and operation of aircraft as well as the inspection of air navigation facilities in the United States.

(B) Independent Police Organizations. Independent agencies are administrative agencies created by Congress outside the framework of existing departments in the executive branch. While they are naturally responsible to the President, they enjoy a relative independ-

---

19. *Ibid.*, p. 173.   20. *Ibid.*, p. 174.

ence from executive control because of the nature of their functions. Also, while some of these agencies like the Federal Trade Commission (FTC) and the Interstate Commerce Commission (ICC), have significant enforcement functions, others, like the Civil Aeronautics Board (CAB) and the National Aeronautics and Space Administration (NASA), clearly have insignificant authority to directly or indirectly affect the daily life of common citizens.

Some independent agencies are quite large. The Veterans Administration, for instance, has about 190,000 employees which makes it larger than most departments. Others, like the Railroad Retirement Board, are fairly small. Also, while most of these agencies have multiple heads (i.e., a board of commissioners), some, like the Atomic Energy Commission, may be headed by single administrators.

Although most independent agencies are set up to deal with particular problems created by emergencies such as depression and wars, some, like the National Labor Relations Board, was created under the pressure of organized interest groups. Still others were established to handle new or technical programs which did not fit under conventional departments, like the AEC and NASA. Another reason for the establishment of independent agencies is the desire to keep new programs out of the hands of hostile or unfriendly departments. The Small Business Administration is a typical example.

Independent agencies, in almost every case, were created on a temporary basis. Once the emergency situation or problem faced was adequately solved, such an agency was supposed to be phased out. However, once these agencies were created they usually manage to rally strong congressional support and justify their permanent existence.

The oldest independent agency is the Interstate Commerce Commission which was established by act of Congress in 1887. Since then the use of independent agencies has escalated and become a popular, as well as effective, administrative instrument for the regulation of economic, scientific, and progressive activities. Some examples of these agencies are mentioned below with the date of their establishment and the areas of their jurisdiction:

(1) Interstate Commerce Commission (1887): railroads, motor carriers, domestic water carriers, and pipelines.

(2) Federal Reserve Board (1913): money, credit, and commercial banks belonging to the Federal Reserve System.

(3) Federal Trade Commission (1914): unfair or deceptive trade practices.

(4) Federal Power Commission (1920): electricity and natural gas.

(5) Federal Communications Commission (1933): telephone, telegraph, radio, and television.

(6) Securities and Exchange Commission (1934): stock exchanges, investment bankers, trusts, holding companies.

(7) National Labor Relations Board (1935): labor-management relations, unfair labor practices, collective bargaining.

(8) Civil Aeronautics Board (1938): air carriers and fares.

(9) Federal Maritime Commission (1962): water carriers and foreign commerce.

Most independent agencies are concerned with those areas of enforcement of laws including preliminary investigation, prosecution of violating parties, informal settlement of cases, and administrative adjudication. Federal police organizations located within these agencies, serve a major function toward the accomplishment of these enforcement goals. Examples of the more pertinent agencies involved in law enforcement activities include:

(A) The Federal Trade Commission is responsible for looking into—and taking appropriate action when necessary—incidents of unfair competition and deceptive and monopolistic practices in interstate commerce.

(B) The Subversive Activities Control Board investigates to determine whether organizations are "communist-action", or "communist-front", or "communist-infiltrated".

(C) The Federal Communications Commission has a Field Investigation Unit which assists in the regulation of interstate commerce. Their personnel are responsible for enforcement of the Communications Act which provides for licensing and regulating of operators and broadcasting stations.

(D) The United States Civil Service Commission has an Investigation Division within its Bureau of Departmental Operations. The Division conducts the Commission's investigative program which includes national agency checks, enforcement of the Civil Service laws and rules, and qualification investigation of applicants for high-level administrative and professional positions.

(E) The Veterans Administration, under the Assistant Administrator for Appraisal and Security, has an Investigation Service, a Security Service, and under the Assistant Administrator for Construction, a Safety and Fire Protection Division.

Organized along lines similar to those of private business corporations, independent agencies were intended to provide more flexibility and freedom from overhead administrative controls and bureaucratic policies, thus becoming more innovative, progressive, and effective.

The general characteristics, therefore, of independent agencies may be summarized:

(a) They are headed by boards or commissions having from five to eleven members, which provides more collegial leadership.

(b) They are engaged in the regulation of semi-private economic activities through common methods of business administration.

(c) They have a measure of freedom from bureaucratic supervision and legislative overhead control.

(d) They are independent in terms of possessing quasi-legislative and quasi-judicial powers and have both policy-making and implementation functions.

(e) They are bi-partisan in nature; therefore, they are more stable.

General Characteristics of Federal Police Organizations

Proper studies of federal police organizations, especially during the last decade, have been significantly rare. Literature prepared for distribution by these agencies, on the other hand, has seemed always abundant. In some cases, like the FBI under Director Hoover, selected writers were reportedly invited to write about the agency and to publicize the great achievements by that organization's leaders and staff. Accurate description of the organizational makeup of these agencies, however, and the roles of the decision making centers which truly ran the administration, beyond the common organization charts, remained mostly a matter of speculation. Probably because of the secretive nature of some of these agencies or the image of secrecy, which some administrators like to reflect, information in this area is considerably limited.

From the available literature and general studies, however, the following characteristics can be drawn:

1 —Federal police organizations are as highly specialized as they are limited in jurisdiction. They are usually authorized to enforce a fairly small number of federal laws.

2 —Federal police organizations seem to maintain a low profile coupled with less visibility. Being mostly in civilian dress, they project a business-like image.

3 —Federal police organizations seem to be more professional than state and local forces because of their higher educational requirements, the strenuous training they undergo prior to and during employment, and the noticeable occupational esteem they enjoy.

4 —Federal police organizations which normally operate from the nation's capital, seem to enjoy a considerable amount of support

and favoritism by the executive and legislative branches of government as well as by the national mass media.

5 —Federal police organizations are more insulated from the gross political interference and pressure usually exerted by local political machines. This apparently increases their effectiveness and their sense of fairness.

6 —Federal police organizations are usually free from the cumbersome duties of operational policing in the streets, and thus escape the common allegations of brutality, discrimination, and wide-spread corruption. This further enhances their sense of public support and legislative favoritism.

7 —Federal police organizations, being securely protected by civil service rules, seem to reflect a sense of job security, organizational stability, and managerial maturity.

8 —Federal police organizations, by virtue of their being the most prestigious police agencies in the nation, exhibit a high level of discipline, stability, and morale.

STATE POLICE ORGANIZATIONS

State police organizations function at an intermediate level between the federal and the local levels. While their geographical jurisdiction extends over the entire state they serve, their legal jurisdiction may be much more limited than that of local organizations.

State police organizations, which employ a total of over 57,000 employees, vary considerably in their size and functions from state to state. In California, for instance, they employ over 7,000 persons while in North Dakota, the force is about one hundred. In a few states, state police officers are relatively limited in their authority (sometimes they live in semi-barracks accommodations) while in other states they enjoy broad police powers and act in effect as a "super police" authority on virtually all matters. In some cases they even exert substantial influence over local agencies and represent them at the courts of federal agencies.[21]

State police organizations are of two types. The first type has a comprehensive jurisdiction (e.g., Texas and Michigan), is clothed with general police powers, and enforces all state laws. The second has limited jurisdiction (e.g., California and New York), specializes in the protection of the motorists, and directs most of its attention to enforcement of laws which govern the operation of vehicles upon the public highways. A description of the organization and management of these types will follow with Texas and California as models representing the two types of state agencies.

21. Norman Swaton and Loren Morgan, *op. cit.*, p. 130.

Comprehensive Jurisdiction Organizations: The Texas Model

Texas State Police, named the Department of Public Safety (DPS), is among the most comprehensive state police organizations in the Union. This should come as no surprise, since the Texas experience with state police predates all other states. This also has made the citizens in the Lone Star State often assume that all Americans must have heard of, and admired, the "Texas Rangers", who have served the state so courageously since 1835.

The Department of Public Safety was reorganized in 1935 from three former divisions—Texas Rangers, Texas Highway Patrol and a Headquarter Division—into a complex bureaucracy with two major line components, six staff divisions, and several levels of managerial hierarchy. The Department also extends its jurisdiction over the state by means of six regional offices located in Dallas, Houston, Corpus Christi, Midland, Lubbock and Waco. Figure 3 illustrates the organization chart of DPS.

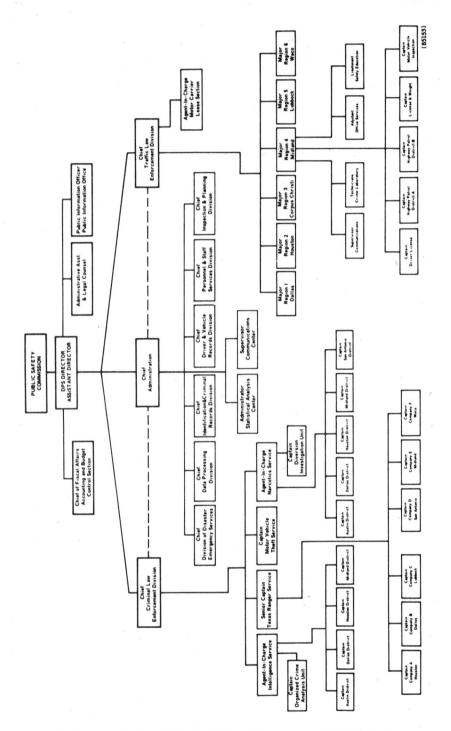

Fig. 3. Organizational Chart of Texas Department of Public Safety
(Courtesy of the Department)

Top management of DPS is vested in a public-safety commission of three members, each of whom serves a six-year term with one member's term expiring each two years. Commission members are appointed by the governor with senate concurrence. The commission names the DPS director and assistant director. The director, who is the chief executive of the force, administers its daily functions in accordance with predetermined guidelines formulated by the Commission. He is also a member of the State Criminal Justice Council Executive Committee and participates in drafting the police standards and goals to be applied by all municipal and sheriff departments in the vast state.[22]

The department's basic functions can be divided into two broad categories—police and regulatory (or nonpolice). The police function involves detecting and apprehending violators of traffic and criminal laws, making related investigations, and assisting in prosecutorial and court procedures. The regulatory function involves administering motor vehicle programs and exercising postlicensing control of drivers through interviews, re-examination and suspension.

As an organization with comprehensive jurisdiction, DPS is required by statute to perform cooperative and supportive functions for other law enforcement agencies. These functions involve educating citizens about public safety and law observance, police training, scientific crime detection, collection and maintenance of police records, and maintenance of a state-wide police communications system.

The DPS, employing about 4,200 officers and civilians and with a 1974–75 budget of $56.7 million, manages programs which fall into three general classes: Traffic Law Enforcement, Criminal Law Enforcement, and Disaster Emergency Services. The first program, Traffic Law Enforcement, is carried out through the Department's traffic division which operates as mentioned earlier from six regional districts. Each regional district is, in turn, divided in terms of specialty into eight offices: communication, office services, safety education, driver license, highway patrol, license and weight, and motor vehicle inspection. Each office is headed by a DPS captain or lieutenant and assisted by an appropriate number of DPS personnel.

Criminal law enforcement consists of the Texas Ranger Service, the Narcotics Service, Intelligence Service and Motor Vehicle Theft Service. These services, beyond their operational activities, provide specialized assistance to local enforcement agencies and cooperate with federal agencies in criminal law enforcement activities.

22. All information presented in this section on the structure and functions of Texas Department of Public Safety is taken from the *1974 Criminal Justice Plan For Texas*, Austin, Texas.

Disaster Emergency Services are administered by DPS for the Governor since the director of the department also serves as director of the Governor's Division of Disaster Emergency Services. This program develops a governmental capacity for the administration of relief and recovery operations during national emergency, natural disaster, and other types of major emergencies. The program coordinates state disaster relief efforts, operates the State Emergency Operating Center located underground at DPS Headquarters in Austin, and provides staff support to the Governor and other officials.

DPS, enjoying such a comprehensive jurisdiction, also provides a host of other supporting services to local police and sheriff's departments. Briefly stated, DPS major supporting services include the following:

1 —It operates six crime laboratories easily accessible to adjacent local police agencies.

2 —It collects crime data from law enforcement agencies across the state and publishes and distributes the information through its Texas Crime Reports.

3 —It collects, analyzes and disseminates data on organized crime.

4 —It operates a statewide teletype communication system with almost 370 DPS and local law enforcement agencies on line.

5 —It runs the DPS academy which trains local law enforcement agencies as well as its own personnel.

Limited Jurisdiction Organizations: The California Model

The California Highway Patrol (CHP) is probably the most famous force of its kind in the nation. The force was created in 1929 in an effort to standardize traffic law enforcement throughout the state. Since that time the department has grown to the point where today over 5,000 officers are employed and located in eight major zones in the state.

CHP is headed by a Commissioner, appointed by the Governor, who is aided by two executive assistants: one for Staff Operations, the other for Field Operations.[23]

The first, with the rank of Assistant Commissioner, supervises and coordinates the Training Division, the Planning and Analysis Division, the Enforcement Services Division, and the Administrative

23. All information presented in this section on the structure and functions of the California Highway Patrol is taken from the department's publication, *The CHP Story* by Dante Lanza, Commissioner, 1976.

Services Division. Each of these divisions is headed by a Commander in charge of middle management and the implementation of policy. Further down the organizational hierarchy, each commander is responsible for supervising component sections. The Planning and Analysis Division, for instance, consists of the Analysis Section, Data Processing Section, Long Range Planning and Operational Planning sections. The Administrative Services Division, in the same manner, consists of a Logistics Section, Communication Section, and Motor Transport Section, in addition to a Personnel Bureau and Fiscal Bureau in charge of Accounting and Budgeting.

The second Assistant Commissioner is in charge of Field Operations and runs a gamet of organizational functions which involves the operational mechanics of the force. His administrative functions directly affect the major body of the force stretched from the southern border of the State of Oregon to the northern borders of the Republic of Mexico. Aided by a commander at each zone, he standardizes and coordinates the traffic enforcement operation in eight zones: Redding, Sacramento, Fresno, Los Angeles, San Diego, San Luis Obispo, and San Bernardino. The Assistant Commissioner carries out the policies worked out by the Staff Operations. He implements the personnel policies, fiscal policies, planning policies, training policies, and—most importantly—the traffic enforcement policies of the agency. The Assistant Commissioner consults with his regional commanders and makes decisions that enhance the effectiveness of the units as a whole, as well as the discipline, morale, and leadership within each zone. Duties regarding the assignments of officers, work procedures, and reporting systems are usually overseen by him and decisions as to the reassignment of officers, disciplining or rewarding their service, etc. are usually recommended by him to the Commissioner's office.

Traffic enforcement duties, the main concern of CHP, is carried out by Field Operations. They include accident control, congestion relief, field inspection, public information, and education and cooperation with outside agencies and governmental bodies involved in traffic control.

The Commissioner's office at the top of the hierarchy is responsible for the overall operations by the units. To facilitate its control function, it is supported by three main staff offices: (a) the office of internal affairs, (b) the office of public relations, and (c) the office of special representation. The latter represents the department with relation to the legislature, the courts, other governmental bodies, and special interest groups. Moveover, it assists local enforcement agencies in areas of traffic legislation, technical fields, and education of traffic personnel.

Figure 4 cited below illustrates the organization of CHP.

[B5205]

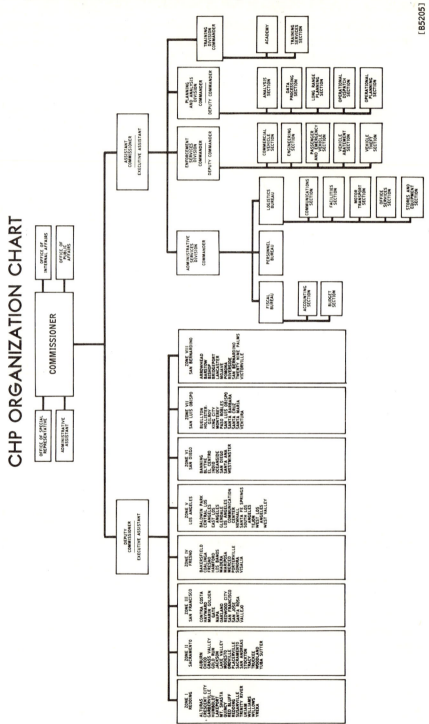

Fig. 4.   Organizational Chart of California Highway Patrol
(Courtesy of the Department)

LOCAL POLICE ORGANIZATIONS

Federal and state police organizations are basically the products of modern political and socio-economic necessities which recently appeared in the American life. Crime and law enforcement, however, existed before these necessities came into being. Since ancient history, and through medieval and modern ages, crime has been regarded as communal in nature, and law enforcement was primarily a concern of local government. Communities varied in their definition of crime, their share of criminal activities, their response to crime, and thus, in the kind of law enforcement they desired. Also, as illustrated earlier in Chapter Three, the advancement in police systems depended primarily on the existence of active communal values, on social awareness, on government responsiveness and on a necessary amount of economic investment in the function of social control.

Throughout the fifty states of the union, local police organizations have been the most visible agencies, and their impact the most predominant on the daily life of most Americans. The average citizen living in an American city, town, or county, today, works confidently every day on the assumption that the local police is safeguarding his home, his place of work, and his children at school, as well as his car on the road. In almost every case, when help is needed the citizen calls the local policeman for assistance. The local policeman, in return, expects the citizenry's cooperation, a fair share of the tax dollar, and the public's constant support.

Local police agencies come in all sizes, shapes and forms. They cover over 3,050 counties, 825 cities 25,000 and over in population, and 3,100 towns with populations under 25,000. The largest police force in the nation is the NYPD with over 31,000 officers (at least until the city's recent financial crisis in 1976), and the smallest are the cities of Etna, California; Albany, Illinois; and Hartford, Kentucky, among many others, with a force of one officer each.[24] The rest of the local forces, municipal and rural, naturally fall between these two extreme sizes.

The major part of local police organizations is centered in the cities. Among the 6,480 cities, the largest cluster of local forces is found in about four thousand highly populated cities. As an informal rule, a police department with a force of over 500 officers is considered large, a department force over 200 officers is considered a medium sized force, and one below 200 officers is considered small.[25]

24. *Uniform Crime Reports*, 1974.

The vast majority of local agencies, nevertheless, consist of smaller numbers of men, sometimes working on a part-time basis, like in small rural communities, compensated by fees, and selected without modern physical, educational, or mental qualifications.[26] Most of these agencies, seem unsatisfactorily trained, supervised, disciplined, and equipped. Concepts of modern organization and management—the two arms of administration—are either unknown, ignored, or not taken seriously. Examples of such disorganized and mismanaged agencies were cited in *The President's Commission on Law Enforcement and Administration of Justice.* The Report on *The Police* frequently found:

> . . . serious deficiencies of internal communications, coordination, supervision, and direction of effort and control. This general dissipation of personnel resources—the scattering of specialized work units about the Department without the essential bond of control and direction of the organization—has reduced the ability of the Department to function as an organized group.[27]

The *Task Force Report* also stated in another reference that, with almost no exception, consultants found serious weaknesses in the administration of forces they surveyed. One consultant noted the following management defects in a middle-size force of 450 personnel:

> Sound management practices apparently are not understood nor used by administrative and command personnel. . . . planning and research are not utilized to resolve present problems of organization, personnel deployment, performance inadequacies . . . nor to prepare programs, procedures and policies for strengthening the [department].

25. While there is no formal rule which identifies the size of police departments with the number of its officers, many authors have developed their subjective criteria. See, for instance, John Kenney, *Police Administration,* (Springfield, Illinois: Charles C. Thomas Publisher), 1972. Kenney indicated that a medium sized department consists of between forty and three hundred personnel. This assumes that the size of a large police department is over 300, and that of a small department is below forty. The 300 figure is hardly representative, however, of the really large departments such as the NYPD of 31,000 which would have to fall in the same category.

26. Germann, Day and Gallati, *op. cit.,* p. 142.

27. Task Force Report, *The Police,* President's Commission on Law Enforcement and Administration of Justice, 1967, p. 45.

Career development programs have not been formulated. Staff inspection as a control device is not known .   .   . and therefore not used.[28]

Such pessimistic views, however, cannot be taken as a rule since some municipal and other agencies (mainly in urban areas) seem to have adequately caught up with the latest in administration theories and management techniques and may be "on the take-off" toward professionalism. A host of new patterns of administration has recently been introduced and are being experimented with by numerous police agencies. Examples of these modern innovations include team policing, organizational development, operations research and management by objectives, among several others. Although it is certainly premature to judge the results of such experiments, the trend toward upgrading police organization and management among local departments seems to be persisting.

A thorough examination of the existing panorama of local police organization is naturally impossible. Emphasis, therefore, will be made on municipal policing in the cities and rural policing in the counties.

Municipal Police Organization

Although there are varying kinds of organizational structures, methods of control, available facilities, assigned functions, and levels of competency and integrity, the Chief of Police of Attica, New York, must face many of the problems that are faced by the Commissioner of Police of the City of New York, albeit on a lesser scale.[29]

All municipal agencies in the country will have to engage in these functions:[30]

(a) Crime prevention activities by educating the public, working with juveniles, cooperating with probation and parole personnel, and providing visible evidence of police availability and ability.

(b) Crime repression activities by investigating crime, by identifying and apprehending offenders, by recovering stolen property and by maintaining constant visible capabilities.

(c) Regulation of noncriminal conduct, by controlling the noncriminal citizen in such areas as traffic (vehicles, parking, pedestri-

28. *Ibid.*   30. *Ibid.*, p. 143.

29. Germann, Day, and Gallati, *op. cit.*,
     p. 142.

ans), public events (crowd control and public places), and social relations (domestic disputes) in order to maintain community tranquility.

(d) Provision of services by rendering information, directions, advice, and general assistance, and through special services such as licensing and registration.

(e) Protection of personal liberty by protecting the individual citizen against unwarranted interference on the part of the state, and by instructing the citizenry in terms of their duties, obligations, rights, and privileges in reference to the law.

While all municipal forces are expected to carry out these functions efficiently and effectively, the administrative patterns applied by each department vary considerably. John Kenney insists that "no singular approach to the study of [their] administration and organization is feasible".[31]

However, Kenney, in his attempt to study municipal forces in America, introduced three basic models: the small department model, the large department model, and the modified police model.[32]

The small department model which includes the majority of municipal forces in America, usually consists of a force between fifteen to forty officers, while much smaller forces are not uncommon. The model provides for a generalist approach to police functions with minimal specialization. Concepts of staff-line-auxiliary segregation do not apply. The department is usually divided into three shifts which handle all police functions. Follow-up investigations or case processings are usually referred to a singular specialist designated by the chief. Another individual is usually assigned to "take care" of the records, property and vehicles. All decisions regarding budgeting, personnel, training, planning, and other managerial functions, are the responsibility of the chief. The organization of small departments is usually paternalistic, supervision is rather informal, communication is mostly verbal, and relations between the personnel is intimate. Most significant decisions are made by the chief in close consultation with the supervising authority at city hall and mostly with high political overtones. Figure 5 below illustrates the organization

31. John P. Kenney, *Police Administration*, (Springfield, Illinois: Charles C. Thomas Publisher), 1972, p. 17.

32. The description of these models as well as the basic ideas expressed are gleaned from John Kenney's analysis, *Ibid.*, pp. 60–65.

chart of Huntsville Police Department as a model of the organization
of small departments.

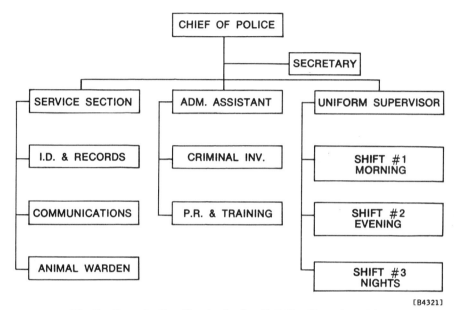

Fig. 5.   Organization Chart of a Small Police Department in
Huntsville, Texas (Courtesy of HPD)

The large department model fits more the characteristics of modern organizations. They meet contemporary specifications in that
they are complex bodies of men, money, methods, and machines.
They are ranked in bureaucratic hierarchies which do not permit
face-to-face relationships. They adhere to impersonal relationships
among specialized offices and maintain a distinct segregation between
line officers, staff members, and auxiliary.

Large departments tend to be highly specialized as well as centralized. The traffic and criminal investigation functions are usually
centralized responsibilities. There is also a high degree of centralization of the vice, narcotics, and intelligence function. Furthermore,
all the administrative staff functions of personnel management, fiscal
management, training, and planning are centralized and supervised
directly by the office of the chief.

The structure of large departments reflects an emphasis on functional specialization. Each major activity is represented by a divisional unit on par with the other. Major divisions are usually patrol,

traffic, criminal investigation, and staff services. Such divisions are the responsibilities of deputy chiefs or commanders who implement the department's policies and supervise their enforcement.

Large departments are also spread out horizontally. They are usually divided in precinct forces or sub-stations. Each precinct is a duplicate of the headquarters' structure except for specialized offices such as intelligence, internal affairs, crime analysis, research or statistics.

While the large department model can find its counterpart in big business, industry, and governmental agencies, many of these departments still maintain the rigidity of traditional bureaucracy. Basically militaristic in their organizational patterns, their willingness and readiess to accept managerial changes seem to be impeded by their long and close association with traditional policing. Even when such willingness and readiness become available, these departments are usually hesitant to go through the agonizing process of selling new ideas to city government and securing its approval to change. Figure 6 illustrates the organization of the Houston Police Department shown here as an example of a large municipal department.

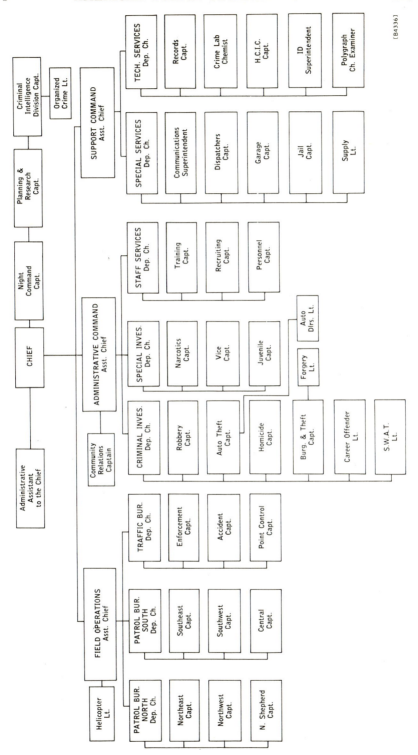

Fig. 6.   Organization Chart of a Large Police Department:
Houston, Texas (Courtesy of HPD)

The modified model is the most common in medium sized departments. The uniformed field officer is the backbone of the department's structure, and the patrol division is the principal and only line unit responsible for performance of all line functions. The detective, traffic, and juvenile units are considered staff only in the sense that their primary responsibilities are to aid and assist the patrol division in the performance of the basic police functions.

The modified model—which Kenney admits is an extension of the simple model created earlier by August Vollmer, Chief of Police in Berkeley, California—calls for a relatively high degree of specialization. Follow-up case investigations are the responsibility of the detective and juvenile units, and vice is commonly an exclusive responsibility of the vice unit. While specialization is emphasized, the overall management of the department can be described as "average". Departments of this size are ordinarily caught between formal and informal organization, impersonal and paternalistic discipline, as well as between the slogans of professionalism and the realities of mediocrity.

Rural Police Organization

Like municipal policing, rural police agencies come in different sizes, forms, and shapes. The county sheriff and county constable generally serve the rural unincorporated areas of the county, and occasionally, extend their services to incorporated areas in the county through request or by contract.[33] The smaller communities, towns, villages, and boroughs have a variety of law enforcement personnel designated as constables, coroners or assessors.

Throughout the United States the multifaceted responsibilities and duties of the sheriff vary from one state to another and even from one county to another within the same state. In virtually all areas, however, the sheriff is responsible for keeping the peace, executing criminal and civil processes, and operating the county jail. His jurisdiction always includes the entire county.

The most striking difference between municipal and rural organizations is the fact that the chief executive of the latter is an elected official and his office, therefore, requires no physical, educational or moral qualifications. No knowledge of law or law enforcement is necessary and, more importantly, no familiarity with public administration or management is required. Consequently, a pattern of parti-

---

33. Germann, Day, and Gallati, *op. cit.*,
pp. 151–157.

san, paternalistic, and mediocre administration ordinarily sprouts. Furthermore, such patterns may abruptly change from one administration to another depending on the electoral forces which "make or break" the sheriff. In large, and usually affluent, counties as well as in advanced communities, the stability of the sheriff system is maintained through the establishment of a chief administrative officer who administers the organization on a semi-permanent basis. To insure continuity, this administrator is usually appointed by the county court and can be removed only by that forum.

The electoral position of the sheriff obviously reflects the democratic aspect of law enforcement administration and holds the occupant always accountable to the public he serves. But the fact that he is elected for a short term (between two and four years) greatly inhibits the continuity of the organization and widely exposes its operations to political interference—one which is classically seen as nonconducive to effective management. In his political capacity, on the other hand, the sheriff enjoys several administrative luxuries unavailable to the chief of police. He can ordinarily deputize anyone that he cares to as a regular deputy, special deputy, or honorary deputy. Civil service for the sheriff's office is extremely rare, and the merit system is seldom present.[34]

Moreover, the functions of the sheriff include some major judicial duties. He is the chief conservator of the peace and acts as executive officer of the district courts. He serves their writs, subpoenas, and processes. Furthermore, the sheriff has charge of the county jail and its prisoners. In counties of less than 10,000 population, the sheriff may also be the *ex officio* tax assessor and collector unless the voters have approved a separate officer for this function.

In most counties, the sheriff's income depends upon fees he collects for servicing court orders and from the management of the county jail. For every writ served, he receives a fee; for every prisoner in the county jail, he receives a stipulated amount of money per meal per prisoner, and often he is allowed to keep the difference between what he spends for food and what he receives to pay for the meals. This naturally raises the question of a conflict of interest: a grave violation of basic personnel management.

While the controversy over the political nature of the sheriff's office continues, it is only appropriate to defend the present system by indicating some of its natural strengths. The system, if properly administered, could be:

(a) most responsive to the desires and expectations of the local community, by virtue of being an elected office;

34.　*Ibid.*

(b) most cooperative with the other components of the criminal justice system, by virtue of its dual function serving law enforcement and the courts;

(c) most influential in correction and rehabilitation services by virtue of its function as keeper of the jail;

(d) free from the complexity of bureaucratic regulation by virtue of its relationship with, and accountability to, only one supervising forum, the county court;

(e) a pioneer in crime prevention projects by virtue of its cordial relationship with the electorate and the strong public support this relationship generates.

Advanced sheriff organizations today, it must be mentioned, are no longer rare. The example of the Los Angeles County Sheriff's Department is worth noting. Since May of 1963, the department has been operating such a superior administration that twenty-seven incorporated cities have requested its services by means of contract. Allocated to the twenty-seven cities are a minimum of eighty-five radio patrol car units manned by a minimum of 124 officers. In a survey later conducted to determine the success of that arrangement, the majority of officials in these cities expressed a favorable view and cited the following advantages for continuing the contracts: [35]

(a) Economy of services rendered: The police service was being delivered at a lower cost than would be the case where cities maintained their own forces.

(b) Professionalism by the highly trained personnel of the department: The larger unit could afford to employ better trained and better educated police officers.

(c) Fairness: The communities received unbiased, non-partisan service in a more appropriate manner than those cities which developed their own forces.

(d) Availability of technical services: The use of crime lab facilities, computerized record-keeping, fully equipped radio cars, etc. greatly enhances local police efficiency.

(e) Immediate availability of emergency reenforcement at no additional cost.

Advanced sheriff departments today provide the same type of enforcement service to the public as do the police departments: patrol, criminal investigation, and special services. In addition, these departments also provide detention and correctional services.

The Patrol Division, which may also be known as the Field Operations Division, Line Operations, Enforcement Operations, or some

---

35. V.A. Leonard and Harry W. More, *Police Organization and Management,* (Mineola, New York: The Foundation Press, Inc.), 1971, p. 114.

other descriptive title pertaining to the functions performed, is the backbone of the sheriff's organization. It may also include a highway patrol in charge of traffic, a marine patrol, or even a helicopter squad. The purpose of patrol in sheriff organizations is based on the theory that an impression of omnipresence created by frequent and conspicuous patrol contributes to the deterrent role of the police and the elimination of the actual or perceived opportunity for successful misconduct on the part of the offender.

The criminal investigation division provides the department with qualified personnel possessing specialized skills, knowledge, and freedom of movement to act in a supportive role toward concluding investigations of major crimes previously investigated by patrol officers on a preliminary basis.

Other units which may be found in modern sheriff departments include a bomb squad, organized crime bureau, polygraph services, evidence and property, criminal offense records and most other specialized services prevalent in advanced municipal forces. Figure 7 illustrates the organization of the Harris County Sheriff's Department as an example of modern sheriff organizations.

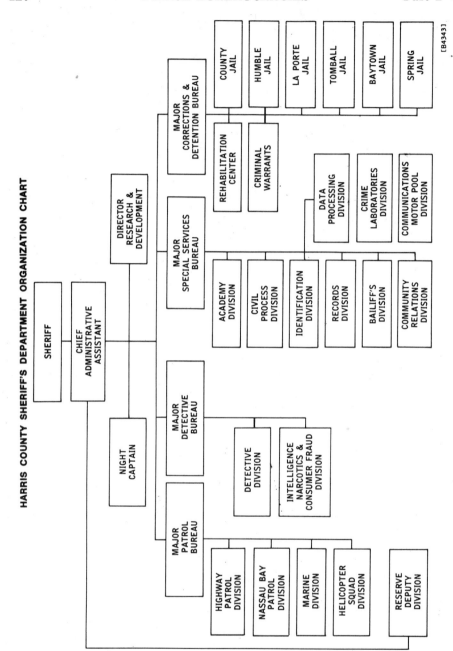

Fig. 7.   Organization Chart of a Modern Sheriff Department: Harris
County, Texas (Courtesy of the Harris County
Sheriff Department)

While the goal is naturally to keep upgrading the "advanced departments", more efforts must be focused on advancing the other departments as well. If the administration of the latter is to rise to an acceptable level of competency and professionalism, major administrative improvements must be undertaken in these areas.[36]

1 —Personnel administration must be upgraded. Men of character, capacity, and ability must be energetically recruited, adequately compensated and appropriately trained, and a viable policy for motivating the officers must be constantly implemented.

2 —Modern management techniques must be used. Systematic planning and scientific research must be undertaken and a serious effort to implement the results of these techniques made.

3 —Legal procedures must be strengthened. The department must work with local and state legislative bodies to revise statutes and to prepare more tenable laws and procedures conducive to more effective service.

4 —Computerized methods for maintaining central records depositories and enhancing communication between units must be developed. Electronic Data Processing (EDP) may be necessary for county-wide effectiveness. Data banks for fingerprint information and criminal histories may be adequate for the time; however, future needs may require more advanced methods for facsimile transmission and the rapid dissemination of operational data.

5 —Public support must be developed. This involves continuous communication and educational effort to eliminate public ignorance, apathy, and probable hostility.

In conclusion, it must be noted that although other areas could be outlined for future reform, sheriff departments must move rapidly toward reorganizing their functions and structures along sound administrative lines. Known theories of organization and management must be seriously applied, and an atmosphere of executive awareness, involvement, and leadership must prevail.

36. Germann, Day, and Gallati, *op. cit.*, pp. 153–155.

PART THREE

THE ADMINISTRATION OF POLICE BUREAUCRACIES

CHAPTER FIVE

POLICE ADMINISTRATION: THE ORGANIZATIONAL COMPONENT

Overview

Since no man can "know the end from the beginning", man has labored constantly with forecasting his ends, defining his goals and devising means for achieving them. These processes of forecasting, defining, and devising clearly take place today under conditions new to the experience of the human race. The development of modern science and technology has created a new "condition of man". Never before has man existed in numbers approaching the four billion mark or have his methods of living—economic, social, and political—been so complex and so rapidly changing. The small, traditional societies of history and prehistory are rapidly replaced by a number of over-sized and complex "societal blocks". Such blocks seem to have turned from the "sacred" to. the "secular", from the "ideal" to the "manageable" and from the "theoretical" to the "workable". Man has long listened to philosophies and ideas. *The transformation of these philosophies and ideas into realistic, tangible and effective action is the essence of administration.* Administrative efforts "do something about" changing the chain of events, and administrators are "involved". Dwight Waldo, a classic student of public administration, accurately addressed himself to the transforming power of administration by saying that, "administration is thus broadly conceived; it is man raising above the blind and aimless forces of his physical and social environment and imposing upon these forces a meaningful pattern".[1]

Each generation may see itself at a crucial moment in time, but it is doubtful if society today can argue that man is entering one of the great transitions in his whole history. The twentieth century's man has already achieved a spectacular success over his environment. He has learned not only how to adjust to nature but how to use it for the discovery and control of new worlds and natures. By "seeking

---

1. Dwight Waldo, *Ideas and Issues in Public Administration*, (New York: McGraw-Hill Book Company, Inc.), 1953, p. 23.

facts and harnessing energy and bending metal and organizing people," man has produced consciously directed change.[2] The enormity and rapidity of this kind of materialistic change coupled with man's inability to administer on a large scale the processes by which one thing leads to another has brought society to its present watershed in human affairs. While man's talents have been concentrated on controlling his physical progress, the complexity "crisis" has been produced by man's "increasing difficulty in understanding and directing his fellow man," a job basic to the achievement of goals in any collective endeavor.

Administration is the *comprehensive effort to direct, guide and integrate associated human strivings toward specific ends or aims.* It is conceived as the coordinated activities of those individuals in an organization charged with ordering, forwarding and facilitating the collective efforts of the group in order to realize defined goals.[3] Modern administration aims at organizing large numbers of people in group associations that can successfully operate highly complex programs and produce rational solutions to man's complicated problems.

Administration as a term can mean either a *system* or a *process.* The former—which for the purpose of accuracy should be called administrative system such as the Carter Administration, the Johnson Administration or that of a mayor, a university president, or a police chief—*refers to formal groupings of selected personnel who are functionally structured, and authorized with legal powers to achieve major goals during a limited term of office.* The latter, such as the administration of justice, police administration, hospital administration, or personnel administration, refers to *the nature and sequence of activities performed in a certain field to direct and facilitate work tasks toward the achievement of prescribed goals.* Throughout this book the term will be used to refer to the latter meaning unless otherwise qualified.

Although the need for administration may not be so discernible in undeveloped communities, it is especially essential in the management of limited resources characteristic in most advanced societies. Without some source of central direction and guidance, individuals in these societies cannot efficiently save energy and prevent wastage. Formal organization of work and a high degree of specialization of labor make administration today imperative as the only means for ensuring optimal utilization of available resources.[4]

2. Harlan Cleveland, *The Future Executive*, (New York: Harper and Row Publishers), 1972, p. 8.

3. Dwight Waldo, *op. cit.*, p. 25.

4. John D. Millett, *Management in the Public Service*, (New York: McGraw-Hill Book Company), 1954, p. 3.

Administration is also a collective term. Individual administration, if such a term exists, can only be an exercise in self-discipline. Administration involves *a group of persons working together in unison and controlled by rules*. It must involve a subject-matter to be administered and a set of management methods to be applied. Administrative agencies, therefore, are charged with "getting the job done" through a formal organization applying rational methods of management. "Administrators" of a public agency are specialists who carry out work tasks along lines set up by the agency in accordance with a prescribed set of management guidelines.

Administration and Bureaucracy

The collective nature of administration has, inevitably, linked the fine art of administration to the hard realities of bureaucracy. As mentioned in Chapter One, bureaucracy is the "long arm of government" and administration is its "subject matter and its reason for being". Bureaucracy, therefore, provides *the formal structure in which administration is performed and translated into action. A bureaucracy without administration would be meaningless, and administration without bureaucracy would be an abstract theory, ineffective and unrealistic:*

Bureaucracy, the physical embodiment of administration, may not truthfully reflect the right framework for how administrative functions should be conducted. Among the terms often used to describe bureaucratic agencies: unimaginative, protectionist, security-conscious, old-fashioned, closed-minded, harsh, aggressive, empire-building, insensitive, and aloof. Such terms have been widely used by elected officials, as well as by political commentators and private citizens. Yet an opposite view of the same agencies indicates such contrasting terms as honest, able, efficient, specialized, dependable, and dedicated to public service. Although an honest evaluation of the role and contribution of bureaucracy in America does not reveal a consistent appraisal by all groups concerned, there is sufficient evidence to suggest that there is a sizable resentment to the bureaucratic ways and means of exercising administration. An efficient administrator, under the circumstances, may accept with considerable difficulty being named a bureaucrat. Jean Couturier, executive director of the National Civil Service League, states that bureaucrats are getting a "bad image" in America. He explained by saying that, "the American people have convinced themselves that the people who run government are bad. You go into a rundown office with a bare light bulb to get a permit from an old lady who wears a green eyeshade and snarls at you—that is how you'll think government is".[5]

5. *U.S. Report and World Report*, November, 1974.

To accomplish a healthy administrative relationship between the administrators and the subordinates, who differ substantially in their abilities, motivation and interests, bureaucracies have been traditionally based on a system of "coercive" authority and "contracted" responsibility. In public service, administration must necessarily be exercised within limits of purpose and procedures fixed by the legislative branch of government. A ladder of authority or a "hierachy" is, therefore, necessary to coordinate the decisions and actions of public employees if they are to carry out a responsible administration. Responsibility, on the other hand, refers to accountability for the results arising from the enforcement of authority. Administrative responsibility imposes internal constraints on the behavior of subordinates, which, if not observed, may result in some sort of disciplinary action. An effective system of authority and responsibility is a principal means of guarding against abuse of administrative authority by subordinates. Without such a system of authority and responsibility, administration would be left to the bare whims of individual workers unrestricted by a routine or a direction of purpose.

Administration and Politics

The field of administration is a field of business. Though the reference here is to government administration, the function of administration must be removed from the hurry and strife of politics. Woodrow Wilson, the 28th President of the United States and an unforgotten scholar of Public Administration, articulated the necessity of maintaining an apolitical framework of administration by saying:

> [Administration] stands apart even from the debatable ground of constitutional study. It is a part of political life only as the methods of the counting-house are a part of the life of society; only as machinery is part of a manufactured product.[6]

Wilson emphasized that administrative questions are not political questions. Although politics sets the tasks for administration, it should not be suffered to manipulate its offices. While Wilson defined politics as "state activity in things great and universal", he described administration as "the activity of the state in individual and small things".[7] Politics is the special province of the statesman, administration of the technician. The broad plans of government are political; the detailed execution of such plans is administrative.

A clear view of the difference between the province of politics and the province of administration ought to leave no room for mis-

6. Woodrow Wilson, "The Study of Administration", *Political Service Quarterly*, Vol. 2, (June, 1887), pp. 197–222.

7. Dwight Waldo, *op. cit.*, p. 72.

conception. Public administration is the detailed and systematic execution of public policy. Every application of general law is an act of administration. For instance, the assessment and raising of taxes, the apprehension of criminals, the transportation and delivery of mails, the equipment and recruiting of an army, etc., are obviously acts of administration. While the formulation of laws directing these activities can be constitutional, legal or political, the detailed execution of such activities is essentially administrative.

Wilson's view of the distinction between the provinces of politics and administration, however, doesn't seem to have much support today. The complexity of today's administrative problems compounded with the increasing necessity of the interdependence of the two domains considerably changed the traditional value of Wilson's theory. Consultations between government agencies and political caucuses have become necessary if not essential. The drive for public interest has intensified the intimacy between administration and politics. If the President proposed an administrative measure for the reduction of crime, for instance, it is not enough to say that his cabinet and chief advisers are certain of its workability; the leading congressional specialists on the subject, together with a spectrum of concerned citizens and groups, must approve its applicability and political convenience.

Also, the growing blurring of public and private enterprise has added to the contemporary trend to ignore Wilson's notion of separation. The conventional line between "public" and "private" can no longer be drawn. Just about all private enterprises today have an obvious responsibility toward the public, and the larger and more complex the enterprise, the more public responsibility it is expected to carry. Executives of both sectors have to face similar problems and consider in their decisions the similar alternatives to hard questions: how to reconcile efficiency with democracy, how to promote full employment without undue inflation, how to beat the high cost of services, etc. Consequently, governments in their attempt to curb their tendency to expand, are obliged to meet the people's expectations through farming out public programs to private organizations (business firms, research organizations, and nonprofit agencies). As an example, most of the nation's taxes today are not collected by the government but by private organizations through the withholding device. Also most of the military production is no longer undertaken by government "arsenals", but through a multitude of private corporations which do most of their business with the United States Department of Defense.

Harlan Cleveland, in his *Future Executive,* refers to modern administration as "a web of tensions" consisting of a mixture of public and private administration. Cleveland describes the state of modern administration as a "complex public/private bundle of relations, held together by constructive tensions". The administrative style, he says, "will have to be adjusted to an environment which is ill-described by drawing square and status diagrams. It will feel more like a continuous chemical reaction in a liquified solution." [8]

THE POWERS OF ADMINISTRATION

Wherever bureaucracy is located at the federal, state, or local level, bureaucrats—mostly unknown to the public at large—make decisions, *or nondecisions*, reaching deeply into the lives of over 213 million Americans. They grant, withhold or revoke licenses, slap penalties on erring taxpayers and direct the public to what they must do. They count bodies, keep records on births, marriages, divorces, deaths, crimes, diseases and hundreds of other facts about *genus Americanus*, and pass judgments on such products as food, medicines, cars and toys. In the view of many writers, bureaucrats have become the "real rulers of America". They argue that bureaucracy, "the fourth headless branch of government", has become as powerful as the elite civil service that served the emperors of China and controlled that nation for centuries.

In a survey of modern government and power in America, Charles Sohner noted that "executive agencies are filled with thousands of experts who are inherently irresponsible because their jobs are so specialized that neither the President, the governors nor the voters can understand what they are doing".[9]

The main source of administrative power is the sheer size of its agencies. Nearly 14 million civilians worked for public agencies in 1974, and another 3 million citizens were members of the armed forces.[10] During the same year they helped spend about 334 billion dollars. In 1976 the estimated federal budget alone was around 385 billion. The salaries, fringe benefits, and work assignments of about 15 percent of the labor force in the nation come from government agencies.

Another source of administrative power stems from the particular roles governmental agencies play. The American people live in an "administrative society", or one heavily influenced by administrative regulations and bureaucratic procedures. As mentioned earlier, the lives and fortunes of the public are governed by the agencies that regulate the economy, public order, and social welfare. Most social

8. Harlan Cleveland, *op. cit.*, pp. 14, 66.

9. *U.S. Report and World News, op. cit.*

10. Ira Sharkansky, *Public Administration,* (Chicago: Markham Publishing Company), 1972, p. 1.

ills, therefore, are naturally blamed on the "overregulation" or the "underregulation" by the bureaucratic establishment.

A third source of administrative power is its "ambiguous" discretion. Administrators can execute the laws to the letter and produce a state of administrative domination, or, on the other hand, they can use discretion and interpret the law in a socially acceptable fashion, therefore promoting reason and harmony. The latter approach obviously reflects a sense of public responsiveness on the part of enlightened bureaucracies.

The fourth source of administrative power is the tremendous influence of administration on legislative bodies. This strength is based on the administration's claim to technology, science, and the mastery of statistical techniques. During the policy-making process, proposed bills are usually referred to the appropriate administrative agency for evaluation and appraisal. Such agencies, in their capacity to provide guidance, can exert considerable pressure on the thrust of the law. Police agencies in several states have consistently blocked legislation which sought to liberalize or decriminalize drug laws, drinking laws and other victimless crime laws.

The fifth source of administrative power is secrecy. Public agencies reach decisions without having to explain how and why these decisions were made or who influenced the decision in this direction or that and why. The right to know is frequently blocked by the executive privilege to maintain secret records, the contents of which cannot be revealed without a legislative investigation or a legal order. Even in the presence of such legislative and legal constraints, bureaucrats have little trouble thwarting their effect by delaying tactics or taking advantage of loopholes in the law. As an example of bureaucratic secrecy, Ralph Nader described his quest for records in the Department of Agriculture by saying:

> The only way I could make my request specific was to get access to the indexes. When I asked for access . . . I was told they were internal memoranda and not available to us. Therefore, I had to make my request in a broad fashion, and they came back with a bill for $85,000 which we regretfully had to run down.[11]

Notwithstanding the obvious powers of administrative agencies, the inevitable dependence upon bureaucracy does not mean that the public is enslaved. There are constitutional and legal controls imposed on administrative agencies to insure their public responsibility. Fundamental to popular sovereignty in a democracy is the con-

---

11. *U.S. Report and World Report, op. cit.*

cept of representative government with elective legislative bodies empowered to control appointed administrators and the administrative process. Such controls, expressed in terms of a "government of laws and not of men", are designed to insure public accountability of administration. Chief controls are either constitutional or legal.

The constitutional controls include three main techniques: (1) periodic reexamination by the legislature of the standards of delegation and the manner in which statutory language has been interpreted in its administrative application; (2) legislative requirement, especially in bills containing provisions authorizing agencies to grant or withhold licenses, that the administrative agency must openly prescribe fully-detailed standards and surrender public records to special scrutiny by legislative committees; (3) the legislative power of the purse by which appropriations can be granted or withheld from administrative agencies; and (4) the congressional power to confirm the appointment of top government administrators.

Legal controls, on the other hand, are imposed on a case by case basis. In addition to the principle of judicial review, groups as well as individuals can sue public administrators for damages incurred by their decisions. Courts, in such cases, can order redress for damage and punishment for the delinquent officials as well as issuing restraining orders to "cease and desist" from enforcing "unfair" regulations.

In addition to the constitutional and legal controls, in a democratic society there is always the force of public opinion and the mass media, along with the inherent right of the people to petition their grievances to the government. These means of exposing and condemning *ultra vires* (illegal) decisions by the bureaucracy have been extremely effective lately in preventing administration from becoming unresponsive, arrogant, or autocratic.

The SCART of Administration

Administration has been described by many as simply an art, while others viewed it as a science. Ordway Tead championed the former view and argued that the essence of administration is the ability to motivate and direct human association toward the accomplishment of stipulated goals. Tead further emphasized that the most common characteristic of administration is cooperation among public officials. Emphasizing the themes of democracy and leadership in government, he described administration as a "body of special talents in a collaborative creation integral to civilized living". Calling administration a science, Tead stressed, would be "less than adequate".[12]

---

12. Dwight Waldo, *op. cit.*, p. 27.

Charles Beard, a leader of the "science" theory of administration, cited the Oxford English Dictionary which defined science as "a particular branch of knowledge of study, or a recognized department of learning".[13] Beard emphasized that administration is as much of a science as economics and physics as long as it involves a body of knowledge wholly deterministic in its rules or axioms. Beard added that modern administration has an enormous body of exact and usable knowledge. If, for instance, it is decided by government to accomplish the purpose of providing compensation at a given rate for men and women employed in a given industry, the administrator, like the engineer, can utilize specific tools of collecting, classifying, and analyzing data to estimate in advance the approximate cost of such a design. He would then have to indicate the types of officers and employees necessary to administer the design and the administrative procedure appropriate to the whole process from beginning to end.

Whether the field of administration is truly an area of rules and axioms (the Beard theory) or a product of individual skill (the Tead theory) is a highly debatable question. Attempts to resolve this question—if at all possible—are of secondary importance to the study of administration since it must obviously consist of a fine, fluid, and well-balanced mixture of both. Hence the term **SCART** (science and art) may be appropriately introduced to indicate such a methodological composite of both.

The term **SCART** will clearly imply a deeper meaning than what its causal application may indicate. The term adds a methodological (rational and systematic) dimension to the study of public administration which can transcend the demarcation line between its scientific and practical aspects. Such a dimension can specially contribute to the stability of the field by capitalizing on its compatibility with science. Moreover, the use of the term can bridge the gap between the practitioners and scientists in the field of administration by promoting a common ground for communication between them, thus enhancing cooperation by both groups. Even more important, the use of the term can bring to the fore the dynamic characteristic of administration by stressing the symbiotic relationship between the two notions of art and science. This would further enhance the capability and effectiveness of the field.[14]

13. *Ibid.*, pp. 77–79.

14. For further information on the SCART concept, see the author's article, "The SCART of Criminal Investigation: A Methodological Approach", the *Journal of Police Science and Administration*, December, 1974.

THE ORGANIZATIONAL COMPONENT

Administration of public affairs has two major components: organization and management. The organizational component is fundamental. Without it, administration could only be seen in the abstract.

Overview

The foremost question that encounters the **SCART** of administration is no longer to organize or not to organize, but rather how to organize efficiently. If college professors will pardon, the formula today is *organize or perish*!

As modern states become increasingly more administrative and communities more structured, the importance of effective organization also grows. Etzioni put it articulately:

> Our society is an organizational society. We are born in organizations, educated by organizations, and most of us spend much of our lives working for organizations. We spend much of our leisure time paying, playing, and praying in organizations. Most of us will die in an organization, and when the time comes for burial, the largest organization of all—the state—must grant official permission.[15]

Organization is the structural framework within which administration is conducted. It provides the framework, tasks and rules for the administrative process. Without a relevant organizational pattern, administration would at best be like the behavior of a free-lance rifle shooter moving around in an arid desert firing his rifle in all directions aimlessly. In all likelihood, his gun would hurt no one, but neither would it benefit anyone either. The freelancer's experience will also have little impact, if any, on the sport of rifle shooting or on his ability to become a better marksman.

Waldo described the relationship between organization, management, and administration as that between anatomy, physiology, and action: organization is the anatomy, management is the physiology, and administration is the action. Each is dependent upon and inconceivable without the other in any existing administrative system.[16] Organization, therefore, if found by itself, would be like the anatomy of a living organism. Management, if found by itself, would definitely be theoretical. Administration, consequently, without its vital components, can only be perceived conceptually. Figure 8 illustrates

15. Amitai Etzioni, *Modern Organization*, (Englewood Cliffs, New Jersey: Prentice-Hall, Inc.), 1964, p. 1.

16. Dwight Waldo, *The Study of Public Administration*, (New York: Random House, Inc.), 1955, p. 6.

the functional framework of administration and shows the relationship between its two major components.

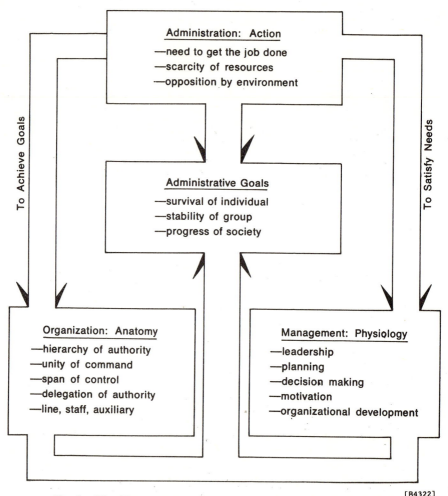

Fig. 8. The Harmonic Integration of Administrative Components

[B4322]

Organization is the structural framework of administration. It is a *blueprint designed to assign functions, positions and tasks.* It sets up the groundwork for the realization of common goals. As such, it becomes a system of work assignments among groups or individuals specializing in particular tasks within a general plan. Furthermore, in public service, organization is more than just a structure of working relationships: it must reflect certain public expectations: constitutional, legal, cultural, social, economic and political. But since public expectations are not necessarily shared by all public servants, certain values projecting these public expectations must be transformed into rules and imposed on the individuals selected to serve in these organizations. To assure compliance with these rules, a system of authority-responsibility must be established. To sustain this system, a hierarchical order must be created and formal methods of supervision enforceable by formal sanctions established. Thus, an organizational network conducive to effective administration is set in motion.

Organizations in the public service are financed by public funds. They, therefore, have to be both efficient, spending the least amount of money possible to do the job, and effective, choosing the most direct means to achieve the goals. Since groups and individuals serving in public organizations cannot consistently and successfully determine the efficiency and effectiveness of public programs, fiscal regulations are imposed and enforced. Also, specialized offices empowered with appropriate means to control public spending, to appraise service cost, and to balance the agency budget, must be created and authorized. Public organizations would thereby be forced to comply with governmental policies of economy and minimization of wastage. Thus a fiscal policy conducive to an economical administration is set up.

Organizations in the public service, as mentioned earlier, must be staffed by individuals capable of efficiently and effectively meeting the administrative goals. But since individuals in public service, both administrators and subordinates, vary in their talents, abilities and potentials, a minimum standard of qualifications must be determined and strictly applied. Moreover, since individuals in public service must earn an equitable living, specialized offices setting compensatory policies and procedures, pay scales and pay increases, must be established. Such offices must also be empowered to handle dismissal policies, reduction in force, retirement, and fringe benefits. Thus, a personnel administration conducive to the humane administration of government employees is set in motion.

Organizations in the public service are expected to be impartial in their dispensation of services. In a democratic society not only do people stand equal before the law, the quality of services they receive must be equally advanced and delivered in an equitable manner. But since public servants who share minimum qualifications at employment time may vary considerably in the quality of services they can later produce, training programs must be devised and implemented. Organizations must, therefore, train their employees so as to be able to produce standard services at a standard quality. Moreover, training bureaus must initiate training programs at all administrative levels to further improve employee productivity. Rules governing the training programs offered, the intervals between each, the amount of knowledge and experience presented in each, and the standards for completing such programs, must be established and periodically evaluated. Therefore, a system by which meaningful training can be matched with particular functions may be developed, thus a reinvigorating capability conducive to the betterment of public services may be always in progress.

The Theory of Organization

It is important to recognize that the very idea of organization stems from the fact that the individual alone is unable to fulfill all of his needs or those of his group. Because he lacks the necessary ability, strength, time or endurance, he must rely on others for helping satisfy these needs.[17] Even in a group of two (the smallest size possible), their efforts must combine toward the same end, even if, as James D. Mooney illustrates, the task is only a short-lived one, such as moving a large stone. "You take this side, and I'll take this side" is a basic plan for the division of work. By the same token, "we'll lift when I count three", is a basic form of coordination.[18] Organization in its simplest form is *basically the appropriate division of work coupled with appropriate coordination*. The purpose naturally is getting the job done effectively and efficiently.

One of the earliest accounts of organization and planning—and of the results achieved thereby—is found in the Book of Exodus. When the Israelites left Egypt, they hadn't even the simplest form of organization. There was one leader (Moses) and a mass of disorganized followers (see Figure 9). Naturally this arrangement proved unwieldy. Moses, the Bible tells us, sat by the people from morning to evening, deciding disputes between them: In consequence, he and his followers made little progress toward the Promised Land in more than forty years.[19]

When a better form of organization was introduced (see Figure 10), the Israelites made as much progress in less than a year as they had in the 39 preceding years.

17. Edgar H. Schein, *Organizational Psychology*, (Englewood Cliffs, New Jersey: Prentice-Hall, Inc.), 1965, p. 7.

18. James D. Mooney, *The Principles of Organization*, (New York: Harper and Brothers), 1947, p. 7.

19. Ernest Dale, *Organization*, (The American Management Association, Inc.), 1967, pp. 10–13.

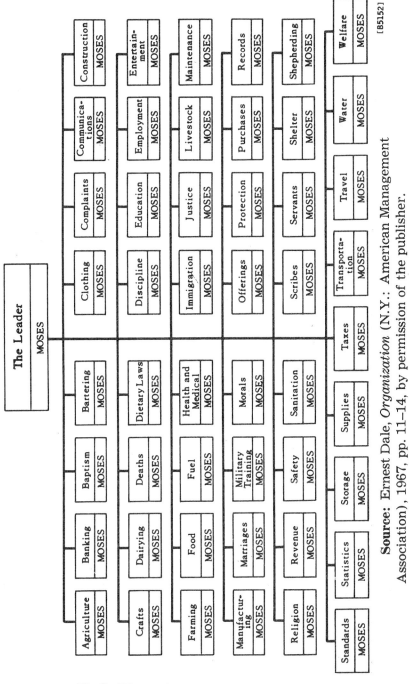

Fig. 9. Disorganization of the Israelite Tribes

Source: Ernest Dale, *Organization* (N.Y.: American Management Association), 1967, pp. 11–14, by permission of the publisher.

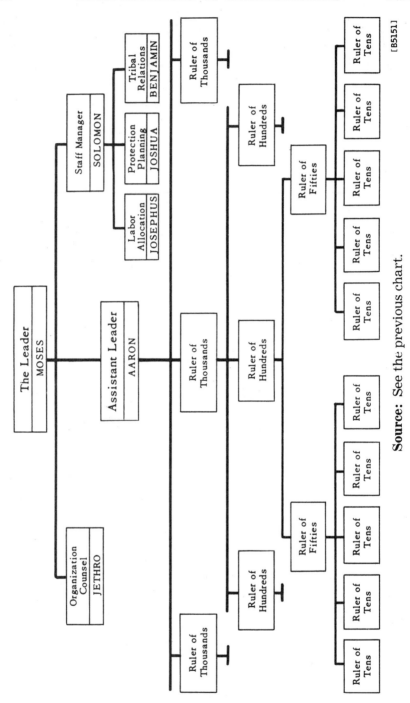

[B5151]

Fig. 10. Later Organization of the Israelite Tribes

Source: See the previous chart.

Society today is the largest grouping of mankind. Through the coordination of the activities of many individuals, society makes it possible for its members to fulfill their needs. Advanced societies, moreover, can only achieve their goals if such division is systematically planned and carefully coordinated. While the division would preferably be done on the basis of individual skills, this is not always necessary since people could be trained to acquire new skills. Thus, an army may decide that it is wise to have some men as combat soldiers, while others are supporters, bringing ammunition, food, and medicine to the fighters. But since the job of fighting and supporting are naturally too complicated, they would be divided in several corps, and each corps would be further divided by function into smaller units which are tied by appropriate coordination.[20]

Basic to the ideas of division of labor and coordination is the need for hierarchy of authority. It is unnatural to man that coordination among so many diverse groups and individuals would be effective without some means of checking, directing, and controlling. The very idea of coordination implies *that each unit submits to some kind of authority for the sake of achieving a common goal.* If each unit pursues its own self-interest and disregards the activities of other units, coordination, would have, by definition, broken down. However, the idea of submitting to organizational authority does not necessarily imply that the authority has to be external. Coordination can be achieved by voluntary compliance and internal self-discipline such as those expected from two children operating a seesaw. While some kind of authority is necessary to affect coordination, the latter can range from complete self-discipline to complete autocracy. The situation obviously varies from one organization to another and from one time to another.

Authority in its simplest meaning is a *working relationship between superiors and subordinates by which the formers direct the activities of the latter who in turn are obliged to comply.* Authority, as a formal means of direction, however, cannot operate in an abstract form. It has to be embodied in a hierarchy of positions and ranks. Each position, defined as an area of responsibility (a division of labor), has the authority to insure that its part of the job will be done according to the blueprint conceived by the highest authority. Organizational blueprints are constructed on rational criteria of how best to divide up the job and to coordinate the units systematically in order to achieve the over-all goals.[21]

---

20. Edgar H. Schein, *Organizational*   **21.** *Ibid.*, p. 8.
  Psychology, op. cit., p. 8.

Organization Defined

Schein defined organization as "the rational coordination of the activities of a number of people for the achievement of some common explicit purpose or goal, through division of labor and function, and through a hierarchy of authority and responsibility".[22]   One important understanding in this definition is that the object of organization is the *coordination of activities, not people*.   From the point of view of organization, it is sufficient to spell out the tasks and functions which must be fulfilled in order to achieve the goal.   Which particular person fills the position may be quite irrelevant to the concept of organization, though it clearly is relevant to how well the agency actually operates.[23]

Ernest Dale defined organization as:

. . . a process of determining what must be done if a given aim is to be achieved [through] dividing the necessary activities into segments small enough to be performed by one person and providing means of coordination so that there is no wasted effort and the members of the organization do not get in each other's way.[24]

John Millett defined organization as "the structural framework within which the work of many individuals is carried on for the realization of a common purpose'".[25]

Police organization may be defined as the *rational coordination of police functions and tasks toward the achievement of goals stated by public policy—in an efficient, effective and impartial manner.*

The Art of Internal Organization

From the previous discussion, it becomes evident that the essence of organization is a technical question.   As such, it is a methodical division of work among specialists in particular phases of a general task to achieve stated goals.   Such a division of work based on "scientific methods" is the most rational way in which laymen can be transformed into a "purposeful and constructive group" of technicians capable of achieving collective goals.

Methodical division of work, as the main feature of modern organization, must be systematically devised in such a way as to promote the realization of the group objectives.   Such a division of work must not only be "purpose related" but also "purpose seeking".

22. *Ibid.*

23. *Ibid.*, p. 9.

24. Ernest Dale, *Organization, op. cit.,* p. 9.

25. John D. Millett, *Management in the Public Service, op. cit.,* p. 153.

Any organizational division which appears to hamper the realization of an agency's stated goal would be obviously dysfunctional. In the pursuit of purpose-seeking organizations, it is imperative that the organizational methods and structural relationships within the organization be so designed as to "capture" the purpose most directly, efficiently, and economically.

A major requirement in the methodological approach to work division is specialization by which work may be divided. One of the minds of the "formal organization school", Luther Gulick, postulated these five alternatives: [26]

(a) **Major purpose organization**—like a defense department or a federal, state or local police agency, which brings under one administrative roof all the component services required to achieve the program goal.

(b) **Organization according to process**—which clusters functions according to specialized skills, for example; the office of legal counsel, the electronic data processing division, the intelligence division of a large police department.

(c) **Organization according to place**—which strives for either geographic specialization (such as the police precinct in a high density crime area so the police can respond to local needs more rapidly and efficiently) or for location economics (the neighborhood fire station with its short run to conflagrations). Examples include the regional offices of the FBI, DEA, or state police agencies.

(d) **Organization according to the "thing"**—provides rather technical specialization around identifiable objects such as the bureau of missing persons, the organized crime unit, or police agencies for juvenile delinquency.

(e) **Organization by clientele**—where political pressures (e. g., veterans, minority groups) or the intrinsic complexities associated with an identifiable group of people generate tailor-made agencies or procedures to cope with such groups. Examples are the Bureau of Indian Affairs, a youth bureau in a police department, or an agency of the Veterans Administration.

On a number of grounds these five bases for organization have been widely criticized. As an attempt at categorizing, they suffer the major flaws of ambiguity and overlap. In police organization, for example, is the office of juvenile delinquency a process, a thing, or a clientele organization? Is the FBI electronic data bank a process, a thing, or a centralized place organization? A second criticism of the

---

26. Luther Gulick and L. Urwick, eds., *Papers on the Science of Administra-* tion, (New York: Institute of Public Administration), 1937, pp. 15–30.

formal organization school is the lack of criteria as to which one should be preferred over another. A third criticism is based on the assumption that such categorization could well be expanded to encompass several more categories by employee stratification, by training, and by source of appropriation, to name just a few. Included in this criticism is the possibility of integrating several of these categories in one organization. The same organization can be divided by purpose, by place, by thing and by clientele at the same time. Police organizations, as a case in question, could be divided simultaneously by purpose (public safety), by process (suppressing crime), by place (breakdown to stations and sub-stations), as well as by thing (special functions), and by clientele (interest groups).

It is not enough, however, to think of organization in technical terms. Organization, after all, involves people working together. In the public service, as in other formally organized groups, the social behavior of people working together affects organizational arrangements. Whenever a group of people are brought together to do a common job, they become in the words of Chester Barnard, "participants in specific cooperative systems".[27] The individual disposition to cooperate with others must be taken as one of the major characteristics of formal organization. This disposition must be cultivated and utilized for effective cooperation. To be sure, much of this individual disposition depends upon personal satisfaction in work and agreeable interpersonal relations with workers who make up the primary work groups. Group solidarity, stability, and loyalty must be reinforced by a sense of worthwhile common purpose. In their intergroup relations, groups tend to develop harmonious adjustment, especially if the constituent group believes that it is receiving ample recognition for its importance.

Group loyalty is especially sensitive to any action which would seem to attack its importance, recognition, or status. Group loyalty is even more concerned with promoting group values in terms of remuneration, customary methods of work, and job security. Tradition also perpetuates many group values. Moreover, the leadership of groups is personally concerned with its individual status, prestige, and struggle for power. In a vicarious way the group, too, participates in this struggle. All these factors make for a certain inflexibility in organizational structure.[28] Modern organization theories based on the importance of human relations techniques, favorable interpersonal relations, and availability of adequate communication channels, can enhance the human relations aspect of organization.

27. Chester I. Barnard, *The Functions of the Executive*, (Cambridge, Mass.: Harvard University Press), 1938, p. 16.

28. John D. Millett, *op. cit.*, p. 201.

The most common organization of government agencies today is bureaucracy. It is based on a "rational" network of authority capable of integrating—through the media of authority and responsibility —men, machines, methods and monies. Complex organizations are sometimes called super-bureaucracies. They combine gigantic numbers of human beings and governmental functions by the means of advanced methodical policies directed toward the achievement of a host of administrative goals.

BUREAUCRATIC ORGANIZATION

Max Weber coined the term bureaucracy to describe modern officialdom. Harold Laski reiterated the same meaning when he described bureaucracy as "a system of government the control of which is so completely in the hands of officials".[29] Oddly enough, the system of modern officialdom advocated by Weber some seventy years ago remains, for all practical purposes, a model for what is practiced today in the U.S. and the western world. With meager attempts at organizational reforms, the example of the Weberian bureaucracy remains predominant.

From a historical perspective, contemporary interest in modern officialdom may have risen as a by-product of medieval, aristocratic rules. Especially in the history of the latter, a disinclination on the part of the aristocracy for active government participation might have led to the transfer of power into the hands of permanent officials who can conduct public service in a stable manner subject to state control. Also, interest in modern officialdom must be viewed as a by-product of the industrial revolution in industrialized communities. Such a revolution, in a way, must have forced advanced societies into creating a tool of government capable of effectively coping with the ensuing problems of industrialization.

From a pragmatic point of view, bureaucracy as a form of modern officialdom can be explained on the basis of the limitations on human rational capacities. March and Simon argued that since the individual could not be endowed with *all* rational knowledge, he had to combine his efforts and cooperate with those knowledgeable in other areas—under a set of qualifying rules—to produce rational decisions beyond the capacity of any single individual. Chester Barnard, arguing along the same lines of March and Simon, also attributed the rise of bureaucracy to man's general biological limitations. Victor Thompson, probably treating bureaucracy as an analogous organ to man's psychological system, named the sickness of bureaucracy "Bureaupathology", and the "psychotic" behavior of bureaucrats as "Bureausis".

---

29. Dwight Waldo, *op. cit.*, p. 36.

Characteristics of Weberian Bureaucracy

Weber perceived bureaucracy as an *ideal* organizational arrangement. Ideal to Weber did not mean desirable, but a "pure form" of organization. Combinations or alloys of various organizational arrangements would appear in practice, but Weber wanted to characterize an ideal type for the purpose of theoretical analysis. This bureaucratic ideal, he thought, would serve as a *normative model* to ease the transition from small-scale undertakings to large-scale professional administration.

Bureaucracy, the formal type of organization, has these basic features. [30]

(1) There is the principle of fixed and official jurisdictional areas which are governed by laws, rules, or administrative regulations.

(2) The regular activities required for the purposes of the organization are distributed in a fixed way as official duties.

(3) A division of labor among offices and individuals is based on authority and responsibility. The offices and positions would be organized in a hierarchy resulting in a chain of command.

(4) All organizational members are to be selected on the basis of technical qualifications through formal examinations.

(5) Bureaucrats are appointed personnel who are expected to serve the organization as career employees.

(6) Officials are kept competent through expert training.

(7) Employees are to undergo a probationary period, the successful completion of which entitles the employee to establish a career employment for life.

(8) Employees work at fixed salaries and guaranteed pensions.

(9) Employees distinctly separate their official activity from their private life. Public monies and equipment are divorced from the private property of the official. Rules and controls are strict, impersonal, and uniformly applied in all cases.

(10) The management of the office is based upon written documents or files which are preserved in their original form.

Contemporary Emphasis in Bureaucracy

Bureaucracy, as originated by Weber, evolved rather slowly in response to the complexity of modern societies. In light of today's

30. Adapted from *From Max Weber: Essays in Sociology,* translated by H. H. Gerth and C. Wright Mills.

highly administrative society which is also heavily affected by the rapid change in science and technology, the emphases of bureaucracy have focused on more contemporary issues:

(1) An abnormal growth in size. As Parkinson humorously puts it, bureaucracy "multiplies like rabbits". The influx of new laws to control individual or corporate behavior requires new bureaucratic organizations which in turn require new super organizations to supervise and keep in line. The 1968 Omnibus Crime Act, as an example, created the LEAA with hundreds of regional offices, criminal justice counsels, coordinating boards, and evaluation units. The Drug Enforcement Administration (DEA) is another prime example.

(2) The evolution of specialized competencies centered around the chain of command. Specialized competencies have grown because of the need to man modern specialized equipment associated with modern techniques. In police work today a new breed of scientists man crime labs, data processing units, electronic communication media, and management units. The traditional "line of command" principle has been relaxed by a structure of "technical interdependence".

(3) Routinization of organizational activity. To secure stability, continuity, and predictability of product or service, the activities of bureaucracy are reduced to procedures or routines. Routinization, implicit in the process of specialization, requires a stable environment and a guarantee of continuity of function. In routinized bureaucracy, the organization can afford to avoid dependence upon individuals by assigning the same routines to whichever specialist qualified to perform them.

(4) A growing dominance of a spirit of rationalism. The classification of divisions and units is to be limited and guided only by empirical verification. Within modern bureaucracy this rationalism expresses itself in a sense of self-scrutiny. The pragmatic test grows not from traditional or charismatic standards, but from such questions as "Does it work?", "How does it promote the organizational goals?".

(5) Bureaucracy as a problem-solving mechanism. This depends on articulation of goals and the factoring of general goals into sub-goals and even into sub-subgoals. These sub-goals are allocated to organizational units and become the goals of these units. Individuals in these units are not given the impossible task, therefore, of examining every problem in terms of the general goals of the organization but only in terms of the particular subgoals allocated to them.

(6) A sense of functional formality. In modern bureaucracy officials perform within a structure of functional relationships. While the specialist performs his function for many and must limit his participation to the area of his speciality, his personal involvement and understanding of the potential and limitations of the agency can reduce the rigidity of formal relations stipulated in Weber's traditional model.

(7) Interdependence. Government today realizes the difficulty of coping with the rapid change in its socio-political and economic environment. Facing the challenge imposed in the sixties by the Civil Rights movement, the police bureaucracy has had to coordinate its activities with the legal bureaucracy and the legislative bureaucracy, especially at the state and local levels, as well as with the departments of HEW, and occasionally with the military. Facing the problem of excessive drug abuse, police organizations have had to rely on the services made available by the Drug Enforcement Administration, Drug Treatment Centers, Probation and Parole agencies as well as other private organizations.

(8) Concern for efficiency. Because of the alarming rise in the cost of bureaucracy and the increasing faith in the scientific solution, bureaucracy today seems forced into the practice of efficiency. Defined as a ratio between input and output, the criterion of efficiency dictates the selection of one or more alternatives of all those available which will yield the greatest return to the organization. Moreover, the organizational objectives today must include a conservation policy directly concerned with the maximization of output, products or services.

(9) System approach to organization. Bureaucracy today emphasizes the need to blend with its social environment. This necessarily enhances its image and generates ample support for its decisions. Modern organizations, therefore, capitalize on the desire to harmonize their goals, structures, and practices with the human needs of the society they serve. Bureaucracy organizes itself along the basic demands of society and operates its functions so as to meet those demands. Products of bureaucracy are returned to the society and in turn are incorporated in fresh social desires and aspirations. This symbiotic relationship between bureaucracy and society provides the former with the needed support and the latter with the appropriate services.

The Dynamics of Bureaucratic Organization

As will become clear later in the discussion, there is no one theory of organization. Neither is there a "best" or a "worse" theory. There are four major organization theories which are consistently cited in the studies of administration: traditional, scientific management, human relations, and behavioral. The existence of other principles or combinations of the aforementioned theories is a known fact and therefore should cause public administrators little or no surprise. Modern organization has lately branched out in a multitude of minor models and ideas which will be referred to later.

Describing administrative theories as "best" or "worse" should be avoided in the academic vocabulary because they are incomplete terms: best compared to what? or worse compared to what? Such terms are especially misleading in the study of organization. Instead, the terms recommended for use are "effective" or "ineffective" since they directly relate to the achievement of specified goals regardless of their nature. For instance, an armed formation which maximized firepower would be effective if used by infantrymen against enemy forces since the goal would be to kill as many enemy as possible. The same formation would be ineffective if used domestically by policemen against rioters since the goal is clearly the preservation of innocent lives.

Organization theories pertain to ideas on structures, patterns for dividing the work, and connecting relationships which can effectively achieve the prescribed goals. The viability and success of these theories mainly depend on their ability to achieve the goals faster, more economically, and with the least side-effects on the morale of the people within the organization or on the support of the public concerned.

The dynamism of organization, its vitality and progress toward the achievement of goals, clearly does not depend on the separate application of one principle or the other. It results rather from the energetic and harmonious interaction of all principles of organization. This is basically the area of difference among organization theories. Some theory may emphasize a broad span of control; another may emphasize a narrow one. A third may, still, emphasize a liberal delegation of authority, etc. The dynamics of organization, therefore, must include the energies of all such principles in harmonious interaction directed toward the achievement of those goals sought at the time. It is obvious that the energies and interaction of a police organization in a tactical emergency situation would be different from those under a regular office situation. The nature of organization, formal-informal, vertical-horizontal, man-oriented or system-oriented, will definitely change with the nature of goals selected under the circumstance.

The Inevitability of Goals

Before getting in a discussion of the elements of police organization, a word on the nature and functions of goals in organizations is necessary. *Organization cannot be divorced from the idea of purpose.* It is not an end in itself but a means to an end. The fundamental reason for an organization's existence lies in the need for a changed "desired state of affairs" which such an agency can realize. Organizations, it must be understood, are not set up like tinker toys to demonstrate administrative dexterity or to be built up only to be torn down.

The Nature of Goals

"Goals" are the administrative translation for needs, and, therefore, without goals there is no rationale in creating or maintaining organizations. If, hypothetically, an agency ceased to have goals, or fulfilled all of them, it would either be abolished or else "recommissioned" to pursue another set of goals—usually under a new name and a new management. In the objective reality of administrative practice, however, this seldom occurs. Once the goals of an organization are determined—usually in flexible language—administrative agencies frequently start emphasizing unforeseen needs and create new goals. The case of the FBI would be a prime example. During the first quarter of this century the FBI's prime goal was to combat social unrest in America caused by anarchists, newly-formed communist enclaves, and misled fascists. During the second quarter the major goal was to subdue the roaming gangs of robbers, kidnappers and extortionists. After the second world war, the FBI emphasized its cold-war goals of guarding against espionage, sabotage and subversion. Finally, under Attorney General Robert Kennedy, the FBI's chief goal shifted to countering organized crime activities.

Fearful of being left "goal-less", modern organizations, and especially police agencies in this regard, develop multiple goals. As an illustration, beside apprehending offenders, the police also emphasize maintenance of the peace and the provision for a variety of community services. "When and if" all these goals are achieved, the police can still claim such goals as traffic control, educating the public, civil defense operations, animal regulation and licensing of motor vehicles among many other activities.

Chris Argyris stresses the need for multiple goals in modern organizations. Whisenand and Ferguson explain that the multiple goal concept increases the achievement of constituent goals and improves recruitment appeal since it provides a wider variety of functions, thus enhancing job satisfaction.

To insure the omnipresence of administrative goals, bureaucratic agencies usually exercise "goal succession" or the replacement of a goal or goals with a sub-goal or a sub-subgoal which happens to be fashionable at the time. An example for police goal succession is the current emphasis on police-community relations, crime prevention projects, police juvenile operations and family-intervention activities. Such sub-goals, which understandably are fashionable today, are used by police administrators to supplement law enforcement goals of arresting offenders, recovering stolen property, and maintaining the public peace.

The Functions of Goals

The goals of an organization can serve many functions. Etzioni asserts that:

> . . . They provide orientation by depicting a future state of affairs which the organization strives to realize. Thus they set down guidelines for organization activities. Goals also constitute a source of legitimacy which justifies the activities for an organization and outsiders can assess the success of the organization—i.e., its effectiveness and efficiency. Goals also serve in a similar fashion as measuring rods for the students of organizations who try to determine how well the organization is doing.[31]

Goals, state Whisenand and Ferguson, are always sought and never attained; "it is a state that we seek, not one we have".[32] In a sense, general goals such as "serving mankind", "curbing violence" and "police professionalism", which are frequently cited in administrative codes of ethics, would fit that pattern. Such general goals are usually in administration for motivational purposes. They inspire personnel, stimulate participation, and induce a sense of commitment. Specific goals, on the other hand, especially those which are tangible and measurable, can be real as well as attainable. For instance, a specific goal of upgrading police education to the baccalaureate level within a given period of time is real, possible, and attainable. Also a police goal such as reducing car accidents at a hazardous intersection through the use of an automatic light is obviously real and possible. The main difference between "attainable" and "unattainable" goals, therefore, is not one of metaphysical significance but rather the availability of numerical or tangible standards by which the attainment of goals can be measured and determined.

31. Amitai Etzioni, *Modern Organization, op. cit.*, p. 5.

32. Paul M. Whisenand and R. Fred Ferguson, *The Managing of Police Organizations*, (Englewood Cliffs, New Jersey: Prentice-Hall, Inc.), 1973, p. 87.

Administrative goals are initially set by the legislative body which created the organization. As mentioned earlier, they are usually "stated" in vague terms to allow the organization the freedom of succeeding or displacing them. Regardless of the formal text, however, stated goals in practice are soon overshadowed by some "real" goals which the administrators believe are more easily achieved and thus reflect credibility and achievement on the organization faster. Such real goals usually emerge in a complicated, but rather quiet evaluation of the state of the organization by the leadership in charge. This usually involves the reexamination of such issues like, (1) philosophy of leaders, (2) subdivisional power, (3) staff recommendations, (4) environmental pressures, (5) size of budget, (6) strength of political control, and (7) efficiency and productivity.

THE ELEMENTS OF ORGANIZATION

All organizational theories, whether they are traditional, scientific management, human relations, or behavioral, agree that the dynamics of organization require the existence and manipulation of the following elements with variable emphasis:

(1) A hierarchy: a network of authority.

(2) Divisionalization.

(3) A trinity of line, staff, and auxiliary.

(4) A unity of command.

(5) A span of control.

(6) A delegation of authority.

(7) A formal communication.

A Hierarchy: A Network of Authority

The term hierarchy originated in Greek to mean a system of church government of priests or other clergy in graded ranks. In administration, the term came to mean "a system of positions based on a subordination—superordination relationship". Positions designated by ranks are arranged in a ladder of hierarchy (e.g. from patrolman to sergeant, lieutenant, captain . . . to chief).

Although hierarchy is directly associated with a system of stratified status, prestige, and pay, the primary and most crucial purpose of hierarchy is to *produce authority*. Without authority, obedience can not be expected. Without a chain of authority—obedience—control, needless to say, organizations, for all practical reasons, would cease to be "organized".

Authority, as defined by Barnard, is not the power to issue orders, but *the power to grant or withhold obedience.*[33]   Herbert Simon used authority to mean *the power to make decisions which guide the actions of others.*   Obedience, in Simon's analysis, is demonstrated when the subordinate deliberately withholds his choice among alternatives and automatically accepts the choice made for him by his superior.

Influence, which may or may not produce obedience, is different from authority.   The verbs "persuade" and "suggest" describe several kinds of influence within an organization.   Influence, which does not have to be within a hierarchial relationship (superordinate—subordinate), can change one's conviction, but still allow one to make decisions and choose among alternatives.   Authority, on the other hand, eliminates the chance to choose.

In the organizational context, hierarchy refers to a set of roles, rather than persons, distributed in terms of a chain of authority. For example, the chief of police, regardless of who he is, makes all policy decisions, and the subordinates, if they are to survive, have to obey.   Obedience to higher authority will ordinarily reflect such elements as fear of unemployment (resulting from dismissal for disobeying orders), fear of administrative sanctions (pay cuts, suspensions, etc.), strong commitment to the agency and its mission, influence of superiors, group norms of compliance, and cultural patterns of respect to authority, among other factors.

In public organizations, and especially in police organizations, the superordinate role is chiefly characterized by *rights* while the subordinate role is chiefly characterized by *duties*.   The boss (e.g. a police chief, a sheriff, or the head of a federal or state unit) is generally considered to have the following primary rights:

(1) to expect obedience and loyalty from his subordinates;

(2) to veto or uphold decisions made by the subordinates;

(3) to represent the organization before other organizations;

(4) to monopolize formal communication both within the organization as well as between it and the outside world;

(5) to see to it that all legislative rules and regulations are effectively executed.

From these primary rights of the superior flow certain secondary rights: the right to determine the personnel of the unit and its organizational form; the right to initiate activities and to set unit goals; the right to assign activities and to confer jurisdictions; the right to settle conflicts and employ arbitration.   The boss' right to control also makes it possible for him to create a non-hierarchial au-

33. Herbert Simon, *Administrative Behavior*, (New York: The Free Press), Second Edition, 1957, p. 126.

thority network by ordering his subordinates to submit to the authority he delegates to a few others.[34]

The duties of the subordinates, in a hierarchical relationship, are basically those which constitute the correlatives of the superordinate's rights. They are the duties of obedience, of loyalty, of deference: the duty to accept a superior's veto without attempting to appeal outside set-up channels.[35]

The rights of superordinates and the duties of subordinates within a hierarchical relationship cannot, however, be seen on an antagonistic course. Actual behavior of superordinates and subordinates must be seen in a cultural context in accordance with the expectations of the total membership of the organization. The roles of subordinate and superior are learned patterns of behavior fostered by the subculture of the organization. For instance, while an army sergeant can be seriously sanctioned for not saluting his captain, a police sergeant is not expected to salute in the first place. More importantly, actual behavior within an organization will be modified by the social process, the type of leadership, and the informal relations within the group of people which compose the organization. Thus, a police lieutenant, for instance, may develop a strong personal attachment to his platoon members and may closely identify with them. Having become their friend, so to speak, he may discover he has assumed the duties of friendship, most of which are incompatible with his hierarchical rights and usually with his duties to his superior. It is not unusual in such a situation for a person so entrapped in informal relations to be considered useless to the hierarchy and to be replaced. A further study of the actual compromise between organizational hierarchy and informal structure will follow later in the book when management theories are discussed.

Divisionalization

The most basic method of dividing work, and one that every police organization uses to some extent, is division by function. A function is generally defined as a *single activity*, but in modern organizations it commonly means *a group of related activities that are placed under a single department head*. Thus, in almost all police organizations today there exists a patrol division, criminal investigation division, special services division, etc. Such divisions are naturally further divided into sub-divisions and, furthermore, into bureaus or offices.

34. Victor Thompson, *Modern Organi-*   35. *Ibid.*, p. 65.
    zation (New York: Alfred A. Knopf,
    Publisher), 1967, p. 64.

The concept of divisionalization is the backbone of any structural arrangement within which the work of many individuals can be carried out for the realization of a common purpose. As such, it is a system of work assignment among groups of persons specializing in particular phases of a general task. But since police agencies are primarily public agencies, using public funds, and expected to produce efficient and effective public services, the structural framework of police agencies has to reflect "optimal" functionalism. Optimal, in this sense must refer to one and only one meaning: to promote agency goals efficiently and effectively.

Divisionalization in many police organizations has not been optimal. Divisions, departments, and offices have frequently followed such lines as tradition, internal pressure, preference or whim of the administrator. The 1967 Task Force Report on the Police stated the following findings as an example:

.   .   .   the scattering of specialized work units about the department without the essential bond of control and direction to hold each such unit to the main objectives of the organization, has reduced the ability of the department to function as an organized group. The ultimate result is a reduction in the efficiency of the total effort.[36]

In another example the Report cited the following:

The department suffers from a deficient organizational structure which contributes to poor management. These weaknesses make it difficult for the Department leadership to exercise full control over the entire police operation; the chain of command is confused and supervision is erratic. The excessive decentralization of the Department's operations into 14 precincts adds to these problems. One of the important consequences of poor organization   .   .   .   is the diversion of police personnel to specialized or administrative assignments, thus unduly curtailing the number of men available for the street operations.[37]

Divisionalization or splitting off the organization into meaningful groupings could be too limited and produce organizational centralization or be too pervasive and produce organizational decentralization. The former has been a trend in police agencies designed to strengthen the control of the chief executive, to make more efficient the use of manpower, and to facilitate the policy-making process by keeping it in the hands of a few. The latter has been a tendency to broaden the police base, to facilitate contacts with the public, and to stimulate expertise through specialized functions.

36. *Task Force Report on the Police,*   37. *Ibid.*
     1967, p. 45.

Either method, conceivably, does not offer optimal functionalism. Appropriate divisionalization calls for an adequate balance between "the need for centralization which is a very compelling need for the administrator [and] the necessity for having a form of organization that facilitates contacts with the community".[38]

To achieve optimal functionalism, some main properties must be considered:

A—The economic state of the organization. The establishment of a new functional department means that a new administrator must be appointed, a number of assistants and staff assigned and a number of subordinates detached from the main stream of the department.

B—The amount of specialization and training required for the members of the new division. If no specialization or additional training is required, then the creation of a new division can hardly be justified. Use of modern technology in police operation clearly induces and often dictates divisionalization.

C—The extent by which the new division would be able to contribute to the realization of the agency's objectives. If the goals of the department are not clearly defined or are lumped in general terms, further divisionalization would not only be unnecessary but also dysfunctional.

D—The amount of overlapping or duplication the new division would create. This, of course, is closely related to the specific identification of goals and objectives. When more than one division is assigned to serve the same goal, the chances are that sufficient duplication and overlapping will take place.

E—The amount of communication disruption which would result from the establishment of a new division. The larger this amount is, the less functional divisionalization would seem to be.

There is naturally no "one best way" for police divisionalism because of differences in size, resources, location, training and public support. Two observations, however, are necessary: (a) any organizational structure which appears to hamper or discourage the realization of an agency's basic purposes would be obviously faulty, (b) while the great majority of police administrators are aware of the merits and disadvantages of the issue of divisionalization, determining the line of optimal functionalism is by no means an easy choice. Such a determination depends not only on the education and expertise of the police chief, but also on the provisions of the city charter, public support for the police, changing conditions in the community, availability of state or federal funds, and the level of professionalism within the agency.

38. *Ibid.*, p. 37.

While optimal functionalism may sound like a hard goal to practically achieve, a "reasonable" level of functional divisionalization can yield these advantages:

(a) It greatly reduces the pressure at the leadership level. Since specialized divisions will have specialized managers who will be held continually accountable, it does not become necessary for leaders to supervise them closely.

(b) It brings the decision-making process to the level of action. It allows division heads to make delegated decisions each at his level of competence.

(c) It promotes the accomplishment of specialized programs through the efforts of specialist groups.

(d) It helps in determining accountability when "things go wrong".

While functional divisionalization can obviously be most beneficial to a large police department, its neglect, on the other hand, can be equally disastrous. Divisions, bureaus, and offices may become so big, independent, or powerful as to pursue individual goals rather than agency goals. Questions of control, supervision and coordination may become too difficult to handle as each division would try to expand at the expense of the other. Agency morale would also drop with the increase in intraagency conflicts and feuds and the general effectiveness of the agency may be seriously undermined.

The Trinity: Line, Staff and Auxiliary

Since its inception, bureaucracy has developed a special interest in the segregation of roles within its ranks. The same interest is still shown today by many organization theories which attempt to maintain a harmonious relationship between three traditionally segregated roles; line, staff, and auxiliary.

In the complex setting of modern organization, with police organizations as a prime case in question, it is important to identify these roles and discuss their basic characteristics. First, line functions are those which (a) carry out the major purposes of police activities, (b) face the clientele, (c) deliver the service, and (d) make final decisions. These tasks include patrol, criminal investigation, traffic control, etc., as well as all supervisory tasks in charge of these functions. Therefore, the patrolman in the beat, the platoon sergeant, the lieutenant, the shift captain, and the police chief himself, must be considered line members since they are in daily contact with the public and make operational decisions concerning the delivery of the police service. They make final decisions as to arrest, to book, to release, as well as to supervise and direct those who make them.

Secondly, staff functions are those which support line activities, operating across the board inside the police agency rather than looking outside. They are highly specialized, mostly in a civilian capacity, and can only make proposals and recommend action to the line personnel without making the final decisions. Staff personnel, often referred to as "steers among bulls" (since they work hard without making final scores), perform advisory and consultative services such as research and planning, budgeting, crime analysis and similar services which do not involve encountering the clientele or making operational decisions relative to the delivery of service. They are usually manned by people behind desks and rarely require contacts with outsiders.

Third, as a result of the contributions of Leonard D. White, the staff category was further divided between staff and auxiliary. While the term "staff" was reserved to describe the functions or offices of government engaged primarily in planning, research and policy advice, the term "auxiliary" was used to denote those in "housekeeping" services.[39] Auxiliary functions, in police organizations, are those in charge of personnel, communication, maintenance, purchasing, jailing, record keeping, and a few others. Auxiliary services are mainly concerned with producing logistical services which keep line workers well equipped and prepared to handle the delivery of services.

As in the case of the "divine trinity," line, staff and auxiliary can be seen separately but must work in unison. The case for segregation is strongly based on four overriding reasons: [40]

(1) Segregation relieves line operators of many headaches extraneous to their main responsibility. For example, each division, (as patrol, detective, traffic) does not have to hire or fire officers, buy their necessary equipment, or maintain government vehicles. Specialized auxiliary services do it for them in accordance with state and city standards and rules.

(2) Segregation saves money by centralizing duplicate services. Examples for this economy argument are legion. Consider, for instance, the costs of letting each police precinct buy and run its own computerized communication system rather than using a central communication center to serve them all.

(3) Segregation provides for adequate planning to get done. One of the most important arguments for segregation is the one

39. Leonard D. White, *Introduction to the Study of Public Administration*, (New York: MacMillan), 3rd ed., 1948, p. 30.

40. These reasons are adapted from J. D. Williams, *Management Begins with Man*, a forthcoming text in Public Administration from Little, Brown, and Company, pp. 41–44.

which underlies the importance of staff services. The concern is simply this: if someone is not pulled away from the day-to-day strife of line operations and given enough time and repose to think ahead and chart the future, adequate planning will always get lost in the shuffle. Since planning, "organizing ahead", is so crucial, then the need for a staff of fulltime "thinkers ahead" is equally crucial.

(4) Segregation provides administrators with a means of getting procedures done uniformly throughout all units. The Federal Bureau of Investigation, for instance, with its 59 regional offices would not be able to apply its enforcement policies uniformly throughout the offices without specialized staff services in the areas of policy making, legal research, training, and technical methods.

On the other hand, the trinity of line, staff, and auxiliary must work in unison if the organization is to remain cohesive and effective. To begin with, the three parts of the trinity must share the mission and philosophy of the organization, its goals and their order of priority. Moreover, the three parts of the trinity must "talk the same language" and maintain adequate communication and exchange of pertinent information at all times. The ultimate purpose must always be the enhancement of the whole organization through the achievement of its goals efficiently, effectively and economically. Figure 11 shows a traditional segregation chart in a large police department.

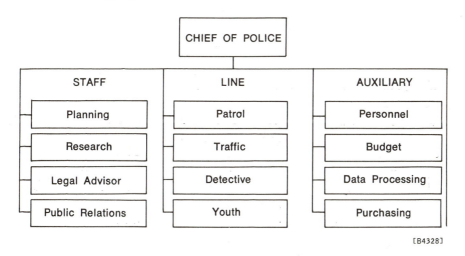

[B4328]

Fig. 11.   Traditional Organization of Line, Staff and Auxiliary
in a Large Police Department

This traditional view of the trinity has not, however, been infallible. It came under direct attack by many critics who consider it unrealistic, dysfunctional, and rather obsolete. O. Glenn Stahl, for example, argued that the traditional concept of "staff"—in its general sense which also includes auxiliary functions—as advisor of, and subordinate to, "line" units "not only should not be the case, but is not and never has been the case".[41] Stahl emphasized that segregation between "line" and "staff" functions is hardly distinguishable. He indicated that staff units in modern organization cannot be treated as "steers" anymore, since they in fact hold ample power, make final decisions, carry out functions of command, and often deliver the final product.

Stahl, in his criticism of the traditional view of the trinity, also emphasized that line and staff operations today are combined in "program" functions which interlace with each other in a harmonious, productive network. The chief executive must, therefore, control his organization by means of both "vertical" line functions and "horizontal" staff functions. Stahl concluded that organizational conflicts between line and staff will further be reconciled and communication facilitated when there is no presumption of unvarying command superiority of line over staff. Figure 12 illustrates the interlacing model of segregation suggested by Stahl. It is adapted from a proposed organization of the Department of State. The figure clearly shows the interrelation of the three functions in a cohesive administrative fabric.

41. Robert T. Golembiewski, "Toward the New Organizational Theories: Some Notes on Staff", in *Readings in* *Public Administration*, ed. by Maurice E. O'Donnell (New York: Houghton-Mifflin Co.) 1966, pp. 65–67.

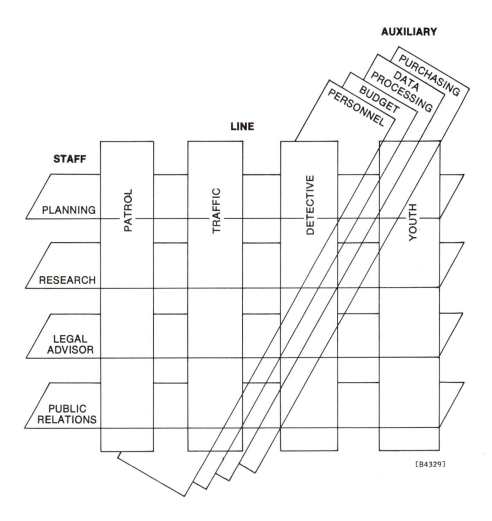

Fig. 12. A Suggested Organization of Line, Staff and Auxiliary in a Large Police Department

Although specialization by trinity is still a favorite organizational method, keeping it active and healthy is necessarily a function of management (the other arm of administration). Appropriate management, through effective leadership, planning, and communication, can maintain a dynamic and harmonious trinity: well-balanced, highly-motivated, and straightforwardly directed toward the achievement of administrative goals.

Unity of Command

Traditional structural analysis has always emphasized that every person in an organization should have one, and only one, superior from whom orders are regularly received and to whom reports are made. This principle of "unity of command" is viewed as the backbone of organizational hierarchy without which straight lines of command from top to bottom could not be maintained. A patrolman, therefore, the traditionalists would argue, must receive his orders from and report to his immediate sergeant and only his immediate sergeant. He should not receive orders from a chief detective, a garage supervisor, a personnel officer or even the lieutenant assistant to the chief for internal affairs.

Gulick, a staunch traditionalist, stressed that the significance of the principle of unity of command in the process of coordination and organization must not be lost sight of. He warned that in building an organizational structure, it is often tempting to set up more than one boss for a man who is doing work which has more than one relationship. Unity of command would keep authority lines straight and avoid conflict situations which might arise under dual or multiple supervision. Gulick, in his analysis, indicated the difficulties to be faced if unity of command is not observed: "A certain amount of irresponsibility and confusion is almost certain to ensue.[42]"

Another problem usually arises when unity of command is not strictly observed. Lower rank officers tend to be carried away in their desire to associate with, and please, the specialists as well as the "self-proclaimed specialists", at the sacrifice of administrative control. Orders might be selectively executed, or ignored and justified upon reported advice by a specialist. In such cases the responsibility of the advisor would be hard to establish and that of the subordinate harder to justify.

Also, if the principle of unity of command is not adhered to, supervisors may end up by being unaware of what their subordinates are doing. This would certainly break down the appropriate line of responsibility within the organization. Consider, for instance, the case of a patrolman assigned by his sergeant to establish a check point outside a crime scene but later advised by a public relations officer to talk to some newsmen and describe the case. As expected, a miserable report would most likely be given. With the patrolman influenced by the PR officer's advice, the sergeant would be left in an embarrassing situation.

---

42. L. Gulick, "Notes on the Theory of Organization", in L. D. White, *Introduction to the Study of Public Administration* (New York: MacMillan Company), 1939, p. 9.

Certainly the principle of unity of command, thus interpreted, cannot be criticized for any lack of clarity or for ambiguity. Simon, however, stated that "the real fault that must be found with this principle is that it is incompatible with the principle of specialization".[43] While the latter embedded in the concept of the organizational trinity (line, staff and auxiliary), is designed to bring about expertise in the making of decisions, strict unity of command simply neutralizes its effect. If staff and auxiliary members cannot reach the line decision-maker when their advice is needed—except through a tall hierarchy of line supervisors—their expertise may never reach the workers at all and if it does, it would most likely be diluted or distorted.

If, on the other hand, dual or multiple supervision by specialized members is widely allowed whenever they feel there is a need, or a desire for it, patrolmen may end up by not only having to "feel the hot breath" of every specialist in the department, but also the "cold stares" of internal affairs personnel, legal advisors, and just about every sergeant in uniform.

Modern organization theories, mainly championed by the behavioralists Chris Argyris and Rensis Likert, deny that unity of command is particularly necessary among enlightened and highly-motivated line members. Their argument is basically made on the assumption that this kind of line member is capable of integrating control with the need for specialized advice—"wisely". They emphasize that well-trained and highly-motivated personnel can receive dual or multiple input and still make the right decisions without jeopardizing organizational accountability. In their conception of organization as a team of colleagues in group interaction, the behavioralists deemphasize the need for a strict unity of command. In return, they seem to emphasize the need for, and training of, management-oriented goal-seekers. An atmosphere of dynamic cooperation, informal cohesiveness, and democratic leadership would lessen the dependence on unity of command. Furthermore, the behavioralists stress that in such an organization, lines of responsibility would be straightened out not necessarily through unity of command but rather because of the workers' concern and their commitment to the organization. In other words, the behavioralists tend to remove the question of unity of command from the area of organization and locate it within the area of management which treats the subject more like a behavioral norm rather than a principle of organizational structure.

This behavioral approach to organization which deemphasizes the principle of unity of command, however, cannot be accepted as applicable to all bureaucracies. While it may work well in professional or intellectual organizations like the AMA, bar associations, universi-

43.   Herbert Simon, *op. cit.*, p. 23.

ty administrations or some select government agencies, its chances to work in the police are low and in the military are just about nil. The dangerous nature of these organizations and the kind of functions they perform cannot afford too much relaxation of the principle. In civilian agencies, nevertheless, the application of the principle can well be liberally relaxed.

With these views in mind, the principle of unity of command in police organizations can perhaps be more functional if narrowed down to the areas of conflicting commands only. In case two authoritative commands conflict, there should be a next determinate person whom the subordinate is expected to obey. If, on the other hand, a conflict occurs between an authoritative command and a specialized advice (e.g., influence by the legal advisor, operations research, or personnel), then the authoritative command must be preserved and the specialized advice subordinated or ignored. Only, however, by the use of appropriate management can such conflicts be removed or expediently resolved.

Span of Control

In traditional organizations—which still include the great majority of police agencies in America—the pyramid shape structure predominates. Held together by a network of authority, organizations consist of a number of positions, or "pigeonholes" as they are commonly referred to. With unity of command giving it length, the span of control gives the pyramid its width.

If each person in an organization were to supervise only one subordinate, then the organization would look like an extremely tall tower or needle. But since rules of efficiency and economics require that each supervisor must be able to supervise more than one subordinate, administrative organizations must look more or less like pyramids with leadership at the top and multitudes of rank and file at the bottom. Although the shape of the pyramid may vary from one organization to another and the pointed head at the top may look flatter, the fact remains that the width can only be produced by the span of control.

The principle of span of control refers to *the maximum number of subordinates whom a superordinate can supervise effectively.* Contemporary management literature is filled with hypotheses on the magic number ideal for effective supervision. They range from three or seven (as complete numbers), to twelve (after Christ's disciples), to thirty (the number of an army platoon) to just about any number the author could, for one reason or another, defend. Unfortunately, no magic number need be devised since "effective supervision" undoubtedly must be seen differently by different organizations.

While the President of the United States can effectively supervise about 250 top bureaucracy officials (white house staff, department secretaries, heads of regulatory agencies, staff generals, etc.), an army corporal may only supervise about ten GIs. In police organizations, the situation is much more atypical. The FBI director, for example, supervises three assistants to the director, thirteen division heads and 59 special agents in charge of the regional offices. In state organizations, the head of the Texas Department of Public Safety, for instance, has to directly supervise an assistant director, three chiefs for traffic, administration, and criminal law, eight administrators in charge of specialized fields, and six regional commanders. In local police organizations, the situation may vary from the New York City Police Commissioner who supervises about 35 top management positions, to the chief of police in Orting, Washington, who supervises the only other man on his force, or Etna, California, where the chief supervises only himself.

The variables which can determine the span of control of a supervisor in a given organization would include: [44]

(1) The physical nature of the work area as it may affect visibility and the need for face to face supervision.

(2) The complexity of functions supervised.

(3) The skill of his deputies (requiring more or less supervision).

(4) The quality of the communication system.

(5) His personal capability, quickness, and skill in managing time.

(6) The organizational culture in terms of legislative statutes, traditions, budget and political support.

The purpose of the principle of span of control is *to increase administrative efficiency*. A smaller span of control is supposed to enhance efficiency by limiting the number of subordinates who report directly to any one administrator. A large span, on the other hand, increases the number of subordinates and, therefore, may reduce efficiency due to the reduction in effective supervision.

The significance of the span of control principle also lies in the organizational headaches which result when it is flagrantly ignored. If the administrator, who theroetically supervises each individual subordinate, were to do just that, then his forty-hour-a-week job would be consumed going over what each subordinate is doing. In the other direction, a too narrow supervisory capability can lead to that administrative oddity known as the "one-over-one-over-one" organization

---

44. J. D. Williams, *op. cit.*, p. 33.

(the needle structure). Figure 13 illustrates a too broad span of control, and Figure 14 illustrates a too narrow span of control.

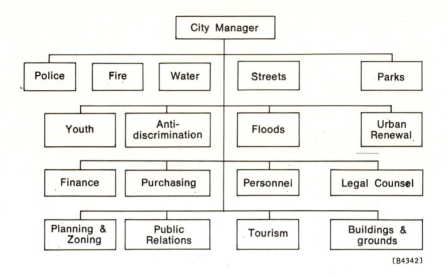

Fig. 13. A Too Broad Span of Control

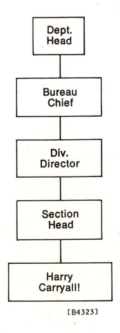

Fig. 14. A Too Narrow Span of Control

There is also the important factor of how spans of control affect those on the receiving end of the supervision, the subordinates themselves. In concentrating on supervisors, the classical writers opted for narrow spans and overlooked the impact which the resulting close supervision would have on rank and file employees. But the behavioralists, like Argyris, Likert, and Golembiewski, have sounded the warning that productivity can be seriously affected by subjecting workers to an almost insulting degree of supervision under narrow spans of control. Consistent with their advocacy for major purpose structuring and for liberal unity of command, the behavioralists make a strong plea for "flat organizations" with broad spans of control.

Delegation of Authority

Organizational pyramids, still the most common among police agencies, could be tall or short, and either shape could be fat or slim. The width factor, as mentioned earlier, is the product of span of control. The length factor, on the other hand, stems from the delegation of authority which determines the number of organizational levels within the context of unity of command.

An example of tall police organizations with numerous organizational levels would be the Texas Department of Public Safety. It is headed by a public safety commission which makes policy decisions and controls the DPS director. The latter superordinates an assistant director who in turn is subordinated by a level of chief administrators. The latter supervise a set of middle managers consisting of majors or "senior captains" who are followed down the hierarchical line with a set of "plain captains". Plain captains, in turn, are in charge of a set of lower managers consisting of lieutenants, sergeants, patrolmen and agents. Tall organizations are necessarily the product of excessive delegation of authority.

Delegation refers to *the conferring of a specified authority by a higher authority*. In its essence it involves a dual responsibility. The one to whom authority is delegated becomes responsible to the superior for doing the job, but the superior remains responsible for getting the job done. This principle of delegation of authority (not power as many students casually use it) remains at the center of all formal organizations. It is "inherent in the very nature of the relationship between superior and subordinate".[45]

When an organization outgrows the possibility of face-to-face supervision, there must ensue an extension of the principle of delega-

---

45. Dwight Waldo, *op. cit.*, p. 91.

tion, which Waldo called *subdelegation*. This means that the leader begins to delegate the *right of delegation* itself, conferring the same kind of authority over others. Thus develops the lengthening of the hierarchial chain of organizational levels which appears in larger organizations of every kind.[46]

The relationship between delegation of authority and the responsibility of the delegator to the matters delegated and to the behavior of the delegate, has some how been left unclarified. Although the traditionalists like James Moony and Paul Appleby stressed that responsibility cannot be delegated down with authority, the fact of the matter cannot be resolved so easily. Would a police chief or sheriff be held accountable to the malpractice committed by each and every patrolman in the force? If the answer is in the affirmative, then simple logic would necessitate that the President would be responsible for the mistakes of each and every employee in the federal government. But since the President in the objective reality of life can not be held responsible for such mistakes, then either the chief should not be held responsible, or the kind of responsibility he may be accountable for should be considered only moral rather than administrative.

It is obvious that the delegator cannot be *totally* responsible for the mistakes of the delegate, especially in cases of remote *subdelegations*. But also sound organization would seriously falter if the delegators could remain immune from *any* criticism, especially if his selection of the delegate was hard to justify, the scope of delegated functions was not clear or precise, or the performance of the delegate was not adequately overseen.

The relationship between delegation of authority and responsibility of the delegator for the mistakes of the delegate would probably be better explained if the concept of administrative responsibility were clarified. If responsibility is the obligation to carry out stated functions according to specified standards or otherwise pay the consequences in terms of prescribed sanctions, then administrative responsibility must be distinguished from moral responsibility which warrants no such sanctions. In this sense the delegator would be administratively responsible—and should pay the consequence in prescribed sanctions—if:

(1) The selection of the delegate was not done according to specified standards.

(2) The scope of delegated functions was not made clear and precise.

(3) The performance of the delegate was not adequately overseen.

46. *Ibid.*

Delegators, otherwise, may be only held accountable for a "moral" responsibility which does not warrant administrative sanctions. Such responsibility, though it may adversely affect the delegator's public career, is chiefly tolerable, mild, and temporary. A sheriff or a chief of police, however, if frequently held accountable for cases of moral responsibility, may eventually find himself losing the public support he needs to retain his position.

Modern organization theorists influenced by the behavioral approach, advocate wide delegations of authority. Championed by Argyris, Likert, and Williams, they argue that such delegations constitute a meaningful way of demonstrating confidence in men, boosting their self-esteem, building commitment through involvement and motivating workers to self-actualization.[47]

Although the concept of delegation of authority has been well routinized in the field of administration, the application of the concept is chiefly managerial. It is commonplace in police organizations today to encounter the managerial syndrome of *inability to delegate*. It often reflects a chief's sense of job insecurity, an exaggerated worry about his deputies' ability to handle responsibility, and on occasion, demands from higher-ups or external groups that compel him to tighten his control within the agency.[48]

Formal Communication

The previous elements are crucial to any organization. By themselves, however, they would remain fragmented unless integrated in a viable organization. Only through effective communication can they become fabric of a viable organization capable of effectively integrating the functions of each element toward the achievement of prescribed goals.

The main difficulty with communication is the problem of understanding. Chester Barnard wrote that "a communication that cannot be understood has no authority".[49] Ordway Tead emphasized the need for understanding communication by declaring that "the underlying aim of communication is the meeting of minds on common issues".[50] Peter Drucker went a step further to say that information is not the problem: information can be provided in carload lots to the supervisors and employees of an organization. Indeed, the larger the organization the more elaborate and extensive usually are the organs for dispensing information. "But the essence of communication," Drucker insisted, is "the ability and willingness to listen and to un-

47. J. D. Williams, *op. cit.*, p. 31.

48. *Ibid.*

49. Chester Barnard, *op. cit.*, p. 165.

50. Ordway Tead, *The Art of Administration* (New York: McGraw-Hill), 1951, p. 185.

derstand the interests and concern of people in various parts of the organization".[51]

Communication is the *nerve* of organization. It is the vehicle for relating decisions to actions, plans to practices, and goals to production. It may be formally defined as *any process whereby decisional promises are transmitted from one member of an organization to another*.[52] It is obvious that without adequate communication there can be no organization, for then there is no possibility for the common sharing of agency goals, for the understanding of policies, for adherence to authority, or for the maintenance of organizational values and standards of performance. Effective communication provides the *thread that binds an organization together by ensuring common understanding, direction, and procedure.*

To communicate—a verb which indicates passing along, transmitting, or sharing—the parties involved must exchange information, signals, or meanings in one form or another. While individuals communicate through methods of sensation directed at the stimulation of bodily organisms (seeing, touching, smelling, gesturing, etc.) organizations cannot afford the risk of using such inaccurate, elusive, and hard-to-interpret methods. Administrative communication must be a language of standardized meanings, documented, storable and retrievable. If a situation of conflict arises between a supervisor and a subordinate, the content of the communication, its format as well as the individual who initiated it, must be traced, and investigated, and responsibilities determined accordingly. To organize and control a communication system within a public agency, appropriate channels must be created, direction and order assigned, and a procedure for registering transmission and receipt of communication established.

Communication in organization is a complex *multi-way* process. It can take place downward, upward, and laterally. It can also follow formal channels or informal ones. Emphasis, however, on the type of communication to be applied in an organization varies considerably. Bureaucratic organizations which are not influenced by managerial techniques limit communication to a two-way process within a formal setting. With an overriding concern to tightening control over the organization and sustaining a perfect chain of command, bureaucratic organizations prohibit lateral communication and discourage all forms of informal contacts. Managerial communication, as will be discussed in later chapters, on the other hand, encourages cross communication and even circular contacts among workers. Moreover, it promotes informal communication as an acceptable means for in-

---

51. John D. Millett, *op. cit.*, p. 81.   52. Herbert A. Simon, *op. cit.*, p. 154.

creasing productivity through the elimination of undesirable steps and unwarranted precautions.

Bureaucratic organizations, which naturally include the overwhelming majority of police agencies, run a two-way flow of communication: downward and upward. The downward flow transmits instruction, and the upward flow returns information. Channels of communication are strictly formal and can be found in the lines of organizational charts. As an example, if a detective needs to use a car kept and maintained by the garage sergeant, he has to contact the chief of detectives who would contact the executive assistant at the chief's office who would—if approved—instruct the head of central services division who in turn would order the sergeant in charge of the garage to provide the requested car. If the detective directly contacted the sergeant, he would be in violation of the regular communication procedure. While such a procedure understandably enhances control over the use of police cars and clearly determines accountability in case the vehicle is abused or involved in a wreck, the procedure is evidently complicated, time consuming, and frustrating. It assumes the lack of proper judgment on the part of both the detective and the garage sergeant. The procedure, as well, may cost the agency a considerable price in terms of man-hours, paper forms, and agency time.

Downward communications in a police agency are of five types: [53]

1 —Specific task directives: job instructions.

2 —Information to produce the understanding of the task and its relation to other organizational tasks: job rationale.

3 —Information concerning organizational standards: job procedures.

4 —Information concerning the subordinate performance: job evaluation.

5 —Information to internalize organizational goals and instill a sense of mission: job indoctrination.

The first type of communication is most often given first priority in police organizations. Instructions about the nature of the police task is communicated to the officers through direct orders, schedules, manuals, training sessions and written directives. The objective is to insure the reliable performance of every individual in the organization. Less attention is usually given to the second type, which is designed to provide the police officer with a full understanding of his position and its relation to other positions in the same organization.

53. Paul Whisenand and Fred Ferguson, *op. cit.*, p. 129.

Withholding information on the rationale of the job not only reduces the loyalty of the member of the organization, but also makes the organization heavily dependent on the first type of information—specific instructions on specific unrelated functions. Job procedures, the third type of information, supplies a prescription of performance standards expected of each officer in discharge of his job. The fourth provides the necessary feedback each officer needs to know about his performance and the administration's appraisal of his contribution. Without continual feedback of that nature, organization members may become indifferent about their job, question their suitability for the job, and become insecure and frequently confused and hostile. The last type of communication, job indoctrination, has as its purpose to emphasize organizational goals, to instill a sense of mission in all workers and to help promote professionalism.[54]

Upward communications are initiated by subordinates and directed through formal channels to the levels of supervisors or administrators: They usually are of five types:

1   —A report about certain actions taken in a specific case or situation.

2   —Response to a particular request for information or explanation of a situation.

3   —Presentation of personal request or grievance.

4   —Proposal concerning what needs to be done or means for doing it.

5   —Request for clarification of organizational goals or standards of performance.

In order for formal communication to be effective, channels of communication must be clearly known to all members of the organization and remain continuously open for their use. Barnard insisted that a "definite channel of communication should exist to every member in an organization", and that the "line of communication should be as direct or as short as possible".[55] Regular (formal) channels are ordinarily used for the two-way flow of information. Unless used in emergency situations, bypassing the formal channel by attempting to use an informal one is strongly discouraged and may call for a disciplinary action by the administration.

In conclusion it must be noted that since most police agencies in America are fairly small organizations, advanced communication systems as an element of internal control have not developed. The police chief, or his deputy in most cases, handles communication direct-

54. This discussion has been gleaned from Whisenand and Ferguson, *op. cit.*, pp. 129–130.

55. Chester Barnard, *op. cit.*, pp. 175–180.

ly with the men. Through the means of manuals, written directives, and occasional memoranda, the job is usually carried out satisfactorily. In large departments, however, where communication becomes much more complex, a communication system is usually created and operated. The major elements of such a communication system can be briefly described as:

1 —A communicator: the sender, the speaker, the issuer, or the suggester of communication.

2 —A transmission procedure: a message center, a telephone, the teletype or the mail.

3 —A form: an order, a regulation, a manual, a letter, a report, or a circular.

4 —A recipient: a position, an office, a group or an individual.

5 —A desired response: a report, a reply, a written or an oral clarification.

CHAPTER SIX

POLICE ADMINISTRATION: THE NEED FOR MANAGEMENT

Overview

All governmental police agencies in the United States, regardless of their titles, functions, claims or slogans, are *bureaucracies*. Their basic organization at the federal, state or local level maintains a heavy tint of Weberianism, the extremely traditional approach. Each agency has a chief administrator (boss) empowered with authority to manage men, machines, methods, and monies. Even in the smallest police unit where the total force consists of one person only, it is not unusual to see him "pulling" the rank of chief. Under the "boss", contemporary police organization calls for a tall hierarchy of positions ranking all the way down to the level of patrolman. All members of the police agency are arranged in a chain of vertical superordinate-subordinate relationships. The network of authority within the police agency is sustained by a set of rules and regulations which stresses the right to command and the obligation to obey. Individuals who entertain notions of disagreement or attempt unorthodox thinking are deterred by a "book" of publicized rules and disciplinary actions. Pursley, in his analysis of the traditional police organization in America, described its classical state of administration by stating:

> Myopically, police administrators tenaciously adhere to their deities of scalar principle (chain of command), span of control and unity of command concepts with no provisions for new aspects of organizational research findings. This classical approach is almost entirely concerned with the organization's anatomy, its structure and the manner in which orders are transmitted through results achieved.[1]

Notwithstanding a few mild attempts to "humanize" police administration and "liberalize" police organizations from the grip of formalistic structures, Weberian bureaucracy in police agencies still dominates, and command appears to be prompt and unquestioning. Such a traditional organization, warned Pursley, will eventually fail in all but the small departments because of its inability to contend

---

1. Robert D. Pursley, "Traditional Police Organizations: A Portent of Future", in William Bopp, *Police Administration* (Boston: Holbrook Press, Inc.), 1975, pp. 83–85.

170

with the contemporary motivation of the new patrolman.   Elaborating on his warning, Pursley stated:

> Under traditional police organization, it is the organization
> that molds the parameters of responsibility and action and
> the individual is required to fit, period!   There exists abso-
> lutely no assessment of human resource potential available
> around which the organization is woven.   However, changes
> occurring today and in the near future will cause this type
> of organizational pattern to fail unless substantial, basic
> modifications are made   .   .   .   The [new policemen] pos-
> sesses different motivational levels, needs, career expecta-
> tions   .   .   .   a rising level of expectations and self-con-
> cept.[2]

Pursley concluded his critique of the current organization of police agencies by calling for a significant departure from traditional
organization in favor of a new managerial concept based on the satisfaction of man, and on his constant motivation which can produce an
"unlimited potential".

Police bureaucracies, like most others today, seem to be suffering from the sickness of "bureaupathy"; a product of an overdose of
organizational control.   Patrolmen seem uncomfortable with departmental policies which they had no voice in formulating;   they are discouraged by the sickening feeling of indifference on the part of their
"politicized" leadership and by the frustrating alienation of their organization from the rest of society.   Police officers seem to realize
more and more their helplessness in effecting meaningful policy
changes or in making their jobs more rewarding and worthwhile.
Police officers, especially the younger and more educated ones who
constitute the majority of police rookies today, are charged with goals,
motivational levels, needs, and career aspirations, different from police
applicants several years ago.   A new administrative culture (effective
leadership, human relations, planning, research, etc.) must be devised
if the hope for a new self-actualized breed of policemen is to truly
materialize.

THE ADMINISTRATIVE DILEMMA

The ultimate goal of organization is productivity, but organizations, mere artificial structures, can not by themselves produce: only
men can.

On the other hand, men in haphazard grouping cannot produce
much either.   While some men are naturally capable of getting some
jobs done, organized men can certainly get complex jobs done in a

2.   *Ibid.*

more organized manner. Organization, therefore, with all its elegant structures is only a catalyst to man's productivity. *Without organization, modern man can still revert to his primitive state of subsistence, but without man organization is dead.*

Moreover, while the significance of organization lies in its abstract nature—formalistic, impersonal, mechanical—the basic values of man are inherently humanistic, individualistic, motivational, and highly emotional. *The inevitable clash between organizational needs and employee needs is the crux of the administrative dilemma.* Successful administration must be able to strike a harmonic mean capable of integrating both needs and elevating employee potential to maximum productivity. This is the function of management.

While man is obviously the key to administration, modern organization has seriously intimidated his need. Traditionalists have always portrayed the "organizational man" as "man the machine". Bureaucracy, which Max Weber saw as a finely tuned mechanism to get the job done, has created too many built-in features which hamper man's efforts to get the job done. Moreover students of administration who since the first decade of the twentieth century have followed Frederick Taylor down the path of "scientific management", have consistently focused on output goals, regimentation and discipline, thus reducing the most sensitive organism on earth—man—to the level of automation.

Fortunately, the portrait of "man the machine" is no more marketable. Management theory and research during the last forty years have finally rediscovered two ancient truths which never should have been lost:[3]

Sophists (of ancient Greece): "man is the measure of all things".

Alexander Pope (of 18th century England): "the proper study of mankind is man".

With these two precepts as guides, the future of the organizational man has to be viewed under different criteria: creativity, motivation and responsibility.

In police administration, evidence of the clash between organization needs and employee needs is particularly obvious. Reports of police strikes (such as in Boston in 1919, Baltimore in 1974, Albuquerque and San Francisco in 1975) or sick-ins and slow-downs are abundant. Incidents of police corruption in which policemen internalize—and compensate for—their frustration with agency policies by

---

3. J. D. Williams, *Management Begins with Man,* a forthcoming text in pub-   lic administration from Little, Brown and Company.

illegitimate means are notorious. Cases of police cynicism in which
alienated policemen separate their own world from the agency's
world sublimating their personal needs in another job or simply accepting their bi-monthly paychecks for their on-the-job burdens, are
commonplace. Police slogans such as "a ticket a day keeps the sergeant away", or "you can beat the rap but you can't beat the ride",
are common police vocabulary which reflects the officers' frustration
with the job and the way it is administered.

THE NEEDS OF ORGANIZATIONAL MAN

Several main breakthroughs are usually cited to indicate that organizational man is after all a "whole" man with feelings and needs
most critical to his job performance. Organizational limitations,
though predominant in most agencies, can not overshadow man's will
to remain free, unique, and important.

(1) The Hawthorne Experiments

The first breakthrough for the rediscovery of man in a work situation came in 1927–33 through experimental studies conducted at
the Hawthorne Plant (Chicago) of the Western Electric Company.
While the research ultimately became highly complex, the basic experiment can be simply described. Five girls employed to assemble
telephone relays were pulled off the regular assembly line and placed
in a segregated test room where observers carefully recorded changes
in production of this "guinea pig" group as working conditions were
altered. Work room illumination, number and length of rest periods,
length of the work day and work week were varied under controlled
conditions. To the surprise of the observation team, productivity of
the five girls seemed to rise (in contrast to the control group on the
main assembly line) regardless of the direction or nature of the
changes.[4]

It was clear that physical surroundings and work hours were not
the central influences underlying the behavior of these five women in
the relay assembly test room. Instead, their "discovery" by management as "persons" apart from the anonymous workers on the assembly line, the opportunity to function as "a small group", and the psychological payoffs that came from being the steady "objects of attention" in the experiment, all served to transform these five girls, to
improve their job attitudes and to increase their productivity.

(2) Maslow's Theory of Human Motivation

The second breakthrough was Maslow's "self-actualized" theory
of human motivation. Most men, Maslow contends, experience five

4. *Ibid.*, p. 3.

fundamental needs.[5] The basic driving need is the physical want for food, sex, elimination, etc. Then arises a concern for security; physical safety, job security, provision for old age. Third is the individual need for love; to belong and be loved, to be accepted by groups and *significant others*. Fourth is self-esteem; his yearning for prestige, status, and to see himself worthy and admirable. And fifth, self-actualization: the innate striving to be creative, to fulfill his potentials and maximize his talents. Figure 15 shows Maslow's scale of human motivation.

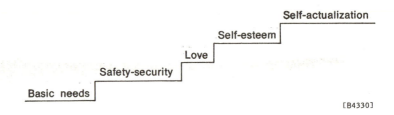

[B4330]

Fig. 15.   Maslow's Scale of Human Motivation

The four lower needs are the demanding ones. Until each one is relatively satisfied, Maslow contends, a person will not strive very hard for the next level of need. Maslow observed that "man does live by bread alone when there is no bread". Reasonably well-fed, secure, loved and confident, a person then has the physical and psychic wherewithal to begin to create, to self-direct, and to accomplish under his own power.

Frustration of the basic needs can be expected to produce compensatory acts and sometimes psychopathogenic behavior. Munro in his study of the police personality stated that "pig and fascist are two of the more printable labels usually affixed to the police". Because he suffers from a generally low level of intelligence, the policeman is accused of being an authoritarian who "attempts to mask his homosexuality with an exaggerated toughness that results in sadistic encounters with his clientele".[6] While Munro's analysis strikes the reader as too militant and perhaps untrue, his study may be useful in exposing the effects of extreme occupational frustration.

5. The reader is referred particularly to Arbrahm H. Maslow, *Motivation and Personality*, (New York: Harper and Row), 1954; and *Eupsychian Management*, (New York: R.D. Irwin), 1965. Also see the helpful summary in Henry Smith, *Psychology of Industrial Behavior*, (New York: McGraw Hill), 1964, 2nd ed., pp. 24–29.

6. Jim L. Munro, *Administrative Behavior and Police Organization*, (Cincinnati: The W. H. Anderson Company), 1974, p. 125.

Failure to reach Maslow's "intermediate stages" of love and self-esteem may force policemen into social isolation. Munro described that situation by saying that "in the life of the policeman it means that the world is composed of cops and civilians".[7] Perhaps this should be phrased "cops versus civilians", added Munro, for the feeling of being, at best, tolerated and, at worst, under siege, is usually encountered among police.

Niederhoffer, basing his information on his study of the New York City Police, noted the negative impact of police organizations on the individual behavior of policemen. He emphasized that the most common personality characteristics in the policemen he studied were "anomie, cynicism, and authoritarianism".[8] Niederhoffer suggested that such characteristics stemmed from "a state of mind in which the anomie of the police organization as a whole is reflected in the individual policeman.[9] One consequence of this cynicism, Niederhoffer proceeded:

> . . . may be an ever deepening disaffection with the values of the police organization. In some cases the extremely cynical officer loses the idealism which he brought with him when he first joined the force and may become a member of the criminal sub-culture.[10]

Self-actualized employees, the most advanced stage on Maslow's scale, must be the goal of organizations. The portrait of self-actualized workers, as drawn by Maslow, shows them comfortable with reality, capable of self-examination without guilt, unpeeved, possessed of great spontaniety and individuality, comfortable alone or with others, committed to human brotherhood, inventive, creative, and reasonable, among other favorable traits. John Gardner vividly described the feeling of self-actualization in the service of public organizations by stating:

> What could be more satisfying than to be engaged in work in which every capacity or talent one may have is needed, every lesson one may have learned is used, every value one cares about is furthered.[11]

(3) Chris Argyris Immaturity—Maturity Theory

According to Chris Argyris, seven changes should take place in the personality of an individual if he is to develop on an immaturity

---

7. *Ibid.*, p. 135.

8. Niederhoffer's definition of anomie is a morbid condition of society characterized by the absence of standards, by apathy, confusion, frustration, alienation, and despair.

9. Arthur Niederhoffer, *Behind the Shield*, (Garden City, New York: Doubleday and Company), 1967, pp. 93–94.

10. *Ibid.*

11. J. D. Williams, *op. cit.*, p. 7.

—maturity scale. Argyris postulated the "healthy" personality develops along a continuum of these steps: [12]

IMMATURITY	MATURITY
From passive	to active
From dependence	to independence
From limited behavior	to multiple behavior patterns
From shallow interests	to deeper and stronger interests
From short time perspective	to long time perspective (present and future)
From subordinate position	to equal or superior position
From lack of self awareness	to awareness and self-control

Argyris postulated that a large majority of the people in the
United States today are treated by social institutions (and especially
by bureaucratic organizations) as immature persons. He argued that
this treatment has in fact caused many of the current organizational
problems.

In examining the widespread worker apathy and lack of effort in
industry, Argyris questions that these problems are simply the results
of individual laziness. He suggests that this is not the case and contends that, in many cases, employees are kept from maturing by the
practices utilized in their organizations. Workers, he concluded, are
given narrow tasks, trivial assignments, and minimal control over
their environment. This encourages them to be passive, dependent,
and subordinate; therefore they behave immaturely. Moreover, in
many organizations, workers are expected to act in immature ways
rather than as mature adults. By virtue of organizational designs
like scientific management, task specialization, chain of command
and span of control, public agencies treat workers as "interchan-
geable parts".

As if in prior agreement with Argyris' arguments, the President's Task Force Report of 1967 raised the question of the need to
improve personnel assignments in the police. It stated:

> Few persons whose ability or academic achievement gives
> them other professional career opportunities are willing to
> spend so many years performing mechanical, undemanding
> duties . . .   in most police departments.[13]

At another section the Report stated that:

> . . .   at the present time, personnel are closely regi-
> mented in most departments and initiative is not encour-

---

12. Chris Argyris, *Personality and Or-*
ganization, (New York: Harper and
Row, Publishers), 1957.

13. *Task Force Report on the Police*,
1976, p. 121.

aged. . . . he is a cog in a machine. Everything seems to be numbered, labeled, covered by rules, and arranged far in advance.[14]

Argyris feels that concepts of formal organization lead to assumptions about human nature which are incompatible with the proper development of maturity in human personality. He challenges modern organizations to provide a work climate in which everyone has a chance to grow and mature as an individual and a member of a group, by satisfying his own needs while working for the success of the organization. The alternative, explained Argyris, would be the demise of the organization at the hands of *childlike personnel.*

(4) Herzberg Motivation—Hygiene Theory

To mature people, needs such as self-esteem and self-actualization become more relevant and important. Frederick Herzberg's studies on motivation—hygiene factors concentrated heavily on these areas. Along with McGregor and Argyris, he thought that knowledge about the nature of man, his motives, and needs could be invaluable to organizations and individuals.

Herzberg and his colleagues at the Psychological Service of Pittsburgh set out to collect data on job attitudes. They interviewed about two hundred engineers and accountants from eleven industries in the Pittsburgh area. The main inquiry was to find out the causes of job satisfaction as well as of dissatisfaction.[15]

In analyzing the data from these interviews, Herzberg concluded that man has two different categories of needs which are essentially independent of each other and affect work behavior. He found that when workers felt dissatisfied with their jobs, they were concerned about the environment in which they were working. On the other hand, when workers felt happy with their jobs, this had to do with the work itself. Herzberg called the first category of needs "hygiene factors" because they describe man's environment and serve the primary function of preventing job dissatisfaction. He called the second category of needs "motivators" since they seemed to be effective in motivating people to superior performance.

Hygiene factors include policies and administration, supervision of working conditions, interpersonal relations, money, status, and security. They are not an intrinsic part of the job but relate to the conditions under which the job is performed. Herzberg, who used

14. *Ibid.*

15. This summary presented above was gleaned from Chris Argyris, *Personality and Organization,* (New York: Harper and Row Publishers), 1957; *Interpersonal Competence and Organizational Effectiveness,* (Homewood, Illinois: Dorsey Press), 1962; and *Integrating the Individual and the Organization,* (New York: John Wiley and Sons, Inc.), 1964. Also see, Paul Hersey and Kenneth H. Blanchard, *Management of Organizational Behavior,* (Englewood Cliffs, N.J.: Prentice-Hall, Inc.), 1972, p. 54.

the term "hygiene" in its medical sense (preventive and environmental), asserted that such factors produce no growth in worker output capacity; they only prevent losses in worker performance due to work restriction.

Motivators, on the other hand, are satisfying factors that involve feelings of achievement, professional growth, and recognition that one experiences in the job that offers challenge and scope. Herzberg used the term because these factors seem capable of having a positive effect on job satisfaction often resulting in one's total output capacity. Figure 16 spells out the two categories.

Hygiene Factors	Motivators
Environment	The Job Itself
Policies and administration Supervision Working conditions Interpersonal relations Money, status, security	Achievement Professional growth Recognition Challenging work Increased responsibility

Fig. 16.   Herzberg Motivation and Hygiene Factors

Herzberg's framework seems compatible with Maslow's hierarchy of needs. While Maslow's basic needs, safety and love, seem to be hygiene factors, self-esteem and self-actualization are obviously motivators. Sense of achievement, professional growth, and recognition is gained through competence and self-discipline.

Herzberg concluded that satisfaction of hygiene factors may eliminate job dissatisfaction but do little to motivate workers. Satisfaction of the motivators, on the other hand, will permit an individual to grow and develop in a mature way, thus promoting work productivity. Naturally, a satisfaction of hygiene factors must be assumed to have had preceded.

In police organizations, hygiene factors seem to be most pervasive and disturbing. The nature of police work itself can hardly be described as dull or detestable. The job provides excitement, a colorful career and a gratifying association with people. The quest for police professionalism and individual satisfaction of officers is, however, frustrated by the bleek hygiene factors encountered on the job. If such barriers are removed, motivators would be easily satisfied.

A variety of police hygiene factors are here gleaned from the Task Force Report: [16]

— If the police service is to be an attractive career opportunity, it must offer compensation that is competitive with other occupations or professions that seek men of education and ability.

— All too often, police precinct conditions are old, cramped and badly maintained.

— Police morale is adversely affected as long as police activities are housed in outmoded buildings and personnel are forced to work with inferior equipment.

— Too often the military aspect of organization pushes the essentially individual character of police work into the background.

— Unnecessary regimentation should be removed, independent judgment should be encouraged, and criticism of existing practices should be solicited.

— In a 1961 survey of status given to occupations, the police ranked 54th out of 90 occupations, which tied them with playground directors and railroad conductors.

The impact of the Hawthorne experiment, Maslow's theory of human motivation and the other human relation studies by Argyris and Herzberg extensively changed the stream of administrative thought in the United States. Since the 1950's a serious plea for "management to begin with man" has evolved and the theory of human relations has "become flesh and liveth in our midst". The elements of this plea consist mainly of these ideas:

1. The raw materials of governmental organizations are human beings.

2. Humans are not automatons simply driven by a single urge to make money.

3. Work is not external to life, but rather deeply intertwined in man's whole search for necessities, for security, for affection, and for himself.

4. Human needs must be met before an agency's output needs can be met.

5. Man's psychic (or ego) needs are as important as his economic needs.

6. Man's associational needs demand a healthy group structure within any bureaucracy.

7. The goal of management ought steadily to be the generation of self-actualizing men.

16.   Task Force Report, *Ibid.*, pp. 134–136.

8. Self-actualizing depends on man's lower needs being met first.

9. Men (whatever their job titles may be, from janitor to department head) are capable of great things.

THE CLASH OF THE PYRAMIDS

While an agency (the Army, FBI, highway patrol, city police departments or a sheriff department) will strive to achieve its goals, the workers will simultaneously be working to achieve theirs. Although it is unlikely in a public agency that a clash does not ensue between agency interests and employee interests, the sharpness of such a clash does not primarily depend on the way the agency is organized but on the manner in which workers are managed.

A police organization, for example, in its attempt to effect and enhance productivity must tighten its control on the means of administrative production—men, machines, methods and monies. In the name of economy, it may strive to cut costs (which may include limiting the number of positions and therefore overburdening the existing number of line workers) to meet legislative and auditive pressure. In the name of organizational discipline, such a department may squelch dissent, and require exact compliance with rules of thumb and untraceable ordinances. In the name of accountability, DEA field agents, for example, may find themselves forced to clear their decisions with a tower of supervisors at the local level, the regional level, the headquarters level and frequently at the Department of Justice level. In the name of specialization, some police organizations are horizontally expanding to provide for technical and staff personnel endowed with "special status" who fail to identify with the patrolman or resent associating with his group.

The organizational pyramid, mostly pointed at the top and broad at the base, can only "stay alive" by reinforcing its constituent elements: authority-command, functions-roles, tasks-supervision, responsibility-discipline, and, at the bottom, productivity-control. Figure 17 shows a diagram of an organizational pyramid.

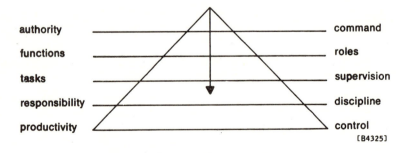

[B4325]

Fig. 17. Organizational Needs of Agencies

Human needs, on the other hand, form an upside-down pyramid, narrow at the bottom (for basic needs—survival) and broad, probably open-ended, at the top (for self-actualization and self direction) with the workers' aspirations flowing upward. In between, in accordance with Maslow's stages of human motivation, workers will strive toward the stages of security-economic stability, love-social acceptance, and self-esteem and personal pride, in this order. Figure 18 shows a diagram of a human needs pyramid.

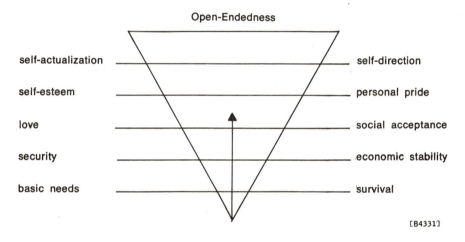

Fig. 18.   Human Needs of Workers

Since the two pyramids are obviously at odds, administrators and workers are always confronted with the clash of pyramids. The organizational pyramid is formal and official. It strongly coerces and threatens employees in order to yield productivity. It is minimally concerned with the "human side of the enterprise", to quote Chris Argyris. Hierarchy is seen by the workers simply as "some people more equal than others". Authority is seen conducive of many sentiments—respect, fear, contempt—but rarely love. The chilliness, aloofness, officiousness, and competitiveness that may prevail in bureaucracies all pose serious barriers to man's needs. Thompson, a master of modern organization, well described the coercive nature of organization as "authoritarian and incompatible with democratic egalitarianism."[17]

The human pyramid, on the other hand, is informal and personal. It emphasizes employee participation in organization. Participation leads to involvement which, in turn, leads to commitment and dedication. The human pyramid demands an organizational atmo-

17.   Victor Thompson, *op. cit.*, p. 64.

sphere conducive to self-actualization: a significant employee voice in agency affairs, meaningful job assignments, broader spans of control, encouragement of small primary groups, and the enhancement of personal prestige regardless of rank, status, or work seniority. Figure 19 shows the clash of the organizational and human pyramids.[18]

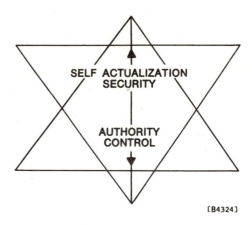

[B4324]

Fig. 19. The Clash of the Pyramids

As a result of the clash bureaucracies may experience bureaupathy, "the sickness of organizations", and workers may consequently fall victims to "bureausis", the bureaupathic syndrome. As mentioned earlier, the former is characterized with low productivity, tense relations, unclear accountability, unresponsiveness, and failure to achieve the prescribed goals. The latter, on the other hand, can be identified with symptoms of worker's frustration, alienation, disloyalty, boredom, poor workmanship, absenteeism, interpersonal hostilities, and occasional insubordination or sabotage.

Organization by itself is incapable of turning the tides of bureaupathy and bureausis. It seems too rigid to adjust to administrative tensions. Moreover, it lacks an adequately sensitive mechanism capable of monitoring bureaucratic performance and appraising productivity. Organization as a set of formal relationships can not determine the need to change, the time to change, or the direction of change. Only management, *the intellectual and human component of administration* can feel the workers' "vibrations" within the organization.

18. The reader may ironically note that the clash shown in Figure 19 resulted in a "Star of David" shape which historically has symbolized peace, love, and harmony.

Through its elements of leadership, appropriate decision making, program planning, and review techniques, can management *take the workers' pulse*, assess the weight of human needs, recommend organizational adjustments, make decisions for remedy and carry them out. Because of the inevitable human involvement of workers in organization, *only management by men can reduce the clash of pyramids* and minimize its collateral implications of bureaupathy and bureausis.

MANAGEMENT: A SEARCH FOR THE HARMONIC MEAN

Throughout the history of managerial thought, managers have always searched for the *harmonic mean to administration*. Although such mean is not expected to prevent or eliminate the conflict between organizational needs and workers' needs (which will always remain as long as organizations are not run by owners), its stabilizing effect in administration has been invaluable. Harmonic means provide administrative agencies with acceptable *trade-offs* between two adversary entities which have to harmoniously coexist or otherwise, simultaneously demise. Harry Levinson described the agency-employee relationship as a two-way street: the agency gives the man a sense of involvement in a major undertaking and reinforces his aspirations; in turn, the worker provides the organization with skills and with personal configuration of the agency's goals, philosophies, and procedures. This *notion of reciprocity* first suggested by Frederick Taylor in his theory of scientific management—maximum prosperity for the employer coupled with maximum prosperity for the employee —remains the essence of contemporary managerial thought. The harmonic mean in its attempt to concoct such a "reciprocity formula" can, in the long range, be most healthy for the organization, the man, and the society at large.[19] As Argyris signifies it in the title of his book, *it integrates the individual and the organization*[20] and can be the only means for amalgamating the two components of administration in a useful and productive fashion.

Harmonic means are sets of "right managerial mix". They are selected management styles which will best reciprocate agency and workers' needs. Naturally, there is no one universally applicable mean of management because of the wide differences in man's abilities, needs and aspirations as well as in the organizational settings and their goals. As cases in point, military administrators, especially in times of war, have always justified what amounts to a dictatorial administration among its ranks. Some basic needs (sleep, sex, physi-

19. Harry Levinson, "Reciprocation: The Relationship Between Man and the Organization", *Administrative Science Quarterly*, (March, 1965), Volume 9, pp. 370–390.

20. See Chris Argyris, *Integrating the Individual and the Organization*, (New York: Wiley and Sons Publishers), 1964, p. 123.

cal comfort, and most obviously, safety needs of the men) are seriously sacrificed for organizational needs. An opposite case to the military administration example would be that of hospital administration or university administration where the needs of doctors and nurses, or faculty and staff can not be, under ordinary work situations, jeopardized and encroached upon by the organization.

Harmonic means even within the same field of activity cannot be expected to be the same. Among the variables which will materially affect the selected mean are the age and maturity of administrators and workers, levels of education and expertise, available skills, complexity of work, allocated appropriations, time pressures, agency traditions, and public scrutiny, among others. A harmonic mean applied by a police chief, for instance, in New York City, Detroit, Chicago or Seattle, may turn out to be *disharmonious*, if applied by the same chief in a Southern county sheriff's department. Also the harmonic mean applied by J. Edgar Hoover during his forty-eight years' control of the FBI was obviously unique and seems most likely unrepeatable in the future of that organization.

The quest for harmonic means of administration by which the interests of the agency and those of the workers could peacefully coexist and be optimized has always intrigued students of public administration. Also, the assumption that one day a ready-made "managerial mix" applicable to all public agencies could be dispensed "off the shelf" contains as much nonsense as the assumption that workers could be turned on by an electrical device. Nevertheless, several models or sets of guidelines have been designed by administration theorists and practitioners. The dominating question which permeated all these models, or sets of administrative guidelines, is clear: How can workers in bureaucracy be lifted to the level of self-actualization in the faithful execution of public policy? Although each individual theorist attempted to introduce a particular format of agency-man relationship, four general groupings were able to leave their everlasting mark on the development of administrative thought:

(a) the traditional approach: the uniformity model;

(b) the scientific management approach: the mechanical model;

(c) the human relations approach: the brotherly model;

(d) the behavioral approach: the systems model.

I. THE TRADITIONAL APPROACH: THE UNIFORMITY MODEL

The traditional approach (also known as the classical, bureaucratic or Weberian) is as old as pyramid-building, perhaps even older. While the ancient Egyptian peasants were by no means experts on administration theories, the gigantic job of building the Gizeh pyramid which involved about 30,000 full-time workers for twenty years must be an administrative miracle. The organizational aspect of the enterprise—the division of labor, the allocation of resources, the engineering methods, the means of transportation—may be simple. But the management, on the other hand, of such numbers of people, keeping them satisfied on the job for so long without major incidents or work disruption, was genuinely brilliant. Whether the basic managerial plan was based on coercion, as some historians report, or on religious devotion and civic responsibility as other historians submit, pyramid-building was basically a model of effective management, discipline, and hard work.

In modern times Max Weber (1864–1920), more than anyone else, has been credited with the development of the traditional approach to management based on the same notions of the pyramid-building plan. Weber, an intellectual of the first degree with far-reaching interests in religion, sociology, economics and political science, justifiably established himself as the father of bureaucratic management. Like ancient Egyptians, he elevated bureaucratic management to the level of religious rituals, military uniformity and idealism. Although his impressions of bureaucracy and authority grew out of his observation of the Prussian civil service in nineteenth century Germany, succeeding generations of European and American public administration students have done very little but modify his original work. Weber's work still stands as the bulwark of bureaucratic management thought in the world. Whether the work requires managing operations at an army regiment, a police agency, a hospital, a state penitentiary or any other public organization, there is always the need for authoritative control to turn "private" individuals into "public men". Attempts to run such organizations on a voluntary basis would require such unlikely questions as "Would you please throw this hand grenade?", or "Would you mind arresting this killer?".

In today's complex police organizations, the Weberian approach to management remains dominant and, perhaps, is still the *sine qua non* method of getting the job done effectively. The regularization of tasks produces speed, predictability, accuracy, and accountability. The clear delineation of line, staff, and auxiliary duties produces specialization and minimizes overlap. Record-keeping and a knowledge of precedents (file-keeping) stimulates expertise which builds on success and avoids past mistakes. Whether the police function is carried out by a traditional sheriff department in Alabama or a progressive manager in Lakewood, Colorado, the traditional model has always been utilized in different degrees.

Weber's principal contribution to managerial thought is based on order and authority. This stemmed from his basic concern with "why individuals obeyed commands and do as they are told".[21] Weber's thesis asserts that workers tend to "orderly work" and "voluntarily obey" as long as they perceive the orders they receive as legitimate. Under an order-authority system, those in the subordinate role see the issuing of organizational rules and directives as ligitimate, therefore appropriate and "obeyable". Hence Weber's study of bureaucratic management focuses on the study of authority relations between designated leaders and assigned workers.

To deal with authority relations and to make them conducive to administrative efficiency and optimal productivity with minimum employee resentment, Weber made the clear distinction between power and authority. The former, defined as *the ability to force people to obey regardless of their resistance,* is personal, capricious and mostly perceived as "unfair". The latter, defined as the *right to command and direct,* is impersonal, codified, routinized and mostly perceived as "fair". Weber's model of bureaucratic management, needless to say, deemphasizes the use of administrative power and stresses the need for institutionalized legitimate authority. Men in the Weberian model would work because the rules are explicit, stable, impartial and fair. The appeal to work would be based on the assumptions of contractual agreements and order. Organizational irritation would be reduced to a minimum because of the supremacy of rules, the climate of stability, and the worker's satisfaction because of job tenure, discipline, compensation, and long-term security.

Weber stated in his introduction of the bureaucratic model that management is "from a purely technical point of view, capable of attaining the highest degree of efficiency and is in this sense formally the most rational known means of carrying out imperative control over human beings".[22] Weber emphasized that his model is "superior to any other form in precision, in stability, in the stringency of its discipline, and in its reliability".[23]

In his famous work, *The Theory of Social and Economic Organization,* Weber described the basic features of his "ideal model" of management as basically consisting of:

    (1) ideal structure;

    (2) legitimate authority;

    (3) rational decisions.

21. D. S. Pugh, D. J. Hickson and C. R. Hinings, *Writers on Organizations,* Second Edition, (Great Britain: Penquin Books), 1971, p. 19.

22. Max Weber, "The Monocratic Type of Bureaucratic Administration", in

Dwight Waldo, *Ideas and Issues in Public Administration,* (New York: McGraw-Hill Book Company), 1953, p. 47.

23. *Ibid.*

Weber's Notion of Idealism

Weber considered the need to establish a coercive basis for the administration of large-scale undertakings and the result was his famous concept of bureaucracy (the power of the office) as the ideal arrangement. Probably because he recognized the dire fallibility of man especially in positions requiring control over other men, Weber had to create the model of the "public man" serving in an ideal set of "prefabricated structure" and insulated from the socio-political environment of the community. To hold this structure together Weber had to use administrative positions as *bricks*, authority as *mortar*, formal relations as *cornerstones* and office rules as *ceilings*. Weber perceived the public man as a special person, well-selected, trained, and disciplined in his public conduct. Weber, in his idealistic ideology, obviously seemed to have failed to take into consideration man's practical needs and his vulnerability to contamination and corruption by the complexities, irregularities and injustices of modern organizations.

"Ideal" to Weber, did not mean desirable, but the "pure form" of organization.[24] And this emphasis on purity is what makes his model of bureaucratic management "a little too ideal" to be applicable to the realpolitik of public service today. While Weber thought that authority would bring order, rules conformity, expertise rationality and continuity of administration, men in public service—especially in democratic societies—are certainly neither angels nor robots. Weber's rather naive imagination of the public man who is "idealistically" stripped of his cultural bias, social prejudice, and selfish concerns for economic welfare, probably never existed in public life and does not seem forthcoming in contemporary bureaucracies. Thus, the modern outcry to divert from Weberian idealism causes one to accept certain amounts of managerial realism and to consider man's needs for motivation and self-respect.

Weber's Notion of Legitimacy

The second feature of Weber's model of bureaucratic management alluded to the kind of authority sanctioned by this theory. Weber was as much obsessed with the legitimacy of authority as he was with the idealism of human organized behavior. To Weber, each supplemented the other and neither could exist separately. For an ideal type of administration to materialize, the controlling force must be appropriate. Such a force was identified by Max Weber as "legitimate authority" or *Herrschaft*. In his ideal type of formal structure (positions, rules, duties) and by virtue of his type of legitimate au-

24. S.M. Miller (edited), *Max Weber*, (New York: Thomas Y. Crowell Company), 1963, p. 10.

thority, Weber envisioned no conflict between administrators and employees. Authoritative controls would be accepted as viable means of maintaining the ideal structure, and the "public man" theory would prevail without implicating personal feelings or private sentiments.

The distinctive feature of Weber's legitimate control is its rational-legal basis, which Weber contrasted with two other bases of legitimacy, traditionalism and charisma, to arrive at his famous threefold typology of legitimate authority.[25]   Although there exists considerable ambiguity in the ways this typology has been interpreted, it is believed that Weber was referring to different types of normative justification for obeying the commands of a power-holder. Such justification, Weber argues, was "much more than a matter of theoretical or philosophical speculation; it rather constitutes the basis of very real differences in the empirical structure of domination".[26]

Obedience to a traditional authority, whatever the motives underlying it in individual cases, is justified by such arguments as "what was good enough for my father is good enough for me", or "that is the way things have always been done". The authority of *eternal yesterday*, as Weber put it, is invoked to uphold compliance with established norms and rules of the present.[27] Traditional authority embodies the fundamental conservative conviction which contains the unspoken premise that "it is right because it is", that is, because it preserves continuity with the past and the values it represented.

Obedience to charisma and charismatic authority, in contrast to the traditional type, involves submission to a *person* allegedly endowed with distinctive gifts—his divinely inspired mission, his heroic deeds, his extraordinary endowments setting him apart from and above other men. Moreover, his followers share with him his belief in his charisma, which literally meant *gift of grace.* For Weber, the prototype of charismatic authority is the leader who says, "It is written, but I say unto you", an appeal that openly challenges the authority of the existing normative order.[28] Weber regarded charismatic authority as an innovating and revolutionary force, obedience to

25. Dennis Wrong (editor), *Max Weber*, (Englewood Cliffs, New Jersey), 1970, p. 41.

26. *Ibid.* This distinction was also developed by Theodore Geiger and is elaborated by J.A.A. Van Doorn, "Sociology and the Problem of Power", *Sociologica Nederlandica*, (Winter, 1962–63), pp. 16–18.

27. *Ibid.*, p. 42.

28. *Ibid.*, p. 43. Political leaders most frequently referred to as charismatic leaders include Hitler, Mussolini, Churchill, Castro, Nasser, and to some extent Presidents Andrew Jackson and John F. Kennedy. Police leaders in this category may include Sir Robert Peel, August Vollmer, John Edgar Hoover, and Buford Pusser.

which could disrupt not only the rationality of the administrative structure but also the legality of its decisional outputs.

Weber's third type of authority and the one requisite in his model of bureaucratic management is rational-legal legitimacy. It affirms the obligation to obey by invoking an existing statute or ordinance that empowers a particular authority to issue commands. Under rational-legal authority the superior is obeyed only by virtue of his *incumbency in an office;* the rights and duties are specified in an abstract and impersonal body of regulations or laws. Similarly, "the person who obeys authority does so   .   .   .   only in his capacity as a member of the organization and what he obeys in only the law",[29] whether the organization in question is a nation-state, a public agency or a church.

Weber's stress on the importance of legitimacy in his model of bureaucratic management is of great significance. A legal system of administration is seen as having "usually been intentionally established to achieve particular administrative or regulatory goals" [30] whatever ultimate affinity may be believed to exist between positive law and that of custom, the will of God, or other supramundane values. Thus, the officials of a public agency under attack for inefficiency or wasteful use of resources are not apt to defend themselves by appealing to a traditional prescriptive right to act as they do, nor by claiming personal qualities entitling them to the loyalty and support of one group or another.[31] Legal authority is associated with bureaucratic forms of organization where efficient and impersonal performance in the service of functional goals is the "major standard legitimizing a particular structure and indeed the very existing of an organization".[32]

As mentioned earlier in the chapter, Weber's concept of legitimacy still dominates managerial thought in public agencies. Although a host of students of management have tended to modify the limits of managerial authority, none has produced a viable substitute to the Weberian concept of rational-legal authority. It is strongly acclaimed as a basis for the continuity and stability of administration, the allocation of managerial responsibilities, the worker's motivation to comply voluntarily and, finally, as an effective tool of achieving managerial effectiveness.

Weber's Notion on Rationality

Weber's third managerial emphasis is rationality. In his attempt to reach a harmonic mean between administrators and work-

---

29. *Ibid.*, p. 42.   31. *Ibid.*, p. 43.

30. *Ibid.*, p. 42.   32. *Ibid.*

ers, Weber stressed the theme of rational management. Such management must utilize specific means expressly designed to achieve predetermined goals. Rational management must be able to operate organizations like a *well-designed machine* with a certain function to perform, and every part of the machine contributes to the attainment of maximum efficiency with minimal waste in time, money or effort.

Rationality is one of those common terms which is deceptive in its simplicity. Rationality of organizations refers to those decisions made by managers in charge of their operation. It means that managers can define their problems, collect information concerning these problems, decide upon the various alternatives which are available, and then select the alternatives whose benefits are greatest and whose costs are least.[33] The crux of rationality lies with *the appropriate selection of these alternatives*.

Weber's primary motive was to build into his model of bureaucratic management the necessary guarantees of rational decision making as safeguards against external political pressures as well as internal prejudicial conflicts. If the image of the public man is to be sustained, the management of bureaucratic organization must be based on "absolutely" rational decisions. Such a basis for operation, Weber thought, would satisfy the needs of workers and managers alike.

Engraved in Weber's notion of rationality is the assumption that individual managers and workers are rational and were selected on the basis of competence to perform their duties. He emphasized that a clear distinction be made between personal and public affairs, and that managerial positions be filled by a contractual method of appointment in terms of technical qualifications for office. Also implied in Weber's notion of rationality is a system of experts, rules, and files capable of providing the manager with adequate means for selecting among options.

Flowing from Weber's notion of rationality are three major principles of bureaucratic management. First is his principle of *rulification*. To maintain a rational management, unencumbered by the personal whims of the leader or by traditional procedures which are no longer acceptable, the management of the office must follow general rules. Such rules must be public, written, stable, detailed, accessible and easy to learn. Knowledge of these rules represents a special technical learning which the official must possess. The reduction of office management to rules is deeply embedded in the very nature of rationalism. Weber's notion of bureaucratic management assumes that the authority of administrators to make decisions does not entitle the official to regulate the matter by commands given for each

33. Jim Munro, *Administrative Behavior of Police Organization*, Cincinnati: The W. H. Anderson Company, 1974, p. 52.

case, but only to regulate the matter "abstractly" by a set of common rules and guidelines.   Rules save effort by eliminating the need for driving a new solution for every situation.   Rulification facilitates the standard and equal treatment of similar situations.

The second principle that stems from Weber's notion of rationality is *systematic division of labor*.   The principle involves: a) a sphere of obligation to perform functions within a rational schema for the division of labor; b) the provision for an incumbent with the necessary authority to carry out these functions; c) the necessary means of compulsion which are clearly defined and whose use is subject to definite conditions.[34]

A third principle that follows from Weber's notion of rationality is *expertise*.   The principle is based on the assumption that rulification regulates the conduct of workers and produces technical norms or patterns of expertise.   If their application is to be fully rational, specialized training must be necessary.   Weber, stressing the need for expertise, emphasized that "only a person who has demonstrated an adequate technical skill is qualified to be a member of the administrative staff   .   .   ." [35]

To conclude this discussion on the traditional approach to administration, it is appropriate to give credit to other philosophers and leading students of management who diligently supplemented and reinforced Weber's authority model.   With obvious approval of Weber's model of authority as a harmonic mean of administration, several neo-traditional students presented some improvements to the model expressed with a few specific emphases.   Alvin Gouldner elaborated on a bureaucratic situation overlooked by Max Weber in his sweeping idealistic model, namely the problem of refusal to consent on the part of the workers in the presence of legitimate authority.[36] James D. Mooney modified Weber's principle of rationality to include his doctrine of *functionalism* by which managerial rules may be determinative, applicative, and interpretative.[37]   Luther Gulick emphasized the functionalism of Mooney by producing his famous *POSDC-ORB* principle which gained considerable publicity in the 1940's and 50's.[38]   Woodrow Wilson emphasized the compatability of administra-

34.   Max Weber, *The Theory of Social and Economic Organization*, Talcott Parsons (ed.), A.M. Henderson and Talcott Parsons (trans.), (New York: Oxford University Press, Inc.), 1947, pp. 329–330.

35.   *Ibid.*

36.   Pugh, Hickson and Hinings, *op. cit.*, p. 25.

37.   Dwight Waldo, *Ideas and Issues in Public Administration*, (New York: McGraw-Hill Book Company), 1953, p. 93.

38.   Luther Gulick and L. Urwick, eds., *Papers on the Science of Administration*, (New York: Institute of Public Administration), 1937.

tion with democracy and democratic features of the United States.[39] Chester Barnard, in his famous publication *Functions of the Executive,* explained the reasons behind workers' obedience to authority in more realistic terms including fear of unemployment and managerial sanctions.[40]

In police administration, the traditional approach is undoubtedly predominant.   The role of authority and rulification is stressed throughout police work all the time.   Relations between police administrators and police ranks are sustained almost entirely by a system of authoritative hierarchy.   Police positions are clear and police tasks seem well-defined.   Patrolmen's obedience to the commands of superiors is based on their trust in the formal process of legitimate authority and rationality of decisions.   When officers put their lives "on the line", as thousands of them do every year, they do so by virtue of their voluntary submission to a higher authority.   While personal motivation and situational zealousness can not be overlooked, the basic harmonic mean which sustains police management today is predominantly Weberian in nature: idealistic, authoritarian, and formal.

II.   THE SCIENTIFIC MANAGEMENT APPROACH: THE MECHANICAL APPROACH

Whereas Max Weber believed that legitimate domination is the harmonic mean for management, Frederick Taylor advocated *science.* He believed that the rules of science would be acceptable to both management and workers since such rules, he argued, are empirical, objective, impartial, quantitative and therefore "fair".   If both the administrators and workers only clung to scientific rules, both would end up "prosperous" and conflict would be greatly reduced.

The acronym stands for:

Planning: working out in broad outline what needs to be done and the methods for doing it to accomplish the purpose set for the enterprise;

Organizing: the establishment of a formal structure of authority through which work subdivisions are arranged, defined, and coordinated for the defined objective.

Staffing: the whole personnel function of bringing in and training the staff and maintaining favorable conditions of work;

Directing: the continuous task of making decisions, embodying them in specific and general orders and instructions, and serving as the leader of the enterprise;

Coordinating: the all important duty of interrelating the various parts of the organization;

Reporting: keeping those to whom the executive is responsible informed as to what is going on, which includes keeping himself and his subordinates informed through records, research, and inspection;

Budgeting: all that does with budgeting in the form of fiscal planning, accounting, and control.

39.   Woodrow Wilson, *The State*, (Boston: D.C. Heath), 1892.

40.   Chester Barnard, *Functions of the Executive*, (Cambridge: Howard University Press), 1938.

Although there is no question that Frederick Winslow Taylor (1856–1915) is considered the father of scientific management, he most probably did not invent the term or originate the approach.[41] Taylor's enormous contribution lay in his large-scale application of the analytical, quantitative approach to improving production methods in industrial organizations. As a young man, he was described as "enamored of scientific investigation, research, and experiment . . . [with] a passion for improving and reforming things on the basis of fact, and early was filled with a divine discontent with anything short of the one best way".[42] He put to careful study and analysis the game of croquet, the best method with the least fatigue of taking a cross-country walk, and devised other ingenious areas of research such as his famous "science of shoveling". Throughout his professional career as an engineer, Taylor developed great empathy for the workers' point of view: "he could swear with the best of them and admired their sense of pride in workmanship".[43] However, he saw about them what he called the "bad industrial conditions" which consisted of workers soldiering on the job, the poor quality of management, and the lack of harmony between workers and managers.[44]

In its essence, scientific management involves a complete mental revolution on the part of the workingmen engaged in any particular organization or industry—a complete mental revolution on the part of these men as to their duties toward their work, toward their fellowmen, and toward their management. And it involves the equally complete mental revolution on the part of those on the management's side—the supervisor, the administrator and the leader of the agency. Taylor stressed that without this complete mental revolution on both sides, scientific management can not exist.[45]

Taylor consistently maintained that through the use of scientific techniques it would be possible to reform the worker's old patterns of work behavior and increase his efficiency. Furthermore, he firmly believed that management, and management alone, should be responsible for putting these techniques into effect. Since he emphasized that it is important to obtain the cooperation of the workers (which he doubted would come forth voluntarily) Taylor did not hesitate to suggest "enforced cooperation" by management.[46]

41. Paul M. Whisenand and R. Fred Ferguson, *The Managing of Police Organizations*, (Englewood Cliffs, New Jersey: Prentice-Hall, Inc.), 1973, p. 155.

42. Daniel A. Wren, *The Evolution of Management Thought*, (New York: The Ronald Press Company), 1972, p. 112.

43. *Ibid.*, p. 113.

44. *Ibid.*

45. Paul M. Whisenand and R. Fred Ferguson, *op. cit.*, p. 156.

46. *Ibid.*

In comparison with Weber's "ideal-type" approach, Taylor's scientific management probably struck the mainstream of managerial thought as "absolutely" pragmatic; emphasizing method over men, and to a large degree totalitarian in design; dehumanizing workers and depersonalizing work steps, work place and work conditions.

The major characteristics of scientific management may be described in the following notions:

    (a) scientification;

    (b) time and motion studies;

    (c) cooperation between management and workers;

    (d) functional supervision;

    (e) efficiency and the first class worker.

Taylor's Notion on Scientification of Work

Taylor meant by science "systematic observation and measurement". While it is doubtful that he believed management could become an exact science in the same sense as physics and chemistry, he believed strongly that management could be *an organized body of knowledge which could be taught and learned*. He also believed that any kind of undertaking could be turned into science by means of systematically observing the sequence of that undertaking, by facilitating the work flow through combining or eliminating some steps, by measuring production by time and motion studies, and by determining an optimum product that a *first-class man* can handle. Scientification consequently required the redesigning of the appropriate tools to be used as well as the necessary training for individual workers and managers.

Taylor pointed out the main problem with "ordinary" management is that neither managers nor workers know what constitutes a fair day's work; a boss therefore has unlimited opportunities for complaining about his workers' inadequacies, and the workers never really know what is expected of them. This can only be remedied by establishing scientific quotas or production standards defining the "largest possible day's work" that could be done by a "first-class" worker under optimum conditions. For this he would receive a high rate of pay—higher than the average worker would receive in "unscientific" management. He would also suffer a loss of income if he failed to achieve this performance.

Taylor's Notion of Time and Motion Study

Time and motion study became the foundation of the Taylor system although some have questioned Taylor's claim to originality. Time studies, nevertheless, were conducted by Taylor in his machine shop at the Midvale Steel Company in 1881. His studies were used for experimental rather than descriptive purposes and consisted of two phases: "analytical" and "constructive". In the analytical phase each job was broken into as many simple elementary movements as possible (useless movements were discarded), the quickest and best methods for each elementary movement were selected by observing the most skilled workman at each, and the movement was timed and recorded. The constructive phase involved building a file of elementary movements and times to be used wherever possible on other jobs or classes of work. Further, this phase led to consideration of improvements in tools, machines, material, methods, and the ultimate standardization of all elements accompanying the job. Taylor's studies emphasized the need to break the job into component parts, to test them, and to reconstruct the job as it should be done. Taylor argued that such scientific study of the job would form a "proof" to the worker to overcome resistance.[47]

Taylor's Notion on Cooperation

Taylor submitted in his famous book, *The Principles of Scientific Management,* that in addition to developing a science by virtue of systematic observations and measurement, management must "heartily cooperate with the men so as to insure all of the work being done in accordance with the principles of the science which has been developed".[48] Taylor later defined the management's "hearty cooperation" as "an almost equal division of the responsibility between the management and the workmen".[49] The management takes over all the work for which they are better fitted than the workmen. This includes planning, verification of methods, quality standards, supervision and control of the worker, as well as data processing and file keeping. There is hardly a single act, explained Taylor, done by any workman in the shop which is not preceded by and followed by some act on the part of the men in management. With this close personal cooperation, under the umbrella of science, the opportunities for conflict are almost eliminated since the operation is not arbitrary—but scientific and therefore "fair".

Taylor's Notion of Functional Supervision (Or Multiple Foremanship)

It was Taylor who originated the term and concept of functional supervision. The concept led to a new managerial technique which upset the previously "Weberian" arrangement of a single boss. Based on the premises of "scientific management" and "hearty cooperation",

47. Taylor, *Shop Management*, pp. 149–176.

48. Frederick Taylor, *The Principles of Scientific Management,* (New York:

W.W. Norton and Company), 1947, pp. 36–40.

49. *Ibid.*

Taylor advocated a system of *multiple supervision* in which workers would receive instructions from several "foremen" at the same time, since he thought that his crews of "first class workers" would be intelligent and well trained as to effectively cope with these work demands. Otherwise, he argued, would be an underutilization of the capabilities of both workers and supervisors.

Taylor divided the responsibility of functional supervision into two major areas: performance duties and planning duties. In the performance segment of supervisory responsibilities, the "gang boss" had charge of all work up to the time that the piece was placed in the machine; the "speed boss" began his work when the material was in the machine and he determined the tools, the cut, and machine speed; the "inspector" was responsible for quality of work; and a "repair boss" was in charge of care and maintenance of the machinery. In the planning segment, which Taylor viewed as important as the actual performance, a "work clerk" furnished written information on tools, materials and other operating instruction, a "time and cost clerk" supervised times taken and cost incurred during the operation, and a "shop disciplinarian" kept a record of each man's virtues and defects and served as a "peace maker" among workers and supervisors.[50] Taylor, however, did not specify that one man had to be in charge of each function; in small units, one man might perform all of the performance tasks, all of the planning tasks or some other grouping of duties. Taylor's functionalization was, in essence, an attempt to decentralize authority and to focus specialized management knowledge on the work.

Taylor's Notion of Efficiency

Since young Taylor had "a passion for improving and reforming things on the basis of fact", it comes as no surprise that he was obsessed with efficiency and filled with "a divine discontent with anything short of the one best way".[51] Taylor's obsession with efficiency and the concept of the one best way became vocal during the hearings ordered by the House of Representatives in October 1911, to investigate the Watertown strikes allegedly due to unsatisfactory treatment of labor resulting from the introduction of the Taylor system. During those famous hearings, Frederick Taylor coined his famous slogan, "Scientific management has no use for a bird that can sing and won't sing".[52] During the same hearings, Taylor reiterated and explained his concept of "the first-class man". He reminded people in management that among every class of workmen there are some balky workmen—physically able to work but simply lazy—who obsti-

50. Daniel A. Wren, *op. cit.*, p. 124.   52. *Ibid.*, p. 138.

51. *Ibid.*, p. 112.

nately refuse to be efficient. Taylor called that class "second-class workmen" because they "underworked", "soldiered", or "hanged it out". The challenge of scientific management was to convert such class of workmen into "first-class workmen" capable of turning out each day his "largest possible day's work".

Under scientific management, efficiency could be increased by: a) an application of time and motion study by which unnecessary work steps as well as slow motions are eliminated, b) a replacement of the hourly work system by a piece-work or a job system, c) the training and development of each individual workman, d) an appropriate planning ahead of each job assignment, e) functional supervision, f) the motivation of the workers by demonstrating to them that maximum prosperity can exist only as a result of maximum productivity.

The gospel of *Taylorism* was not a passing wave in the development of managerial thought in America. Carl Barth and Henry Gantt were among Taylor's closest disciples. Others like Henri Chatelier, Horace Hathaway, Morris Cooks and Frank Gilbreth joined the earlier apostles in spreading the movement of scientific management by developing such practices as "the task and bonus system", the "habits of industry" and "graphic aids to management".[53]

In police administration today, scientific management seems least influential in comparison to other managerial approaches. Taylorism succeeded and prospered mainly as a practice of shop management fairly confined to limited grounds and in the business of producing tangible items. Police administration, on the other hand, is basically a practice of street management, unconfined, unique, dynamic, unpredictable and in most cases unmeasurable. Also, while scientific management is adamantly obsessed with efficiency (cost of output over input), police organizations are by definition of their roles service-oriented—obsessed with the achievement of goals regardless of cost. Furthermore, while products of scientific management are quantifiable items which were mathematically measurable, the service produced by policemen on the street by and large defies quantification and measurement. As long as the police are handling human matters which affect human lives and basic interests, no dollar mark can be easily placed on police services, neither can scientific comparisons be safely conducted.

Moreover, Taylorism, as a set of concepts designed for business management, could not have been exposed to the cultural, social and political pressures focused on contemporary police organizations.

53. H.L. Gantt, *Work, Wages, and Profits,* (New York: Engineering Magazine Company), 1916, p. 33.

Such pressures certainly add to the realm of environmental variables police agencies have to manage in their system of administration.

Turning to the other side of the coin, however, principles of scientific management did influence contemporary police administration in several areas. First, they stimulated and supported a system of functional supervision in police administration which seems to be in the process of replacing the traditional concept of unity of command. Police agencies, especially those applying team-policing systems, seem to appreciate multiple supervision by the team sergeant, by the planning unit, by the legal advisor and by the intelligence unit simultaneously. Second, principles of scientific management have stimulated police planning in almost every facet of police activity and have resulted in today's areas of strategic planning, organizational planning, operational planning, and tactical planning, etc. Third, Taylor's principles have aroused a genuine concern among police organizations to apply technology and science to reduce physical motion and reliance on human judgement. Crime lab techniques, sophisticated communication methods and advanced data processing are only a few examples. Fourth, scientific management undoubtedly aroused an awareness for efficiency in police administration to be coupled with the original drive for effectiveness in meeting goals. Current concern for cost-benefit analysis in police administration is only one evidence of the impact of scientific management.

III. THE HUMAN RELATIONS APPROACH: THE "BROTHERLY" MODEL

The Weberian theory of bureaucratic management and Taylor's theory of scientific management have come under severe fire in the United States since the end of World War II for the same reasons. Beginning perhaps in 1946, the largely unquestioned "harmonic means" put up by the Weberians behind the shield of "authority-uniformity" and the Taylorists behind the shield of "science-cooperation" came in for scathing criticism from the "humanists" led by Elton Mayo, Victor Thompson, Douglas McGregor and others.

Whether it is bureaucratic or scientific management, the damaging accusations focused on Weber's and Taylor's lack of understanding man and his needs. With the former stressing authority, conformity and rules, and the latter emphasizing science, time and motion studies and output goals, the most sensitive organism on earth, *man,* is reduced to the level of automation. What emerged from those wonderings (bureaucratic and scientific) was a portrait of a shambled man which looked like this:

—work is a drudgery, an unpleasant necessity that is external to life;

—economic motives make man tick; men work solely for money;

—workers should be constantly supervised by a tight hierarchical control;

—man-to-man competition should be encouraged and informal work groups discouraged.[54]

The "humanists" who championed the "brotherly" approach to management emphasized that that portrait of "man-the-machine" must not be allowed to prevail. They accused bureaucratic and scientific management of sacrificing man, the raw material of management, on the altar of artificial structures alien to his habitat. Arthur Fisher Bentley, the father of the small group theory, best stated the theme of the humanists by saying:

> The raw material (of government) . . . is never found in one man by himself; it can not even be stated by adding man to man . . . It is a relationship between men . . . the action is the given phenomenon . . . the action of men with or upon each other. We know men only as participants in such activity.[55]

Bentley's main argument emphasized the need for "natural" human interaction among people in management and labor.

Humanists accuse the Weberian approach and the Taylorist approach of imposing a "fabricated" facade of relationships on man under different names. Such facade, however, may be translated in only one way: *You will cooperate on our terms or else!* Consequently man is often intimidated and frequently exploited. In both bureaucratic and scientific management the attempt to reconcile organizational needs and employee needs have backfired. The coldness and impersonality of big organizations that resulted, in addition to red tape, waste and frustration, became managerial characteristics. Also, the tendencies to define people in terms of what positions they occupy or tasks they perform have further tarnished the image of human equality. Furthermore, the barriers to communication posed by hierarchical levels and status symbols in bureaucratic and scientific management can seriously undermine Weber's and Taylor's hopes for precision, speed and the reduction of conflict. Finally, the humanists accused bureaucratic and scientific management of often becoming so convinced of their own goals that resort is made to any means to achieve them, with ethics getting badly skewed in the process.[56] The humanists insist that the value of man may not be degraded by artifi-

---

54. J.D. Williams, *Management Begins with Man*, a forthcoming text in public administration from Little, Brown and Company, 1971, p. 2.

55. Arthur F. Bentley, *The Process of Government*, (Evanston: Principia Press), 1908, p. 176.

56. J.D. Williams, *op. cit.*, p. 4.

cial structures. It is human motivation, aspiration, morale and natural interaction with others that yield productivity and efficiency. Artificial managerial structures, the humanists argue, *won't work because they are alien to man's nature.*

The champion of the human relations approach was George Elton Mayo (1880–1949). Mayo was an Australian who studied and later taught logic and philosophy. With keen interest in medicine and psychopathology, he grew as an industrial researcher. He studied "pessimistic reveries" of the workers at a textile mill near Philadelphia and was able, through the introduction of work pauses, to reduce turnover from 250 percent to 5 percent and improve efficiency, morale and productivity among the workers. Joining the Harvard faculty in 1926 as professor of industrial research, he was about to embark on an intellectual journey that would reshape the course of management thought.[57]

Intrigued by the initial results of the Hawthorne experiments and subsequent research, previously discussed in this chapter, Mayo perceptively noted that "a remarkable change of mental attitudes in the group" was the key factor in explaining the Hawthorne mystery.[58] In his opinion, the test room girls became a social unit, enjoyed the increased attention of the experimenters, and therefore, developed a sense of participation in the project.

Mayo's development of the "social man" model became the milestone of the human relations approach. The humanists argue that the employee has physical needs to satisfy, but more importantly, he has social needs. These needs arise from early social conditioning and persist through organizational life in his relations with fellow workers and others in the organization. Events and objects in the physical work environment "cannot be treated as things in themselves; instead, they have to be interpreted as carriers of social value".[59] For example, a regular desk has no social significance, but if people who have desks are the ones who supervise others, then the desk becomes a status symbol and a carrier of social value. Humanists stress that *organizations are in fact social systems based on human sentiments and interactions.* Informal organization not only becomes necessary but crucial. If the goal of management is optimal productivity, then informal organization is the vehicle for effective human cooperation. The objective must be the restoration of a social code by which human adjustment to administrative life may be enhanced.

---

57. Daniel A. Wren, *op. cit.*, p. 278.

58. *Ibid.*

59. Fritz J. Roethlisberger and William J. Dickson, *Management and the* *Worker,* (Cambridge, Mass.: Harvard University Press), 1939, p. 557. It is also interesting to note that the word desk in Arabic is the same word to mean office.

By informal organization, the humanists refer to *the actual groupings of human beings in a work situation, together with their value systems, customs and myths, their affiliations, likes and dislikes, and the authority network and human interaction patterns resulting from all of these.*[60] Informal organization therefore embraces the totality of interpersonal relations and arrangements that prevail in an agency. They range all the way from shifting dynamic friendship groups and ad hoc groups on up to the rather institutionalized associations of workers such as the department's bowling league and the wives' gourmet club. In attempting to map out the informal organization of an agency, one strives to convey the actual lines of authority, the natural groupings of employees, and the patterns of obedience which prevail among the work force. Such a chart, it must be noted, can never be done with accuracy because so much of the relations are introspective and in flux.[61]

To develop his thesis for human collaboration based on informal organization, Mayo signified Emile Durkheim's concept of *anomie* (lack of purpose, identity, or ethical values in a person) as the basic consequence of formalism. Bureaucratic and scientific managements, through their widespread division of labor, rulification, regimentation and specialization, have destroyed man's social solidarity inherent in his domestic system and which is built around the informal organization within his family and kinship. The result was a normless, rootless mode of life which seriously affected man's overall capability of personal achievement and organizational cooperation. Mayo emphasized that only through "informal organization" can this "social lag that causes the widespread sense of futility and the resultant social disorganization"[62] be eliminated or reduced. Although Mayo or his associate humanists never envisioned or expected a totally informal organization, Mayo hastened to note that *informal organizations must be viewed as an interdependent aspect of the formal organization.* Viewing the organization as a "social system", rather than an "authority system" or a "scientific system", would enable management to attack the conflict between the "logic of efficiency" demanded by formal organization and the "logic of sentiments" crucial for human interaction.[63]

To pursue a harmonic mean, Mayo stressed the role of management in "maintaining the equilibrium of the social organization so that individuals through contributing services to the common purpose obtain personal satisfaction that makes them willing to cooperate".[64] For Mayo, one of the major tasks of management is to organize spon-

60. J. D. Williams, *op. cit.*, p. 70.

61. *Ibid.*

62. Daniel A. Wren, *op. cit.*, p. 292.

63. *Ibid.*, p. 290.

64. Daniel A. Wren, *op. cit.*, p. 290.

taneous cooperation, thereby preventing the further breakdown of formal organizations.   Conflict, competition and disagreement between individuals is to be avoided by management which understands its role for providing the basis for group affiliation as well as individual satisfaction through group membership.

As a result of Mayo's contribution to the humanist school focusing on the "social man" approach, many humanistic studies were conducted by humanist scholars like Victor Thompson and Douglas McGregor, with the latter perhaps gaining as much publicity as the founder of the school.   Thompson warned administrators of the *tyranny* of formal structures strategically located in the practices of bureaucracy, authority, hierarchy and specialization.   Such practices, Thompson stressed, have the tendency of becoming *dramaturgical* or blown out of proportion by the superior, the subordinate or other role players.   Thompson, further, warned that the result of employee dissatisfaction with the dramaturgical aspect of formal organization is the development of *bureaupathic behavior* expressed in terms of employee insecurity, anxiety, stagnation, inefficiency, insubordination and perhaps sabotage.   Thompson concluded his study by emphasizing the dire *need for organizational cooperation based on informal organization, group identification, common conscience, love, co-operativeness, and informal management.*[65]

McGregor's Theory Y and Participative Management

Douglas McGregor walked the path of the humanist school still further in his book, *The Human Side of Enterprise*.   In the book, a clear view of the working man ("Theory Y") emerged in sharp contrast to the older schools of bureaucratic and scientific management which he referred to as "Theory X".   As axioms of this theory, McGregor contended that: [66]

—The average man does not dislike work.

—Man will exercise self-direction and self-control in the service of objectives to which he is committed.

—Commitment to objectives is a function of the rewards associated with their achievement, *e.g.,* ego satisfaction and self-actualization.

—The average man learns, under proper conditions, not only to accept but to seek responsibility.

—The capacity to exercise a relatively high degree of imagination, ingenuity, and creativity in the solution of organizational problems is widely, not narrowly, distributed in the population.

65. For more information on Thompson's approach see his famous thesis, *Modern Organization,* (New York: Alfred A. Knopf), 1967.

66. Douglas McGregor, *The Human Side of Enterprise,* (New York: McGraw-Hill), 1960.

—Under the conditions of modern organizational life, the intellectual potentials of the average man are only partially utilized.

—Human needs must be met before an agency's output needs can be met.

—Man's psychic (or ego) needs are as important as his economic needs.

—Man's associational needs (small groups) demand a healthy group structure within the organization.

—The goal of management ought steadily to be the generation of self-actualizing men.

—Self-actualization depends on man's lower needs being met first.

—Men (whatever their job titles may be, from janitor to department head) are capable of great things.

McGregor's "Theory Y" aimed at the integration of individual and organizational goals for the achievement of one would mean the achievement of the other. Under "Theory Y", it is the essential task of management to *unleash man's potential* so that he can achieve his goals by directing his efforts toward those of the organization. The primary motivation of the workers would come from their commitment to the objectives of *their* organization. Managers who accepted "Theory Y" as a harmonic mean to management would not structure, control, or closely supervise the work environment. Instead, they would *attempt to aid the maturation of subordinates* by giving them wider latitude in their work, encouraging self-control, and motivating through the satisfaction which comes from the challenge of work itself. The use of authoritative control by management would be replaced by getting people committed to organizational goals because they perceived that this was the best way to achieve their own goals. While a perfect integration cannot naturally be possible, McGregor hoped that an adoption of "Y" assumptions by managers would certainly improve existing managerial techniques. Workers would enjoy being involved, involvement would increase commitment, and commitment would increase productivity.

As excellent example of the appropriate application of the human relations approach to the management of police organizations is the case of the FBI. Amid the exceptionally formal and hierarchial organization of the FBI, there blossomed an outstanding humanist pattern based on the need for friendship, moral support, compassion and *esprit de corps*. Don Whitehead in, *The FBI Story*, after describing the strict disciplinarian approach of the organization in terms of fixed tasks, close supervision, and tight control of the agents, attributed the basis of the FBI success to its form of the brotherly model that permeated the formal structure. Whitehead referred to top management in the FBI:

> Hoover trusted them to make decisions. In turn these men repaid the trust with loyalty and fierce pride in the FBI. They accept without question the FBI policy of anonymity. Their names are not widely known beyond the doors of the FBI headquarters. And yet they hold in their hands much of the responsibility of the nation's safety.[67]

Whitehead furthermore referred to the humanist approach in the FBI as applied to common employees by relating the story of a new FBI female worker:

> Mary had the FBI telephone number in her purse and she called the personnel section. She was immediately taken under the FBI wings. A woman from the Housing Unit helped her find a room in one of the approved homes, with another FBI girl who wanted someone to share expenses . . . . One of the girls who worked with Mary went to lunch with her and saw that she met other employees . . . Mary's name and home town were posted on the bulletin boards and she began meeting other girls from her home state, who gave her advice.[68]

In another reference, Whitehead reported:

> A family-type magazine called the Investigator serves as a kind of small-town newspaper, reporting the doings of FBI folk in sports, social affairs, special activities, promotions, and incentive awards. And the FBI Recreation Association (FBIRA) promotes outside activities such as dances, excursions, moonlight cruises, sports competition and camp shows. And there have been clubs for camera, drama, flying, writing and pistol enthusiasts. More than 13,000 FBI employees are members of the FBIRA and pay annual dues of $1.50 each.[69]

The case of "humanism" within the famously "tough" FBI is by no means unique. In every formal organization, a humanist subculture must evolve based on friendship, mutual likes and dislikes and the strengthening of former relations or current interests. In all police organizations, at all levels the members of the "outfit" develop a special sense of solidarity which transcends the formal inhibitions by rules and regulations. Adequately harnessing these informal ties and loyalties and utilizing them positively toward the achievement of

67. Don Whitehead, *The FBI Story*, (New York: Random House), 1956, p. 120.

68. *Ibid.*, p. 125.

69. *Ibid.*, p. 126.

agency goals are summarily the primary purposes of the human relations approach.

IV. THE BEHAVIORAL APPROACH: THE SYSTEMS MODEL

Elton Mayo's human relations approach, like bureaucratic and scientific management before it, came under severe criticism by theorists and managers seeking a more harmonic mean to management. The basic criticism was the humanists' "pampering" of workers at the expense of work. Managers were accused of abandoning their primary goal of productivity and wasting their time on rehabilitating "a bunch of unhappy workers". Workers, the critics argue, must after all be considered a "means to an end" which is output production. Secondly, critics argue that even with the humanists' lamentation and overconcern for organizational mysticism and evangelism, their rationale that "contented workers make more productive workers" does not necessarily hold true in real life. Daniel Bell elaborated on this criticism: "To think that contented workers were productive workers was to equate human behavior with cow sociology; contented cows give more milk".[70] Third, critics of the human relations approach insisted that no matter how idealistically the Mayoists feel about human motivation, it is an apparent fact that workers, by and large, work at least largely and perhaps exclusively for monetary gain and for the other economic benefits of employment.

A final, though indeed serious, attack on the human relations approach to management came from William Fox, who attacked the premise of the "brotherly model" as expounding a naive view of intraorganizational conflicts. According to Fox, the Mayoists assumed that a communality of interests could transcend the conflicts between workers and leaders, workers and workers and leaders and leaders. This would keep everyone happy in a *conflict-free* state of equilibrium with resultant worker-management "marital-bliss". Such a cult, reiterated Fox, which preached participation, permissiveness, and democracy for all, misled the manager to think that a conflict-free state would automatically lead to the organization's success. Fox concluded that while organizational tensions and conflicts are inevitable in every human situation—and are frequently considered necessary— "happy" relations can not be substituted for well-defined goals, policies, standards and subsequent administrative functions essential for goal attainment.[71]

The behavioral approach emerged as a successor to the human relations school. While it does not dispute the utility of bureaucratic

70. Daniel Bell, *Work and its Discontents: The Cult of Efficiency in America*, (Boston: Beacon Press), 1956, p. 25.

71. William M. Fox, "When Human Relations May Succeed and the Company Fail", *California Management Review*, Vol. 8, No. 3, Spring, 1966.

management, scientific management, and human relations, behavioralists accuse them all of lack of comprehensiveness, scientific objectiveness, and failure to reach an appropriate balance between the emphasis on work and workers. The behavioralists argue that earlier models were merely *recipe-like* recommendations shaped after the subjective philosophies of their concocters. The models lacked the consideration of environmental relationships, influences, and constraints. The behavioral approach, on the other hand, attempts to *integrate human behavior with quantitative measurement toward the achievement of prescribed goals.* The approach focuses on the phenomenon of causes and effects in a conceptual fashion. The interaction, for instance, of a patrolman with an armed robber results in an effect on the patrolman himself as well as on police effectiveness in general in terms of a higher clearance rate. But, it is also the cause of another interaction between the patrolman, his colleagues, his sergeant, his chief and perhaps the city manager in terms of service output, quality of policing, need for tactical training and extra protection . . . and probably higher pay for police personnel.[72]

Behavioral methodology, or behavioralism as it is commonly referred to, grew in the early 1950's as a systematic approach to inquiry into areas of human activities whether they were sociological, political, judicial, economic, administrative or otherwise. The major characteristics of this approach are:

(a) It is based on the application of empirical evidence: that which can be sensed, learned or recorded by any of the five human senses.

(b) It requires the utilization of scientific theories comparable to those applied by natural scientists in the fields of physics, chemistry, mathematics, etc.

(c) It is interdisciplinary in nature, blending information from the fields of sociology, psychology, economics, statistics and others.

(d) It aims at the enhancement of human life through a problem-solving pattern.

(e) It tends to be quantitative by developing statistical models relative to possibilities, probability ratios, percentages, etc., thus adding to the preciseness, orderliness and predictability of research.

(f) It works with recognized tools within the realm of, or in close conjunction with, system theories and analyses.

---

72. Gleaned from Alan R. Coffey's discussion on systems in *Administration of Criminal Justice: A Management* *Systems Approach,* (Englewood Cliffs, New Jersey: Prentice-Hall, Inc.), 1974, p. 7.

Behavioralism and the System Theory

Behavioral methodology and the system theory supplement each other like military strategy and tactics. The former can only be manifested in terms of the latter which, in turn, would remain as a futile exercise outside the framework of the former. In other terms, behavioral methodology is the philosophy of comprehensiveness, empiricism, science and objectivity, while systems approach is the study of means by which methodology becomes functional.

For all practical purposes a system may be defined as "a purposeful, organized interrelationship of components in which the performance of the whole exceeds the individual outputs by all the parts". Study of systems so defined would (1) facilitate understanding of the organization as a whole rather than as a chaotic arrangement of parts; (2) permit the analysis of resource flows toward objectives; (3) describe the manager's job in terms of the allocation and utilization of resources; and (4) reveal an awareness of the environmental forces which affect managerial decision making.[73]

Systems could be seen as *physical, behavioral* or *both.* A physical, biological, solar, or mechanical system is a set of interdependent components working together in equilibrium, *steady state,* toward the achievement of common goals. A behavioral, social, psychological, or administrative system is a chain of causes and effects governed by a goal-oriented mechanism capable of achieving prescribed goals. The criminal justice system and the police subsystem must be viewed as a combination of physical and behavioral systems. They are physical in terms of their physical components (men, monies, methods and machines) as well as behavioral in terms of their cause-effect relationships (commands, influences, resentment, etc.).

Whether they are physical or behavioral, functional systems must have these key characteristics:

(a) The system is a totality, not just the sum of its component parts.

(b) It is open: it exchanges information, energy, or material with its environment as well as other systems. Like biological systems, *the human body,* or social systems, *a police force,* it has constant interaction with its environment. These interactions shape the condition of the system components and the relationships between them.

(c) It has boundaries that separate it from its environment. Boundaries, however, in an open system are not rigid, impenetrable, or closed.

(d) It is responsive, having the flexibility to respond to disturbances and stresses it receives from its environment and other systems.

73. *Ibid.*

(e) It is adaptive, capable of coping with the environments by regulating the behavior of the components, transforming the internal structure and even going as far as remodeling the goals and objectives.

(f) It is equilibristic, capable of maintaining a "steady state", *homeostatis*, with its environment as well as its components. If extreme pressure develops, an open system must be able to return to a state of stability. If it fails to equilibriate, a system ceases to function as a unified entity and thus collapses.

(g) It is dynamic; it is constantly in motion.

(h) It is conversional, capable of changing the amounts of inputs, demands and supports into outputs, services and decisions.

(i) It is communicative, capable of transforming information among the components as well as relating outputs with inputs through a feedback mechanism (cybernetic cycle).

(j) It is hierarchical; with the exception of the whole universe, all systems have subsystems and are parts of a supersystems.

The behavioral approach assumes that human interaction (proaction—action—and reaction) does not occur in a void. It takes place within a physical or conceptual "system framework" and within a given environment. All interaction—social, political, administrative, economic or otherwise—must be viewed as a system imbedded in an environment which affects and is affected by the system itself. Any phenomenon under investigation must be considered in relationship to its entire environment at the time.

The following is a simplified model of an open system.

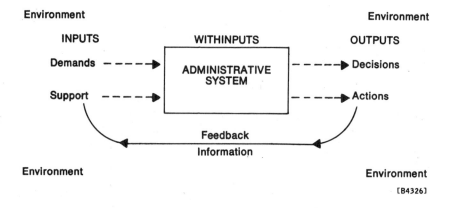

[B4326]

Fig. 20. A Simplified Model of an Open System

When applying the behavioral approach (the systems model) to daily activities, one would be amazed by the nature, the diversity and number of systems today in existence. The molecule, the cell, the organ, the individual, the group, the society are examples of systems. Also, as mentioned in Chapter Two, systems come in a hierarchy of levels—super systems, systems and subsystems. Examples would include the United Nations, the United States of America, the Federal Government, the Department of Justice, the FBI field office, an FBI team of agents, etc. Each of these organizations may view the higher level as a supersystem and the lower one as a subsystem. Environments, in the case of this example, would include influences from the international community of nations, the socio-political community of the United States, the legal community of the Department of Justice, the congressional sub-committee reviewing the activities of the FBI as well as the psychological background of its members, along with an unknown number of influences by pressure and interested groups and individuals.

Behavioral management of police organizations lies within this gamut of interrelated systems and environments. Not only does behavioral management address itself to this large number of components, relationships and influences, but also it manages to cope with the dynamic changes which constantly occur between these forces and the subsequent alternatives available for the production of services and decisions.

A key variable in the behavioral approach to management or the systems model is the distinction between efficiency and effectiveness. Police organizations have to be both efficient in their processes and effective in achieving their goals. Though both words are used interchangeably, their managerial significance is indeed different. To understand the difference, consider an automobile as a system. In terms of efficiency, the engine may be well-tuned, the transmission and power column perfectly synchronized, and the torque pounds of wheel turning power delivered to the axle all in sufficient harmony. The automobile then would use a reasonable amount of gasoline. It can provide the passengers with all the city driving they need for a "cheap" cost. This car would be efficient, which *is an economic term simply meaning more output for the input invested in it* or $\frac{output}{input} =$ 1 plus. Effectiveness, on the other hand, *is an administrative term referring to the achievement of goals whatever they are at any cost.* Therefore, if this extremely efficient car got stuck in the mud and was unable to reach its destination on time, the car would be considered ineffective. The systems approach to the management of police organizations attempts to achieve the harmonic mean by scientifically examining and quantitatively proving that the organization is both efficient and effective. Furthermore, system analysis constantly aims at "efficiencizing" the organization by reducing operational costs to a minimum. This should simultaneously take place without lowering the effectiveness rate of the system or generating negative side effects concerning the levels of motivation, morale, discipline, and harmony among the workers.

Systems models, tools of the behavioral approach to management, are numerous and vary considerably in application but not in theory. They chiefly follow the basic assumptions of the behavioral approach in attempting "the placing of significant human interaction in a logical design that permits measurable results".[74] The value of these results is assessed in terms of efficiency and effectiveness. Managerial techniques are acknowledged by these models only in terms of the value of results they achieve. Focus on philosophy rather than on results is, from the systems view, likely to obscure output, *or what it is that the organization does,* as opposed *to who does it and how,* under former approaches.[75] The integration of human behavior with achievement of quantitative results is, therefore, the crucial theme of systems models.

To pursue this theme, the behavioral approach, through systems models, attempts to *define* the goals that are to be achieved by an organization, to *devise* the operational techniques needed to achieve these results, to *assign* the most effective personnel capable of achieving the desired results, to *utilize* the most effective methods toward the achievement of results, and to evaluate the efficiency and effectiveness of these managerial functions within the overall purpose of the organization.

Pioneer behavioral scientists who helped found the behavioral approach are Rensis Likert, Chris Argyris, J. D. Williams, and with particular interest in the fields of criminal justice and police administration, Alan R. Coffey.[76] While the first three prominently laid the foundations of the behavioral approach to management in general

74. *Ibid.,* p. 44.

75. *Ibid.,* p. 45.

76. For a deeper insight into Likert's contribution to system analysis and its impact on modern management, see Rensis Likert, "Motivational Dimensions of Administration", *America's Manpower Crisis,* (Chicago: Public Administration Service), 1965; "Developing Patterns of Management", Part I, *General Management Series,* No. 178, (New York: American Management Association), 1955; also *New Patterns of Management,* (New York: McGraw-Hill), 1961. On Argyris' contribution see, Chris Argyris, "The Organization: What Makes it Healthy", *Harvard Business Review,* 36, No. 6, (November-December), 1958; "We Must Make Worthwhile", *Life,* (May 5, 1967); also *Integrating the Individual and the Organization,* (New York: Wiley), 1964. On Williams, see J. D. Williams, *Management Begins with Man,* a forthcoming text in Public Administration from Little, Brown and Company; on Coffey see, *Administration of Criminal Justice: A Management Systems Approach, op. cit.*

terms, Coffey must be credited with developing one of the most detailed and advanced systems models for the management of law enforcement and criminal justice agencies. A brief discussion of these authors' contributions is vital to an understanding of the behavioral approach.

Management, according to Likert, is always a relative process. While emphasizing the role of the managerial leader, Likert stated that no specific rules can work in all managerial situations. There are "only general principles which must be interpreted to take account of the expectations, values and skills of those with whom the manager interacts".[77] Sensitivity to these values and expectations is a crucial leadership skill, and organizations must create the atmosphere and conditions which encourage every manager to deal with the people he encounters in a manner fitting to their values and expectations.

Likert designed a set of *interviewing variables* for the measurement of managerial effectiveness: (1) the amount of member loyalty to the organization; (2) the extent to which the goals of groups and individuals facilitate the achievement of the organization's goals; (3) the level of motivation among members; (4) the degree of confidence and trust between different hierarchical levels and between different sub-units; (5) the efficiency and adequacy of the communication process; and (6) the extent to which each superior is correctly informed of the expectations, reactions, obstacles, problems and failures of his subordinates.[78]

These variables, which could be statistically quantified by assigning a figure value along a measurement scale, enable the manager to know and adjust his agency's state of "interaction-influence" system. Through the regular examination of his chart of interviewing variables, the manager should be able to take his organization's *temperature*, and make the necessary changes to increase effectiveness to the desired standards. Likert contended that employees need to have their attitudinal temperatures taken long before falling output confirms the organization's sickness. However, he correctly warned that "the measurement of these variables is a complex process and requires a high level of scientific competence . . . it cannot be done by an untrained person".[79]

Chris Argyris, a former professor of industrial administration at Yale and of education and organizational behavior at Harvard, consistently studied the relationships between the personal development

77. D. S. Pugh, D. J. Hickson and C. R. Hinings, *Writers on Organizations*, (Great Britain: Hazell Watson & Viney Ltd.), 1975, p. 148.

78. *Ibid.*, p. 149.

79. Rensis Likert, *New Patterns of Management, op. cit.*, p. 196.

of individual workers and the kind of situation in which each individual worked.   Argyris sees each individual worker as having a potential which can be fully realized, *self-realization*, and thus benefits not only the individual but also the organization in which he works.   Unfortunately, remarks Argyris, business and other organizations are usually run in a way which positively prevents any such benefits.[80]

Argyris remarks that there are three axes to this question: (1) the development of the worker toward personal and psychological maturity; (2) the degree of interpersonal competence within the system; and (3) the nature of the organization itself.   As in Likert's work, each of these axes could be measured, quantified and compared. What complicates the equation is the amount of interfacing between the axes which to a large degree prevents the isolation of these ingredients.   For example, the lack of interpersonal competence within the working system would result in preventing, or delaying, the workers becoming mature in outlook and would fail to arouse their psychological energies.   This would certainly affect the structure of the organization by persuading management to "tighten ship", which, in turn, would cause further interpersonal stresses, and the cycle goes on.

This situation, warns Argyris, is common in organizations, which he labeled "not axiologically good".   His term "axiologically good" described a highly advanced and systematic organization in which "all its parts are well coordinated and related to further the overall objectives and are able to respond to internal and external need for change".[81]

Faced with "not axiologically good" organizations, managers, as mentioned earlier, "tighten ship" by becoming more autocratic and directive.   Their "linking" influence would be turned into managerial controls, thus depriving the workers of participation in the important decisions of their work.   This leads to feelings of psychological discontent and, simultaneously, output failure.

J. D. Williams, a professor of political science and public administration at the University of Utah,[82] followed the Likert-Argyris lines of the systems approach to management.   The goal of this kind of approach, insists Williams, *is the optimization of output* through the "generation of creative, self-actualizing men and women in government with a strong commitment to their agencies".[83]

80. D. S. Pugh, D. J. Hickson and C. R. Hinings, *op. cit.*, p. 135.

81. *Ibid.*, p. 137.

82. The author had the privilege of being a graduate student and a disciple of Professor Williams at Salt Lake City, Utah.   So many ideas in this book may be traced to the inspiration and support implanted in the author during his association with Professor Williams.

83. J. D. Williams, *op. cit.*, p. 104.

Williams, in his search for the "right managerial mix", examined all possible quantitative variables within the context of public administration. Leaving "no stones unturned", Williams suggested the inclusion of such variables as the age and maturity of administrators, clients, available skills, complexity of work, time pressure and resources available. Counter-balancing these "production-oriented" variables, Williams emphasized *the need to examine and quantify* those variables which are basic to "all men everywhere", namely physical well-being, security, love, self-esteem and growth. Such equations would certainly provide managerial "uniformities", patterns or styles. A "right managerial mix" model, however, must leave room for modifications dictated by the same variables which are not always constant.[84]

Eschewing any universally applicable model of government administration, Williams outlined nine themes that might produce a "harmonic mean" in "our kind of culture": [85]

(1) Major purpose organization at all levels.

(2) Meaningful job assignments.

(3) Broadened spans of control.

(4) Encouragement of natural work groups and winning their loyalty to agency goals.

(5) Significant employee voice in agency affairs.

(6) A democratic leadership style.

(7) Demanding the impossible of everyone in the agency.

(8) Satisfying a whole range of ego needs of employees.

(9) Satisfying basic economic and security needs of employees.

Alan R. Coffey, a practitioner of criminal justice and a notable academician at California State University at San Jose, developed perhaps the only advanced theoretical model for criminal justice operations known today. His model is applicable to police management as well as to the management of probation and parole, courts and correctional agencies.

Coffey's model of "systematic management" is complex, consisting of a multiple facet design of conceptual notions and different levels of considerations. The model does not limit itself to the common application of the systems approach to management, but also introduces the dynamic concept of "interfacing", or overlapping, as a tool for examining actual managerial effectiveness. By integrating his systems approach (input-process-output) with the interfacing relationship between roles and functions in criminal justice, Coffey at-

84. *Ibid.*, p. 104.   85. *Ibid.*

tempted to reach some appropriate managerial equations. The following discussion will briefly describe the four basic facets integrated in Coffey's model.

(A) Analytical Facet: Results, Whats, Who and How

In accordance with the system approach, Coffey attempted to measure the effectiveness of the criminal justice system by measuring the inputs to the system, the conversion process, and the outputs of the system and its subsystems.

In this facet, Coffey delineates four measurable components the integration of which affects the optimal managerial yield: [86]

(a) Results: administratively defined goals. They include the expectations of the system as well as its environments—community, government, industry, business, etc. Determining results is a function of top management.

(b) Whats: operational determination of what is needed to achieve results, along with precise measurement. They include tasks, time spans, cost, production alternatives, operational planning, and methods of program evaluation.

(c) Who: managerial determination of operational staffing. This includes personnel planning, job classification and task assignment. Determining operational staffing is a function of middle management.

(d) How: supervisory determination of methods. This includes the functions of control and supervision, training and guidance, ways and means, influence, morale, discipline, etc.

Coffey, in this facet, attempts to measure the effectiveness of agency output by examining its major elements, namely goals (results), operations (whats), personnel (who), and quality control (how). The increase in efficiency and effectiveness of these elements must lead to an increase in agency outputs.

(B) Elements Interfacing Facet: Roles and Functions

Since the elements of Results, Whats, Who and How, are indisputably man-created, then the study of individuals in management becomes necessary. But since the study of management can not accurately determine the individual abilities and styles of managers beyond the minimum standard qualifications, the determination of such abilities and styles can only be viewed within the generalizations of the sociological concepts of roles and functions.

86. Alan R. Coffey, *Administration of Criminal Justice*, (Englewood Cliffs,   New Jersey: Prentice-Hall, Inc.), 1974, pp. 61, 70.

Coffey, in line with role theorists, Sarbin, Shibutani, Williams, and others,[87] remarks that regardless of any particular "management package", the concepts of roles and functions occupy a strategic position in successful management. Through the study of the "interfacing relationship" between these two concepts, management could reliably standardize and predict the expected behaviors and tasks of men in public agencies. Roles would determine *the expected behavior of each position occupant* and functions would delineate *the tasks to be accomplished by these roles.* The development of managerial roles and functions thus creates a common cosmology (view of reality) among all managers based on a common understanding of their expected behaviors and duties. This would clarify the management environment and facilitate the flow of systems operations. Managers and workers alike, within their assigned roles, would perform predetermined functions in predetermined manners.

Coffey defined managerial roles as the expected performance of occupants of managerial positions taking into consideration their status—position, rank, or obligation toward the group.[88] Examples of such role levels in police administration include those of chief, deputy, inspector, supervisor, patrolman, etc.

Managerial functions, on the other hand, are tasks or duties having special purposes required by the role.[89] In police administration such functions would include decision making, directing, organizing, budgeting, planning, filing, jailing and patroling among a multitude of other functions.

The interfacing facet ties in roles and functions. The number of roles (rank/status) involved determines how many functions will be performed by their occupant. Larger departments assign a single managerial function to a single managerial role (specialization). Smaller departments assign several managerial functions to each managerial role (generalization). The interface process between functions and roles would be valuable when the role allows enough overlap of interrelated functions to permit ample exchange of information and managerial flexibility, but not, however, so much overlap that would distort the role or role structure.[90] Interfaces hold (or fail to hold) the department's balance of organizational control and managerial flexibility. Too many roles with a few managerial functions would produce a tall hierarchical organization with a frustrated,

87. For more information on role theory, see Theodore R. Sarbin, "Role Theory", in *Handbook of Social Psychology*, (Englewood Cliffs, New Jersey: Prentice-Hall, Inc.), 1961, and J. D. Williams, *Management Begins With Man, op. cit.*

88. Alan R. Coffey, *op. cit.*, p. 83.

89. *Ibid.*

90. *Ibid.*

under-utilized staff. While this naturally increases the Whos and Hows, it clearly limits the Whats and the Results. The outcome would represent too much accountability and too little responsibility. The agency output may thereupon lack both efficiency and effectiveness.

Too few roles with too many managerial functions would not, on the other hand, increase either the efficiency or effectiveness of output. Such an interface would produce a flattened organizational structure with an overextended staff. While such an arrangement would increase the Results (goals) and the Whats (operations), it would naturally limit the number of the Whos (personnel) and the influence of the Hows (quality controls) over them. The outcome in this case would be too much responsibility with too little accountability, and the agency output may, likewise, be neither efficient nor effective.

A well-balanced interface should create the right number of functions at each role level taking into consideration the realities of goals, operations, personnel and quality. The following equation should explain the appropriate balance:

$$\frac{R \ (Roles)}{F \ (Functions)} = \frac{R \ (Results) \times W \ (Whats)}{W \ (Whos) \times H \ (Hows)}$$

In police administration, the equation would provide a sensible means of dividing labor among workers. Each role, *whoever the occupant is,* would be assigned the necessary functions, whatever their *nature is,* in order to achieve agency goals, *however stated,* in a predetermined operational manner, *however developed.*

The interfacing process would become even more significant when the department undergoes organizational "dislocation" or suffers of "system disequilibrium" due to substantial changes in manpower, budget, leadership, or environmental support. Such cases frequently occur when the department loses favor with city hall, encounters civil disorder in the streets, is threatened with a police strike, or experiences internal leadership conflict, to mention a few occurrences. In such cases, police departments, as in New York City during its financial exigencies, Detroit and Albuquerque during their latest strikes, or Houston during their 1975 turmoil of leadership, would have to adjust to new equilibriums by relocating their interfaces between functions and roles. Chiefs may assume more control functions, deputies may be assigned additional supervisory functions, captains may be required to get into the planning function and sergeants might be assigned to supervise more patrolmen who may be directed to carry out community relations functions above and beyond patrolling "extended" beat clusters.

Unless the interfacing process could provide the police department with the necessary flexibility without, as Coffey warned, "distorting roles and role levers", systematic management would cease to influence the agency which would almost certainly revert to bureaupathic existence.

(C) Managerial Skills Facet: Conceptual, Program, Human and Political

Coffey used the sociological concepts of roles and functions to resolve the problem of individual uniqueness of managers. The purpose was to standardize "managerial capabilities" within an acceptable framework of "perception of reality".

Managerial capabilities alone, however, can not produce desired outputs. The systems approach requires real skills capable of making functional decisions. Coffey's model, therefore, provided a third facet to his systematic management approach. This facet explains managerial skills in terms of conceptual skills, program skills, human skills, and political skills.[91]

While this facet may suggest that managerial skills operate independently, the fact of the matter remains that they could only be isolated analytically. Coffey identified these skills as follows:[92]

(a) Conceptual skills are the manager's ability to integrate theoretical abstractions and possibilities with the pragmatics of experience, tradition, and resource limitations. While casually they might be referred to as "imagination" or "creativity", such skills provide the talent to see issues, variables and options through the blurs of a long complicated and monotonous story. Conceptual skills are frequently the underpinnings of the other three managerial skills. They are essential at the top management role levels where determination of "results" is a major function. Goals, objectives and order of priorities are the main products of conceptual skills.

(b) Program skills are the manager's ability to translate a concept into specific plans. Program skills are usually required once goals and objectives are set. A goal of police professionalism may be pursued in a program, *package of plans,* consisting of educational efforts, training efforts, public relations, internal control, etc. Program skills are essential at the middle management role levels where determination of "whats" is the major function.

(c) Human skills are the manager's ability to communicate freely and to relate to employees in the organization. While human skills naturally permeate all aspects of communication within the organization, they are particularly necessary at the lower management role level which regularly handles the "who" questions. Human

---

91. *Ibid.*, p. 81.   92. *Ibid.*

skills provide the element of informal organization: worker motivation, morale and commitment to the achievement of goals.

(d) Political skills are the manager's ability to weigh the consequences of his actions and to distinguish between a "solution" *per se* and a "feasible solution". Like in the case of human skills, political skills permeate all role levels of police functions. They provide the manager with the necessary "sensitivity" to environmental stimuli whenever discharge of discretion is required or allowed. Contrary to the common belief that political skills must stem from the top, political skills, in police administration, include the behavior of line, staff and first line supervision in avoiding "exchanges or transactions" that cross the system "boundaries".

(D) The Measurement Facet

With regard to measurement, Coffey's model referred the user to the concept of a linear system. Measurement may be quantitative, qualitative, or both, but above all, it must be explicit.

Although Coffey did not elaborate on his system of measurement, some general principles were suggested by the model:

(a) Measurement must focus on the end results in terms of productivity and cost.

(b) Measurement of results must be computed in terms of several solutions or choice among "whats".

(c) Each decision must be examined in terms of cost-benefit analysis; the cost of "whos" plus "hows" compared to the price of results.

(d) The interfacing process between roles and functions should provide multiple cost estimates.

(e) Final decisions must be selected on the basis of the effectiveness of "whats" and efficiency of "hows" without jeopardizing the normative well being of "whos".

To sum up this discussion on the behavioral approach to management, it seems necessary to compare it with its predecessor, the human relations model. The main differences are:

(a) While human relations emphasize dealing with workers as individuals, the behavioral approach emphasizes their role as members in small groups or teams of experts working in unison; planning team, communication team, analysis, etc.

(b) While human relations emphasize informal relations among workers, the behavioral approach limits that to intra-group activities while maintaining authority and formal relations among groups.

(c) While human relations emphasize a semi-permanent association among workers, the behavioral approach assumes that groups co-exist on temporary basis and only to accomplish specific results. When results are achieved and goals are no longer replaced by others, the association must be broken up.

(d) While human relations emphasize that communication within the agency can be downward, upward and diagonal, the behavioral approach treats communication as a scientific element of the system and therefore must be used as freely as necessary including formal, informal and circular communication through face to face conferences within the teams as well as among them.

(e) While human relations overemphasize workers' happiness and job satisfaction, the behavioral approach overemphasizes results. The happiness and job satisfaction of workers come second and only as a means of achieving those results.

(f) While human relations emphasize the social harmony of the agency, the behavioral approach seeks first its economic balance based on the cost-benefit analysis of its programs. These must be constantly evaluated, compared and upgraded.

A further discussion of the behavioral approach and its utilization in police administration will follow in Chapter 14 where the subject of productivity and organizational development will be presented.

CHAPTER SEVEN

POLICE ADMINISTRATION: THE MANAGERIAL SIDE

Overview

The art of management is as old as man. Formal studies in management, however, are relatively new with police management among the latest additions to the field. Consequently most police administrators today are unaware of the growing need for police management. Moreover, among those exposed to modern management, quite a few unfortunately lack the necessary skills or training to utilize it effectively and have thus turned their frustration into a "who needs management" slogan.

Police work is still viewed by the "old school" of police administration as the "black and white" application of authority prescribed by a conventional "book of rules" and enforced by a massive hierarchy of ranks "forever" routinized by an agency's organization chart. This, of course, reflects the myth of administration—one singularly based on traditional organization without appropriate managerial latitude. If strong attachment and adherence to organization principles is the key to agency success, one may wonder why some police organizations are effective and others are failures. What is it that causes one police department to be exciting, interesting, and challenging while another is boring, suffers from high turnover rates, and is basically losing its battle against crime?

The major difference between the effective and ineffective must naturally be traced to the management of the department and more specifically to the difference in managerial skills of those in charge of administration.[1] Such differences may be seen in the degree of realistic planning, sound decision making, stimulative leadership, problem solving techniques, program evaluation and review techniques, organization development, effective communication, and research, along with corollary managerial abilities such as creativity, critical thinking, imagination and initiative.

Public service is the product of past and present cultural forces, and the field of management is a natural product of the economic, social and political forces of the past and present. The economic facet relates to the relationship between man and his environment's scarce resources. The social facet relates to man's need to deal with a vari-

1. Ronald G. Lynch, *The Police Manager*, (Boston: Holbrook Press Inc.), 1975, p. 7.

ety of people of differing values, needs, and abilities. The political facet of management alludes to man's understanding of democracy and constitutionalism and his beliefs in the basic freedoms and civil liberties of his fellow men. Management must therefore be viewed as a cultural activity which brings together the effective acquisition, integration, and utilization of human efforts and physical resources in order to accomplish man's goals of survival, stability, and progress.

Management is the process of rational adaptation which must take place as long as organizations consist of *neither angels nor robots*. It is man's way of reconciling the myths and realities of human socialization, motivation and will in order to cooperate and achieve common goals. Such myths, argue the proponents of organization theories, stress that men are equally capable and willing to perform assigned functions at an equal level of proficiency and dedication. The realities of human life, on the other hand, clearly indicate the fallacy of human uniformity and signify his diversity in capability, motivation, understanding and temperament. Thus, the study of management provides the field of administration with some behavioral tools capable of integrating individual contributions and promoting group efficiency regardless of human diversity, changing conditions, and environmental pressures.

Practically everyone has some conception of the meaning of the term "management," and practically everyone is conscious, to some extent, that management requires abilities distinct from those needed to do the work that is being managed. Thus a person may be a first-class engineer but unable to manage an engineering company successfully, just as a superior sergeant may make an unsuccessful lieutenant. Many cases have been cited in which an enterprise failed not because its owner did not know his field, but because he was a poor manager. Thomas Edison, for example, was a superb inventor, but he lost control of the business based on his inventions through poor management.[2]

Management Defined

A single definition of management does not exist. Tom Borns put it accurately when he stated that "the beginning of administrative wisdom is the awareness that there is no one optimum type of management".[3] In fact, the discipline of management may be better off without a single definition since it is too flexible and too rapidly changing to be contained in a fashionable slogan. Furthermore, the field of management is growing to encompass much more than the traditional areas of industry, business and personnel. Some of the

2. Ernest Dale, *Management Theory and Practice*, (New York: McGraw-Hill Book Company), 1965, p. 3.

3. D. S. Pugh, D. J. Hickson and C. R. Hinings, *Writers on Organization*, (Great Britain: Penquin Education), 1975, p. 17.

new areas now involve behavior management, computer management, ecological management, energy management, court management and, of course, management of police services. Nevertheless, some definitions by leading authorities in the field can shed light on the role and scope of modern management: [4]

> To manage is to forecast and plan, to organize, to command, to coordinate and to control.—Henri Fayol

> [To manage is to have] an understanding of the structure and dynamics of the thing acted upon .   .   . so that the chain reaction of change in one part coursing through other parts can be calculated.—E. Wright Bakke

> [Management is] a process of continual readjustment to physical, biological and social environments as a whole.—Chester Barnard

> [Management] depends on information, estimates, and expectations that ordinarily differ appreciably from reality.—R. M. Cyert and J. G. March

> [To manage is] to depersonalize the giving of orders, to write all concerned in a study of the situation, to discover the law of the situation and obey that.—Mary Parker Fallet

> [To manage is] to design the environment that the individual will approach as close as practicable to rationality in his decisions.—Herbert A. Simon

When a person becomes a manager, he may not continue to do part of the actual work but must take on new functions that are entirely managerial in character. He must make policy decisions by which maximum effectiveness can be achieved, organize the tasks of work groups by which maximum efficiency can be reached, lead and motivate his men so that maximum productivity can be attained, and constantly monitor and evaluate the progress of his organization.

Knowledge of the work will, of course, help the manager, but he will need something more. Even when he knows exactly how he would go about the job if he were to do it himself, he may be unable to explain to others how it should be done or to decide on the best sequence when several people are to handle parts of it. He may find that people resent his orders and are apathetic toward their work no matter how hard he tries to arouse their enthusiasm. The question, therefore, of whether the manager should be an insider or an outsider can naturally be difficult to resolve without examining each organization on a case by case basis. This would require a study of the or-

4. *Ibid.*, pp. 57, 95.

ganization's history, climate, needs, goals and above all—the managerial skills of its members.

The study of management, compared to organization, is like the study of physiology compared to anatomy. Management is a dynamic process of "priming" an administrative system to affect change. Dwight Waldo in his definition of management stressed the term "action". He defined management as "action intended to achieve rational cooperation in an administrative system".[5] It involves the *continuous output of decisions pertinent to the maintenance and progress of an organization.* Like physiology, it reaches out to all segments of the organization turning on and harmoniously uniting the operations of men, methods, monies and machines. Through effective management, administrators are able to predict and detect the weaknesses of work groups and diagnose, as well as correct, the failure of public agencies by the use of rational methods. Unmanaged organizations, on the other hand, remain static, hard and dry. They erode by exposure to physical environments, internal conflicts and lack of energy. They may catch the disease of *bureausis* (sickness of the bureau) and become an administrative *flop* in need of constant treatment to remain alive. They may fall victims to frequent administrative *comas* or breakdowns with little or no power to rebuild the damaged parts. Effectively managed organizations, in this sense, can easily head off conflicts, adjust to internal stresses, and maintain a strong administrative stamina.

Management, like education or government, is a continuing process. There are always new ideas to implement, fresh minds to stimulate, and more events to cope with. And the satisfaction of needs today invites higher aspirations for tomorrow. Thus, new problems crop up before old ones are solved. For purposes of analysis, management studies obviously focus on a single problem—or just one series of action that leads to a specific end, but in practice, management "deals with a wide variety of problems, each in a different stage of resolution".[6]

Management is the personal side of administration. While organization is clearly impersonal, marked by sets of positions, ranks and rules unidentifiable with a particular incumbent, management operates through individual styles of leadership, of harnessing manpower, informal communication, and of making smart decisions. Professional managers become known by name rather than by position. Endowed and trained to "manage complexities", such managers

5. Dwight Waldo, *The Study of Public Administration*, (New York: Random House Inc.), 1955, p. 6.

6. William H. Newman, Charles E. Summer and E. Kirby Warren, *The Process of Management*, (Englewood Cliffs, New Jersey: Prentice-Hall, Inc.), 1967, p. 9.

not only "get things done through other people" as they are normally charged with doing, but also handle such difficult, abstract work like "building institutions", "sharpening values", and "professionalizing agencies". Effective managers are not just special people who can "bring people together in organizations to make things happen; they live and work in the midst of events they help create".[7] Future managers, as Harlan Cleveland described, will consequently be "brainy, low-key, collegial, optimistic, and one thing more—they will positively enjoy complexity and constant change".[8]

MISCONCEPTIONS ABOUT MANAGEMENT

As must be already understood, management has no body of its own. It cannot exist outside an organizational context. Like the human body, where physiological processes cannot function outside a physical form, the managerial process cannot take place without an adequately established organization. Therefore, while most police organizations can exist without police management, the process is not reversible.

A second major misconception of management stems from the semantics jungle that often confuses the use of the term. Perhaps the greatest single semantics confusion lies in mistaking "management" to mean the function of organizing. A few writers, especially of the management process school, use the word to define the establishment of the activity-authority structure of an enterprise. Also many practitioners believe that they are "organizing" when they create or promote a framework of informal activity groupings and working relationships. In both cases, they confuse organization, the formal structure within which functions are to be carried out, with management, the latent *priming operation* which follows, once a formal structure has been established.

Other semantic entanglements might also be mentioned. Leadership, an ingredient of management, is often made synonymous with "headship" which is an ingredient of organization. Decision making, the sequential methodological and scientific tool of management, is often mistaken for the organizational method of keeping control and maintaining discipline. Also communication, the managerial means of *mutual understanding*, is frequently limited to its structural use in organization by which it refers to the exchange of reports, memoranda, and tabulated forms.

A third misconception of management is its perception as fundamentally successful. The term must only be viewed as situational:

---

7. Harlan Cleveland, *The Future Executive*, (New York: Harper and Row Publishers), 1972, p. 7.

8. *Ibid.*, p. 89.

an intellectual effort to straighten out organizational complexities by rational means. It neither has a best way nor is always effective. It can work or fail depending on some vectors representing the strength and direction of its ingredients: (1) the adequacy of the organization it operates in; and, (2) the ability and expertise of its members. The quality of management may be characterized as effective if it achieves its prescribed goals, or ineffective if it fails. Therefore, a managerial style used by the New York police department may not necessarily be effective in such departments like Atlanta or Dallas, and vise versa. But, while management, as mentioned earlier, is not a panacea to all administrative ills, effective management has always paid off abundantly in administrative dividends and positively contributed to the solution of human problems whether they entailed pyramid building, peace keeping, moonlanding, or war.

A final caution is necessary, however. There is *no effective management without effective managers.* Management has to begin with man since he is its only component capable of rational thinking. And naturally, since nobody is born rational, it follows that effective management is an acquired ability. It takes native intelligence, training, education, expertise, understanding of human nature, and imagination, among other unidentifiable qualities.

CURRENT NEEDS FOR POLICE MANAGEMENT

Most police agencies in America today, whether at the federal, state, or local level, are bureaucracies functioning at the organizational level. Quite a few, especially those at the local level, are essentially static organizations mostly running *hard and dry.* They operate by virtue of their structural inertia with little or no managerial capability. Bereft of an effective management capable of lifting the plane *up, up and away* in defiance of *organizational gravity,* these agencies will keep *taxiing around* unable to take off to "new horizons" of administrative achievement.

To illustrate these new horizons which effective management could offer to traditional organizations, Robert Tannenbaum presented these leads for possible managerial changes: [9]

1 —From a mechanistic, formalistic view of organization to an organic, systems-oriented view.

2 —From linkage between individual units by organizational charts to linkage by organizational needs.

3 —From motivating the individual from the outside in, to motivating him from the inside out.

9. Harry W. More, Jr., *Effective Police Administration,* (San Jose, California: Justice Systems Development, Inc.), 1975, p. 53.

4 —From the use of formal authority, to developing an atmosphere conducive to freedom, creativity and growth.

5 —From telling people, to listening to them.

6 —From a primary concern with the isolated individual, to a concern with teams.

7 —From inter-individual and group competition, to collaboration.

8 —From maskmanship (hiding one's thoughts and feelings), to a more appropriate degree of openness.

9 —From a primary concern for the immediate utilization of individuals, to a greater concern for their development.

Some major areas of police reform which need urgent management intervention include the following:

(a) the increasing unrest and discontent among police officers;

(b) the sectarian occupational fraternity which often develops;

(c) the increasing job dissatisfaction among police ranks;

(d) the growth of militant unionism;

(e) the inadequate value systems concerning police roles and goals;

(f) the quest for police professionalism;

(g) the absence of effective police leadership.

(A) Increasing Unrest and Discontent

No thoughtful manager can neglect the changing feeling and attitudes of Americans since World War II. During the last decades the motivation and the general psychology of people inside, as well as outside, bureaucracy have changed considerably. Generally speaking, Americans today: (a) have a rising set of expectations; (b) have experienced many personal frustrations; (c) are less satisfied with their lot in life; and (d) have altered their attitudes about one another and have questioned the integrity of the government institutions that control them.

These changes in attitudes have had a major impact on police service in America. They have influenced how police officers look at the nature of their work; how they view social and political change; how they respond to their superiors and fellow officers; and how they feel about various people and groups within the communities they serve. An increase in the tensions within the department has complicated these changing attitudes and behaviors. The troubled self-image of many police officers today has produced troublesome kinds of internal discontent, mounting frustration, occupational isolation, group factionalism, severe anxiety and regrettable withdrawal from social norms giving way to substantial allegations of police brutality and corruption.

Although the subject of police corruption will be discussed in detail in a later chapter, it is appropriate to refer to the problem at this time and explain its dismal relationship with conventional organization. While police organizations attempt to reflect a public image of the policeman as efficient, honest and fair, they fail to show him, in realistic terms, how to achieve and maintain high levels of efficiency, honesty and fairness. The situation becomes even more complicated when policemen who suffer from low salaries, real or imaginary community hostilities, intolerable political intervention, dishonest superiors, and ambiguous enforcement policies receive little or no managerial guidance. Organization of police agencies, as explained earlier, only provides a set of rules which tells the policeman, as an abstract entity, *What* ought to be done, but seldom shows him *How,* as an individual, the job can be done "best". Organization—especially the traditional type—has always been particular regarding the *What* question, but elusive as to the *How* question of administration. Policemen, consequently, are expected to figure out on their own a way for maintaining their balance within a gamut of state laws, civil service rules, and department regulations.

Individual policemen, on the other hand, are unique persons who interact with their changing environments whether social, political, psychological or economic. They observe other occupations and compare what they get with what others get. They realize their declining economic condition in an inflated economy. They are particularly conscious, for instance, of the increasing number of officers killed and injured "in the line of duty" and how much streetsweepers in San Francisco make per month. Consequently, and justifiably so, they question the utility of an organization unresponsive to their needs and unable to "understand" their aspiration for a more privileged social life. Faced with what they perceive as a conspiracy by "corrupt politicians" and a "hostile community", they seek work gratification (both as individuals and in small groups) by illegal means. Careful not to violate the organizational rules, they quietly pursue a policy of selective enforcement by which they can accomplish an acceptable degree of occupational stability and, at the same time, an ample leeway to social recognition. Thus a large number of policemen become, in fact or by allegation, corrupt officers. To add to the problem, as long as such officers are not caught and as long as the organization's reputation is not publicly smeared, the leaders of these agencies do not really seem to care.

Corrupt practices in which policemen are allegedly involved vary widely in character. The most common are acceptance of gratuities or bribes in exchange for nonenforcement of laws (particularly those relating to gambling, prostitution and liquor offenses); the fixing of traffic tickets; minor thefts; and occasional burglaries. The President's Task Force Report attributed the background of the problem of police unrest, discontent, and corruption to these factors:

1 —political domination;

2 —lack of clear enforcement policies;

3 —dishonest superiors and fellow officers;

4 —lack of public participation;

5 —inadequate compensation;

6 —police isolation and decline in morale.

According to a study by William H. T. Smith and Drexel A. Sprecher, increasing numbers of police administrators and social scientists today anticipate a continuing period of unrest and uneasiness within police forces coupled with a substantial decrease in effectiveness and an increase in corruption. The study emphatically called for the need to "analyze the nature of internal unrest and to find ways of coping with it".[10]   The call obviously is one for effective management, and the assignment is to research police behavior and their views of the polity, the community, and their organizations.   Only through a dynamic managerial program can self-content among officers be restored, morale uplifted, ethics reinforced, community relations enhanced, leadership promoted, and an atmosphere of professional performance reestablished.

(B) Sectarian Occupational Fraternity

Most police organizations, especially the larger ones, have long fostered and accommodated some informal group norms as a means of coping with the strains of formal rules and restrictions. In many departments this has become a kind of unofficial code governing relationships between fellow officers as well as within the official hierarchy. The most harmful aspect of these norms lies in the fact that they tend to overlook the public interest *accidentally* or intentionally. In the former case such norms would lead to sheer incompetence, in the latter to outright corruption. In either case, unprofessional norms can seriously disrupt to machinery of the organization by promoting in-group loyalty, resentment to authority, and bureaupathology.

Unprofessional norms by sectarian fraternities evolve as a method of "organizational escapism" to compensate for internal unrest by simulating an artificial code of organizational ethics. Under such a

10. William H. T. Smith and Drexel A.   (Washington, D.C.: Leadership Re-
     Sprecher, *The Police Leader Looks at*   sources Inc.), 1974, pp. 3–4.
     Unrest   Within   the   Department,

code, these norms serve (a) personal aspirations, (b) relations with peers, and (c) relations with superiors.[11] Policemen involved in these fraternities in effect develop their own functional system of management. The first group of norms, serving personal aspirations include these:[12]

　　—Try to get out of uniform and into a plain clothes job, whether by ability, hard work, or *pull*.

　　—Succeed by *pull*, which is generally approved if not actually admired.

　　—Learn to make your own minor misconduct appear legitimate under the rules; have a *good story* when called to account.

　　—When possible avoid involvement in enforcement activity while off duty.

Examples of the second group of norms include:[13]

　　—Say little about the behavior of other policemen, especially your squad partner, even if that behavior involves brutality, corruption, or other forms of malfeasance.

　　—Do not, except in the most unusual cases, bear witness to dereliction of duty by other officers—again especially by your squad partner.

　　—Make peace with your sergeant, whether he is right or wrong, before you complain to a higher rank.

Examples of the third group of norms include:[14]

　　—Avoid open criticism of the way superiors discharge their responsibilities.

　　—Expect superiors to exercise the prerogatives of their rank for *rank hath its privileges*.

　　—Regard incumbent superiors as holding these privileges in trust for the next generation, which may include you.

While these norms of sectarian fraternity may seem functional to many members of police organizations, from the administrative and professional perspective they have a number of serious and long-range disadvantages. They help *cover up* many police crimes and justify illegal and unethical behavior by individual policemen. They offset genuine feedback within the system as to how personnel really felt about police functions and services. And finally, they may further encourage police isolation and withdrawal from its natural environment.

11.　*Ibid.*, pp. 4–5.

12.　*Ibid.*, p. 5.

13.　*Ibid.*

14.　*Ibid.*

(C) Job Dissatisfaction Among Personnel

Part of the corrective role of management is its active role in helping police personnel surmount their job-related barriers to the satisfaction of their psychological needs and aspirations.

All public employees encounter substantial daily barriers to goal achievement, and a police officer certainly is no exception. Inertial organization, as mentioned earlier, can produce and augment bureaupathic behavior, thus making some people "sick". The special nature of the police function frequently becomes intolerable, thus making some police personnel even "sicker". Examples of such conditions which cause this "sickening" feeling include: [15]

(a) the constant pressure of having to encounter weird persons in open streets—everywhere you go;

(b) the use, or possible, use, of a fire arm as an essential part of the job to defend yourself and members of the public;

(c) the requirement that police officers must enforce laws with which they might disagree;

(d) the flagrant intervention of politicians in the administration of the department;

(e) changing legal requirements pertinent to what policemen can or cannot do in dealing with criminal suspects;

(f) lenient sentences and the extensive use of probation and parole techniques;

(g) special constraints frequently placed on policemen by chiefs and supervisors who flatly submit to community pressures;

(h) unfair practices within the department relative to promotions, assignments, rewards, and disciplinary actions;

(i) depressing work conditions which include smallness of pay, irregularity of work hours and the lack of public respect of police practitioners.

Faced by these "sickening" conditions each day, police officers seem to be constantly suffering from anxiety, frustration and conflict. If the obstacles are minor, the policemen usually manage to overcome them promptly, to ignore them, or to live with them. In such cases irritation is usually short lived and in quite a few cases may stimulate special energy and imagination. This could help the tolerant police officer cope more effectively with his feelings of job dissatisfaction.[16]

15. Patrick V. Murphy and David S. Brown, *The Changing Nature of Police Organizations*, (Washington, D.C.: Leadership Resources Inc.), 1973, p. 13.

16. William H. T. Smith and Drexel A. Sprecher, *op. cit.*, p. 11.

If these "sickening" conditions appear insurmountable or persistent, the policeman's *cope-ability* with his organizational environment becomes seriously reduced; he feels frustrated, torn, and may even turn schizophrenic. He expresses sentiments of tension, anger and may behave in desperate ways. Assuming the tension is not reduced or relieved by effective managerial treatment, a policeman may: [17]

—show increasing nervous strain and irritability expressed in signs of alienation, skepticism, boredom and poor performance;

—respond compulsively and irrationally to tasks, problems, and people by goofing off, brutality, interpersonal hostilities, insubordination and sabotage;

—internalize stress, developing migraine headaches, ulcers, a heart attack or even becoming an alcoholic or a drug addict.

Curing the problem of job dissatisfaction through reduction, relief or alleviation is a necessary function of management. Effective police management, through the concepts of organizational development, informal communication, and evaluation and review techniques can turn around job dissatisfaction among personnel by occasionally "taking the officer's temperature", and launching a morale-boosting campaign aiming at restoration of self-confidence, relaxation of unreasonable organizational constraints and promotion of professionalism.

(D) Growth of Militant Unionism

One of the major movements which developed in America around the turn of the century to protect the interests of workers was the establishment of labor unions. They swept private organizations and public organizations as defense mechanisms against the so-called "intransigence" of management. The term referred to such practices as exploitation of workers, denial of workers' rights and lack of reconciliation between their interests and those of enterprising groups and individuals.

From an administrative point of view, the alleged "intransigence" of private bureaucracy which became notorious during the 1920's and 30's reflected poor familiarity with what modern management is all about. Owners of private industry eventually had to learn the hard way that profit could be sustained and even increased while the interests of workers are secured. Only through effective management—the art of rational compromise—could these adverse interests be simultaneously maximized.

The issue of police unionization today is not as volatile as the issue of labor unions in the 20's because major disputes between state

17. *Ibid.,* p. 12.

and local governments and the police over the right to form unions have been resolved. There are only five states and the District of Columbia in which statutes specifically prohibit police from joining labor unions.[18]

Militant unionism among police ranks can be a sharp double-bladed sword. On one hand, unions such as the Fraternal Order of Police (FOP) and the Police Benevolent Association (PBA), can be extremely helpful in advancing the interests of police personnel. They can enhance job security, career building, training qualifications, and other welfare benefits to police officers and their families. They can play an active role in espousing a variety of social activities and bringing together police organizations and officials of local government.

On the other hand, militant police unions and associations can be counter-productive (if not damaging) to both police and public interests. To mention just one example, the infamous Boston police strike of 1919 would not have occurred had the AFL not incited and misled the members of the police force. That notorious strike, which left the city with virtually no protection, caused extensive damage and looting. When it ended, the strike left at least four people dead, ten wounded, and over 1,100 striking officers jobless.[19]

Despite specific prohibitions against strikes in many police manuals, police "benevolent" associations occasionally support unprofessional group actions. Such actions include "blue flu" epidemics, when large numbers of officers call in sick, and "job actions" by slow-downs, reducing arrests, permitting or even encouraging traffic snarls, and the like.[20]

Few police administrators today believe that the trend toward unionization (at different levels of militancy) will be reversed. On the contrary, most feel that unionization movements will expand to encompass most smaller cities as well as other law enforcement agencies yet untouched by unions. Moreover, these administrators concede that more and more police discontent will become expressed in unusual union actions. This will, of course, add another burden to the task and responsibility of management in coping with future police unrest.[21]

18. Hervey A. Juris and Kay B. Hutchison, "The Legal Status of Municipal Police Employee Organizations", Working Paper Number 3, Center for Law and Behavioral Science, University of Wisconsin, p. 4.

19. Harry W. More, Jr., *Critical Issues in Law Enforcement*, (Cincinnati: The W.H. Anderson Company), 1972, p. 282.

20. William H. T. Smith and Drexel A. Sprecher, *op. cit.*, p. 9.

21. *Ibid.*

Without getting into a detailed discussion of police unionization, it is perhaps safe to state that the "old school" of police administration, *the organizationalists,* have always viewed union activities not only as illegitimate and incompatible with the "sacred" mission of police forces but also as an invasion of the exclusive "prerogatives" of the police leadership.　In contrast, the role of effective management, without taking a stand on the legality of police unions, could eliminate or reduce this increasing militancy among the ranks.　Effective management can, by spotting and adequately remedying the causes of internal unrest, by resolving conflicts, and by responding to the just demands of police personnel, preempt illegal union actions, harness the surplus energy and turn it into a constructive and stabilizing force.

(E) Inadequate Value Systems About Police Roles and Goals

The strength of organization lies in its uniformity, continuity and impartiality.　Necessary as these characteristics are, however, organization can hardly escape the inevitable consequences of inflexibility and the consequent allegations of unresponsiveness to changes of times and values.

Police organizations, like all traditional agencies of government today, have been under considerable criticism for their failure to adapt to the social, political, and legal moods of the nation.　They, especially, seem to have difficulty adjusting to the values of the post-Vietnam era, the dynasty of the youth, the rising sexual and drug revolutions, among several other growing movements.

From an administrative point of view, police departments maintain an authoritarian approach to the handling of domestic tranquility.　The large majority of police departments still retain a para-military appearance rather than a benign professional one. This has perpetuated, at least among populaces of the lower economic class and among minority groups, the image of a police army of occupation, alien to the indigenous problems of poverty, discrimination and rising expectations.　In today's age, characterized with social unrest, economic crunch, massive unemployment, and juvenile crime, the social role of the police as protectors of the public good has not noticeably changed.　Whether this role is in fact true or not makes little difference in this reference as long as large segments of the public perceive it that way.　The police are probably seen by the lower and middle income classes today as: [22]

　—servants of the influential minority—the wealthy, politically powerful and socially prominent;

22. This information was gleaned from William H. T. Smith and Drexel A. Sprecher, *op. cit.*

—conductors of differential treatment of violators because of race, political pressure or corrupt practices;

—self-acclaimed "defenders of the faith" sadistically devoted to the harassment of the young, the blacks and moral offenders;

—trigger-happy custodians of "law and order" heavily armed primarily to protect their own lives.

Organization theories, it must be noted, cannot be blamed for such unpleasant perceptions. As mentioned earlier, it is not the function of organization to change, or even consider changing, institutional or departmental values established by statutory policies. Moreover, organizations are not *self-cleansing systems* designed to periodically wash off *administrative dust*. Nevertheless, old policies in time become obsolete, agency values become burdensome and personnel behavior becomes more and more anomalous.

Studies in value displacement have always lacked in accuracy, reliability and conclusiveness. Establishing and promoting a set of new values in public organizations, therefore, must be considered a highly specialized and complicated task. Given, as mentioned earlier, the functional inadequacy of police organizations to cope with changing social values, the instillment of new police values must be considered an important managerial function.

Effective police management, through the processes of leadership, attitudinal analysis, performance evaluation, feedback, and decision making, can systematically monitor, survey, correct, and enforce new value systems in police organizations. Such a value displacement program requires the harmonious integration of societal sentiments, latest legal rulings, economic trends, departmental values, and the personal and professional values of personnel in charge of police supervisory positions.

The manner in which a harmonious integration of these values can be worked out is naturally one of the principal distinctions between an effective manager and a less effective one, regardless of differences in the size, type, or structure of their respective organizations. The effective manager must naturally be attuned to local demographic surveys, population distributions, social and religious traditions, local legal ramifications, and changes in morality within the community. Mainly a product of intelligent orientation, familiarity with statistical readings, and sound prediction, effective management would have little trouble shaping up police roles along modern professional values.

(F) The Quest for Police Professionalism

It is certainly commonplace today to refer to practically any effort that is aimed at improving law enforcement as a contribution to police professionalism. Thus improving police performance by reducing response time to crime reports, by the application of the computor to police work, by the improvement in communications systems, and even by an increase in police pay have all, at one time or another, been cited as contributing to police professionalism.[23]

Without attempting to explain in detail, at this junction, the concept of police professionalism, the concept obviously pertains and must be restricted to the attitudes and behaviors of policemen. Professionalism is an *elevated state of mind by which policemen can distinguish between fair and unfair practices regardless of their personal bias or institutional prejudice.* A professional policeman will naturally abide with the former and avoid the latter. Improving police performance, therefore, by any means which does not also help elevate his state of mind must not be mistaken for police professionalism. While cases of unprofessional practices by police are obviously too common to enumerate, a few examples would include the following:

—the lack of a sense of mission in discharging police duties;

—the use of intimidating language or demeanor with suspects, witnesses or members of the public;

—the lack of police compassion especially necessary in handling the aged, the sick and the poor;

—discrimination in the treatment of the public based on bias or prejudice;

—allowing "loose" discretion in initiating, or failing to initiate, the criminal justice process with little or no regard to legal and administrative criteria;

—diversion from the codes of police ethics regarding the private and social life of policemen.

Organizational theories, as referred to earlier, are not by definition much concerned about professionalization. Furthermore, by virtue of their structural approach, classification of tasks, and discipline, they can do little to enhance professionalism within the bureaucracy. The impact of organizations on the worker's mentality or his attitudes toward his job is minimal. Especially under traditional organization, which still dominates most police departments today, questions concerning the mental and emotional framework of practitioners are of little concern. The major purpose of police organizations today is mainly to do the job, regardless of whether the workers believe or disbelieve in how the work quota is produced or the quality of the service rendered.

23. Herman Goldstein, "Police Policy Formulation: A Proposal for Improving Police Performance", *Michigan Law Review*, Vol. 65, No. 6, April, 1967, pp. 1123–1146.

Effective management, on the other hand, treats the worker as a "whole" man. It seeks his attention for, and concern about, the work produced as well as the attitudinal framework by which he delivers it. Under effective management, workers become inspired and highly motivated. Their hearts as well as their minds become devoted to the achievement of their product or service.

Without the need for comprehensive and detailed rules, effective management expects—and labors to create—dedicated and highly motivated workers capable of handling discretion wisely and in a professional manner. Toward these goals, effective management emphasizes the need for informal communication, feedback analysis and continual testing of workers' attitudes, and a special effort is constantly made to transform workers into professional agents attuned to the needs of their community and responsive to the social expectations of their clientele.

(G) Absence of Effective Police Leadership

Most top-ranking officials in charge of police forces in America today can certainly qualify for the titles they hold whether chief, superintendent, commissioner or the like. Only *a few*, however, would qualify as police leaders.

Although the subject of police leadership, like that of professionalism, will be discussed in detail in a later chapter, it is necessary at this junction to call attention to the current shortage in police leadership.

Consider for a moment and answer this question—name five nationally-known police leaders in America. No doubt you will have a hard time replying to the question. The difficulty is not only one of numbers but also of substance. With approximately 40,000 police organizations in America, it should be safe to expect a large number of police leaders. This, unfortunately, is far from being accurate. Although we certainly could count 40,000 police *headships,* only a small number of them can be considered as "leaderships" capable of introducing constructive change and managing their agencies in an efficient business-like manner. Law enforcement organizations today are suffering from a leadership shortage which is primarily responsible for the present stagnation in police administration. Police reforms, remarked the International City Managers' Association, "has been advancing faster at the bottom of the enterprise than at the top; great efforts have been devoted to the improvement of the patrolman and the detective, but little attention has been given to the development of competent police executives".[24]

24. The International City Manager's Association, *Municipal Police Administration*, 1943, p. 52.

Police *heads* today are abundant and local governments have no problem finding and employing them. By way of contrast, police "leaders" are rare, and traditional police agencies which ironically need their services most are reluctant to hire them even if they became available. Political machines often fear that hiring *strong* police leaders will instigate organizational, operational, and community conflicts which, for purposes of survival and dominance, such machines prefer to keep dormant.

Organizational "headship" is routine *foremanship*. It is the exercise of statutory control and organizational supervision over the conventional areas of headquarters administration, patrol duties, radio communication, records and other functions of law enforcement. Police *foremen* seldom have an interest or training in the fields of executive management, behavioral sciences, public finance, productivity analysis or human relations. Their administrative ability to control large numbers of people can carry them only as far as the basic principles of organization can apply to the simple pigeonholing of submissive workers. Beyond that point, the police foreman would be confronted with managerial decisions and techniques peculiar to his limited ability and orthodox training. Consequently, it is not unusual that the personnel he commands, especially if familiar with the technical aspects of management, will deny such an office head the respect and confidence which are necessary for effective executive control.[25]

Organizational *headship* in the police is also an inert exercise of power, shrewdness and opportunity. Raymond Fosdick, a pioneer in modern police systems, perceptively described this common type of police foremanship by saying:

> The chances are rather that he is unfitted for the task. Lacking in administrative experience with scant appreciation of the larger possibilities of the position, and often without imagination or resourcefulness, he has little chance of success, and it would be unwise and cruel to saddle him with the responsibility . . . But the task, particularly in large cities, is so much broader than routine and involves activities of such vital consequences that only a high order of creative intelligence can cope with it.[26]

If police management were merely a matter of assignments, promotions, and discipline, or if it had to do only with the ordering of a

25. V. A. Leonard and Harry W. More, *Police Organization and Management*, (Mineola, New York: The Foundation Press, Inc.), 1971, p. 42.

26. Raymond B. Fosdick, "Police Administration", Part III of the *Cleveland Foundation Survey of Criminal Justice in Cleveland*, 1921, pp. 16–17.

well-defined routine, commented Fosdick, "any capable man who himself has been through the mill might be well adapted to handle it".[27]

Police *headship,* which represents the majority of police agencies in America today, comes in all shapes, types, and forms. It, however, can be identified by these general characteristics:

—insistence on formal ranks, titles and privileges;

—emphasis on command and control measures;

—emphasis on written documents and manuals;

—overemphasis on work hours and specific tasks;

—immersion in minute details;

—absence of adequate delegation of authority;

—reactive response to events and incidents;

—response to crises when they occur;

—emphasis on a continuous reporting process;

—monopoly of all outside contacts;

—a closed door policy and meetings by appointments;

—absence of department or staff meetings;

—factionalism among the workers;

—an air of suspicion and confusion.

Police leadership, on the other hand, requires a special talent and a number of managerial skills that are not necessarily acquired in the course of ordinary police training or service. The police manager deals with community problems in the large. He is familiar with the underlying forces responsible for the need of police service. Constantly before him must be the conception of the department as an agency for problem-solving and the consequent relationship of his work to all activities—social, economic, political, and educational—operating to that end. He must be able to interpret public opinion and to anticipate his agency's moves. Above all, he must be able to see his agency as a whole and inspire his workers toward the achievement of common goals.

Effective police leadership is primarily managerial. It requires originality, sensitivity, sufficient intelligence to be innovative, and enough self-assurance to be flexible.[28] It emphasizes a goal-oriented approach and an optimistic attitude. It focuses on results with less concern for methods as long as it is within acceptable legal and moral limits.

---

27. *Ibid.*

28. Jim L. Munro, *Administrative Behavior and Police Organization,* (Cincinnati, Ohio: The W. H. Anderson Company), 1974, p. 10.

Effective managerial leadership in the police is proactive, antici-patory, and adaptive. Proactivity entails *the consideration of the problem at hand without being stifled by the risk involved in making a decision.* It emphasizes innovation and creativity in dealing with problems and the use of behavioral analysis and modification in re-solving conflict. The proactive leader of today uses modern research and group dynamics in stimulating departmental cohesion and set-tling organizational differences.

Anticipatory leadership is based on intellectual enrichment, sys-tematic planning, management by objectives, and the appropriate se-lection of alternatives in the decision making processes. Anticipatory leaders must always keep in mind the philosophy of the organization and its goals and consider all the scientific methods by which they can assist their personnel in achieving these goals.

Adaptive leadership is *the executive flexibility to adapt to the changing condition of laws, environments, and methods by using a variety of leadership styles.* Such variety extends from a dictatorial to a democratic style and the adaptive police leader must devise the appropriate style to meet the existing conditions.

Whisenand, Fox, and Chamelin in their discussion of police lead-ership stated that:

> The most important ingredient in any recipe of organi-zational success is good leadership. Good leadership means motivation of others to form a management team, and then prudently leading the team. Further, good leadership as-sumes that a police administrator is prepared to devote a substantial portion of his time to effecting change.[29]

Examples of managerial techniques in police organizations today include: (1) collegiality of command, (2) organizational develop-ment, (3) redistribution of responsibilities, (4) strategic and opera-tional planning, (5) employee-centered administration, (6) decentrali-zation of authority, and (7) participative problem-solving—just to name a few.

While effective leadership has been able to utilize some of these techniques in a few large police departments, there is no reason why effective leadership in smaller size police forces cannot follow suit. The first move, however, must be toward the creation of a manage-ment environment above and beyond the organizational level.

29. Paul M. Whisenand, Vernon Fox, Neil C. Chamelin, *Introduction to Criminal Justice*, (Englewood Cliffs, New Jersey: Prentice-Hall), 1975, p. 103.

THE NEED FOR A POLICE MANAGEMENT THEORY

Management, like all behavioral sciences, is an "inexact" science. The term here is used to distinguish the field of management from areas of "exact" physical sciences like chemistry, physics or mathematics. While management is an inexact science, it has grown in a convincing manner to the status of being perhaps the most exact behavioral science. While the true criterion of exactness lies in the quantitative confirmation of a theory by statistical proof, which of course would be most desirable in the emerging field of management, there is no rational use in waiting for such proof before giving credence to a theory which can obviously improve the conduct of human endeavors.

Theory is a *systematic grouping of interrelated principles*. Its task is to tie together significant knowledge collected by the application of principles and give them a general reference. Principles *are concepts or fundamental truths,* or "what are believed to be truths at a given time, explaining relationships between two or more variables".[30] Fashionable managerial principles, for example, include Parkinson's Law, which states that work tends to expand to fill the time available for its completion, or the Peter Principle which states that in a hierarchy every employee tends to rise to his maximum level of incompetence. Examples of effective police management principles include team policing, neighborhood watch, the legal adviser, community participation, PPBS (Program Planning and Budgeting System), among others.

Management theory is *the systematic arrangement of principles so as to relate their ingredients or meanings in a logical sequence of events*. Scattered data such as the miscellaneous numbers or diagrams used to indicate crime indexes, clearance rates, manpower percent distributions, efficiency ratios and differentials, etc., can have no significance unless the police decision maker applies a theory which explains their relationships in a meaningful manner. Only a management theory can offer a rational scheme for the integration of these principles and suggest how they can be put to the test in practical situations.

Management principles are *causal relationships* which help explain management behavior. They are formulated to predict results in a given circumstance, thus indicating whether the outcome will be efficient and effective in the attainment of department objectives. For example, the principle of team policing forecasts that if a group

30. Harold Koontz and Cyril O'Donnell, *Management, A Systems and Contingency Analysis of Managerial Func-* *tions,* (New York: McGraw-Hill Book Company), 1976, p. 12.

of motivated patrolmen are assigned daily to the same district under flexible conditions, they will be more effective in preventing crime, apprehending criminals and maintaining law and order.

Management principles are either "descriptive" or "prescriptive". The former relate to those which *merely describe a relationship between variables.* They are theoretically "sensible" but their effectiveness varies since they do not propose firm steps to be taken. Like team policing or S.W.A.T., they may not be necessary for all police forces, their effectiveness has not been proven "across the board", and their utility thus remains partial. Descriptive police management principles are therefore only recommended for consideration by police department.

Prescriptive principles, on the other hand, are stated in such a way as to *indicate what steps are to be taken and what results are to be expected.* They are of a proven success based on a quantitative verification like in the application of advanced crime lab techniques or communication systems, or on undeniable experience like police education, budgetary procedures, or legal advisement. Prescriptive principles in police management are therefore required by national task force reports "for use . . . by every police chief executive". Examples would include, besides those already mentioned, a commitment to research in the police, police-community relations, and state mandated minimum standards for the selection of police personnel.[31]

Knowledge of the basic principles and techniques of police management obviously has a tremendous impact on the improvement and professionalization of police practices and procedures. It is certainly invaluable to effective police executives. It allows one to observe and relate indications which otherwise would remain unseen. The kind of experience on which a traditional police policy-maker usually relies is the variety of problems he has experienced in the past, which are never exactly duplicated. Knowledge of management theories, on the other hand, can provide the modern policy-maker with *fundamental causal relationships applicable to the solution of new problems* without engaging in original laborious research or the risky practice of trial and error.[32]

---

31. *The Task Force Report*, 1973.

32. In *General and Industrial Management*, (New York: Pitman Publishing Corporation), 1949, pp. 14–15, Henri Fayol bemoaned the lack of management theory as he said, "Without theory no teaching is possible". Likewise, Chester Barnard in *The Functions of the Executive*, (Cambridge, Mass.: Harvard University Press), 1938, pp. 290–291, deplored the lack of "an acceptable conceptual scheme with which to exchange thought". Also, L. Urwick in *Elements of Administration*, (New York: Harper and Row Publishers), 1943, puts it aptly by saying "and we should not forget that in the field of management our errors are other people's trials".

Adoption of a management theory in police administration could help the policy-maker to intelligently and systematically:

(a) understand the nature and goals of the current organization;

(b) figure out the major forces and issues contributing to current performance;

(c) explain the causes contributing to present performance;

(d) spot the problem areas in need of management intervention;

(e) evaluate the strengths and weaknesses of intervening variables;

(f) predict the scope and value of possible changes;

(g) establish standards for modified operations;

(h) plan a detailed program for improvement;

(i) determine implementation stages in sequential patterns;

(j) select personnel;

(k) implement programs;

(l) evaluate successes and failures against the pre-set standards.

The mere knowledge of management theory in police administration, however, may not be quite sufficient in long term operations. The police manager need not only know management, but *think* management, *practice* management, and *live out* his public office in a management mentality. Future police managers must be able to see the agency as a whole, to conceptualize its boundaries and sensitively assess the environmental pressures over its activities. Because police organizations in the future will be more horizontal, police managers will have to reach decisions in a collegial, consensual and consultive manner. They will have to be brainy, intellectual, low-key, optimistic and, above all, have a talent for strategic planning and a tolerance for scientific research. The manager will have to initiate change, follow it through, and in a sense "make dreams come true".

THE POLICE MOVEMENT TOWARD MANAGEMENT

The need for a clear concept of police management and for a framework of related theory and principles was recognized many years ago by distinguished practitioners and scholars. Foremost among those in the United States were Leonard Fuld, Raymond Fosdick, Bruce Smith, and, of course, O. W. Wilson. Works by these pioneers presented early and strong warnings to police decision makers all over the nation. Notwithstanding these warnings, however, very little change seems to have taken place. It wasn't until the release of the first Task Force Report in 1967 that police chief executives seriously started to experiment with management techniques and improve police performance.

In 1967, the Task Force Report came up with some blunt and harsh condemnations of the current lack of management theory. It pointed out serious weaknesses in police organizations and called for a "fundamental change in attitude on the part of many police administrators and local officials".[33]

Apparently frustrated by the lack of substantial change, the 1973 report by the National Advisory Commission on Criminal Justice Standards and Goals had to *order* some major changes. The report, using phrases like "every police agency should immediately . . .", attempted to establish concrete managerial guidelines by which police agencies could *snap out* of their traditional methods and embark on a serious program of managerial change. The "should orders" entailed areas such as development of goals and objectives, establishment of policy, cooperation and coordination, a commitment to planning, fiscal management, measures of effectiveness, among many others.[34] The appropriate integration of these principles can certainly establish a viable police management theory.

This section will survey the development of police managerial thought in America during three periods:

    (a) the early warnings (1909–1967);

    (b) the "would you please shape up" (1967–1973);

    (c) the "thou shall shape up" (1973–present).

(A) The Early Warnings: (1909–1967)

Influenced by the works of Sir Robert Peel and August Vollmer, several leaders in police administration released valuable studies pertinent to the area of police management in the United States. The following are certainly the most famous and authoritative.

Leonard Fuld. In 1909 Fuld released his critical study of police organizations. Although his work seems to be forgotten by many of the more recent critics, it is decidedly a monumental work.[35] He stressed that in all problems of police administration, two main factors must be constantly borne in mind: efficiency and humanity. He believed that before a police organization could be effective, the police commissioner or chief has to be a strong executive. Critical of the non-professional heads of police departments, Fuld expressed the belief that in order to be efficient, police policy-makers must act quickly and decisively, particularly in times of emergency.

---

33. *The Task Force Report*, 1967, p. 44.

34. *National Advisory Commission on Criminal Justice Standards and Goals*, Washington, D.C., 1973, pp. 5–15.

35. Leonard Felix Fuld, *Police Administration*, (New York: G. P. Putnam's Sons), 1909, p. 304.

Fuld was particularly concerned with the selection and training of police officers and stated emphatically that all political considerations should be eliminated during the selection process.[36] Fuld's principal focus was on the management process of controlling, for he felt that man would only work effectively when closely supervised. He emphasized the problem-solving approach to police management and suggested that such an approach could only be utilized by strong police leaders competent in the application of management techniques.

Raymond Fosdick. In 1915 Raymond Fosdick released a comprehensive study of seventy-two cities in the United States with populations in excess of 100,000.[37] He identified numerous gaps in police management such as the political control of police, inadequate police leadership, organizational rigidity and lack of supervision. Fosdick suggested that in order to have sound police management, it was necessary to fulfill three conditions: [38]

(a) The relationship between supervision and work must be well balanced.

(b) The different parts of the system must be adjusted to each other.

(c) The whole system must be adapted to its task.

Fosdick was especially concerned with the role of personnel management and called the attention of police executives to the need for a more humanistic approach to management. He stated that:

> In the final analysis, police business is but the aggregate of personal enterprise, and the observation, knowledge, discretion, courage and judgement of the men, acting as individuals, who compose the various units of the organization.
> . . . only as the training of the policemen is deliberate and thorough, with emphasis upon the social implications and human aspects, can real success in police work be achieved.[39]

Fosdick criticized the old Weberian school of police administration in which the prevailing disposition was one of a "mechanism created to operate automatically". He concluded that such an emphasis on the mechanical side of organization, rather than on the "initiative and imagination of the individual officer", would stifle effective police work.[40]

---

36. *Ibid.*, p. 41.

37. Raymond B. Fosdick, *American Police Systems*, (Montclair, New Jersey: Patterson Smith), 1969, pp. 382–383.

38. *Ibid.*, pp. 189–190.

39. *Ibid.*, p. 306.

40. *Ibid.*, pp. 314–315.

Bruce Smith. In 1940, Bruce Smith released the first edition of his book, *Police Systems in the United States,* and stated that the "major aspects of police management were often neglected or ignored".[41] Smith found that the vast majority of American police agencies continued to function according to patterns laid down several years ago. He expressed the belief that the broad management principles which had become commonplace in industrial organizations had a definite application to police organizations. He explained that the failure of police agencies to utilize modern management techniques was because of the sudden growth of police organizations into large complex structures and the lack of experienced police leadership.

Implying a situational approach of management, Smith emphasized the need for an *elastic* organization in which the span of control is determined by an *informed opinion* in each specific situation. He suggested a broad type of organization not only based on the conventional divisions of patrol, traffic, and criminal investigation, but including some novel divisions like property management, personnel management, crime prevention and morals regulation.[42]

With reference to the common problem of the generalist-specialist conflict, Smith expressed his concern for the prospect of overspecialization in police organizations. While he acknowledged the increase in complexity in several areas of law enforcement and the need for specialization, he emphasized the importance of a reasonable balance. Such a balanced policy, he asserted, must be determined and maintained by a flexible and open-minded leadership sensitive to the needs for cooperation and coordination.

O. W. Wilson. In 1950, O. W. Wilson released his monumental work, *Police Administration,* which later became the *bible* of many police administrators in large cities. In his subsequent editions (1963 and 1972) Wilson expanded his views on major management principles. He emphatically expressed the need for adequate police leadership sensitive to the needs of a changing community. He stressed rational consolidation of police functions and the application of behavioral tools to the practice of policing.

Wilson's early writings were primarily in line with the traditional school of administration. He started out by classifying police duties by their objectives. He determined the immediate objectives of the police as: (1) prevention of crime, (2) repression of criminal activities, (3) apprehension of criminals and the recovery of stolen proper-

41. Harry W. More, Jr., *Effective Police Administration,* (San Jose, California: Justice Systems Development, Inc.), 1975, p. 25.

42. Bruce Smith, *Police Systems in the United States* (New York: Harper and Brothers), 1960, pp. 219–220.

ty, (4) regulation of noncriminal activities and (5) the performance of a variety of regulatory services.[43]

Based on his determination of police objectives, he suggested these principles: [44]

1   —Police tasks are to be organized by purpose, process, place, thing, or clientele.

2   —Duties of police units are clearly drawn by precise definitions which are made known to members of the agency.

3   —Communication channels are to flow down in terms of orders and up in terms of reports.

4   —Unity of command is established.

5   —Span of control is maintained.

6   —Assignment of clear tasks are designated to specific persons.

7   —Supervision of line personnel is constant.

8   —Responsibility of personnel is commensurate with their assignments.

9   —Persons to whom authority is delegated are invariably held accountable for its use.

Wilson described the purpose of police management as necessarily directing, coordination, and controlling the members of the force. At each level of authority, Wilson emphasized the need for planning and inspection in order to (1) ascertain whether the task was being performed as outlined; (2) learn whether the anticipated results are being attained; (3) discover whether the resources are effectively utilized and (4) reveal the existence of need for further planning and inspection.

(B) The "Would You Please Shape Up" Era: (1967–1973)

Despite the early warnings of these practitioners and scholars, most police agencies at the federal, state, and local levels kept their administrations at the organizational level. Especially among local agencies, police administrators showed little or no concern for the emerging management movement. It seemed safer to carry on the traditional norm than to experiment with *liberal* types of change. In particular, from the point of view of an "unenlightened" and "insecure" police chief, managerial change presented a series of unnecessary risks which he was neither equipped for nor willing to take. To change his authoritative style of leadership and solicit the workers'

43. O. W. Wilson, *Police Administra-*   44. *Ibid.*
tion, (New York: McGraw-Hill, Inc.),
1950, pp. 2–3.

input in *his* decision making process would mean opening the door wide-open to irresponsible and liberal views and *inviting a breakdown in authority*. This he must have viewed with a lot of skepticism and with considerable mental anguish. Given the fact that most police administrators in the 1940's and 50's were "depression policemen" who had received their positions by political appointment, a sudden shift in administrative policies must have sounded administratively illogical and politically unwise, if not foolish. In addition to these skeptical sentiments on the part of those depression administrators, they probably realized that there was no compelling reason to change their policies voluntarily. In the absence of a pressure to change, there naturally was no serious need to abandon a "secure" system of administration which had been in operation for centuries "without default".[45]

In the meantime, the face of America had changed drastically since the pre-depression days. It turned from a collection of predominantly rural and independent jurisdictions to an industrialized urban nation. Yet in several respects law enforcement had not kept pace with the change. The policing of America had since grown into a disorganized bureaucracy causing an immense overlapping in responsibilities and duplication in efforts and producing serious handicaps in the overall capability to apprehend criminals.

With the rapid change in post WWII America, it became apparent that serious deficiencies retarded the development of functional police systems and threatened the demise of the nation's main defense line against crime and anti-social activities. During these years the problem of crime seemed to have risen to unmatched levels in the nation's history. The President's Commission on Law Enforcement and Administration of Justice of 1967, warned that, "the existence of crime, the talk about crime, the reports of crime, and the fear of crime have eroded the basic quality of life of many Americans".[46] In the commission's study conducted in high crime areas of two large cities, some shocking findings about the scope of crime were revealed: [47]

—43 percent of the respondents say they stay off the streets at night because of their fear of crime.

—35 percent say they do not speak to strangers any more because of their fear of crime.

—21 percent say they use cars and cabs at night because of their fear of crime.

—20 percent say they would like to move to another neighborhood because of their fear of crime.

45. *The Task Force Report*, 1968, p. 48.   47. *Ibid.*

46. *The Task Force Report*, 1967, p. v.

The report in a subsequent reference proceeded to say that in a national survey, the findings generally supported the previous local survey. The report corroborated these findings by stating that: [48]

—One-third of a representative sample of all Americans say it is unsafe to walk alone at night in their neighborhoods.

—Slightly more than one-third say they keep firearms in the house for protection against criminals.

—Twenty-eight percent say they keep watchdogs for the same reason.

In the meantime, police systems in America seemed to have further declined in their capability to prevent, contain or suppress crime. They lacked adequately trained and qualified personnel, crime prevention techniques, effective police-community methods, modern technology, leadership, morale, and, above all, management skills capable of introducing constructive change in police systems.

Like American industry, business, or warfare, the outcry was one for basic change in police attitude toward effective management. Faith in management has consistently been the answer in attempting to solve all American failing endeavors. Sixty British businessmen who once visited the United States for nine months have reportedly stated: "if there is one secret about all of the American achievements in productivity, then it is to be found in the attitude of American management". The Britishers were impressed with an attitude that "seems to engender an aggressive management which believes that methodical planning, energetic training, and enthusiastic work can solve any problem".[49]

No wonder, therefore, that the 1967 President's Task Force Report on the police strongly called for a "fundamental change in attitude on the part of many police administrators and local officials".[50] In the police world, as anywhere, the report continued, "significant reform requires imagination, labor, and sacrifice".[51]

In another section, the report emphasized in the strongest language the need for police managerial reform by stating:

In general too many police departments appear unwilling to abandon outmoded concepts . . ., or to encourage per-

---

48. *Ibid.*, The report is the work of 19 commissioners, 63 staff members, 175 consultants, and hundreds of advisors. The commissioners, staff, and consultants came from every part of America and represent a broad range of opinion and profession. In the process of developing the findings and recommendations of the report, the Commission called three national conferences, conducted five national surveys, held hundreds of meetings and interviewed tens of thousands of persons.

49. William H. Newman, Charles E. Summer and E. Kirley Warren, *The Process of Management*, (Englewood Cliffs, New Jersey: Prentice-Hall, Inc.), 1967, p. 7.

50. *The Task Force Report*, 1967, p. 44.

51. *Ibid.*

sonnel to show initiative or offer suggestions . . . Every activity of police administration [must] require new ideas effectively put into practice to meet new conditions. This is practically true within the area of police management . . . This prevailing attitude *must* change if the police is to meet the changing conditions of police service.[52]

The Task Force Report, moreover, criticized the attitude of the "old school" of police administrators for their lack of comprehension of the new managerial concepts in police administration.　Pointing to the sad consequences of that situation, the report clearly indicated that:

> Sound management practices apparently are not understood nor used by administrative and command personnel. . . . planning and research are not utilized to resolve present problems of organization, personnel deployment, performance inadequacies, nor to prepare programs, procedures, and policies for strengthening the [department].　Staff inspection as a control device is not known . . . and therefore not used.[53]

In another part, the report regretted the apparent *bankruptcy* in police managerial thought today by saying:

> Many police departments do not have the expertise to recognize their shortcomings or to correct them when they are recognized . . . and some cities are not interested in reform even when it is desperately needed.　These are some of the reasons for the wide disparity in the effectiveness and efficiency of law enforcement agencies.[54]

Referring to the apparent *resentfulness* on the part of many police administrators which causes them to block the advent of effective management and its incorporation in police administrative programs, the report, in a clearly frustrated language, "blew the whistle" on the police bureaucracy by raising such questions like:

> Why should a department be denied access to fresh outside executive talent of proven ability?　What is there about management of police resources that causes it to be different, in this respect, from all other professions?　Why only in the police field, are the managerial skills not regarded as transferable? [55]

---

52. *Ibid.*, p. 48.

53. *Ibid.*, p. 45.

54. *Ibid.*, p. 48.

55. *Ibid.*, p. 45.

The 1967 Task Force Report concluded its sharp criticism of the *total absence of police awareness of managerial concepts and practices* by pointing out the unfortunate constitutional and legal consequences of this deficiency. Making reference to the fundamental principle of "equal protection" in the American democracy, the report alerted the police community to the fact that "citizens within the same state or even within the same country do not receive the same quality of police service because of differences in agency management".[56]

The recommendations of the Task Force Report exceeded 200 specific subjects and covered a wide variety of issues including (1) community relations, (2) personnel, (3) organization and operations, and (4) resources and services. For the purpose of this discussion, only management related recommendations will be listed.[57] On Promoting Police Organization and Operations:

—Develop and enunciate guidelines for exercises of law enforcement discretion.

—Clarify police authority.

—Include police in community planning.

—Provide state assistance for management surveys.

—Employ legal advisors.

—Strengthen staff control.

—Create administrative boards in larger departments.

—Establish internal investigation units to maintain police integrity.

—Experiment with team policing.

—Explore consolidation of law enforcement in all counties or metropolitan areas.

—Provide areawide communications and records coordination.

On Enhancing Personnel Management:

—Divide functions and personnel among three kinds of officers; police officer, police agent and community service officer.

—Assess manpower needs.

—Recruit more actively especially on college campuses and in inner cities.

—Increase police salaries to competitive levels.

—Set a goal requirement of a baccalaureate degree for general enforcement officers.

56. *Ibid.*, p. 48.   57. *Ibid.*, p. xi.

—Improve screening of candidates.

—Encourage lateral entry to specialist and supervisory positions.

—Improve training methods.

—Require probation and evaluation of recruits.

—Establish police standard commissions.

The President's Commission on Law Enforcement and Administration of Justice concluded its report by calling for "a revolution in the way America thinks about crime". The recommendations called for basic changes in the operations of police, prosecutors, defenders, social workers and prisons. The recommendations also called for a greatly increased effort on the part of the federal, state and local governments in developing new procedures, tactics and techniques. Such efforts, concluded the report, could lead to "a safer and more just society".[58]

The report, unfortunately, had no mandatory provisions to force change. Recommendations were left to state Commissions on Law Enforcement Officer Standards and Goals to consider their possible implementation. No sanctions were attached for failure to comply. Other than the "loss of face" and possibly the denial of requests for financial grants by the LEAA (Law Enforcement Assistance Administration) or its affiliate agencies, there was no real harm in ignoring the report's recommendations altogether.

The value of the report and its impact on police management thought, nevertheless, were of some significance. Hardly any police chief or administrator overlooked its recommendations, or so they claimed. The report, which was also directed to members of the polity and the public at large, opened the eyes of these groups (police, polity, and public) to the seriousness of the crime problem in America and to the gravity of the police inadequacy to cope with it. The answer had to be an organized and methodical effort to implement modern police management with political backing and public support. The burden was naturally on the police to initiate, plan, research, lead, and change.

The most valuable outcome of the President's Commission on Law Enforcement and Administration of Justice, however, was the establishment of the LEAA. It was created by Public Law 90–351 as a product of the findings cited by the report criticizing the "near helplessness" of state and local governments in their administration of police agencies and in their fight against crime. The act authorized the United States Attorney General to make grants to, or contract with, public or private nonprofit agencies to improve the train-

---

58. *Ibid.*, Summary, p. v.

ing of personnel, to advance the capabilities of law enforcement agencies, and to assist in the prevention and control of crime. The act also authorized the Attorney General to conduct studies, to render technical assistance, to evaluate the effectiveness of programs undertaken, and to disseminate knowledge gained as a result of such projects.[59]

The LEAA has also endeavored to bring together the police and academic worlds. Many of the police management projects conducted lately have involved the use of systems experts from college faculties who have worked closely with practitioners in many police departments. Several programs described at the end of this chapter were developed by the help of management professors from the academic world upon the request of interested police organizations.

(C) The "Thou Shall Shape Up" Era, (1973–Present)

The 1967 President's Commission on Law Enforcement and the Administration of Justice was only a preliminary document and did not spell out, except in general terms, what police management would really involve. By contrast, the 1973 report by the National Advisory Commission on Criminal Justice Standards and Goals, is a massive management guide which stated the "should's and oughts" that had to be implemented "immediately" in the areas of Criminal Justice. The report defined "immediately" as "implementation as soon as practical and without unnecessary delay".[60]

Within the reference of immediate reform, the 1973 report addressed its efforts directly to the managerial aspects of the administration of criminal justice systems. The primary aim of the National Advisory Commission, the report stated, was the development of a planning capability below the federal level that would bind together a highly fragmented criminal justice system and its environment. The report also introduced some technical approaches to management like program budgeting, performance measurement and evaluation, and integrated information systems. The first section of the volume on police dealt with planning; the second, information systems; the third, education and training; the fourth, criminal code revision; and the last dealt with research. All except the fourth dealt with basic managerial functions without which an effective system of police management could not evolve.

---

59. A. C. Germann, Frank D. Day, and Robert R. Gallati, *Introduction to Law Enforcement and Criminal Jus-* *tice*, (Springfield, Illinois: Charles C. Thomas, Publisher), 1970, pp. 285–286.

60. *Task Force on Police*, 1973, p. 5.

Compared to the 1967 report on the police, the 1973 document was more comprehensive, management-oriented, and committing. While the report made no claim to the discovery of viable formulas to solve all police problems, it approached the problem of crime reduction as primarily "the achievable product of police efficiency and effectiveness". The report aimed directly at cure-related matters which offered "workable and practical standards for police".[61] The National Commission had ordered that the Police Task Force direct its efforts at a "basic course of action" which "must be taken this year to begin reducing crime".[62] In compliance, the report carefully identified seven basic objectives designed to improve police management and designed specific standards to be applied in support of each. It was the considered judgment of the Task Force that the seven objectives and their corollary standards would be "most efficient" in improving police management and reducing crime.[63]

The seven objectives are:

1 —Maximizing the police capability to apprehend offenders.

2 —Promoting police interaction with the public.

3 —Promoting police interaction with the other components within the criminal justice system.

4 —Clearly determining all local needs and the realistic establishment of goals and priorities.

5 —Maximizing the utilization of police human resources.

6 —Maximizing police technological capability.

7 —Maximizing police responsiveness to public needs.

The Task Force Report followed its statement of objectives by *ordering* each chief executive to insure that an implementation plan is developed for each objective. In this reference it firmly stated:

> Every police executive should insure that an implementation plan is developed for each objective . . . Where budget funds are required, they should be sought immediately. If grant funds are necessary, they should be applied for at once. When possible, implementation should be tied to a schedule.[64]

To insure that the achievement of these objectives is done uniformly across the board, the report developed certain sets of stan-

61. *Ibid.*, p. 3.　　　　63. *Ibid.*

62. *Ibid.*　　　　64. *Ibid.*

dards to be used as checklists. The following will present the relevant sets of standards, as cited, next to each objective: [65]

1. **Fully Develop the Offender-Apprehension Potential of the Criminal Justice System.**

Immediately develop and apply all available police agency, community, and other criminal justice element resources to apprehend criminal offenders. This may be implemented through the following standards:

Standard 1.1   Identification of Priorities.

Standard 3.2   Neighborhood Security Programs.

Standard 5.1   Providing 24-Hour Police Service.

Standard 8.1   Minimum Response Time.

Standard 8.3   Deployment of Patrol Officers.

Standard 9.4   State Assistance.

Standard 9.7   Criminal Investigation.

Standard 12.2 Crime Laboratory.

Standard 23.1 Rapid and Accurate Telephonic Communication.

Standard 23.2 Rapid Processing of Emergency Calls.

Standard 23.3 Two-Way Radio Communications.

2. **Get the Police and the People Working Together as a Team.**

Immediately develop and apply community resources to the reduction of crime through formal crime prevention and police support programs. This may be implemented through the following standards:

Standard 1.1   Local Definition of Police Functions.

Standard 1.2   Accountability to the Public.

Standard 1.4   Communication with the Public.

Standard 1.6   Public Understanding of the Police Role.

Standard 3.1   Developing Community Resources.

Standard 3.2   Community Crime Prevention.

Standard 16.4 Police-Public Workshops and Seminars.

Standard 19.2 Responding to Personnel Complaints.

3. **Get the Criminal Justice System Working Together as a Team.**

Actively pursue criminal justice system coordination and effectiveness to serve society. This may be implemented through the following standards and recommendations:

Standard 4.1   Cooperation and Coordination.

65. *Ibid.*, p. 5.

Standard 4.3   Improving Police Effectiveness in Criminal Justice System.

Standard 4.4   Diversion from Criminal Justice System.

Standard 4.6   Criminal Case Followup.

Recommendation 4.1   Alcohol and Drug Abuse Centers.

Standard 5.2   Combined Police Services.

Standard 12.4 The Detention System.

Standard 23.1 Accepting Misdirected Telephone Calls for Emergency Service.

4.   Clearly Determine and Act on the Local Crime Problem.

Immediately identify specific local crime problems and set crime rate reduction goals. This may be implemented through the following standards:

Standard 1.1   Establishing and Revising Priorities.

Standard 1.4   Communicating with the Public.

Standard 3.1   Neighborhood Meetings to Identify Crime Problems.

Standard 9.1   Analyzing Crime to Determine Specialization.

Standard 9.11 Use of Intelligence Information.

5.   Make the Most of Police Human Resources.

Immediately develop and apply every human resource to stop crime and apprehend offenders. This can be implemented through the following standards:

Standard 10.1 Civilian Police Personnel.

Standard 10.2 Selection and Assignment of Reserve Police Officers.

Standard 13.1 Police Recruiting.

Standard 14.1 Police Salaries.

Standard 14.2 Position Classification Plan.

Standard 15.1 Educational Standards for the Selection of Police Personnel.

Standard 16.3 Preparatory Training.

Standard 16.5 Inservice Training.

Standard 17.1 Personnel Development for Promotion and Advancement.

6.   Make the Most of Police Technological Resources.

Immediately develop and apply every available technological resource to stop crime and apprehend offenders. This may be implemented through the following standards and recommendations:

Standard 23.1 Police Use of the Telephone System.

Standard 23.2 Command and Control Operations.

Standard 21.3 Radio Communications.

Standard 24.3 Data Retrieval.

Standard 24.4 Police Telecommunications.

Recommendation 23.1 Digital Communications System.

Recommendation 23.2 Standardized Radio Equipment.

Recommendation 23.3 Frequency Congestion.

7. Fully Develop the Police Response to Special Community Needs.

Immediately develop and apply all available resources to respond to community needs. This may be implemented through the following standards:

Standard 1.4   Communicating with the Public.

Standard 1.5   Training in Community Culture.

Standard 1.6   Participating in Youth Programs.

Standard 13.3 Minority Recruiting.

Standard 16.4 Interpersonal Communications Training.

Standard 17.4 Lateral Entry.

Throughout the discussion of these specified standards, the police executive was expected to implement those standards not yet in effect within his agency. The report explicitly held police "chiefs, sheriffs, superintendents, colonels, directors, or commissioners, along with competent top level staff" responsible for the accomplishment of the standards. As to remove any further doubt about the role of effective leadership in police management, the report stressed the following:

> [Effective police chiefs] are the key to positive change needed within the police service to reduce crime. Effective police agencies are led by successful police chief executives who are surrounded by competent top level staff all of whom actively seek new ways to reduce crime and serve the community.[66]

Attaching even more significance to the necessity of effective leadership, and at the same time subtly warning police chief executives across the nation, the report concluded by stating that "complacency and incompetence have no place in the American police service".[67]

66. *Ibid.,* p. 4.   **67.** *Ibid.*

MANAGEMENT OF TECHNICAL AREAS

In addition to the report's strong emphasis on the role of committed leadership as the prime mover of police management systems, it introduced, as mentioned earlier, three technical areas as requisites for steady and effective management:

(a) program budgeting;

(b) evaluation and performance measures;

(c) developing information systems.

(A) Program Budgeting

The implementation of a plan is not a part of the planning process. It only begins after the plan has been put together, adopted, and funded.

Between planning and implementing, therefore, lies the vital process of budgeting or allocation of resources, without which a plan would forever remain an expressed theory. Simple plans may need simple budgeting techniques, but advanced plans have to be supported by an advanced budgeting system. The Task Force Report emphasized the need for a "symbiotic relationship" between planning and budgeting which current police administration has seldom recognized. The report indicated that while police planning has been either sporadic or nonexistent, budgeting for police functions always followed a traditional line item approach, focusing on fixed categories of expenditure such as equipment, salaries and supplies.[68] Although the overriding purpose of the line item budget is obviously fiscal control, namely, *the determination of whether funds are spent by authorized persons for authorized purposes,* such a purpose no longer is serviceable for complex program planning. Useful as it may be for control purposes, line item budgeting was not originally designed to relate to planning. Line budget issues commonly involve comparisons between past and present item requests. Program planning, on the other hand, involves multiyear forecasts far beyond the annual budget potential.

The report recommended that Program budgeting (also known as Planning-Programming-Budgeting, Planning and Budgeting, or Program Planning and Budgeting System—PPBS) be used by criminal justice and police agencies. In Program Budgeting, management plans are grouped in systematic programs, and resources are allocated toward objectives through needed programs *regardless* of an annual budget cycle.

68. *Ibid.,* p. 12.

The report suggested several management techniques which are associated with Program Budgeting systems: [69]

1 —Goal setting: the formal establishment of intermediate and long-range goals and objectives. It becomes more meaningful when associated with quantitative objectives. Beside providing a purposeful framework for police planning, goal setting is closely tied to the principles of police efficiency, effectiveness, economy and accountability.

2 —Program definition: with the articulation of objectives, the kinds of activities designed to reach goals are considered and in turn broken into smaller parts in a hierarchical structure; programs, categories, subcategories and elements.

3 —Multiyear forecasting: the long-term prediction of results. This requires program planning and budgeting for several years in advance. It necessarily involves a systematic prediction of future social, economic, and governmental trends.

4 —Performance measurement and evaluation: the establishment of evaluation criteria is necessary to assess the achievements of various programs. It is based on the selection of a unit of measurement of police service and relates its effectiveness to its cost, thus becoming a standard unit for measuring police efficiency and effectiveness.

5 —Program analysis: the identification of program alternatives and the projection of costs and benefits. Though difficult to determine in the areas of police services, program analysis naturally depends on the appropriate selection of standard units for measurement and the presence of adequate information systems.

A further discussion of this technical area will follow later in the chapter.

(B) Evaluation and Performance Measures

One of the most disturbing characteristics of present police operations is how little is known about what works and what does not work. Whether a one-man patrol serves "better" than a two-man patrol is not known for certain. Whether police unionization harms the cause of professionalism is not clearly established. Whether employment of minority group officers—at some sacrifice of the minimum standards—enhances the police image in the public eye varies from one community to another and from one police chief to another.

Because of similar doubts about the effectiveness of police practices, the National Commission undertook at the outset of its effort a

---

69.   *Ibid.*, pp. 12–13.

survey of innovative criminal justice projects throughout the country, both federally and non-federally funded. The commission staff queried more than 400 agencies for information and the responses corroborated the doubts previously raised. The report stated:

> The agency responses, although often enthusiastic, were nonetheless not particularly useful. Many evaluation reports contained ill-defined objectives providing no specific standards by which to judge the project. Claims of success were generally couched in subjective and intuitive statements of achievements. Even when quantitative measures were used, they frequently were not accompanied by analysis and by adequate explanation.[70]

The Task Force Report therefore emphasized that performance evaluation *is and should be* an integral part of the planning and resource allocation process. Evaluation provides feedback on the results of previous planning efforts, prevents planning from becoming unrealistic and provides a corrective device to enable modification of previous efforts that were unsuccessful.[71]

The report stressed that evaluation *can and should* take place at various levels. A statewide program to reduce burglary, for example, can be evaluated by specific reductions in the incidence and cost of burglary. At the local level, the relative effectiveness of various program strategies for reducing burglary can also be assessed; comparisons can be made concerning the relative worth of offender reintegration, reduction of target vulnerability, and increased risk of apprehension strategies.[72]

The report identified at least three key functions that must be performed: (1) definition of program objectives and impact/output measures of performance; (2) development of evaluation plans and design of evaluation studies; and (3) dissemination and use of evaluation findings. Of particular interest, the Task Force Report stated, is the function of impact/output measures of performance since it may be the most difficult to accomplish and is certainly the most controversial. Impact measures are *indicators used to describe the effect police activities have* on major criminal phenomena. Such indicators assess the fear, costs and incidence of particular crimes. Output measures, on the other hand, are *indicators that describe the police response to the same criminal phenomena.* They include measures of deterrence, apprehension, or conviction.[73]

In the future, the report concluded, planners at all levels will have to become more concerned with the construction and interpreta-

70. *Ibid.*, p. 14.   72. *Ibid.*

71. *Ibid.*   73. *Ibid.*

tion of performance measures in evaluation efforts. Effective evaluation will require the clear definition of objectives, performance measures, and adequate data analysis in the initial stages of any program.

(C) Developing Information Systems

Possibly the greatest obstacle to program planning involves the use of information. Sophisticated blueprints in other areas of domestic research, such as transportation or industry, were only possible after planners were well financed and able to obtain large amounts of data that could be analyzed by computers. The Task Force Report insisted that the same requirements must be applied to criminal justice and police agencies.

The report emphasized that police planners must develop a capability to build and handle mathematical models. Such models would be invaluable aids in projecting the workload, personnel requirements, and cost of the police function. Properly structured, mathematical models could suggest which policy alternatives—law enforcement, peace keeping, or public relations efforts—would have the "best" results in reducing the crime rate in a certain area. Toward developing such a planning capability, the report stressed the need for adequate information bases.[74]

Although a number of states, the report stated, have invested block grant money in information systems since the late sixties, the report required the establishment of criminal justice data collection systems in each state. Future funds, the report assured, will be made available for information systems in these areas: [75]

1 —State criminal justice data centers.

2 —Management and administrative statistics systems.

3 —Uniform Crime Reporting systems.

4 —State technical assistance capabilities.

If federal assistance continued and was accepted, the report concluded, it is reasonable to expect that within 10 years planners would have a tremendously expanded information base.

INNOVATIVE POLICE MANAGEMENT PROJECTS

This section will describe a number of innovative police management projects. By and large, the projects have been initiated and tested in one form or another by at least one police department. However, since most of these projects are still undergoing modification in the light of further testing and evaluation, it is recommended that they are not to be applied indiscriminately in disregard of pre-

74. *Ibid.*, p. 15.   75. *Ibid.*

vailing conditions or organizational limitations. On the other hand, since these projects have already been of substantial help to some police agencies, there is no reason to believe they cannot be applied elsewhere. With effective managerial skills, courage, and foresight, it is hopeful that police agencies will be successful in redefining and reconstructing their basic themes and in modifying them for local use.

(A) Team Policing

By the early 1970's team policing had become a popular concept among many police administrators. The term, although varies slightly from one city to another, relates to the *reorganization of the conventional beat approach into an integrated and versatile police team assigned to a fixed district,* thus becoming more capable of responding to the local needs of that community. Team policing was experimented in several cities under different names: in Detroit, it was called Beat Commander; in Dayton, Ohio, Team Policing; in Syracuse, New York, Crime Control Teams; and in Los Angeles, The Basic Car.

The concept is basically a management compromise between conventional patrol requirements and the community outcry for more responsive policing. Implementation of the concept, therefore, calls for three major operational changes: (1) geographic stability of patrol, (2) maximum interaction among team members, and (3) maximum communication among team members and the community.[76]

The first change, geographic stability, was carried out in Detroit by a team of 21 officers, under a sergeant (beat commander), who were made responsible for 24 hours for a small high-crime area. In Dayton, 10 to 12 patrolmen, together with 5 or 6 community service officers, were likewise assigned. In Syracuse, each team—composed of 8 officers and a sergeant—covered an assigned area for a 24-hour period. In Los Angeles, the team consisted of 9 and serviced the assigned area on a 24-hour basis.[77]

The second change, maximum interaction among team members, was implemented in these cities with considerable variation. Basic in the concept is the maximum exchange of information. The most common method applied was the scheduling of team conferences at regular intervals in an analogous fashion to that practiced by doctors, attorneys and accountants. Police teams which attended these conferences found that in many instances, criminal activities were

76. Lawrence W. Sherman, Catherine Milton, Thomas Kelly, *Team Policing,* Police Foundation, 1973, p. 3.

77. Paul M. Whisenand and R. Fred Ferguson, *The Managing of Police Organizations,* (Englewood Cliffs, New Jersey: Prentice-Hall, Inc.), 1973, p. 183.

continuing problems covering more than one shift and required a great deal of strategic planning and team coordination.

The third change, maximum communication among team members and the community, was primarily carried out by regular meetings between the teams and the community. The meetings provided for adequate cooperation in the areas of crime prevention, in the flow of information, and in the identification of community problems. The meetings also served as a vehicle for eliciting community involvement in the peacekeeping function. Another technique involved the participation of community members in police work through auxiliary patrols, through information leading to arrests, and through a community voice in police policy-making. Yet another technique of police-community participation involved a system of referral of non-police problems (such as civil complaints, drug related questions, juvenile offenses, etc.) to appropriate community-service agencies.

In addition to these operational changes, team policing as experimented by these cities required a number of managerial adjustments:

1 —Stability of supervision: Different supervisors controlling an area during the course of a day can create inconsistent police policies and approaches to community problems. It may be difficult, for example, for a group of young boys to understand why one officer allows them to play baseball in the street between 8:00 a.m. and 4:00 p.m. while another forbids them from 4:00 p.m. to midnight. In order to maintain coherent and consistent police performance, it was preferable that one supervisor be responsible at all times and that his orders be obeyed.[78]

2 —Lower-level flexibility in policy-making: Interaction among team members proved to be most productive when the team had the flexibility to carry out its own collectively-reached decisions. For example, decisions about mode of dress and duty schedules which were traditionally reserved for higher-ups were pushed down to the team level where information about neighborhood needs was most accurate.[79]

3 —Lower-level assessment of service needs: This related to the team's responsibility to assess what kinds of police services are needed in the neighborhood. This included the team's power to decide when specialized police units are needed, for what purpose, and for how long. Although this should not deny the value of specialist skills, it only stressed the ability of the team generalists to decide when those skills are needed.[80]

---

78. Sherman, Milton and Kelly, *op. cit.*,   80. *Ibid.*
    pp. 3–6.

79. *Ibid.*

4 —The total-policeman function: As a part of the team-policing concept, team members were expected to perform a larger unified delivery of services. The most common kind of these services involved a combined investigative-patrol function. A more advanced practice combined peace-keeping functions, community relations, conflict disorder assessment among others.

(B) The Lakewood Experiment

Lakewood is a middle-sized town with a population of about 130,000 people, located on the eastern slope of the Rocky Mountains in central Colorado. For the last few years, the Lakewood Department of Public Safety has become a model in police management and has attracted the attention of the police community across the nation. While the supporters consider Lakewood DPS as the most progressive type of police management "ever exercised", critics maintain it is only an elaborate exercise in managerial "window dressing". Notwithstanding the controversy, most police philosophers and practitioners today carefully keep an eye on the department as a leading experiment in police management worthy of close observation and study. The experiment has grown so famous as to foster the concept of *Lakewoodism,* which every policeman in America today is assumed to have heard about one way or another.

The essence of Lakewoodism is *progressive management.* Its objective is the application of the behavioral approach to police administration. Leadership is configurated in the role of a courageous, rational, systematic police manager, who is also employee-oriented and familiar with the scientific approach to the solution of problems. Officers, all with baccalaureate degrees, are organized in teams of generalist-specialist experts, assigned to carry out well-planned programs in response to well-defined community needs. Organization is no longer dependent on the use of traditional authority but on the predominance of a management atmosphere conducive to flexibility, creativity and growth. Individual and group competition is replaced by collegial collaboration. The primary concern of the department is not limited to the effective utilization of officers but also to the development and growth of department members.

The basic managerial changes introduced by the Lakewood Department of Public Safety include: [81]

1 —Replacement of police uniforms with blazers and title of officers with "agents."

81. Gleaned from an address by Pierce R. Brooks, Director of Department of Public Safety, before the Tenth Annual Interagency Workshop, June 2–13, 1975. The text is available through The Institute of Contemporary Corrections and the Behavioral Sciences, Sam Houston State University, Huntsville, Texas.

2 —Approval of lateral entry of officers from other police agencies at the same rank.

3 —Requirement of a baccalaureate degree as a minimum credential for service.

4 —Establishment of the generalist concept of policing by which the agent would operate as a patrolman, detective, traffic officer, community agent, all in one.

5 —Application of team policing with team rotation each three months to coincide with changes in school semesters.

6 —Evaluation of agents by peer group supervision.

7 —Open-ended training of agents in areas of law or liberal arts.

8 —Increasing financial compensation, which makes the department one of the highest paid in the country.

9 —Remodeling leadership along the lines of a board of directors with the chief as chairman.

10 —Establishment of a staff position of legal advisor.

11 —Enhancing research through services of competent experts in administrative science.

12 —Management of internal discipline through the strict investigation of all complaints against agents.

The Lakewood management experiment, which also came to be known as the "Lakewood Innovation", caused as much publicity within the police community as the "Hawthorne Experiment" did to the industrial community forty-four years earlier. And like the "Hawthorne Experiment", humanistic management "even by super cops" seemed to have failed in turning Lakewood into a "Utopia P.D.". Human motivation, job enlargement, sincerity, openness and other fundamentals of the human relations approach did not substantially increase the productivity of the Lakewood police force, and no drastic expectations seemed to be forthcoming.

The results of the Lakewood experiment are rather premature to assess at this time since its basic policies are still undergoing fundamental changes and especially after Pierce Brooks, Director of the Department, has openly attempted to defuse the "inflated" picture of its success. Brooks has indicated that the changes at Lakewood were rather too big and perhaps too fast for the force to adapt to. In his analysis, Brooks stated:

You can imagine what happened. There was an attitude problem . . . . The problem was change for the sake of change alone. They did not plan change . . . . Some of the old-timers were sitting around . . . chuc-

kling and saying give it back to the sheriff .   .   .   there
had to be change .   .   .   it was a bit drastic.[82]

Brooks explained the traumatic myth of the generalist approach
of policing by saying:

> The theory here was that you could take the hundred
> finest young police officers in the United States, all-Ameri-
> can supercops, and start a police department, telling each su-
> percop, "you are everything, so go out and take all the calls,
> respond to the calls, follow up on the investigations, handle
> the traffic accidents, and write citations." .   .   .   This was
> supposed to inspire motivation, and it just decimated the
> department.[83]

Brooks further stressed that the generalist approach was a catas-
trophe and was abandoned in favor of reverting to a more traditional
approach. He stated that the agents who were inclined to be investigators were following up on their cases, "but there was no patrol in
their areas at all". The generalist approach to policing, he stated, vi-
olated and confused the basic logic of police organization. He illustrated by saying:

> Under this theory the police agent who is patrolling
> that area responds to the call, and then he's supposed to fol-
> low up on it, now he's become the investigator in this vi-
> cious crime. Later he's still taking statements, he's got one
> witness in a hospital, he has got some at the market, the
> stolen car has just been located in Denver .   .   .   and
> suddenly he realized it's one-thirty, and he's due in court on
> a traffic ticket he wrote a week ago.[84]

In addition to the failure of the generalist approach, the Lakewood experiment had to do away with peer group supervision by the
establishment of a promotional exam. The director concluded after
a few years of the experiment that: [85]

> People need to be supervised whether or not they have
> a college education. A fellow who was President not too
> long ago tried to work without a boss, and we found out he
> certainly needed a boss. So if the President of the United
> States has to be supervised, certainly young police officers
> must be .   .   ..   First line supervision is the backbone
> of the police organization.

82. *Ibid.*   84. *Ibid.*

83. *Ibid.*   85. *Ibid.*

According to other testimonials by Director Pierce, the "Lakewood Innovation", after a few years, had to undergo a state of "regrouping" and develop its own "balanced approach" to police management.[86]   Open-ended training was abandoned in favor of a police oriented educational program.   Team policing was adjusted to provide ample supervision within, as well as over, the team.   Several other modifications also had to take place.

While the Lakewood experiment in progressive management is not the only one of its kind, it is certainly the most publicized.   The management lesson to be learned is obviously not one "of change for the sake of change" but of *"change to fit"*.   Managerial innovation must, after all, stress cope-ability, realism, and acknowledge human limitations.

(C) Program Planning and Budgeting System: THE Dayton Experiment

On August 25, 1965, President Lyndon Johnson announced to his cabinet members and agency heads that he was introducing a new Planning—Programming—Budgeting System (PPBS) for all departments and agencies in the federal government.   In his statement he indicated his conviction that the "system will improve our ability to control our programs and our budgets rather than having them control us.[87]   Under the PPB system each department must:

> Develop its objectives and goals, precisely and carefully; evaluate each of its programs to meet these objectives, weighing the benefits against the costs; examine, in every case, alternative means of achieving these objectives; shape its budget request on the basis of this analysis and justify that request in the context of a long-range program and financial plan.[88]

Regardless of whether PPB truly constitutes a radical reform of the fiscal system of government, and many experts argue that it does not, it placed considerable emphasis on program results and the managerial tools by which they can be accurately achieved.   The use of such tools is no longer limited to federal agencies.   It has recently spread among many state and local governments and large police agencies today are among those agencies which finally turned to

86. *Ibid.*

87. Fremont J. Lyden and Ernest G. Miller, *Planning Programming Budgeting: A Systems Approach to Man-*   *agement*, (Chicago: Markham Publishing Company), 1970, p. 5.

88. *Ibid.*

their use. The Dayton Police Department in 1971 was the first to apply PPBS.

The basic concept in PPBS is that of "programming". The concept was used for the first time in fiscal administration to refer to the integration of planning and budgeting, elements which historically had little relation to one another. In police agencies, as mentioned earlier, planning seldom involved relating agency goals to resources. Beside the fact that the responsibility for allocating police resources has always been delegated to persons completely outside the agency, usually in city hall or county court, police budgets customarily consisted of line item requests for materials and services, e. g. salaries, vehicles, uniforms, training or maintenance, etc. A budgetary program that related agency outputs (crime prevention, apprehension of criminals and provision of services among others) to resource inputs never really existed before.

Without reiterating what was said earlier on the same subject, PPBS as a method of fiscal management seeks purposefulness and clarity. To insure accountability and facilitate legislative scrutiny, PPBS capitalizes on the crucial relationship between agency goals, planning, and budgeting. The system relates them in a program easy to supervise and evaluate. Programs comprise a number of interrelated plans selected on the basis of cost-effectiveness analysis and results are computed in advance. A realistic criterion for appraisal of performance is set up, and allocation of resources is clearly earmarked to insure the appropriate funding of plans at the anticipated level of quality performance.

The way PPBS works is as follows:

(a) determine the goals and objectives of the agency, as well as the subgoals and activities necessary to obtain their primary goals;

(b) examine alternative methods of attaining the goals and the costs and effectiveness of each method;

(c) select the "best" alternative method or combination of methods for the achievement of the most effective goals at the cheapest cost;

(d) present these alternatives and their cost in a well-planned long-range program clearly identifying stages of implementation and resource requirements (budget) for each stage.

The Dayton PPBS project was established with the assistance of the Dayton Pilot Cities Team. It involved a team of police specialists, who carried out the planning research, pooled their knowledge of program analysis and presented the chief with independent estimates of the department's program.   The program development consisted of four components: [89]

1 —A program structure which identified measurable achievement of program objectives.

2 —A budget structure which identified the cost of achievement of program objectives.

3 —A program budget reporting system (management information system) which identified the relevant problems and the cost of achieving program objectives.

4 —A planning system which formulated, evaluated, and selected optimal solutions for the relevant problems identified.

The first two components refer to functions; the other two, to systems.

1.   A program structure:

The stated goal of a police department is frequently identified as "to protect life and property and to maintain public order".   Such a generalized goal, however, is too vague to be of any value to PPBS. Goals under the new system are to be spelled out in much more detail so as to provide "quantitatively measurable" objectives capable of being ordered on a priority scale and of being compared with future programs or those managed by comparable agencies.

The development of a program structure, therefore, requires that police administrators analyze the major goals of their organization and break them down in terms of "service areas" which the public needs.   In the Dayton Police Department the police goal of security of persons and property was broken down into these service areas: [90]

   (a) decrease unreported crimes;

   (b) decrease notification time;

   (c) decrease apprehension time;

   (d) increase of reported crimes;

   (e) increase successful prosecution;

   (f) increase recovery of stolen property.

As an example, traffic control was broken down to: [91]

   (a) decrease reported traffic congestion;

   (b) decrease accidents caused by traffic violations;

   (c) increase successful prosecution of persons arrested for traffic violations.

89. Gary Pence, "Program Planning Budgeting System", *The Police Chief*, Vol. 38, No. 7, July 1971, pp. 52–57.

90. *Ibid.*

91. *Ibid.*

For the purpose of developing such a program structure there are no "golden rules" that a police administrator must follow. Therefore, in the case of the Dayton police it was developed so as to:

(a) reflect community needs;

(b) comply with statutory provisions;

(c) promote efficiency and effectiveness;

(d) enhance cooperation with other public agencies;

(e) ensure rationality and realism in decision making;

(f) project a managerial concern for workers' welfare;

(g) reflect critical thinking by people in a democratic society.

2. A budget structure:

The purpose of the budget structure is to identify and establish a reasonable price tag for each service area selected for the program. The budget structure is built around budget units of "activities". An activity is simply a *manageable task* which requires a certain amount of resources (dollars) expended. The cost of a "service area" (identified objective) is calculated on the basis of the cost of production of these units. The number of units desired, multiplied by the cost of each would determine the cost of each service area. In budget structuring, this would be a budget activity.

Estimating a price tag for a service unit in police management is admittedly a difficult task. In contrast to the production of shoes or ice cream cones, it is next to impossible to attempt to measure the worth of a policeman's smile in a police-community program unless it is reflected through the achievement of a specific and measurable unit. A viable monetary measurement must be relative to "something" which can be measured by an increase or decrease. Hence, in budget structuring for a police PPBS, selected units are usually in terms of response time, processing a criminal violation, handling drunks or jailing procedures. In some sophisticated systems, handling a midemeanor or solving a felony case was successfully designated as PPBS units.

Unlike itemized budgets, the cost of a selected unit, and consequently a budget activity, is not estimated only in terms of how much it costs in salaries, supplies, or gasoline—direct cost. It is also estimated in terms of the indirect cost of total man-hour effort, which includes overhead cost, direction, supervision and other services. A burglary investigation unit, for example, would include:

1   —cost of field service (by patrol and detective divisions);

2   —cost of supervisory service (first line supervision and middle management);

3 —cost of direction (by the chief's office);

4 —cost of special services (crime lab and jail, etc.);

5 —cost of staff and auxiliary services (training, planning, evaluation and coordination, etc.).

The Dayton Police Department, consequently, ceased to budget for needed paper clips and ammunition and instead prepared their budgets in terms of cost-effectiveness of "activities" designed to accomplish "service areas" in a whole package or a program.

3. A budget reporting system:

The purpose of a program budget reporting system is to provide the police administrator with significant and relevant data by which he can make his budgetary decisions. While this traditionally was the function of one or more part-time employees in charge of preparing an itemized budget, with the advent of PPBS it became the duty of a specialized and well-trained group of system analysts. Managing such a system requires the full-time responsibility for data collection, analysis, and interpretation, and for the manipulation of modern data processing techniques.

In Dayton, the personnel in charge of the Budget Reporting System developed a "public need survey" to assist budget personnel in the determination of service areas, the consideration of alternative cost plans, and the establishment of priorities. The budget reporting system in addition, monitored and evaluated the requests and desires of various groups which had an impact on the formulation of the PPBS program: (1) government officials, (2) pressure groups, (3) department personnel, (4) other criminal justice administrators, and (5) community leaders.[92]

The primary functions of the reporting system are to:

(a) prepare a budget structure;

(b) establish service priorities;

(c) provide viable alternatives;

(d) identify and resolve program problems.

4. A planning system:

Once police objectives are identified in "service areas", and costs are estimated in "activities", then the PPBS planning facet is invoked. The purpose is to select which services, at which costs, are to be selected for the police program. Since programs are normally prepared for a period of two to five years, careful planning becomes a crucial facet of PPBS; otherwise, the agency would have to put up with unbalanced programs for long times.

92. *Ibid.*

Through this planning facet only the desired services at the appropriate cost are selected to form an optimal program. Problems exist, however, within a police department when either the kind of services selected for the program are not the most desirable or the most desirable services cannot be afforded. For these reasons, effective planning must be able to put together the most desirable services at a most economical cost. If this becomes prohibitive, then alternatives at the next priority level must be considered. If a police administrator is not offered ample alternatives by his planning staff, his programming effort will most likely be doomed to failure, a situation any effective planning system must always avoid.

Like other management innovations, the results of the Dayton experiment with PPBS are not conclusive. The fact that it was later applied in New York, Los Angeles, Chicago and in most large police departments indicates its usefulness and suitability to progressive fiscal management in large police agencies. Except for the prohibitive cost of its installation in middle sized and small agencies, PPBS should be recommended to all police departments across the nation.

OTHER LOCALIZED INNOVATIONS

In addition to the previous significant experiments, many local agencies have initiated their own brand of managerial changes. Most of these changes are tailor-made to suit local needs or upgrade their particular police organizations. Examples of these innovations include:

(1) The Pilot Precinct—Washington, D. C. This was designed to improve police community relations through citizen participation in policing. It provides for a 17-member, elected, citizens board to meet at regular intervals and to be consulted by police managers concerning the formulation of policy and the conduct of operations within a precinct. Officers assigned to the program were required to take several hours of weekly training in company with community residents. The training stressed relevant local problems. The results of this project are neither final nor conclusive. It has been reported, however, that the more militant members of the board have been frustrated by their inability to expand their role from one of advice to one of control.[93] On the police side, however, the problem seemed to be primarily one of attitude—how to change from "no confidence and trust" to "complete confidence and trust in all matters". To both groups, the public and the police, the resolution of the conflict obviously lies in the existence of an effective management capable of creating an environment conducive of smooth attitudinal adjustment.

93. Paul M. Whisenand and R. Fred Ferguson, *The Managing of Police Organizations*, (Englewood Cliffs, New Jersey: Prentice-Hall, Inc.), 1973, p. 184.

(2) The "Fourth Watch"—Various cities. The concept is an effort to get away from some of the limitations of the traditional three shift practice. It provided for the organization of a special group (or watch) of officers available for assignment to high crime areas during the hours of peak crime.

This watch normally works from early in the evening until early in the morning (usually between 6 p.m. to 2 a.m.) overlapping two of the usual three shifts. Members assigned to this division may even work different hours if the peak times of crime differ substantially in particular areas. The geographical assignments of this watch also vary and may involve parts of more than one precinct or district.

A number of advantages are claimed for this approach: [94]

(a) greater saturation and therefore more police effectiveness;

(b) reduction in the amount of manpower on regular watches and therefore a reduction in the overtime otherwise required for special assignments during peak hours of crime;

(c) availability of difficult and challenging assignments for those officers wanting more action;

(d) improvement in the public image of the department by having its men in the right place at the right time.

(3) Lateral Entry of Specialists—various cities. One of the President's Commission's major recommendations was the supplementation of department personnel by lateral entry of professionals and experts of various kinds: planners, programmers, statisticians, chemists, attorneys, computer analysts, accountants, and public relations experts, among others.

Obviously many of these highly trained specialists are not readily available from the ranks of uniformed personnel. Accordingly, most larger departments are revising upward their demands for lateral entry of civilian specialists and are trying to work out arrangements with city officials to make this possible at compensation rates which will draw first class people.[95]

Although the principle of lateral entry has been controversial lately, especially among police ranks which perceive it as primarily an occupational threat, the principle has some definite advantages:

1   —It reflects and strengthens the role of police management as a specialized field based on the cooperation between experts.

94. Patrick Murphy and David Brown,   95. *Ibid.*, p. 29.
    *The Changing Nature of Police Organ-
    ization*, (Washington, D.C.: Leader-
    ship Resources, Inc.), 1973, p. 27.

2   —It improves the police image and raises its level of professionalization in the public eye.

3   —It improves the department's capability of making sound decisions by broadening its base of qualified decision makers.

4   —It improves the department's planning and programming efforts furnished by specialized staff.

5   —It provides legal and scientific advice to all levels of police cadres.

6   —It provides an opportunity for field training to officers working with specialized staff.

7   —It stimulates serious research in crime related areas which for decades have been taken for granted by inside crews.

8   —It enhances the police problem-solving capability.

(4) Central Police Dispatch (CPD)—Muskegon County, Michigan. The Central Police Dispatch consolidated the radio dispatch services of nine law enforcement agencies. Until CPD, the agencies' services were limited, confused, inefficient, and costly.[96] For instance:

1   —Eight of the nine departments operated on a single radio frequency independently of each other.

2   —Only four of the nine departments had around-the-clock dispatch service seven days a week.

3   —Nearly 10 percent of the combined personnel in the agencies were assigned to dispatch services.

By pooling the radio dispatch resources of the agencies, CPD provided all nine departments with around-the-clock, seven day service, eliminated confusion and duplication, and reduced the number of dispatch personnel required. Moreover, the centralized service helped implement the 911 emergency system in sparsely populated areas.

Spurred by the success of their combined managerial effort, the nine agencies have pooled their resources to create a Central Narcotics Unit (CNU) and a Crime Prevention Bureau (CPB).

(5) Citizen Dispute Settlement Program—Columbus, Ohio. The CDS program provides an out-of-court method for resolving neighborhood and family disputes through mediation. The program saves many police lives and the enormous man-hour efforts by uniformed policemen distracted from the original stream of fighting street crimes. At the same time, the program also spares regular prosecutors, judges, and courtroom staff the workload of a multiplicity of mi-

---

96. *The Exemplary Projects Program,* a publication of the National Institute of Law Enforcement and Criminal Justice, Washington, D.C., December, 1975, p. 5.

nor criminal cases. The average cost per case handled by the program is about $27 compared to $100 for regular prosecution and trial procedures.[97]

Cases in the program are screened and referred by the local prosecutor's office for a hearing within a week after the complaint is filed. Law students trained as mediators meet with the disputants during convenient evening and weekend hours to help them solve their problems without resorting to formal charges and court procedures.

(6) Police Legal Liaison Division—Dallas, Texas and Other Cities. The Dallas Police Legal Liaison Division successfully integrates two components of the criminal system that often operate in isolation—the police and prosecutor. Its primary purpose is reducing the number of cases "no-billed" or dismissed due to police error, therefore increasing the efficiency and effectiveness of police work in Dallas.

Since 1973, assistant city attorneys in Dallas have been on call 24 hours a day to advise Dallas police officers on case preparation. In addition, the attorneys provide regular training for police in the elements of various offenses, proper search and seizure procedures, and other aspects of the law.

To achieve its stated goal, the division has established a case review system. All prosecution reports are reviewed for legal sufficiency before they are submitted to the DA's office. As a result, the number of "no-bills" due to police error have dropped from 13.8 percent to 4.3 percent during a two year period. Similarly, felony dismissals resulting from police error were reduced from 6.4 percent to 2.6 percent during the same period.[98]

Increased convictions, although important, are not the only measure of the project's success. More informed decision-making by police in such sensitive areas as arrest and search and seizure certainly means greater respect for the constitutional rights of individuals and the fairness of the department.

97. *Ibid.*, p. 7.   98. *Ibid.*, p. 3.

PART FOUR

ELEMENTS OF POLICE MANAGEMENT

Introduction

While management started as the younger sister of organization, it has undoubtedly grown to be a maverick agent with unlimited potential. The successful maintenance and growth of today's complex administration must be attributed to the proliferation of *management unlimited* rather than to organization theory.

While organization still provides the foundation for any administrative endeavor, effective management has evolved as the prime mover of administrative action. Further, while it is evident that organization consistently sought the preservation of the administrative status quo, management consistently pursued breakthroughs that produced administrative reform and coped with insoluble problems. As proven by the victory in WW II and by the overwhelming expansion in government services ever since, management today has become the potent instrument of change in public and private administrations. It generated new ideas and figured unorthodox means for implementing them. It proposed new functions for bureaucracies and offered new methods for operating them. Management thought today has influenced modern organizations, dominated all successful programs, and distinguished competent executives. By so doing, the management component of administration has brought organization theories to a near maturity. It has helped bring about the ultimate reason for their being: the optimal achievement of goals along with the maximum enrichment of workers.

Thomas Philips perhaps best described the crucial role of management, when he said:

> Every individual, organization or society must mature but much depends on *how* this maturing takes place. A society (organization) whose maturing consists simply of acquiring more firmly established ways of doing things is headed for the graveyard—even if it learns to do these things with greater and greater skills. In the ever-renewing (organization) what matures is a system or framework within which continuous innovation, renewal and rebirth can occur.[1]

1. Thomas P. Philips, *Roots of Strategy*, (Harrisburg, Pennsylvania: Military Science Publishing Co.), 1955, p. 23.

The *major elements* of management, within which a "continuous innovative, renewal and rebirth" of administration can occur, are:

I   —Planning.

II   —Decision-making.

III   —Communication.

IV   —Leadership.

CHAPTER EIGHT

MANAGEMENT OF POLICE PLANNING

Overview

The term planning originated in the Latin word *plánus,* meaning "flat". The word was so used perhaps with reference to the shape of the earth and other "planets", which were considered at the time to be flat. The term later meant "clear", "evident", or "obvious". The contemporary use of the term refers to the "flattening" of a project or *making it clear* by devising a scheme of action, a draft, or a forum.

Throughout history man always needed a necessary amount of planning. The more complicated man's problems the more he needed planning for his survival, stability, and growth, and the more sophisticated his planning techniques had to be. Man needed planning in order to fill a crucial gap in his daily pursuit of individual and group accomplishments—to calculate and avoid risks. The gap was created by (1) his need to prepare for tomorrow's business and (2) his inability to know the future. The only logical reconciliation between these two situations is the concept of planning. It offers the only hope for rational thinking into the unknown.

Appropriate planning depends upon appropriate knowledge. While planning itself is a neutral term which could mean either "good" or "bad" planning, effective planning has to rely on the collection of facts, the understanding of their meaning, and the construction of a future pattern by projecting trends or drawing reasonable generalizations about those facts. Modern planning in administrative institutions therefore requires an elaborate inquiry into their economic prospective, their social environments, their legal implications and their value systems, among other factors. Today, due to the continuous need for administrative reform and the availability of all sorts of computerized data, management planning has become essential to the appropriate direction and growth of public agencies.[2] Katz and Kahn emphasized that "any organization that does not have a four, five or a ten-year plan is risking destruction or a series of continuing crises in its operation".[3]

Planning is a process of everyday life. No longer restricted to administrative purposes, planning has become a societal necessity.

2 Daniel Katz and Robert Kahn, *The Social Psychology of Organizations,* (New York: John Wiley and Sons, Inc.), 1966, p. 272.

3. *Ibid.*

Because of the rapid change in human needs, conditions and resources, individuals and groups have diligently sought to increase their productivity by reducing economic waste and unnecessary pain. To achieve such a high degree of efficiency and effectiveness, individuals and groups must make appropriate decisions which minimize their risks and maximize their gains. It became common, therefore, to hear and watch people today practice career planning, insurance planning, health planning, family planning, recreational planning and even burial planning. At the administrative level, the most common types of planning include economic planning, policy planning, strategic planning, operational planning, procedural planning, personnel planning among others.

Planning is an attempt to read the future. It deals basically with the prediction of future trends. In French the term used for planning is *prevoir* which means "seeing ahead". Management planning, therefore, cannot deal with present or past events except in terms of their significance as relevant data to be used as research materials. The time span involved in planning projects varies from one case to another. While planning in the U.S.S.R. usually involves periods between five to seven years, most American plans are concerned with one or two years at a time. Naturally, the longer the time span involved in the plan, the less accurate it will be because of the difficulty in calculating the number and impact of changing variables in the remote future. Although most budgetary plans today are still limited to a one year period, quite a few agencies operate on a biennial budgetary plan, and several police organizations have devised a five-year plan for improving police performance and reducing crime rates.[4] The problem with five-year plans for police is obviously the lack of reliability since they must depend on assumptions and unsubstantiated prediction.

What distinguishes planning from fortune-telling is the fact that the former must be an intellectual process, well-organized and carried out in a methodical manner. For planning to be worthwhile, it has to be based on fundamental facts regarding resources that are carefully assembled and thoroughly analyzed and upon an examination of the various factors which must be brought together to form a unified direction for action.[5] As an intellectual process, planning is thus *the rational determination of courses of action*—the basing of decisions on purpose, facts and considered estimates.[6]

4. See, for instance, the five-year plan for the Dallas, Texas, Police Department released in 1973 by Chief Frank Dyson.

5. Charles E. Merriam, "The National Resources Planning Board", in G.B.

Galloway, (ed.), *Planning for America*, 1941, p. 486.

6. Yehezkel Dror, "The Planning Process: A Facet Design", in *Planning, Programming, Budgeting, A Systems*

Planning is not an end in itself. If it is, it would only become a game of intellectual forecasting. The purpose of management planning is simply to *help make sound management decisions.* Planners are staff members who make no policy decisions. They only study, research, and recommend alternative courses of action. Their influence on the decision-making process stems basically from the depth of their research, the realism of their plan, and the wide variety of decisional options they can offer. Aside from their managerial skill in "selling" the plan and standing by it during the implementation stage and the evaluation stage, proficiency in planning is indicated by the merits of each plan. Given the necessary talents and training, planners (analysts, advisors, or consultants, as they are sometimes called) can become exceedingly sophisticated in the use of quantitative analysis, research methods, problem identification, and problem-solving techniques.

The SCART (science and art) of planning deals mainly in estimates. Even the most effective plan, when implemented, may vary slightly from reality. As long as planners, especially in the areas of behavioral sciences, use human values and judgment, the subjective evaluation by planners must be expected to be less than exact. For example, the famous plans suggested by the President's Commission on Law Enforcement and the Administration of Justice in 1967 and 1973 never quite worked as planned. By the same token, state and local criminal justice plans all over the nation which aimed at the reduction of crime by certain percentages never really met their prescribed goals. Like other plans in the areas of economics, employment, and environmental control, highly elaborate plans, while proving viable in the aggregate, never turned out to be mathematically exact. Nevertheless, the value of planning even with an admissible margin of error has always been invaluable.

Management planning is the optimal use of reliable predictions for administrative purposes. It is a serious attempt to apply foresight to administrative decisions. Administrators cannot wait until all conditions are brought under man's complete control in accurate forecast before they decide to build a dam, set up an employment compensation scheme or operate a police department. Administrators, for all practical purposes, would be waiting indefinitely for exact projections, which are unlikely to come about. Management planning must then be viewed as only a SCART capable of producing valuable estimates. The value of those estimates, however, is usually enhanced by the skills and the reliability of the individual planner.

Approach to Management, ed. by Fremont Lyden and Ernest Miller, (Chicago: Markham Publishing Company), 1968, p. 97.

Planning Defined

Planning has been defined as:

. . . the systematic, continuous, forward-looking application of the best intelligence available to programs of common affairs.—National Resources Board[7]

. . . the process of determining the objectives of administrative efforts and of devising the means calculated in achieving them.—John D. Millett [8]

. . . definition of the objective of an enterprise, formulation of policies governing its achievement, designing a system of procedures whereby the objective is achieved precisely and with minimum waste of the energies employed. —H.S. Person [9]

. . . the working out in broad outline the things that need to be done and the methods for doing them to accomplish the purpose set for the enterprise.—Luther H. Gulick [10]

. . . the fullest and most rational utilization of all work and of all the material resources of the community, in the light of a scientific forecast of the trends of economic development and with strict observance of the laws of social development.—A Soviet economist [11]

Yehezkel Dror in his brilliant analysis of the planning process probably presented the most comprehensive and articulate definition of planning. He divided his definition into seven distinct parts. Planning, he said, is: [12]

1 —The process (. . . a continuous activity in sequential order).

2 —Of preparing (. . . furnishing with necessary provisions).

3 —A set (. . . a group of interdependent elements).

7. National Resources Board, *A Report on National and Public Works*, 1934, p. 83.

8. John D. Millett, *Management in the Public Service*, (New York: McGraw-Hill Book Company), 1954, p. 55.

9. H.S. Person, "Research and Planning as Functions of Administration and Management", in Dwight Waldo, *Ideas and Issues in Public Adminis-*

tration, (New York: McGraw-Hill Book Company), 1953, p. 396.

10. Luther H. Gulick, "Notes on the Theory of Organization", *Papers on the Science of Administration*, 1937, p. 13.

11. Yehezkel Dror, *op. cit.*, p. 97.

12. *Ibid.*, pp. 99–100.

4 —Of decisions for action (. . . choices among possible alternatives to be carried out).

5 —In the future (. . . emphasis on uncertainty and the need for prediction).

6 —Directed at achieving goals (. . . emphasis on reaching defined objectives).

7 —By optimal means (. . . selecting the most effective methods at the least cost).

In summary, planning may be defined as *the process of facilitating management decision-making by clarifying agency problems and by recommending rational courses of action for their solution through means of systematic, intellectual research.*

Police Planning

Serious planning is one of the most needed functions by the police today. A police force cannot be effective, or even survive, if it is administered on a day-to-day or crisis-to-crisis basis. Perhaps because of the frequent life and death activities by many policemen or because of the long-lasting, and often awesome, consequences of the decisions they have to make on the street every day, police agencies need all the planning they can develop to minimize their errors. Effective police planning can save the lives of both policemen and the private citizens. It can also improve the quality of police services; streamline police operations; increase police productivity; enhance the police image; improve police-community relations; economize in cost, time, and effort; and, above all, reduce crime. The failure of a police executive to recognize the need for administrative planning certainly disqualifies him as a manager, let alone as an effective one. And his department will have to suffer the consequences of his lack of understanding, resentment to adaptation, or pure ineptness. The following definitions makes this even more evident.

Police planning:

[is] the process of developing a method or procedure or an arrangement of parts intended to facilitate the achievement of a defined objective.—O.W. Wilson [13]

. . . means using a rational design or pattern for all departmental undertakings rather than relying on chance.— John Kenney [14]

. . . involves the marshalling of facts relevant to the solution of particular problems, evaluation or alternative so-

13. O.W. Wilson, *Police Planning*, (Springfield, Illinois: Charles C. Thomas), 1952, p. 3.

14. John Kenney, *Police Management Planning*, (Springfield, Illinois: Charles C. Thomas), 1959, p. 7.

lutions, and detailing in advance the action to be taken toward implementing desired changes.—John Ashby [15]

Police planning is thus an intellectual attempt to upgrade police activities and enable the police organization to cope with internal changes as well as within its environments. *It is a step by step analysis of police goals and functions and the devising of optimal means to make them realities.*

Police planning is a primary managerial function. It requires a closer look into *all* aspects of police activities: procedural, operational, organizational, tactical, financial, or developmental. Improvements of this nature cannot be accomplished in a haphazard manner or at the whim of the chief executive. They require the continuous, systematic, and forward-looking exercise of planning. Effective planning is not only necessary to develop new plans but to review the operations of the department and to modify them or replace them when needed.

No police agency can afford to remain static while the community is changing. Even when no noticeable change takes place in the size of the community, changes in the composition of the population occur. Changes in the age and sex composition, changes in the way people earn a living, changes in status of residents, and physical changes in the community all are factors affecting current police policies and operations. Without planning for these changes, the police agency will certainly be caught unprepared.[16]

THE POLICE PLANNER

Effective police planning requires effective police planners. Although modern computers can be programmed to collect, classify, and probably analyze data, the role of the planner is still irreplaceable. He is the one who programs them in the first place. Also, only human planners can assess the human, cultural, social, and behavioral data which enter the planning process "in pursuit of rational courses of action". To carry out this function of interpreting the data, police planners must also engage in research and analysis. Crime trends must be studied as well as the intervening factors associated with them. Experimental projects must be devised to test novel police policies and techniques on a limited scale and under controlled conditions. Models for innovative police operations must be introduced and resulting findings evaluated. A whole atmosphere of critical thinking, rational reasoning, and methodical outlook must prevail. Police planners must, therefore, be selected from among the most

15. Harry More, *Effective Police Administration*, (San Jose, California: Justice Systems Development, Inc.), 1975, p. 181.

16. John Ashby, James L. LeGrande, and Raymond T. Galvin, "The Nature of the Planning Process", *Law Enforcement Planning*, (Washington: U. S. Government Printing Office), 1968, pp. 1–3.

competent, educated, and trained personnel. A combination of a
background in behavioral sciences with adequate training in quantitative research and ample police experience seems exemplary. Planners with less qualifications (who constitute the large majority of police planners today) evidently need further training. The 1973 Task
Force Report criticized the present state of police planners by complaining that: "planning assignments are often assigned to personnel
without adequate training in planning processes or techniques." The
report further charged that personnel are often assigned to planning
units or are given planning assignments for reasons other than their
expertise in planning." [17]

> The report later emphasized the need for trained police planners:
>
> Every police agency should provide training necessary for
> all personnel to carry out their planning responsibilities
> . . . . If there are planning needs that cannot be satis-
> fied by agency personnel, the police agency should satisfy
> these needs through an appropriate arrangement with an-
> other police agency, another government agency, or a pri-
> vate consultant.[18]

To insure the competence of police planners, the report stated
that every police agency should determine the qualifications of such
personnel, establish these qualifications in writing, and provide procedures for the evaluation of candidates for such assignments. In compliance with these stipulations, police agencies have recently started
"to do something about it." The results have led to a mosaic of different types, forms, and shapes of planning units. While in the large
metropolitan departments the planning function is handled by a highly specialized group of well-trained and well-paid specialists, in small
departments the function is still usually perceived as an additional
headache assigned to the chief, his deputy, or "one of the clever boys
—whenever he has the time to get around to it."

The Police Planner vs. the Outside Consultant

While the use of outside consultants in police planning processes
is on the increase, such fashionable practice is certainly not without
reproach. Many large police departments today take pride in hiring
"big name" planners for diverse reasons. Foremost among these reasons are elevated prestige, availability of grant funds, and obsession
with technological systems. While hiring outside consultants does
not necessarily create an air of euphoria among the rank and file of
the department, plans produced by such consultants do not necessari-

17. *Task Force on Police*, 1973, p. 119.   18. *Ibid.*, p. 117.

ly prove invaluable either.   There are, however, five obvious advantages of the outside consultants.

1   —They are highly specialized in research methodology.

2   —They have an objective view uninfluenced by local practices and traditions.

3   —They are independent by virtue of being removed from departmental chain of command.

4   —They are neutral in the sense of having no particular interest in the outcome of the process.

5   —They add to the prestige of the department.

On the other hand, outside consultants usually share these disadvantages:

1   —They are not attuned and are generally uncommitted to the local cultural and social environments.

2   —They tend to have difficulty collecting the necessary data, especially from disenchanted department personnel.

3   —They tend to use sophisticated language alien to the department members.

4   —They tend to suggest the same solutions they discovered in previous projects elsewhere.

5   —They are not around to take the blame if the plan proves unsuccessful.

6   —They tend to become hostile if their plan is not adopted by the department.

Without any need for repetition, the advantages and disadvantages of the inside police planner could easily be understood by comparing them with those of the outside consultant.

The Need for Planning

Virtually every aspect of police activity lends itself to management planning. It is no surprise, therefore, that the Task Force Report cited earlier insisted that "every police agency should develop planning processes which will anticipate short and long-term problems and suggest alternative solutions to them." [19]   Only through effective planning can the management of police services be synchronized in a predictable and systematically-designed pattern.

O.W. Wilson, a police leader who championed administrative planning over a quarter of a century ago, insisted that the planning unit must examine "the minute detail of every aspect of police organization, operation, and management," and attempt by analysis and contemplation "to increase the effectiveness of police efforts and the

19. *Ibid.*

economy of their operations in every field." [20]   John Kenney, like Wilson, emphasized the need for police planning by declaring that it combines all aspects of the department and that it "relates patrol operations to investigation, to records, to reporting, to communications and to all other aspects of departmental work." [21]   Lack of effective planning would leave the department as an aggregate of *aimless divisions and units* bereft of a central guidance mechanism capable of uniting their efforts and directing their activities toward the achievement of prescribed goals.

Aside from its role as a central guidance mechanism for the department as a whole, effective planning can be of direct assistance in these specialized areas:

1   —Police policy-making: by examining future trends and necessary changes in department rules and regulations which entail the definition of department goals, institutional values, effective control, supervision techniques and general areas of department effectiveness and efficiency.

2   —Police role-taking analysis: by proposing the necessary changes in the present police role in the community; orienting the department on issues such as "victimless" crimes, selective non-enforcement of laws, juvenile justice, community participation, and other crime prevention techniques.

3   —Police recruitment and selection: by suggesting required standards for employment; balancing representation on the force, upgrading educational requirements, and providing for a fair system for selection among applicants.

4   —Police training: by examining the adequacy of present pre-service and in-service programs; developing minimum curriculum requirements; certifying police training centers and establishing minimum qualifications for instructors; inspecting and periodically evaluating all training programs to insure compliance with training standards.

5   —Police operations: by planning for the functional responsibilities determined by department policies;· coordinating a 24-hour-a-day police service by those assigned to specific tasks, such as patrol, traffic, criminal investigation, etc.

6   —Fiscal control: by initiating annual budget planning with a detailed statement on budgetary needs, performance measurement, cost-effectiveness analysis, and efficiency control methods.

7   —Police-community relations: by analyzing social trends, community expectations, public support; proposing programs for informing the public; soliciting community participation and involve-

20.   O.W. Wilson, *op. cit.*, p. 12.   21.   John Kenney, *op. cit.*, p. 8.

ment in the crime problem and devising means for stimulating police-community cooperation.

8 —Police personnel management: by researching the areas of
police morale, loyalty, and bureaupathy within the force; revising old
personnel regulations; providing meaningful incentives; suggesting
promising career ladders and introducing a fair and a motivating
schedule for pay, promotion and compensation.

The Police Planning Process

As of yet, modern technology hasn't been able to produce a planning machine capable of accurately predicting the future or "rationally" selecting among alternatives. While the "computer community"
claims it has the technological ability to process and analyze planning
data, the sensitive evaluation of human needs will aways remain with
planners. Therefore, while the basic steps in the police planning
process are initially the same, several authors have presented them
with different emphasis. While some have limited the process to its
basic steps, others extended them to include some pre-planning and
post-planning steps.

O.W. Wilson explained that the planning process encompasses
five basic steps: (1) the need for the plan to be recognized; (2) a
statement of the objective to be formulated; (3) relevant data to be
gathered and analyzed; (4) details of the plan to be developed; and
(5) concurrences to be obtained from organizational units whose operations may be affected by the proposed plan.[22] Although Wilson
did not get into a detailed analysis of each step, he nevertheless emphasized these characteristics of the planning process:

a —the practicality of the plan under present conditions;

b —the feasibility of the plan as determined by external factors like community resources, attitudes, and cooperation by
affiliated agencies;

c —the ability of the planning staff to research and recommend
a "complete plan";

d —the orientation of the operating personnel to the planning
process and their competence in carrying it out;

e —the organizational flexibility of the agency to delegate authority and place the necessary responsibility for implementing the plan [23].

John Kenney explained the mechanics of the planning process in
nine steps which he stated "would provide an orderly means for the
development of plans, be they large or small, long-range or short-

22. O.W. Wilson, *op. cit.*, p. 14.   23. *Ibid.*, pp. 17–20.

range." [24]   Kenney presented his model as a framework for the consideration of any planning process. His nine steps are: [25]

1 —Constructing a frame of reference for the plan by examining the situation for which the plan is being developed.

2 —Clarifying the problem by identifying its record and its possible solutions.

3 —Collecting all pertinent facts.

4 —Analyzing the facts.

5 —Developing alternative courses of action which appear to be logically comparable to the needs of the situation.

6 —Selecting the most appropriate alternative.

7 —Selling the plan.

8 —Arranging for execution of the plan.

9 —Evaluating the effectiveness of the plan.

Compared to Wilson's model, Kenney's model of the planning process is more comprehensive and detailed and covers several pre-planning and post-planning steps. The model, which in fact furnishes a "plan for planning", emphasizes these requisites:

a —There is a need for a frame of reference which integrates agency needs, concerns, opinions and ideas by operating officers and configurates the collective desire of the members to effect some type of management change.

b —There must be an emphasis on collection and analysis of factual information. Only such facts that have relevance should be considered. No factual information may be discarded or overlooked unless truly considered immaterial or irrelevant.

c —There must be an emphasis on the role of the planning staff as successful businessmen selling their product. Any plan, regardless of its prospective effectiveness, indicates an explicit or subtle need to change the normal course of action. This arouses natural fear or doubt on the part of the operating subdivisions and of the members to be affected by change. The planning staff must then spread a reassuring environment and generate an optimistic view conducive to the rational approval of the anticipated change.

d —There must be active promotion of the executive plan. Although technically not a part of the planning process, Kenney emphasized the need for the issuance of orders and directives to involved units and personnel, the establishment of a schedule, and the provision of manpower and equipment for carrying out the plan.

24.   John Kenney, *op. cit.*, p. 21.   25.   *Ibid.*, pp. 21-23.

e —There must be an assessment of the plan. The results of the plan should be determined in order to know whether a correct alternative was chosen, whether the plan was correct, which phase (if any) was poorly implemented, and whether additional planning is necessary.

Harry More added another model for the process of planning. He suggested that the scientific approach be recommended in all the fields of police planning. While the model did not add to the ingredients presented by Wilson and Kenney, More capitalized on an integrated model that combined the highlights of both. More's model involved: [26] (1) the discovery of the problem, (2) the isolation and clarification of the problem, (3) the collection and analysis of pertinent data and opinions, (4) the identification and evaluation of alternatives, and (5) the selection between alternatives. Immediately following his listing of steps, More added that "it may be necessary to sell the plan, arrange for its execution, and evaluate its effectiveness." [27]

Yet another model was presented by O'Neil, Bykowski, and Blair. They focused on the causative relationships in the planning process. They viewed the process as a continuous effort of research, change, and improvement. They proclaimed that the planning process does not even have to begin with a problem. Rather, the process develops from the inescapable relationship among causative factors, problem and need determination, and plan development.[28] The authors identified the causative factors as relating to external influences from the community and internal influences from within the police department itself. The need determination is established by the study of the existing difficulties that persist as a result of the causative factors and the anticipated solutions that would remove these difficulties and make the situation more acceptable. Plan development is the process of devising methods for the attainment of objectives and the achievement of specific and recognizable results.

The Police Planning Process: A Facet Design

Although the beforementioned models by Wilson, Kenney, More, and O'Neil—Bykowski—Blair have adequately described the planning process and devised some guidelines for its completion, the models seem to have overlooked a major aspect of the planning process: *its multi-dimensional nature.* The police planning function is certainly

---

26. Harry W. More, Jr., (editor), *Effective Police Administration*, (San Jose, California: Justice Systems Development, Inc.), 1975, pp. 185–192.

27. *Ibid.*

28. Michael E. O'Neil, Ronald F. Bykowski and Robert S. Blair, *Criminal Justice Planning*, (San Jose, California: Justice Systems Development, Inc.), 1976, p. 30.

much more pervasive and interdependent than the simple task of following a certain set of steps or procedures. The planning process, if it is to be effective, must carefully examine *all* the factors which could contribute to the appropriate development of the plan. Therefore, a plan for a police-community project, for instance, must consider the police facet involved in the project with its values, ideologies, power-groups and resources as well as the community facet with its background, demographic, social, cultural and economic factors. But these are not all. The successful preparation of such a plan will also have to depend on the ability of the planning unit, the expertise of its members, its institutional attitude, status and power. Finally the appropriateness of planning will also have to depend on the form of plan to be arrived at, such as long-term, short-term, fixed, conditional, or otherwise. The police planning activity today must recognize the nature of planning as a *methodology of rational thought and action* rather than a specific blueprint for one set or another of planning steps. Modern police planning is a very sensitive operation which is shaped and conditioned by many intervening variables. Without the thorough examination of each facet, the planning process would most likely fail to materialize as a realistic design for successful action.[29]

Following the concept of facet as originally developed by Louis Guttman, effective police planning must be viewed in terms of a composition of some primary facets. Each of these primary facets is the product of a number of secondary facets which in turn are the product of a series of tertiary facets, and so on. For example, the police-community in question would be a primary facet. Secondary facets would include the physical layout of the district where the community resides; community background in terms of its social composition, ethnic differences, religious beliefs, etc.; community resources in terms of manpower, capital, knowledge, etc.; and the terms of reference within which the community identifies its goals, objectives, desires and expectations. Tertiary facets in this example naturally refer to the components of each of these secondary facets.

In order to carry on a meaningful discussion of the police planning facet design and analyze it in terms of primary and secondary facets, the same example of the police-community project will be used throughout this analysis as a basic frame of reference.

---

29. This discussion is based on Yehez-kel Dror's article, "The Planning Process: A Facet Design," *International Review of Administrative Sciences*, Vol. 29, No. 1 (1963) pp. 44–58. Among the most significant contributions to the study of the planning process is; Le Berton and Henning, *Planning Theory*, (Englewood Cliffs, N.J.: Prentice-Hall, Inc.), 1961; also see the files of the *Journal of the American Institute of Planners*, which include a number of valuable papers on the function, sequence, and characteristics of the planning process.

The four primary facets of the police planning process are: [30]

Primary Facet A: The general environment of the planning process.

Primary Facet B: The subject matter of the planning process.

Primary Facet C: The planning unit.

Primary Facet D: The form of the plan to be arrived at.

Primary Facet A: The General Environment of the Planning Process

While quite a few police plans are *transplanted* plans, the effectiveness of such plans is later determined by their acceptance by the environment or the amount of resentfulness mustered against them by those assigned to carry them out. This naturally explains why a police-community project, for instance, would work in one city in the Northeast but fail in the South. On one hand, the planning activity is shaped and conditioned by various environmental factors; on the other hand, planning is in many cases directed at that environment trying to shape it to a greater or lesser extent.[31]

In the case of the police-community project, Facet A will then have to include two secondary facets:

FA–C, the environment of the community (C)

FA–P, the environment of the police (P)

Each secondary facet, FA-C or FA-P, will consist of several tertiary facets. Therefore, FA-C for instance will include these:

FA–C$_1$	Basic physical, demographic, ecological, cultural, geo-physical, geo-economic factors.
FA–C$_2$	Community resources in manpower, capital, industry, education, etc.
FA–C$_3$	Community values, ideologies, beliefs, sentiments, etc.
FA–C$_4$	Community goals, demands, expectations, desires, etc.

Secondary facet FA-P could obviously be assessed in terms of tertiary facets similar to those cited for FA-C.

Primary Facet B: The Subject Matter of the Planning Process

The subject matter in the case of a police-community project is obviously the improvement in attitudes, sentiments, and behavior of

---

30. Yehezkel Dror, "The Planning Pro-   31. *Ibid.*
     cess: A Facet Design", *op. cit.*

the police and the community. Its purpose is the development of a mutually favorable and responsive relationship that emphasizes the role of the police as a part of, not apart from, the community they serve. The subject matter could, therefore, be as comprehensive as to involve the total orientation of the police organization. It could obviously influence and possibly change the organizational and managerial techniques of all the units in the police department, not merely in a specialized bureau or office within the department.

The subject matter of the planning process in the example of a police-community project can be viewed as consisting of seven secondary facets:

FB₁   The scope of the activity subjected to planning in terms of public relations, community service, community participation, etc.

FB₂   Its significance in terms of urgency, need, and societal or legal pressures.

FB₃   The extent to which the subject matter is predetermined by constitutional, statutory, legal, traditional, religious or moral constraints.

FB₄   The extent to which the subject matter has already been subjected to planning. This refers to the relationship between the planning process and previous plans prescribed by higher levels in the criminal justice system, the judiciary, or legislative bodies.

FB₅   The orientation of the subject matter toward the planning process. Planning for a police-community project can naturally have a more meaningful and positive result today than it would have had fifty years ago. This is due to the presence of more institutions and groups involved in the subject matter and the availability of various theories which could lend themselves to the planning process of the subject matter.

FB₆   The degree of penetration into the details of the subject matter. The planning process, in the case of a police-community project, can naturally penetrate today into socioeconomic issues and subjects which were considered too sensitive fifty years ago. Examples would include racial integration and representation among members of the police force. Other subjects, nevertheless, are still planned with a superficial level of penetration. These pertain, for instance, to issues of forced busing and racial violence.

FB₇   The time-span available for the completion of the planning process. The selection of an optimal time-span that provides for ample research and thorough examination of the intervening factors of the subject matter is crucial to the planning process. Without the allotment of such an optimal time-span, which is commensurate with the complexity of the subject matter, the planning process may turn out to be incomplete, superficial or hasty.

Primary Facet C: The Planning Unit

The characteristics of the police planning unit can be detrimental to the effectiveness of the planning process. In the absence of a qualified staff with distinguished expertise in the areas of behavioral methodology, quantitative analysis, and objective reasoning, the planning process may turn out to be another exercise in group prejudice, irrational thinking, slanted prediction or interest-motivated conclusions.

The characteristics of the planning unit are the product of six secondary facts:

FC_1 The basic nature of the planning unit. This refers to the education, training, and expertise of the members of the planning unit. Special attention must be focused on the institutional mood of the planning unit which is the composite configuration of all individual members of the unit and not identifiable, therefore, with that of any particular member. The institutional mood may be described in terms of enlightenment, progressiveness, optimism, or otherwise, in terms of closed-mindedness, indifference or pessimism.

FC_2 Primary or delegated planning. The former relates to planning conducted directly by the planning unit within the department. The latter refers to planning conducted by another unit—usually a specialized unit within the criminal justice system—or by outside consultants.

FC_3 Status of the planning unit. A unit with a high status can usually muster more power in terms of acquiring more resources which can be mobilized for the planning process and resisting external pressures directed at the planning process.

FC_4 Values and character of the planning unit. The planning process in all its phases calls for consistent judgment involving the value systems, the professional integrity, and character of the planners. The effectiveness of the planning process depends on the level of honesty maintained by the police planners, their ability to uphold high moral values and to suppress natural bias and tendencies to be swayed by political pressures.

FC$_5$ Resources and means. This refers to the manpower, equipments, methods and funds at the disposal of the planning unit. Abundance of resources and sophistication of means have a definite influence on the success and effectiveness of the planning process.

FC$_6$ Organizational structure of the planning unit. Especially in larger units, the planning process is influenced by its organization in terms of hierarchical levels, specialization, control, and supervisory techniques. Naturally when the unit is organized along flexible lines and plans are thought out in a consensual fashion, the planning process would be considerably enhanced.

Primary Facet D: The Form of the Plan to be Arrived At

As stated earlier, the form of the plan to be arrived at is a major facet of the planning design. Planning units are seldom assigned to develop final plans since plans are technically never final. Therefore the success of the planning process has to hinge on the form of plan pursued by the planning unit to fit the purposes stipulated by the police department.

The form of the plan to be arrived at is the product of at least three secondary facets:

FD$_1$ The realism of the plan. While most police plans seek genuine solutions to present or anticipated problems, it is not uncommon for police departments to initiate plans directed at political advantages, capturing a lucrative grant, face-saving, or for mere training objectives. Leaving such "quasi-planning" aside, the effectiveness of a police-community project must coincide with a realistic approach to problem solving coupled with a serious intent to utilize the plan for the proclaimed purpose. "Phoney" planning is not only deceptive, unprofessional and probably illegal, it undermines the planning process by adulterating the subject-matter and demoralizing the planning unit.

FD$_2$ The type of plan. This secondary facet includes various types of plans such as long-range plans, short-term plans, or contingency plans to be executed at a given occurrence which might or might not happen in the future. As will be discussed later, police plans vary also by the nature of their purpose. They include strategic plans, procedural plans, operational plans, organizational plans, and various other types.

FD$_3$ Degree of details. The plan to be arrived at can be more or less detailed. In general, the longer the range to be covered by the plan, the more it will include general frameworks and directions, leaving details for shorter range plans or delegated planning. A related element of this facet is whether the plan will be a single alternative process (providing for one course of action) or a multi-alternative process (providing different courses of action for later selection in the light of developments).

To conclude this part on facet design planning, the planning process can then be regarded as:

P (planning) = A (general environment) x B (subject matter) x C (planning unit) x D (form of plan)

or

$$P = A \times B \times C \times D$$

Each primary facet in turn is the product of a number of secondary facets, namely:

$$A = AC \times AP$$

Each secondary facet is in turn a product of tertiary facets, therefore:

$$AC = AC_1 \times AC_2 \times AC_3 \times AC_4$$

The effectiveness of the planning process, therefore, could be quantitatively determined in advance by assigning a numerical value (on a scale of 1 to 10 for instance) to each primary, secondary and tertiary facet involved. The total value compared to the possible value would indicate the amount of effectiveness.

Typologies of Police Planning

Police plans may be classified in a number of ways. O.W. Wilson offered a typology of five kinds of plans: [32]

a —Procedural plans. They include every procedure that has been outlined and officially adopted as the standard method of action. They constitute standard operating procedures to be followed by all members of the department under specific circumstances, regardless of where and when the circumstances arise. Procedural plans relate to office, headquarters, and field operations. Examples include uniform regulations, reporting regulations, record-keeping procedures or booking procedures.

b —Operational plans. They include the work programs for the line divisions. They relate to work procedures necessary

32. The five kinds are taken from O.W. Wilson, *Police Planning*, (Springfield, Illinois: Charles C. Thomas), 1952, pp. 4–7.

to accomplish the purposes of patrol, crime investigation, traffic, vice, etc. Operational plans seek to analyze such work programs from the point of view of the nature, time, and place of the component tasks and to measure them in terms of manpower and equipment requirements.

c   —Management plans. They relate to the problems of equipping, staffing, and preparing the department to do the job, rather than to its actual operation as an organized force. They include the organization chart, the budget, personnel, accounting, training, rating, selection for promotion, discipline, etc.

d   —Tactical plans. They are methods of action to be taken at a designated location and under specific circumstances. They represent the application of procedures to specific situations such as cases of jail emergencies, hostage taking, or riot control procedures. They also deal with special community events such as athletic contests, parades or political rallies.

e   —Extra-departmental plans. They include those plans that require action or assistance from persons or agencies outside the police department or that relate to some form of community organization. Examples would include plans for cooperation with other criminal justice agencies, local government, or community boards interested in crime prevention, juvenile reform, treating drug addicts or alcoholics, etc.

John Kenney classified his typology of administrative police planning in four kinds: [33]

a   —Policy planning. They refer to the process whereby ideas, events, individuals and innumerable factors are combined in the police department to meet the needs for governing its affairs. Policy defines the goals, objectives, methods and resources of the agency and stipulates what should be done and why. Policy planning sets up the general rules by which organizational and operational activities are guided.

b   —Organizational planning. In a sense similar to Wilson's management planning, organizational planning relates to the structure of the department. It applies to the creation of units and sub-units, to jobs and grouping of jobs and to inter-relationships between hierarchical and divisional levels. Organizational planning is ordinarily governed by guidelines dictated by the local needs of the department.

c   —Operational planning. As a combination of Wilson's operational and tactical plans, they are developed to carry out all

33.   John P. Kenney, *op. cit.*, pp. 14–15.

police functional responsibilities. They control such activities as patrol, traffic, investigation, communication, as well as specialized operations described by Wilson as tactical.

d —Program planning. It integrates police organization and operational plans. It is the consolidation of all other plans into a program package that spells out what the department expects to accomplish, how, when, and at what cost. Most planning agencies at the federal and state levels emphasize program planning since it provides adequate integration of all other functions and responsibilities which would otherwise remain separated from the main mission of the agency.

Yet another typology of planning most applicable to police activities was presented by Robert Anthony. His classification included three kinds of planning which added a new role for the planning process. His typology emphasized the role of planning as a control technique which serves as a yardstick for measuring the effective disposition of allocated resources as well as the efficient use of these resources.

Anthony's classification consisted of three kinds: [34]

a —Strategic planning. It is the overall, long-range, comprehensive planning which requires a series of sequential decisions to be made upon further collection of information and consideration of anticipated moves by opponents. Strategic planning follows a general rule for deciding on objectives of the organization, on changes in these objectives, on the resources used to attain these objectives, and on the policies that are to govern the acquisition, use, and disposition of these resources. Anthony's strategic planning is a combination of Wilson's procedural planning and Kenney's policy planning. The concept of strategy, in addition, distinguishes police plans which are made in response to criminal activities or in anticipation of their probable occurrence.

b —Management control planning. It is the process by which managers assure that resources are obtained and used effectively and efficiently in the accomplishment of the organization's objectives. While this type of planning is analogous to Wilson's management planning and Kenney's program planning. In his analysis, planning establishes certain resource quotas along with measurements for effectiveness and efficiency to be applied by all personnel in charge of op-

34. Robert Anthony, *Planning and Control Systems* (Boston: Harvard University), 1965, pp. 24–71.

erations. The power of the plan therefore becomes a significant control element.

c —Operational control planning. Analogous to Wilson's tactical planning and Kenney's operational planning, Anthony's type is the process of assuring that specific tasks are carried out effectively and efficiently. Operational control planning covers both general tasks, such as patrol, criminal investigation, or vice, and specific tasks such as bank robberies, hostage taking or riot control operations.

CHAPTER NINE

MANAGEMENT OF POLICE DECISION-MAKING

Overview

Management is the art of rational change for administrative purposes. Change must be well-planned ahead and plans must be well-researched in advance. Planning and research, by themselves, however, cannot affect change in administration. While they may influence the minds of people, they fall short of directing their actions. Sophisticated as it may be, planning still remains a staff function and planners can only submit recommendations for change. Administrative change can only begin, however, after plans are selected, authorized and communicated within the organizational structure of the agency. Submitted plans are only theories which have to be studied and compared before a selection among the possible courses of action they offer is made. This process of selection based on appropriate study and comparison is the essence of decision-making.

Decision-making is an elaborate intellectual process. While man is considered a decision-making animal, his superior intellect sets him apart from his friends and relations in the animal world and is responsible for his constant domination over them. In the development of human civilization, man began with a biological decision-making mechanism which enabled him to survive hunger and natural disasters. As civilization grew, so did man's ability to develop cultural mechanisms for making decisions. Decisions were simply based on the pooling of experience that man obtained. Instead of decisions being limited to the experience of one individual or his family, the cultural pattern combined the experience of hundreds of individuals. Also, in this way the young were advised on appropriate actions to take in a variety of situations. The development of cultures preserved man's discoveries and transmitted them to successive generations.

The decision problems presented by civilization, however, later became more complex, and neither the biological nor the cultural mechanisms were adequate to handle them. Since the number of situations requiring decision-making became too large, and since that number was multiplied manifold with the advent of organized communities, it became increasingly difficult to specify in detail the appropriate course of action for every situation. As a result, a rapidly growing number of ritual responses were developed, and some superstitious patterns for the decision-making process were established to prevent chaos. Such superstitious patterns were based on soliciting decisions from gods and idols or by performing some magical litany to figure out the appropriate course of action to be taken. By applying this *devil theory* of decision-making, certain courses of action were ruled out, as likely to incur the wrath or disfavor of the deities who "controlled events and determined man's choices."

With further development in human civilization, mysticism and the devil theory were criticized by the "enlightened man" for their fabricated alibis, ambiguities, and metaphysical constraints. The age of reason, based on Aristotle's rules of logic, introduced a more realistic means for decision-making. As a convincing method of persuasion, reason gradually grew and became the most rational, reliable, and acceptable decision-making procedure. While not without reproach, the use of reason represented a substantial advance beyond the devil theory. It regarded the events of the real world as the products of causes not necessarily explainable through identical mediums. Explainable causes were considered "material"; unexplainable causes were considered "natural".

The successor to reason was science. It was viewed as capable of explaining the "natural causes", which were taken for granted by the reason theorists. Science provided new techniques of experimentation and measurement, as well as a symbolic language capable of testing, comparing and verifying facts. Science supplied the modern decision-maker with a "scientific method", which very quickly demonstrated its power in an irresistible manner. Statistical decision-making today is the most intellectual and powerful mechanism used by managers, and its exercise seems to have yielded many proven results.

Decision–Making Defined

There are three major definitions of decision-making:

. . . that thinking which results in the choice among alternative courses of action.—Donald Taylor [1]

Choices from among alternative courses of action; they help to shape the outputs that the units produce.—Ira Sharkansky [2]

A decision-maker is considered to be a machine. Into the machine flows information; out of the machine comes a recommended course of action.—Irwin Bross [3]

1. Donald W. Taylor "Decision Making and Problem Solving", in *Handbook of Organizations*, ed. James G. March, (Chicago: Rand McNally & Co.), 1965, p. 48.

2. Ira Sharkansky, *Public Administration*, (Chicago: Markham Publishing Company), 1972, p. 41.

3. Irwin D. J. Bross, *Design for Decisions*, (New York: The Free Press), 1953, p. 32.

Nature of Decision–Making

Decision-making is a purposeful process. Purposiveness brings about a recognized sense of direction to the behavior of workers in the absence of which their efforts would be spontaneous and aimless. Since administration strives on "getting things done" by groups of people, purpose-oriented decisions provide a principal criterion for determining what to do, when to do it, and who will do it. Managers in public service respond to the changing demands of their environments, as well as to the needs of their workers, by making purposeful decisions. External inputs from the environment include conflicting demands by the citizens and by members of the executive, legislative, and judicial branches of government. Internal needs include the expectations of workers to have favorable working conditions, adequate pay, stable relations, defined responsibilities and standards of performance. Decisions, therefore, lie at the center of the administrative process. They provide the basic control mechanism which governs the conduct of administrative agencies. Through the decision-making process, managers can determine the amount of input that enters the system, the way it is converted into output or services and the manner in which these services are delivered to the consumers.

As a dynamic purposeful process, James Rosenau described the decision-making process by saying:

> Decision-making sustains bureaucracies, dominates legislatures, preoccupies chief executives and characterizes judicial bodies. Decisions lead to policy, produce conflict, and foster cooperation.[4]

Decision-making is the art of compromise. All decisions in public service are made in relation to other possible choices. If a manager is faced with a situation which offers him no choice among alternatives, then the manager is not truly making a decision. His resolution in that case would be an act of administrative capitulation to events and the management of the agency would be seriously jeopardized. The opportunity to choose, which is the crux of the decision-making process, must provide the manager with at least two alternatives. Naturally the larger the number of options, the more appropriate the selection could be. The function of planning and research is primarily to widen these options for the decision-maker and, thus, make compromise and trade-offs among options both safer and easier.

Decision-making is a continuous process, which takes place all the time in public agencies. For the agency to survive and grow, management decisions regarding men, monies, methods and machines may have to be made periodically—on a daily or an hourly basis, or

4. James N. Rosenau, "The Premises and Promises of Decision Making Analysis", *Contemporary Political Analysis*, (New York: The Free Press), 1967, p. 195.

even much shorter.   For instance, the surgeon operating on a patient in a general hospital, the pilot flying a passenger plane, or the policeman cruising a heavily trafficked highway may have to make split-second operational decisions in order to protect the lives and properties of citizens.   Not only do administrative decisions shape the organization and its capability to deliver public services, they continuously have to address the questions of effectiveness, legality, morality, and economy of all transactions between public agencies and the clienteles they serve.

Decision-making is a rational process.   While public agencies in the past often exercised the administrative power of government through arbitrary decisions and capricious whims by administrators, the conduct of government today has tended, *or has been forced,* to follow a line of rationality, objectivity, and adherence to reason. Contemporary decision-makers are compelled by the forces of modern management to think in terms of the public interest, to make their decisions within the constraints of available resources, and to apply democratic principles to their selection process.   While absolute rationality is, of course, impossible, future decisions nevertheless will be more systematic, open to public scrutiny, and justifiable.   Harlan Cleveland projected that decision-making in the future will become "more collegial, consensual and consultative." [5]

Decision-making is a hierarchical process.   The concept of responsibility dictates the notion of a hierarchy of decisions—each level down the hierarchy ladder must abide in its decisions with the agency policies and standards set at the top.   In traditional organizations, the hierarchy of decisions consists of three levels: top management, middle management, and lower management.   The first deals with making decisions, the second with the supervision of decisions, and the third with the implementation of decisions. Modern management, however, seems to have amalgamated the three levels in a flexible chunk of *intraorganizational* decision machine with interlocking advisory committees, review boards, and staff feedback.   Cleveland described this complex machine of the decision-making process by saying: [6]

> At the upper levels of the bureaucracy the executive seldom writes a letter he signs, or signs a letter he writes   .   .   .
> On matters where he makes the 'final decision', he is surrounded—or prudently arranges to surround himself—with an intricate network of lateral clearances—personal relationships   .   .   .   veto groups and political personalities

5.   Harlan Cleveland, *The Future Exec-*   6.   *Ibid.*, p. 34.
utive, (New York: Harper and Row Publishers), 1972, p. 13.

whose views must be reconciled, offset, or discounted before a decision at that level will 'stick'.

The executive, described Cleveland, who is by function and temperament in motion, must see each decision as simply a milestone in a long and highly dynamic trip. Each decision is "the sequel to earlier and the prologue to his later moves and those of others." [7] Under modern management a policy decision by a chief of police, for instance, must take into consideration the demands, views and expectations of the rank and file, the sergeant group, and the lieutenants and captains. In addition, the chief's decision, if it is to be effective, must consider the views and expectations of people in city hall, interest groups and the mass media, among many others.

Finally, the decision-making process is necessarily one based on applied values. The function of knowledge in the process is, after all, partial. It only pertains to the understanding of consequences which would or could follow a certain choice among alternatives. The appropriateness of selection, moreover, depends on the appropriateness of values incorporated in the process. Such values provide a "criterion for choice" by which public decision-makers must abide. They naturally include values of democracy, constitutionality, legality, morality, and economy. While knowledge of the possible consequences of a decision can furnish the practical aspects of the decision-making process, abiding with applied values would provide the ethical part of the process. To determine whether a proposition is correct, and therefore ought to be selected, the decision-maker must equally examine its ethical content as well as its factual premises. For instance, a decision by a police "commissar" in the Soviet Union to prevent crime by banishing or locking up indefinitely all would-be criminals could be a most effective decision based on factual propositions. In the United States, such a decision would be strongly denounced because of its lack of moral value and legal foundation. Similar examples could be easily cited from the annals of American heritage, democratic tradition, and basic ethics.

While in theory, however, it might be easy to divide the decision-making process in terms of factual and ethical considerations, in reality it is extremely difficult since there are usually no clear lines of demarcation. Whether the commander of a riot control unit would decide to use major force against a group of rioters to achieve instant law enforcement, or use negotiation with the riot leaders to maintain peace and reflect a restrained police attitude, or decide to use nonlethal gas or riot batons to reinforce police authority with moderation would depend primarily on the commander's sense of judgment and his view of what is happening. While there are natu-

7. *Ibid.*, p. 35.

rally some general guidelines which should enter into the police commander's calculation of what is factual and what is ethical, in the final analysis it is his value judgment that could reconcile the boundaries of facts and values in an appropriate decision. Closely related to the mechanics of the decision in the commander's judgment must be the notions of "ways and means," "right and wrong", "legal" and "illegal", and perhaps "good" and "bad". While the process by which judgments are formed has been very imperfectly studied, judgment in decision making can be improved by managerial expertise, collegial consultations, education, and most importantly the decisions maker's sensitivity to events.

Inherent Limitations in Organizational Decision-Making

Not only do the conceptions of decision-making place a heavy emphasis on judgment and rationality, but such emphasis is even more complicated by the organization's limitations on the decision-making process. Anthony Downs cogently states that public officials "operate in a realistic world" and thousands of decisions have to be made by administrators within the existing constraints of bureaucratic structures. Some of the limitations which Downs cites are: [8]

a   —Each decision-maker can devote only a limited amount of time to decision-making.

b   —The functions of most administrators require them to become involved in more activities than they can consider simultaneously; hence, they must normally focus their attention on only part of the major concerns, while the rest remain latent.

c   —The amount of information initially available to every decision-maker about each problem is only a fraction of all the information potentially available on the subject.

d   —Additional information bearing on any particular problem can usually be procured, but the cost of procurement and utilization may rise rapidly as the amount of data increases.

e   —Important aspects of many problems involve information that cannot be procured at all, especially concerning future events; hence, many decisions must be made in the face of some ineradicable uncertainty.

To add to Downs list of organizational limitations, one may also note that:

(a) Bureaucratic officials are not particularly trained in the areas of research, logic and the use of advanced reasoning;

---

8. Anthony Downs, *Inside Bureaucracy*, (Boston: Little, Brown and Company), 1967, p. 75.

hence, their decisions usually lack the in-depth analysis of intervening variables based on thorough isolation and evaluation of issues.

(b) Public problems are by definition controversial problems which touch heavily on conflicting social, economic, or moral issues; hence, there usually is no consensus on how to approach them, and proposed decisions may vary by as many decision-makers as are involved in the process of decision.

(c) Public officials do not have the independence necessary for making objective and impartial decisions. Especially in strategic or policy decisions, considerable pressures are focused on decision-makers by politicians, civic leaders, interest groups and other bureaucrats.

(d) Important public decisions necessarily commit public funds which are controlled by independent legislative bodies. Since public funds are usually scarce and are in great demand by competing agencies, public decisions are in most cases tailored to fit the available or promised funds. Costly decisions may be too hard to justify and defend.

THE MICRODYNAMICS OF DECISION-MAKING

A most problematic question in decision-making is the "how" question. Everyday people make thousands of decisions which are mostly "habitual" or do not require intentional thinking at the moment. Examples of these habitual decisions involve shaving in the morning, showering at night, riding a bus, or turning the ignition key to start a car. "Particular" decisions, on the other hand, require intentional thinking and involve non-habitual situations requiring a selection process of options. The raw material for decision in both cases is information either stored in the brain, as in the case of habitual decisions, or accumulated at the time of the decision, as is the case in the latter. Embedded in the stored information, however, in the case of habitual decisions, is a value scale which is accepted at face value. In cases of intentional thinking, a desirability scale has to be devised on a case-by-case basis and applied to each separate situation.

Managerial decisions are primarily particular decisions which require a process of intentional thinking. Such decisions are made to produce outcomes or anticipated changes in desired directions. In its simplest form the decision-maker is considered to be a machine. Into the machine flows information; out of the machine comes a recommended course of action. The purpose of managerial decision-making is to achieve the most desirable outcome with the least amount of uncertainty. The decision-making process, therefore, calls for the use of, (a) a desirability scale to determine value, (b) a prediction system to determine possibility,[9] and (c) a probability system to determine likelihood. The relationship between data, decision and outcome is further illustrated in Figure 21.

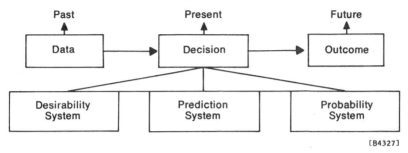

Fig. 21. The Microdynamics of Decision-Making

Appropriate managerial decisions must be made based on the highest possible levels of desirability and predictability. Less than appropriate decisions may mean outcomes which are less desirable or less likely to occur, or both. While individual managers can not claim the infinite wisdom of being able to determine desirability or accurately reading the future in order to determine the predictability of their decisions, the integration model offered by Bross can certainly be most helpful.

A.   Desirability System

Studies of desirability scales fall basically within the field of values, which is not only considered as nonscientific and hard to measure numerically, but also intrinsically subjective. How desirable, for instance, is it if policemen are instructed to smile when they hand out citation tickets to traffic violators? Naturally nobody can accurately tell. Moreover, it would be almost impossible to attempt to put a numerical value on the policeman's smile in such a situation. Such a value judgment must be seen from the policeman's point of view, from the violator's point of view, as well as from the point of view of noninvolved passers-by. On the other hand, it is not difficult for a police manager to determine the value of replacing squad cars in terms of dollars and cents or to measure the utility of establishing a team

---

9. The essence of this discussion is taken from Irwin Bross, *op. cit.* The study by Bross is probably one of the most informative inquiries made in the area of decision-making. The way he integrates past data with future outcomes through the decision-making process in the present, hasn't yet been matched by any other study in the field.

policing system. While there is obviously little agreement among experts on general procedures for assigning values, three broad techniques for measuring desirability could be discerned: [10]

(1) Dollars and cents: It is based on the market value of commodities and services. While there is not much in common between a new car and a bushel of apples, both can be evaluated on the same scale; that is, in terms of dollars and cents. Market values represent a consensus value system (except when monopoly conditions exist) which is applicable to matters in the police decision making process. It is commonly used in situations pertaining to buying police equipment, increasing or decreasing the police force, determining overtime duties of policemen, establishing new communication systems, or even adopting, or declining to adopt, a crime prevention program or a community-relations project.

(2) Utility: If dollars and cents could not offer a viable means of assigning values to a proposed service or function, a utility scale may be functional. While utility is an acceptable tool for measuring values, it is admittedly much lower in significance and accuracy than dollars and cents. The process must involve a comparison between two commodities or services of the same kind. A simple example would be measuring the utility of a confection like gum drops by comparing it with chocolate kisses. A child would be offered a choice of either kind. If he took the chocolate kiss, he would then be offered a choice between a chocolate kiss and two gum drops. If he still took the chocolate kiss, he would be offered a choice between a chocolate kiss and three gum drops. By increasing the number of gum drops, a point would be presumably reached at which the child might make either choice; a sort of a balance point or "the point of indifference". The utility scale of a chocolate kiss may then be seen as 4 to 1 compared to gum drops. By the same token, a policeman's utility of a flak vest, for example, may equal that of an air conditioning system in his squad car, or an air conditioner plus a shot gun, or an air conditioner, a shot gun, and a modern communication gadget, etc. At the department level, each officer may be asked whether he or she would choose between a flak vest or an air conditioner in the squad car and the utility ratio would then be calculated as 40:30, 55:75, etc. depending on the officers' assessments of the item's utility.

Introspective as it may be, the application of this principle, in the absence of a dollars and cents scale, has often been helpful in assigning desirabilities to decisional options and

10. *Ibid.*, pp. 89–98.

positively contributed to the determination of hard-to-measure utility items.

(3) Preference: Still another value scale which is worth noting is mere preference. The impetus of this principle has come mainly from the world of business especially from corporations in the food processing field. The general process of setting up a preference scale is fairly simple. For example, a company may wish to make a decision as to whether the public would like their product of strawberry ice cream. Do they like to have large servings? Do they want creamy mixtures or a solid kind? To establish a preference scale, the company would gather a group of tasters who would then be randomly selected. The panel would taste the proposed product and indicate their preference. By the same token, a decision to change the starting time of a patrol shift could be valued by the preference of a sample of officers chosen randomly from the force. Other examples concerning the police booking process, pay raises, or vacation schedules could be handled in the same way.

B.　Prediction System

While, as mentioned earlier, man can not claim the ability to read the future, man has to make decisions with "his eyes beyond today and into tomorrow." The only answer to man's search in the future must come from his studies of the past. Even in the mysterious and erratic world of today there exist tangible threads of continuity; amidst the atmosphere of uncertainty which engulfs public agencies today, there is an element of assuring stability. Prediction of future events must therefore begin with the search for stable characteristics which have persisted over a period of time. Four techniques are commonly used for predicting the future: Persistence Prediction, Trajectory Prediction, Cyclic Prediction, and Associative Prediction.[11]

(1) Persistence Prediction: It is the simplest method of predicting the future. It means nothing more than the prediction that there will be no change. Persistence prediction works surprisingly well in weather forecasting, life insurance tables and other relatively stable or slowly changing situations. In police management it can certainly help predict the size and type of police budget, size of the force, amount of turnover, attitudes and beliefs of the officers toward the public and toward themselves, efficiency rate, clearance rate, and many others.

(2) Trajectory Prediction: It assumes that although there will be change, the extent of which will be stable. This tech-

11. *Ibid.*

nique has been helpful in artillery fire control, in weather forecasting, in short-range stock market predictions, and in predicting the size of human populations. In police management it can be helpful in predicting crime rates, increases in the use of illicit drugs or juvenile delinquency, rise in the educational levels of officers—along with their tendency to become more organized, specialized and perhaps professionalized.

(3) Cyclic Prediction: It is based on the principle that history repeats itself. It assumes that patterns of events repeat themselves in cycles. The technique is certainly helpful in predicting the occurrences of eclipses, sunspots, and other astronomical events. It is used extensively today in predicting wars, economic recessions, stock prices and clothes fashions. In police management it can be helpful in predicting cycles of riots and civil unrests, trends of supreme court rulings, seasonable increase in crime rates, ups and downs in organized crime activities, etc.

(4) Associative Prediction: It differs from the foregoing in that it uses the data from one type of event to predict a second type. It establishes a relationship between at least two events. The first event would be a cause affecting the second event. It is used in politics, economics and everyday life. For example, war causes a large national debt and overproduction causes unemployment. In police management, associative prediction can help foretell racial disturbance if the department has engaged in racial discrimination against minorities, can predict an increase in the motor vehicle accident rate if the speed limit goes back up to 70 miles per hour, and may indicate an increase in clearance rate if the supreme court relaxes its restrictions on rules of evidence, etc.

C. Probability System

Prediction techniques discussed above, it must be noted, are far from being infallible. They are primarily a stop-gap technique and still remain unscientific, nonnumerical and primarily subjective. To back them up and validate their use in decision-making situations, a probability system must be devised. A probability system is developed by following these steps: [12]

(1) Collect a series of situations which are similar to the situation to be predicted. Each situation in the series is called a case.

12. *Ibid.*, p. 55.

(2) List the outcomes which have occurred for each case.

(3) Count the number of occurrences of each type of outcome and also the number of cases.

(4) Calculate the probabilities by this rule:

$$\text{Probability of outcome (P)} = \frac{\text{Number of occurrences of outcome (NOO)}}{\text{Total number of cases (TNC)}}$$

Combining a prediction system with a probability system would produce a Probability-Prediction System capable of providing the manager with ample insight into future outcomes.

The micro-dynamic model of decision making, in the absence of a mathematical model, is probably the most useful and the most applicable to the decision-making process in public and police agencies.

THE POLICE DECISION–MAKING PROCESS

Law enforcement agencies cannot remain static and still serve the public adequately. Administrative change by the police community, however, must be done in an organized, stable, efficient and effective manner. The only way to effect such change is through sound decision-making.

Law enforcement today is a gigantic operation. To control it efficiently and streamline its organization, management must permeate all its levels, review its policies, modernize its procedures, upgrade its performance, motivate its personnel, and constantly evaluate its effectiveness. Nothing of this could be accomplished without a network of qualified decision-makers at all levels. The task of "deciding" must, therefore, pervade the entire police organization from policy-making at the chief's level to the foot patrolman's decision to stop by and "just have a look" on the street. At both levels, as well as all those in between, Chief William Parker perceptively noted decisions must be backed up with careful investigation. Describing the appropriate decision-making process, he said:

> All police administrators are constantly called upon to make decisions: the wisdom of these decisions will depend, in large measure, upon the information and advice available to them. If decisions are made without proper analysis of facts, or without regard for standard practices developed as the result of change, the chances are that they will be mediocre decisions.[13]

In making decisions, the police manager seems to be hampered by many conditions which particularly exist in the field of law en-

13. William H. Parker, "Practical Aspects of Police Planning", a paper delivered at the 61st Annual Conference, International Association of Chiefs of Police, New Orleans, September 27, 1954, p. 7.

forcement. First, the police decision-maker usually functions under the handicap of public distrust and criticism. While decisions by a corporation may be shared by the stockholders at yearly meetings and those of a public agency revealed occasionally to legislative bodies, police decisions are critically examined by the public they serve with almost every edition of the local newspaper.[14]

Second, police decisions often involve matters of life and death. While some judges, military personnel and prison guards may find themselves sometimes confronted with similar decisions, they are usually privileged with ample time to make such critical decisions, adequate staff input by jurors, advisors or superiors, and in most cases, a comfortable early warning.

Third, police decisions, contrary to modern managerial thought, are still considered quasi-political decisions. While policy decisions made by appointed chiefs of police are fairly independent from the political grip of local politicians, the case is certainly not so in sheriff's departments, at the constable level, and the like. Police decisions at these levels, and in many cases at the former as well, often have to be checked with the local political machine, with leaders in the community and with influential individuals. If some decisions fail to receive the approval of these "significant others" at the local level, they usually would have to be rectified or replaced.

Fourth, there is the lack of sufficient policy guidelines for the police decision-making process. Especially for policemen on the street, discretion seems too vast, and demarcation lines between what is appropriate at the time and what is not are mostly vague and ambiguous. In a situation where danger is commonplace, justifiable reason is usually mixed, vision is blurred, emotions are high and motives are obscure. Consequently, in the absence of clear guidelines, the situation may easily get out of hand and further impede the policeman's ability to make sound decisions. Resulting decisions could easily be described as hasty, overreactive, or "brutal."

Fifth, there is the common effect of fatigue and nervousness on the hard working policemen. "Self-control" and "self-discipline" are merely the cultivated ability to make decisions in spite of occupational or personal difficulties. Obviously, the state of mental alertness necessary for making an appropriate selection among choices would be considerably impaired by the long, exhaustive, and risky hours a policeman puts in daily while on the job. Not only are a large portion of police decisions made on the street reached by exhausted officers, the general feeling of danger, alienation, and job dissatisfaction shared

14. *Ibid.*, p. 10.

by so many officers today contributes to the state of overreaction common in so many of their decisions.[15]

Sixth, still another condition which adversely affects decision-making by traditional police administrators is their lack of management training. Most policemen at the chief executive, middle management, supervisory, or operational levels, have not received any formal education and/or training in the crucial area of decision-making. Either because of their short tenure on the force, their lack of interest, the remoteness of a training facility, or their overreliance on personal intuition, most policemen today are not equipped with the basic analytical tools of decision-making. In the absence of such specialized education and training, police decisions today, unsupported with adequate assistance by qualified staff, tend to be spontaneous, contradictory, hard to justify, and often "sloppy".

Bristow and Gabard, in their most realistic description of the "sloppy" practice of decision-making by some police administrators perhaps demonstrated several of these factors by saying:

> The usual pattern of the inability to make decisions is as follows: the administrator, due to fatigue and/or nervousness, experiences indecision; he finds that concentration, beyond a brief time-span is difficult; as a result of this realization, he tries to compensate for his inabilities by putting forth more effort; this merely creates tension and irritability . . . he experiences impulsiveness, and this, he finds increases his burdens; realizing that he is becoming incapacitated, he makes quick decisions rather than attempting to produce accurate, well-thought out decisions; this creates a sense of guilt, which in turn adds indecisiveness to future decisions, thus tempting the subject to avoid decisions, and convincing him of his own unworthiness; insecurity results.[16]

POLICE DECISION-MAKING MODELS

In police agencies, as in all public agencies, sound decision-making is imperative. With or without the help of advanced technology, data processing equipments, or computers, police decisions both within the department or on the street have to be made by qualified ad-

15. For more information on the occupational behavior of policemen see, Martin Symonds, "Emotional Hazards of Police Work"; Hans Toch, "Psychological Consequences of the Police Role"; Jerome Skolnick, "A Sketch of the Policeman's Working Personality"; Arthur Niederhoffer, "Police Cynicism", published in Arthur Niederhoffer and Abraham Blumberg, editors, *The Ambivalant Force: Perspectives on the Police*, (Waltham, Massachusetts: Ginn and Company), 1970.

16. Allen Bristow and E. C. Gabard. *Decision Making in Police Administration*, (Springfield, Illinois: Charles C. Thomas Publisher), 1961, pp. 7–8.

ministrators. Even if "supercops" were ever able to build "deciding machines" capable of reading "appropriate", "inappropriate", or "does not compute", policemen will still have to make decisions on how to program the machine, what the criteria of appropriateness are, and whether the machine can adjust to different people in different cases at different times and places.

While decision-making is primarily an individual process that depends on the maker's level of intellect, training, values, and expertise, the process also assumes an institutional character. Rational police decisions must take into consideration the philosophy of the department, its size, structure, location, capability, resources, leadership, and training, among other orientation factors. To maintain a credible posture and reflect sound organizational values, decision-making within a police agency must be consistently legal, impartial, economy-oriented, and, above all, effective; the decisions must work. Nothing harms an agency's capacity to survive and progress like the frequent making of wild decisions, which are irrational, unplanned, unpredictable, or impractical. Such decisions certainly smack of instability, contradiction, and restlessness and would rapidly lead to a sharp decline in efficiency, effectiveness, and, consequently, in morale and public support. The next step would naturally be the total collapse of the organization.

To avoid such dire consequences, management had to step in and introduce a number of decision-making models, or sets of procedures, which reconciled individual ability and freedom of choice with the need for organizational character and consistency. While, of course, the areas requiring decisions and the frequency and level of decisions vary according to each law enforcement organization, management has produced some models which can contribute equally to the upgrading and refinement of the decision-making process in all law enforcement agencies.

But while the suggested models should be functional to all agencies of public service, some seem to be more functional than others. The degree of "functionability" in this reference can only be explained in terms of idealism and pragmatism. The most rational-comprehensive model, for instance, by which a highway patrolman would have to collect *all possible data* about a suspicious vehicle ahead of him on the freeway (before he decides to stop it) and consider *all* the legal, professional, and moral implications involved in such a decision, may sound too idealistic and therefore dysfunctional. On the other hand, allowing the same highway patrolman to stop any passing vehicle based on merely a "hunch" or "gut decision", would be too superficial and, therefore, dysfunctional as well.

Most functional decision-making models must, therefore, fall between the extremely idealistic "rational comprehensive approach" and the extremely superficial "gut feeling approach." Realizing the apparent dysfunction of both extremes in most situations, management emphasizes the need for the moderate models in between. While a decision to apply a specific model can further be predetermined for the police manager, attempting to do so would intolerably jeopardize the requisite flexibility and judgment latitude intrinsic in the selection aspect of the decision-making process. At this level, management theory relents and relies on the professionally acquired and nurtured judgment of managers.

Major decision-making models are:

1 —Rational Comprehensive.

2 —Pragmatic Rationality.

3 —Mixed Scanning.

4 —Gut Approach.

1 —**Rational Comprehensive:** Its use is claimed by most police departments today and is a part of most police management literature, especially in large departments committed to police professionalism. It may work effectively in the areas of policy decisions, strategic decisions and those concerned with the philosophical roles of the police. Also, chiefly limited to decisions made by top administrators, the rational comprehensive model does not lend much utility to administrators at the middle management level and below.

The model was suggested and expounded by Herbert Simon, who insisted that the "principle of efficiency" must be paramount in decision-making. Simon emphasized that for decisions to qualify as "rational", they must "maximize the attainment of certain ends with the use of scarce means." [17] He further stressed that the notion of rationality lies, in particular, in the "selection of effective means." [18]

Rationality, however, is but one component of Simon's model. The other is "comprehensiveness", which extends the area of selection to include almost *all* imaginable means. In this reference, however, Simon quickly qualified his earlier statement:

The word 'all' is used advisedly. It is obviously impossible for the individual to know all his alternatives or all their consequences, and this impossibility is a very important departure of actual behavior from the model of objective rationality." [19]

17. Herbert Simon, *op. cit.*, p. 39.   19. *Ibid.*, p. 67.

18. *Ibid.*, p. 61.

The original version of the rational-comprehensive model as presented by Simon involved only three steps: [20]

(1) the listing of *all* the alternative strategies;

(2) the determination of *all* the consequences that follow upon each of these strategies;

(3) the comparative evaluation of *all* these sets of consequences.

Simon's three steps were further expanded in subsequent literature and discussed by several authors in different fashions, naturally without altering the basic parameters prescribed by Simon. As an example of this literature, Ira Sharkansky presented this extended model: [21]

1 —Identify the problem.

2 —Clarify the goals and rank them as to their importance.

3 —List *all* possible means for achieving each of these goals.

4 —Assess *all* the costs of the benefits that would seem to follow from each of the alternative means.

5 —Select the package of goals and associated means that would bring the greatest relative benefits and the least relative disadvantages.

As Sharkansky clearly indicated, decision-makers who follow this model should inform themselves about *all* possible opportunities and *all* possible consequences of each opportunity. This further supports the notion that such decisions must be limited to top administration levels since decisions of this nature should:

a —afford ample time for study, planning and research;

b —have adequate intelligence and report information;

c —use consultation and perhaps public hearings;

d —be documented, preferably in a written form;

e —prove useful to quantitative transformation and data processing;

f —affect the organization as a whole;

g —have a lengthy impact on the agency;

h —be worth the trouble.

---

20. *Ibid.*

21. Ira Sharkansky, *op. cit.*, p. 43. For other examples see William Newman, Charles Summer, Kirby Warren, *The Process of Management*, (Englewood Cliffs, New Jersey: Prentice-Hall, Inc.), 1967, pp. 312–317; Harold Koontz and Cyril O'Donnell, *Principles of Management, A System Analysis of Management Functions*, (New York: McGraw-Hill Book Company), 1972, pp. 173–178; Paul Whisenand and Fred Ferguson, *Managing Police Organization*, (Englewood Cliffs, New Jersey: Prentice-Hall, Inc.), 1973, p. 234.

The rational-comprehensive model, which is the most formalized and perhaps the most difficult to fully achieve, has come under serious attack because of its "too idealistic" premise. The model seems to have assumed that public agencies have unlimited time and resources that could be used to gather intelligence about every possible problem. It also seems to have assumed that personnel are not sufficiently committed to or against any one set of goals and policies and can make unbiased selection based solely on information systematically collected. While naturally these assumptions strongly divert from the real world of administration, the following five features of practical administration could be cited as major road blocks to the fulfillment of the rational-comprehensive model in police administration: [22]

1   —The multitude of problems, alien to the education and training of police administrators, which must be faced daily and decided upon quickly.

2   —Barriers to collecting all the data required by the model.

3   —The human weakness of administrators: their personal interests, bias, commitments, inhibitions, and attitudes.

4   —The pressures both from within the agency as well as without.

5   —The deviant behavior of individual administrators.

2   —**Pragmatic Rationality:** Total and complete rationality is a hard-to-achieve ideal. It is unattainable in all public decisions except for the most stable and philosophical kinds of problems.[23] Not only does it require public officials to "make every human effort" to discover all the unknown alternatives, it is also too costly and time consuming. Decision-makers in the real world of law enforcement obviously neither have the funds nor the time to overcome the limitations of that "tight" model.

Simon, the exponent of the rational-comprehensive model, ironically also provided for a more relaxed approach to public decision-making based on his further interpretation of the notion of rationality. Certainly aware of, and perhaps concerned for, the limitations of his orginal model, Simon accepted an amount of pragmatic rationality, which would suffice with the selection of a *satisfactory or good enough* course of action. Felix Nigro followed suit and presented the "incrementalism approach" to refer to pragmatic rationality. Also, Whisenand and Ferguson referred to the same approach of *qualified rationality,* using the term "bound rationality".[24]

22. Ira Sharkansky, *op. cit.,* p. 44.

23. *Ibid.*

24. See Felix Nigro, *Modern Public Administration,* (New York: Harper and Row Publishers), 1970, p. 183, and Whisenand and Ferguson, *op. cit.,* p. 235.

Simon's change in his original position was explained in terms of his identification of four overlapping categories of rationality: [25]

A —Objective rationality—or the maximization of *all* possible values, which is the basic notion incorporated in his rational-comprehensive model.

B —Subjective rationality—based on the *actual* knowledge of the issue at the time of decision without the need for further research or analysis.

C —Organizational rationality—limited to the achievement of the *organization's goals* as they are known to be at the time of the decision.

D —Personal rationality—based on the public official's *individual goals* which is primarily a reflection of his perception of his public role.

In police administration, as in most other public agencies functioning at a lower level of management, these areas of rationality are identifiable with particular levels on the managerial hierarchy. Objective rationality, for instance, is clearly more identifiable with top management-level decisions dealing with policy-making and policy modification than with any lower level of management. On the other hand, personal rationality seems to be more evident at the operational level, at the bottom of the hierarchy, than at any higher level. Moreover, it must be noted, that the four areas of rationality naturally overlap to some extent within each individual decision-maker, as well as, in different proportions, in different size police agencies. The following chart will demonstrate how these areas generally correspond with the hierarchical levels of police administration.

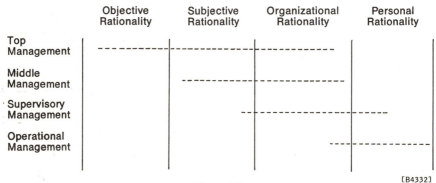

Figure 22

[B4332]

25. Herbert Simon, *op. cit.*, pp. 76–77.

Top management levels: While they often claim full objective rationality, they often make their decisions without being fully aware of *all* the political, social, or economic implications of *all* the issues. In large departments, top management levels seem more objective in their decisions, since they usually enjoy more advanced staff services and appear to have more access to city information and technological facilities.

Middle management level: It seems like the most systematic police level of decision-making. Decisions at this level are neither claimed to be "objective" nor carried out in a "personal" manner. Middle management seems to exercise mostly a subjective and an organizational rationality.

Supervisory management level: It seems fairly within the realm of organizational rationality while its decisions often smack of the personal rationality of the decision-makers at this level.

Operational management level: It is the bottom level of the administrative hierarchy as carried out by patrolmen and detectives on the street. While decisions of this nature should be absolutely organizational, they are mostly carried out in a personal rationality approach.

The pragmatic rationality approach calls for these steps: [26]

1 —Instead of attempting a comprehensive survey and evaluation of all alternatives, the decision-maker focuses only on those means within the context of his rationality area.

2 —Only a relatively small number of alternatives would then be considered.

3 —For each alternative considered, only a restricted number of outcomes are evaluated.

4 —There is no one final decision or one "right" solution, but a never-ending number of remedial decisions geared to compensate for the lack of a rational-comprehensive method.

In pragmatic rationality, decisions would be made more realistically by focusing only on the issues that are common within the administrative realm rather than on "reviewing the entire sky" as proposed by the rational-comprehensive model. Also, the alternative means selected would be among the main alternatives the decision-maker can see in view of his conception of administrative goals.

3 —**Mixed Scanning:** It is yet another approach proposed by Amitai Etzioni, in 1967, as a means of using a combination of the rational-comprehensive model and the pragmatic rationality approach. The idea is to flexibly employ two levels of decisional scanning, de-

---

26. Felix Nigro, *op. cit.*, p. 183.

pending on the problem. In some cases "high-coverage" scanning would be desirable, in others the more "truncated view" would be in order. Explaining the model, Etzioni illustrated by saying:

> Under mixed scanning, two cameras would be used: a broad-angle camera that would cover all parts of the sky but not in detail, and a second one which would zero in on those areas revealed by the first camera to require more in-depth examination.[27]

The broad-angle camera in Etzioni's illustration is naturally the pragmatic rationality approach, which would reduce the unrealistic aspects of rationalism by limiting the details required by the rational-comprehensive model. But when trouble spots are discovered, the rational-comprehensive approach would be called in and used for an in-depth examination of the contained trouble spot, considering *all* possible alternatives for its solution. By so doing, the use of the rational-comprehensive approach would be limited to overcoming the simplistic slant of pragmatic rationality.[28]

4 —**The Gut Approach:** This approach has been the only guide for ancient man probably for thousands of years. In modern administration, it has been consistently condemned and its application has always been discouraged. In police work, reliance on hunches or gut feelings indicates a sign of organizational underdevelopment, personal immaturity, and absence of training.

In 1964, William Gore, however, revived the ancient notion of "gut decision-making", in the form of his "heuristic model". Gore argued the utility of the ancient practice as a valid approach, calling it "a grouping toward agreements seldom arrived at through logic." [29] The very essence of the heuristic approach is that the facts, validating a decision, are internal to the personality of the individual, instead of external to it.[30] Gut feelings *reach backward* into the memory and *forward* into the future. They touch any number of people at any time and place. Moreover, the gut decision-making approach takes advantage of the unseen emotional motivations that energize the organizational system. It adds the human dimension to the decision-making process and thus fills the gap created by Aristotalian logic, mathematical decision-making, and later computer analysis. Futhermore, in the heuristic model, the police administrator can also

27. Amitai Etzioni, "Mixed Scanning: A Third Approach to Decision-Making", *Public Administration Review*, XXVII, No. 5, December 1967, pp. 386–387.

28. *Ibid.*

29. William Gore, *Administrative Decision Making: A Heuristic Model*, (New York: John Wiley & Sons, Inc.), 1964, p. 11.

30. *Ibid.*

bounce the problem and the gathered data off other administrators and gain their responses based on their conglomerate experiences.[31]

Discarding Gore's analysis as too unreliable, the gut approach to decision-making in the police could complicate existing situations, promote spontaneity, discredit the role of training and delay the advent of professionalism.

31. Paul Whisenand and Fred Ferguson, *op. cit.*, p. 237.

CHAPTER TEN

MANAGEMENT OF POLICE COMMUNICATIONS

Overview

Contrary to common views expressed by "pet rock" lovers, rocks *can not* communicate and, therefore, will always remain *rocks*. Consequently, a *society of rocks,* so to speak, capable of protecting their population, organizing their affairs, and promoting their collective interests, will never materialize.

Man's ability to speak, read, write, and communicate is perhaps the most significant feature that sets him apart from all other creatures. Through such media of communication, man, in a strategical sense, discovered his strengths and weaknesses in relation to other populations, learned to overcome natural hazards, to organize his forces, to invent sophisticated defenses and to maintain a viable position. Nevertheless, in the tactical areas of inter- and intra-organizational affairs, such as society, government, justice, etc., *effective* communication seems to be one of man's least developed abilities. Ironic as it may sound, man's dazzling success in establishing interplanetary communication across virtually millions of miles has perhaps dulled his ability to reach out and communicate effectively with his neighbor across the street.

Only since the early 1900's have any real efforts been devoted to studying communication, to seeking to understand what it is, how it is done, and how to improve it. Effective communication has since proved to be not only necessary but also crucial to the organization of people and groups in today's complex world. Without it man would exist on a very primitive level for complex organizations would be impossible.[1]

Nature of Communication

In public organizations, people generally do not get a chance to choose their co-workers, let alone their superiors. They are therefore compelled to work and cooperate with people who happen to be there at the time but who may not share with them the same habits, beliefs, views, and, in many cases, language (the U.N., for instance, at the political scene, or Interpol at the police scene). Without a system of communication common to all concerned within the organization, workers will not be able to share the organization's reason of being, its goals, and its policies. Furthermore, cooperation among

1. Herbert G. Hicks, *The Management of Organizations: A Systems and Human Resource Approach,* (New York: McGraw-Hill Book Company), 1972, p. 327.

workers would be next to impossible since man hasn't yet learned to read the minds of one another. It is no exaggeration, therefore, to say that communication is the *nerve* by which organizations are unified. Whether the organization in question is a family, a church, a business enterprise, or a police force, the clear and effective transfer of information among all members is absolutely essential to keep the organization together.

Chester Barnard, one of the first and best-known authors to give serious consideration to communication, viewed it as the means by which people are linked together in an organization in order to achieve a central purpose.[2] Group activity becomes impossible without a standardized system of information transfer. Without it, Barnard explained, common understanding and coordination of activities cannot be effected, and the achievement of goals would be impossible. Naturally, with the size and complexity of modern organizations the way they are today, the communication process can be expected to be a particularly difficult one.

In the previous chapter, decision-making was described as the intellectual activity which selects the direction and means for organizational activity. Without effective communication, however, these directions and means, crucial as they are, would remain unrelated to the rest of the organization and may thus stay forever mute. As in the function of human nerves, administrative communication relays the decisions made by the decision-making centers to a multitude of "energy cells" grouped in certain organs in control of the administrative system. Once the right channel is activated and orders are transmitted, the receiving organs would start to respond and the designed action would take place.

The communication process in organizations, however, can not be treated so simply because neither the decision-making centers nor the receiving organs are really mechanical. Both consist of unique people, who cannot transmit or receive on a standard frequency. Peter Drucker insists that the essence of communication "is the ability and willingness to listen and to understand the interests and concern of people in various parts of the organization".[3] While the level of ability and willingness naturally varies from one individual to another, in public organizations, nevertheless, a standard method has to be designed and applied in the interest of the whole organization, its coordination, its harmony and its stability.

The responsibility for devising and applying such a standard method of communication is basically one of management. Only

2. Chester I. Barnard, *The Functions of the Executive*, (Cambridge, Massachusetts: Harvard University Press), 1938.

3. Peter F. Drucker, *The New Society*, (New York: Harper and Row), 1949, p. 191.

management can combine the formal means traditionally required to transmit organizational authority with the informal means designed to motivate energetic and receptive personnel. While the former emphasizes uniformity and limited knowledge, the latter focuses on creating a meaningful dialogue between a concerned leader and his dedicated workers. Developing such a special blend of formal and informal means, conducive to the promotion of the efficiency and effectiveness of both the organization and the workers, is the main goal of communication management.

Communication Defined

Communication has been defined as:

.   .   .   an exchange of facts, ideas, opinions, or emotions by two or more persons.—Newman and Summer [4]

.   .   .   intercourse by words, letters, symbols, or messages; and as a way that one organization member shares meaning and understanding with another.—Bellows, Gibson, and Odiorne [5]

.   .   .   the ability of the various functional groups within the enterprise to understand each other and each other's functions and concerns.—Peter Drucker [6]

.   .   .   a meeting of minds on common issues.—Ordway Tead [7]

.   .   .   a two-way flow of instruction and information.— John Millett [8]

Communication takes place in many ways, shapes and forms. It can be verbal or written. It can also be in signs, symbols, or gestures. Signs include "traffic signs", "billboards", and sometimes pictures and cartoons. Symbols include mathematical information, computer language, and charts. Examples of gestures are plenty. They include a pat on the back, a nod of a head, or a raised eyebrow. While the use of verbal and written communication may not be effective enough in some public contacts, the use of signs, symbols, and gestures can obviously be a most elusive, misleading, and misinterpreted type of communication.

4. W.H. Newman and C.E. Summer, Jr., *The Process of Management*, (Englewood Cliffs, New Jersey: Prentice-Hall, Inc.), 1961, p. 59.

5. R. Bellows, T.Q. Gibson, and G.S. Odiorne, *Executive Skills*, (Englewood Cliffs, New Jersey: Prentice-Hall, Inc.), 1962, p. 59.

6. Peter F. Drucker, *op. cit.*, p. 191.

7. Ordway Tead, *The Art of Administration*, (New York: McGraw-Hill), 1951, p. 185.

8. John D. Millett, *Management in the Public Safety*, (New York: McGraw-Hill), 1954, p. 83.

Most communication in public agencies is verbal which makes the process of understanding considerably complex.   Unlike the "loose" areas of politicizing or sermonizing, words in administration can be a poor vessel for expressing the right thoughts and intentions. Even if thoughts and intentions are adequately expressed, it may be hard to tell how they will be interpreted by the recipient, if they are heard at all.   To dramatize the difficulty of verbal communication, Whisenand and Ferguson introduced their chapter on communication by this statement: [9]

> I know you believe you understood what you think I said, but I am not sure you realize that what you heard is not what I meant.

Verbal communication in public agencies, therefore, is often considered informal, suggestive, "off the record", and less authoritative.

Written communication, on the other hand, is more formal, more instructional, "on the record" and more authoritative.   While written communication is strongly believed to be a dependable means of communication in government, it is certainly not without pitfalls.   Its major shortcomings are:

1 —bureaucratic jargon and the use of "officialese" or "gobbledygook" as it has sometimes been called;

2 —the rigidity of the written word which is referred to sometimes as the "tyranny of words";

3 —the tendency to "formalize" simple meanings by complicating their expression.

As a result, written communication, if carried to an extreme, can become "overexact, overabstract, and overimpersonal".   For example, Rudolf Flesch stated that a nice simple statement such as "I love you" would never do in an "official" communication,   It would become, as Flesch translated it, something like this: "Complete assurance of maximum affection is hereby implied." [10]

Written communication can be found in terms of orders, circulars, directives, inquiries, fliers, memoranda, notes, records, recommendations, manuals, etc., as well as in a host of upward reporting messages.

ORGANIZATIONAL v. MANAGEMENT COMMUNICATION

Organizational communication, the forerunner of management communication, is traditional and is mostly used as an instructional

9. Paul Whisenand and Fred Ferguson, *The Managing of Police Organizations*, (Englewood Cliffs, N.J.: Prentice-Hall, Inc.,) 1973, p. 122.

10. Rudolf Flesch, "More About Gobbledygook", *Public Administration Review*, Vol. 5, (Summer, 1945), p. 242.

device. It was designed basically to control administrative agencies by circulating authoritative policies and formal procedures about what was to be done, when, where, how, and by whom it was to be done. The *why* question which might clarify the rationale behind a given policy was usually avoided lest the workers "would know as much as their bosses!" Non-procedural information was rarely given voluntarily; thus, the process of communication was generally bereft of any significant information. Under organizational communication, orders *descended* in much larger amounts than *ascending* information. Reports were not particularly necessary unless required to account for a particular incident or to assure the administrator that the recipients of the communication had in fact received and read it. Feedback, as a means of reviewing the organization's assessment of past performance, was required only when *things went wrong*. Non-vertical communication (horizontal and lateral) was rare, if at all permitted. To insure its documentation, mostly for the purposes of accountability but more so to justify taking a disciplinary action, organizational communication was mostly written. Non-written communication was considered informal which made it "less accurate, less important, and less binding". Thus, it was generally discouraged and often prohibited. As a whole, the concept of organizational communication overemphasized the roles of authority, formality, secrecy and control. While the concept is still practiced in a wide majority of public agencies today, the increasing influence of management theories has caused a considerable shift toward the recognition and adoption of managerial communication.

"Managerial communication", on the other hand, is based on the social concept of "no man is an island". It assumes that few of the worker's needs, if any, can be satisfied without his becoming part of, or interacting with, the organization. Managerial communication is a system of *information-sharing* designed not only to keep the organization efficient but also to affect the lives of workers and make them more productive. It contends that the most significant factor accounting for the "total behavior" of the organization is the *humanity* of its communication system and the sense of involvement and commitment it generates among its members. The goal of managerial communication, Harlan Cleveland indicated, is providing agency members with "a working knowledge of interorganizational complexity." [11]

Unlike organizational communication, managerial communication is less formal, less impersonal, less structured, and less secretive.

11. Harlan Cleveland, *The Future Executive*, (New York: Harper & Row, Publishers), 1972, p. 32.

While its ultimate goal is naturally the achievement of organization goals in an efficient and effective manner, managerial communication pursues that goal even further through "touching the personal aspects of the lives of workers". This stimulates the workers' sense of participation and keeps up their collective interest in the outcome of their administrative effort. This, in turn, leads to furthering the efficiency and effectiveness of a *dynamic* organization.

Managerial communication can be written or oral, over the telephone, inside the office, in the hallway, on the golf course or anywhere. It is not limited to vertical contact (downward and upward) but allows for horizontal, diagonal, and circular exchange of information. In whatever form it may occur, managerial communication does not consider formal titles, positions, and ranks as essential or even necessary. Rigid impersonality could be a barrier to the effectiveness of communication by suppressing personal opinions and spontaneous responses. In terms of the amount of information circulated and the classified nature of some of its parts, managerial communication limits only the circulation of those materials which could hamper the effectiveness of the organization and the productivity of its workers.

Certainly not a product of administrative "liberalism" or "weakness" toward workers, managerial communication is so designed as to maximize organizational interaction among workers and enhance their shared understanding of goals, while at the same time minimizing human and organizational barriers to effective communication. Toward the achievement of these goals, managerial communication attempts to:

a   —motivate the workers by keeping them informed of the total picture of the enterprise and its progress;

b   —unite the workers in affiliated interpersonal groups, i.e., golf clubs, cooking clubs, boating teams, little dribbler's leagues, etc.;

c   —educate the workers through the media of books and periodicals, attendance of conferences and symposia, or the like;

d   —solicit fresh ideas through personal association and one-to-one encounters;

e   —stimulate workers' feedback and assessment of past experience;

f   —clarify controversial issues or misunderstood subjects and thus reduce organizational factionalism, feuds, and unfair competition among workers;

g   —facilitate the petition of grievances on the part of unhappy workers and expedite the redress process.

MANAGEMENT OF POLICE COMMUNICATION

Police communication may be defined *as any process whereby decisional premises are transmitted from one member of the department to another.* Without police communication there can be no coordination of police efforts, and without the latter the whole concept of police organization would collapse or revert to a loose group of paid vigilantes.

The maintenance of effective communication between superiors and subordinates at all levels of the police hierarchy, as well as between persons at the same level, is considered by many to be the biggest single problem of police management.[12] No matter how highly educated and well-trained the members of a police department may be, or how advanced they are in the areas of criminal investigation, patrolling, community-relations, etc., without an effective system of communication, such a department would always be distorted, disoriented, unbalanced and often jerky. Undoubtedly, the unacceptable behavior by a few FBI agents during the later years of Director Hoover or by those officers occasionally indicted by local grand juries for gross police overreaction must be seen as a breakdown in effective communication, or in some cases, the result of blunt miscommunication.

A well-balanced police department must consist of synchronized divisions and sub-divisions which act and react harmoniously within a well-understood framework of goals and objectives, ways and means, and prescribed standards of performance. For these police units to function as such, top management, middle management, first line supervisors and the rank and file must share three basic ideologies:

(a) A common understanding of the "professional ideology" of law enforcement in a free society. This encompasses the knowledge of the constitutional, legal, social and cultural backgrounds of the policing function.

(b) A common understanding of the "institutional ideology" of the department they serve. This consists of the knowledge of departmental goals and objectives, values, beliefs, habits, and attitudes.

(c) A common understanding of the "work ideology" of the department. This consists of policies, procedures, regulations and standards of performance.

12. N.F. Iannone, *Supervision of Police Personnel*, (Englewood Cliffs, New Jersey: Prentice-Hall, Inc.), 1975, p. 52.

In order that these basic ideologies become known, understood, and practiced by all policemen within the organization, "open", "free", and "serviceable" channels of communication must be always available. Through such channels flows a constant stream of information that appropriately feeds the receiving centers in the divisions and subdivisions and keeps the department in "functional equilibrium", a balance of professional, institutional, and work knowledge.

An excellent testimony to the importance of effective communication as it relates to the "functional equilibrium" of departments was expressed by Robert Hampton:

> But good government [police work] requires more than good people. It requires good management of these good people. And too often, managers tend to spend great time and effort on their program responsibilities and their monetary resources while leaving their people-management responsibilities and opportunities to take care of themselves. This type of imbalance must be stopped.[13]

Toward the achievement of this "functional equilibrium" the Task Force on Police, 1973, demanded the following:

> Every police agency immediately should act to insure understanding and cooperation between the agency and all other elements of the criminal justice system . . . should provide for the instruction of police personnel in the functions of all criminal justice agencies in order to place the police role in proper perspective.[14]

Communication: System and Process

As the underlying theme of this book may have indicated, this discussion on the management of police communication will not touch on the *formalistic* type of communications used over police radios, teletype, computer printout, and the like. Bereft of any intellectual theory, this type of police communication is of a mechanical nature, is used as a standard operation procedure by all departments, and is easy to learn "off the manual" at any police academy training class.

Management of police communication, the focus of this discussion, however, is *substantive*. It treats the internal relationships between officers in the department and their impact on the survival, stability and progress of the whole police organization. It is interwoven with the concepts of managerial planning, managerial decision-making, and managerial leadership. It is concerned *with the*

13. Robert E. Hampton, "Special Feature—Dialogue for the 70's", *Public Personnel Review*, October 1970, p. 295.

14. *Task Force on Police*, 1973, p. 73.

sharing of minds by workers and leaders for the achievement of maximum productivity.

Management of police communication can be viewed as a *system* or as a *progress*.

As a *system*, police management communication is an aggregate of identifiable components within the agency through which available information is efficiently and effectively transmitted, processed and received. Regardless of the size, such a system exists in every police department, unless it is a one man force. A management communication system consists of five elements:

(a) A communicator: A sender, speaker, issuer, or suggester. Ordinarily the communicator in police management is at the top management level, and most communications are issued in the name of the chief even when prepared by a staff member and never actually seen by the chief executive himself. There certainly is much to be said about this practice by the chief. If the communication is too insignificant for the chief to give it the necessary attention, then the facade of putting his name on the communication means little, or nothing, to the receivers. This practice by chiefs may indicate an unhealthy interest in trivial matters. Moreover, if the communication is found to be in error, then the chief will have to take the blame and might have to "cover up" for the faults of the original communicator. Furthermore, the practice might induce "unprofessional" staff members into exerting illegitimate or undue power over the department under the blanket protection of an uncommunicating chief. The effective management role in this situation is to decentralize communication and let every manager communicate in his own right, within prescribed areas and delegated authority, as long as the managers at the higher levels are kept informed of the nature, purpose and content of the communication.

(b) A transmission procedure: Although management communication, as explained earlier, recognized a various media for communicating information, it is desirable to have a more or less routinized procedure in order to ensure proper delivery and distribution. Although organizational communication, especially in large police departments, requires the establishment of an official communication center with review and clearance powers, management communication does not require such a need. Routinized transmission procedures include—beside formal means—reliable informal means, especially among reliable managers within the organization.

(c) A communication form: This ordinarily is linked to the purpose of communication. If it is intended to direct and control, then the form is usually an order, directive, regulation, manual or the like. If it is intended to educate, then the form is usually a circular, a flier, a ruling or the like. If it is to inform, then it is usually a letter, a note or a message. Solicited communication is primarily in the form of a request, and feedback communication is either a request for a response or simply a performance report.

(d) A recipient: It is not always easy in a police organization to determine who should receive what communication. The organizational solution is likely to fall at the extremes of too few or too many. The management solution emphasizes the need for relevance, selectivity and economy. The management solution therefore contends that every communication should go to all whose behavior is to be affected by the communication. To restrict distribution is to run the risk of communicating with too few and blocking the anticipated cooperation by others. To distribute communication widely is expensive and overwhelms many persons with materials that do not interest them. This may distract from the workers' attention on relevant matters and perpetuate the bureaucratic perception of communication as superficial, trivial, and worthy only of the wastebasket.

(e) A desired response: Unless some definite effort is made to determine whether the intended communication has influenced administrative behavior, the effectiveness of a communication system cannot be evaluated. Moreover, the response of the recipient of a communication is crucial since it activates the feedback flow of information in the police organization and completes the information cycle basic to an effective communication system.

As a *process,* managerial communication is characterized with flexibility, selectivity, intelligence, and mutual confidence. It assumes the presence of a will and a desire to communicate on the part of all officers, from chief to patrolman. Moreover, it assumes the shared perception of the basic ideologies: professional, institutional and procedural. Notwithstanding the common and inevitable differences in opinion, success in managerial communication depends primarily on the mature attitude of managers and officers and their desire not to sacrifice straightforward talk for bureaucratic jargon, directness for officialdom, and "taking the hint" for "putting it down in writing". An excellent example of this mature attitude was presented by Pierce Brooks, the veteran director of the Lakewood police department:

> Any police agent, any person in the department, can make a suggestion, and it follows a flow chart . . . to the top and then back to the agent or civilian who initiated the suggestion. After one year we evaluated the program and found that 63 percent of the projects suggested by the police agents were approved.[15]

N. Iannone, another veteran police manager from California, described the process of police management communication as an "expression-absorption" exchange of information between officers. He stated that officers express themselves by words, gestures, inflections, and actions. The recipient then absorbs what he perceives, interprets it, and reacts by word or action. Iannone proceeded by saying that the "communicator then responds to the recipient's reactions". "If this sequence of interaction is distorted or unbalanced," warned Iannone, "it may result in a failure on the recipient's part to respond as expected," or worse, "in no action at all." [16]

Unless the Brooks-Iannone management approach to police communication prevails, expands, and is ultimately adopted by American law enforcement agencies, the communication process within police agencies will remain rigid, abrupt, artificial and counter-productive. As an example of the deficiency of the old organizational approach to communication, a case study of the California Highway Patrol revealed that:

> Commissioner Crittenden once issued a statewide directive that was so variously interpreted as it passed down the hierarchy that its meaning had become altogether different by the time he next encountered it on a remote patrol officer bulletin board.[17]

The next discussion on the types of police management communication will explain how the communication process works.

---

15. Pierce R. Brooks, "Lakewood, Colorado: Change Agent in Police Administration and Organization", Proceedings of the Tenth Annual Interagency Workshop, Sam Houston State University, Huntsville, Texas, June 2–13, 1975, p. 58.

16. N.F. Iannone, *Supervision of Police Personnel*, (Englewood Cliffs, New Jersey: Prentice-Hall, Inc.), 1975, p. 53.

17. Phillip O. Foss. "Reorganization and Reassignment in the California Highway Patrol:, in Frederick C. Mosher (ed.), *Government Reorganizations: Cases and Commentary*, (Indianapolis, Indiana: Bobbs-Merrill), 1967, p. 195.

Typology of Police Management Communication

Police management communication may be analytically categorized, first, by *kind* and second, by *direction*. The former relates to the nature of communication used: *formal-informal*. The latter pertains to the organizational relationship (or hierarchical level) between the communicator and the recipient: *vertical, horizontal, diagonal,* or *circular*. Vertical communication is further broken down into *downward* and *upward* directions. Figure 23 illustrates this typology.

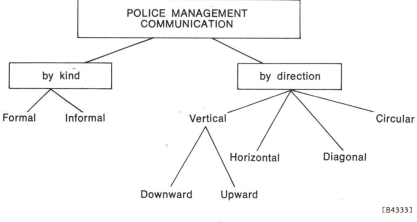

Figure 23

These two main categories, however, are not exclusive and neither can be found without the other. There is, therefore, downward formal and downward informal communication, upward formal and upward informal, horizontal formal and horizontal informal, etc. The following discussion will explain each category and identify the characteristics of its subcategories.

Kinds of Police Communication: Formal-Informal

Regardless of how advanced the management of a police department may become, an inevitable amount of formal communication will always be necessary to sustain the organized nature of the agency. The "regular system" or the *channels,* as formal communication is often referred to, is basic because it establishes the ground rules for the whole operation. It identifies the statutory purposes of the agency, its organizational structure, and its legal, social, and administrative responsibilities. Through the formal channels, the agency transmits its basic governing policies, its standard operation procedures, its fiscal and budgetary procedures, its personnel qualifications, and training requirements among others.

Almost without exception, formal communication is written and addressed from one position to another regardless of the occupants of those positions. Hence, one typically sees communication expressed in policy directives from the chief, official correspondence between the various divisions, department records and manuals, and reports from individual officers to their supervisory and leadership levels.

Formal communication, from the communicator's point of view is safe, functional, and authoritative. It tends to finalize matters and spare the embarrassment of face-to-face contact. From the recipient's point of view, however, formal communication indicates a rather serious situation. Because of its impersonality, recipients often fail to identify the motivation behind it or the real message hidden between its lines. Because of its official nature, the details behind it are in most cases kept secret, and inquisitive officers are commonly rebuffed and directed "to mind their own business". As a result, few formal communications are seen by the subordinates as motivational or inspiring. Agency insistence, therefore, that policemen follow formal communications can have a stifling impact on the department and create a bureaupathic attitude usually attributed to the "ineptness of the brass" at the top and their failure to communicate effectively with their men.

This stifling impact of formal communication can obviously cause considerable harm to the police department. The police chief and his "brass associates" may find that pertinent information does not flow to them in the usual way and suddenly realize that they are the primary victims of their own rigid system of information dissemination. They may discover, rather too late, that the "old gang" is no longer as friendly as they used to be and that their offices have become wrapped in cellophane boxes that isolate them from the department's realities. They may hear rumors of conflicts among the men and of friction among the divisions, witness an increase in disciplinary actions taken for absenteeism and "goofing-off", or observe an increase in turnover among the ranks. What adds to the misery of the situation is that when the "brass associates" ask for causes, they generally receive little or no meaningful information.

In every formal organization, an informal system of communication develops, and attempts to prevent it or suppress it have always failed. The reason for this is obvious: social gregariousness is basic to mankind and antedates modern organizational associations. No matter how elaborate a system of formal communication is set up, or how hard it is protected by the "brass associates", informal channels of communication will always develop and survive.

Informal communication systems revolve around the social relationships of the members of the police organization. A high school friendship between the patrol sergeant and the head of the detective division, a neighborhood relationship between the police chief and the garage sergeant, or membership in the same church by the intelligence head and the head of internal investigation, are all bases for informal organization and informal communication. Such social relations certainly create occasions for close interpersonal contact and foster mutual loyalty. They may further give rise to an authority relationship parallel to, and sometimes stronger than, the formal organizational authority prevalent in the police department. From this arises the common phenomenon of police cliques, groups that build up an informal network of relations and use it effectively for maintaining power in the department.[18] It is, therefore, not uncommon in law enforcement agencies (especially in sheriff's departments) to have a small number of lieutenants, and patrolmen, who exert more power and enjoy more privileges than their peers. Such a group of well-connected officers can have a strong say in the policy-making of the department, undermine formal authority, extend their protection to a sizeable number of "loyal friends" in the department, and advance their personal aims.

The greater amount of informal communication in police organizations, nevertheless, is "non-conspiratorial" in nature. Supervisors, detectives, dispatchers, and, of course, patrolmen go out together for breakfast, chat over coffee, or grab a "brown bag" and "gossip" during lunch hour. Whether this type of information exchange takes place inside the department building or outside, such informal communication, or "subformal", as described by Whisenand and Ferguson,[19] can play a constructive role in interrelating work units and improving work relations.

Informal communication, which is nonconspiratorial in nature, can yield a definite advantage to police management. Because it is nonofficial, and therefore nonincriminating, it can be an adequate platform for genuine ideas, for creative plans, and for a flow of thoughts free from authority. Through informal communication, new officers can be "broken in" and taught the ropes of the police organization, informed of the cultural, social, and political features of the community they serve, and guided through their green years of police service. By means of informal communication, officers can clarify the behind-the-scene reasons and motives for new policies and procedures. Officers can also heal the breaches that might develop among their units. Of particular importance is the role of informal

18. Herbert Simon, *Administrative Behavior*, (New York: The Free Press), Second Edition, 1965, pp. 160–161.

19. Whisenand and Ferguson, *op. cit.*, p. 127. The authors break down informal communications to subformal, personal task related, and personal nontask directed. While in reality it is almost impossible to isolate such areas, for analytical purposes it can be acceptable.

communication in supplying management with adequate feedback, which can help it make more realistic decisions on future problems. Finally, a major use of informal communication could be the strengthening of cohesion among department members and the unification of their stands against external encroachment by other agencies of criminal justice, by pressure groups, and by unfair press attacks.

As if to emphasize the importance of informal communication in police agencies, the Task Force Report of 1973, stated:

> Every police chief executive should provide for maximum participation . . . this participation should include . . . input from all levels within the agency— from the level of execution to that of management—through informal meetings between the police chief executive and members of the basic rank, idea incentive programs, and any other methods that will promote the upward flow of communications.[20]

Directions of Police Communication: Vertical, Horizontal, Diagonal, Circular

As mentioned earlier, either kind of police communication, formal or informal, can not possibly exist without a direction. A directionless communication would not only be ineffective but also meaningless.

In police agencies, management communication could be vertical, horizontal, diagonal, or circular (conference type). A brief discussion of each type will clarify strengths and weaknesses.

Vertical communication refers to information that "descends" directly from top to bottom through superordinate—subordinate levels of hierarchy, as well as that which "ascends" directly upward through the same channels. It is the most traditional approach to administrative communication and is based on the assumption that decisions made solely at the top and "dropped in the chute", so to speak, are expected to slide smoothly down the hierarchy.[21] If any hitch develops in the implementation of the decisions at any point in this downward trip, it is attributed to the shortcomings of the workers concerned. Upward communication, on the other hand, is the transmission of reports and opinions by the rank and file up the same hierarchy, traveling the reverse route. Beside the traditional "authoritative effect" of vertical communication, its effectiveness can be seriously hampered, especially in large police departments, by the ex-

20. *Task Force on Police*, 1973, p. 53.   21. Felix Nigro, *Modern Public Administration*, (New York: Harper & Row, Publishers), 1970, p. 189.

cessive number of hierarchical levels between communicators and recipients. The case of Commissioner Crittenden of the California Highway Patrol, described in the inital discussion of management communication, would certainly be an excellent case in point. That example, in which Commissioner Crittenden discovered that his orders were altogether altered by the time they reached the patrol office bulletin board, indicates the major handicaps of vertical communication. They can be summarized as: [22]

1 —physical distance and slowness of movement;

2 —dilution or distortion at each level;

3 —difference in attitude among supervisors;

4 —inferior status of subordinates;

5 —natural resentment to downward communication.

Horizontal communication refers to information exchanged between administrative supervisors at the same level of authority. Examples would include such messages, notes, or oral information exchanged between the day patrol commander and his night counterpart, between the head of the criminal investigation division and the head of the intelligence division, between the head of the intelligence and the legal advisor, or between patrol sergeants in charge of different precincts of town. Although most such communication is informal in nature, the use of written notes among such peers is not uncommon. Horizontal communication, unless abused as a buddy-buddy system in pursuit of its own power, can be most effective in facilitating operational coordination among units. The practice, however, can also be organizationally harmful and dysfunctional if the "brass associates" at the top are not kept informed of the purpose and content of the exchanged information. Copies of this information, therefore, should be sent upward to the management level in charge of overall coordination of the agency. Unless there is a veto at the leadership level, horizontal communication may be carried on as an effective and fast channel of managerial communication.

Diagonal communication is a novel channel introduced by police managers to circumvent delay, redundancy, and repetition. It is based on the concept that officers are capable of handling multi-directional communication effectively. Instead of limiting officers to vertical channels, diagonal communication allows one to contact and to receive information from superiors and subordinates outside the direct line of vertical hierarchy. Within diagonal communication a patrolman may contact the head of detectives, the assistant legal adviser, the garage sergeant, or the captain of SWAT, without having to go through traditional vertical channels first. It allows police practi-

22. *Ibid.*, p. 190.

tioners to exchange fast information with others of different levels who are not in a superior-subordinate relationship.

Diagonal communication is most effective in emergency situations when going through vertical channels would waste valuable time and produce little or no relief from the direct supervisor. The patrolman at the scene of a crime, for example, may have to contact the head of criminal investigation or the captain of SWAT directly regarding a rapidly changing situation and can do so without the need to go through his sergeant, lieutenant and captain. He may also receive direction or guidance from these individuals without further delay. Dangers involved in such a hypothetical example may include:

1   —the lack of experience on the part of the patrolman and his need for close supervision;

2   —a conflict of communication between what he may receive diagonally and vertically;

3   —the inaccuracy of the diagonal contact;

4   —the difference in training, ideology and working language between the two parties;

5   —the unfair implication that the vertical supervisor has failed to render his assistance effectively when needed.

Diagonal communication naturally assumes that parties to the contact are intelligent, highly trained, cooperative and attuned to the same set of goals, policies and procedures.

Circular communication is the latest innovation in the management of police communication. Often referred to as management staff or operating "conference", it pertains to the exchange of views among police practitioners through face to face association, seated around a table. Members of such conferences may be permanent, temporary, or a combination of both. They may consist of only supervisors seeking information on a certain subject or on an agenda of subjects, or a number of policemen and civilians called to represent themselves or their concerned groups. Participation by these members is normally determined by their need to know and their ability to exchange information intelligently.

In management-oriented police departments, especially the larger ones, a special room in the building is usually designed for conference meetings where circular communication takes place. Not limited to top or middle management levels, circular communications may take place among first line supervisors or patrolmen in the process of discussing a coordinational or an operational problem at their level.

Circular communication may be formal or informal. Two usual differences between them exist. First, informal conferences meet on irregular occasions whenever summoned by the administrator and do not have any fixed participation. Secondly, proceedings of informal conferences are not recorded, while formal conferences are usually taped or their minutes taken and circulated.

Management of police communication suggests that these conferences have three basic uses: (1) to gain awareness of a problem; (2) to help in problem solving where it is desirable to explore different points of views and to reveal the extent of these differences; and (3) to gain acceptance and execution of a decision by explaining purposes and answering questions.[23] Conferences may also be used to help promote a sense of unity among the management group at a particular level of hierarchy or among the various operating officials.

Circular communication in police agencies can obviously have some advantages and disadvantages. It offers advantages in that:

1 —It provides a democratic setting for exchange of information that is contrary to the traditional environment of authoritativeness and militarism.

2 —It provides a demythicized image of police chiefs and "brass associates" in the eyes of subordinate participants.

3 —It provides an opportunity for creative and imaginative personnel to express their views and argue their cases.

4 —It provides an instant feedback to police managers and an opportunity for reasoning and for rebuttal of charges.

5 —It provides for adequate representation by all concerned with the police decision-making process.

6 —It provides fast resolution of controversial issues without needless waste in the preparation and circulation of papers or in waiting time for answers.

7 —It overcomes the common difficulties of expressing one's views in writing, on one hand, and comprehending the sentiments and motives of report writers, on the other.

8 —It boosts the morale of lower-ranking participants by giving them the satisfaction of addressing general questions which concern the department as a whole.

9 —It is probably a more economical method of communication, especially in the long run.

Some disadvantages of the circular communication approach are:

1 —Its success depends primarily on the selection of participants, which is left almost entirely to the chief.

23. Martin Kriesberg and Harold Guetzkow, "The Use of Conferences in the Administrative Process", *Public* *Administration Review*, Vol. 10, (Spring 1950), p. 93.

2 —Its effectiveness corresponds positively with the levels of intelligence and motivation of participants.

3 —Its success might be seriously hampered by technical questions, such as the lack of a quorum, an attempt at filibustering, or a conflict in committee rules.

4 —It provides an opportunity for opposing cliques to seek private gains and privileges overlooking the institutional interests of the agency.

5 —It might turn into lengthy and endless sessions which can consume many regular work hours which can be used for more important matters.

6 —It may turn into an oratorical platform reminiscent of election campaign efforts, especially in sheriff's department, where the chief executive has to run periodically for reelection.

7 —It may give nonparticipants the impression that their contribution is not really welcomed.

While the use of circular communication in police agencies is still novel and its usefulness is uncertain early reports indicate its success. Egon Bittner asserted that "whenever police officers are furnished an opportunity to discuss their work problems around a conference table, they generally display a thoughtful approach that amazes outsiders." [24]

Bittner proceeded to defend the circular communication in police agencies by saying that:

> Some people might say that the idea of 'burly' policemen having staff conferences at every change of the watch in the precinct house is absurd, presumably because they are by the nature of their background, especially their low education and inarticulateness, not prepared for it. This view is almost certainly mistaken.[25]

BARRIERS TO EFFECTIVE POLICE COMMUNICATION

Maintaining an effective network of communication within a police agency is a vital managerial function. Every human act or thought within a police organization depends one way or another on the effectiveness of communication. Without such a vital function, a police agency would revert to a *pet rock status, in which it can not communicate, change, or grow* to quote Robert Di Grazia, former Commissioner of Boston.

24. Egon Bittner, *The Functions of the*   25. *Ibid.*
  Police in Modern Society, (New York:
  Jason Aronson), 1975, p. 68.

Barriers to effective police communication are either behavioral —*caused by the failure of individual officers* to communicate effectively, or organizational—*caused by the failure of the agency* to establish adequate managerial techniques. The former could be corrected through the processes of education, training, motivation, supervision and leadership. The latter can be remedied by the installation of a sound management communication system.

Behavioral barriers include the following:

1 —**Lack of human concern:** Whisenand and Ferguson noted that the effectiveness of communication tends to be directly proportional to the degree to which both the sender and receiver regard and treat each other as human in the personal context of the event.[26]

2 —**Human intransigeance:** Egon Bittner noted that the real obstacle with effective police communication is a fraternal understanding among those who have information not to cooperate. That is, the uniformed patrol as a whole, and the various bureaus, are opposed to having any of their members hobnobbing with detectives from the intelligence unit in accordance with the general maxim of brotherly obligation to keep things one knows to oneself.[27]

3 —**Failure to listen:** Iannone noted that a principal obstacle to effective communication is the failure to listen to what others are saying.[28] This may result from lack of interest, personal problems causing mental preoccupation, egocentricity, or other psychological conditions which cause inattention or inability to concentrate.

4 —**Status differences:** Gilkinson, Paulson, and Sikkink reported that the more prestigious the communicator is, the more apt the receiver is to listen and obey the transmitted information.[29] Policemen, by and large, seem to be more resentful of orders issued by first line supervisors and middle management than those issued by the chief.

5 —**Fear of criticism:** Many policemen at all levels avoid making, or writing, clear communication statements because they fear being criticized. As a result, they often couch their expressions in vague and abstract wording, always leaving "an

26. Whisenand and Ferguson, *op. cit.*, p. 140.

27. Egon Bittner, *op. cit.*, p. 67.

28. N. F. Iannone, *op. cit.*, p. 54.

29. H. Gilkinson, S. F. Paulson, and D. E. Sikkink, "Effects of Order and Authority in an Argumentative Speech", *Quarterly Journal of Speech*, 40, (1954), pp. 183–192.

open back door" through which they can retract their statements, if challenged.[30]

6   —**Psychological preparation:** Policemen, like most communication receivers, interpret the communication they receive in terms of their past experiences, present needs, and future expectations. Therefore, if the communication contains a threat to his conditioned state of sentiments and attitudes, a policeman would tend to understand the communication in a slanted meaning.

7   —**Filtering:** This refers to the distortion or dilution of the content of a communication as it is passed from one individual to another.[31] It results from the tendency of individuals to focus on the part of information that has the most impact on them, leaving the rest of the information to mean what it may to the next receiver. In time, the original communication may mean something totally different from what it was intended to mean.

8   —**The "just fine" syndrome:** Good news, especially what is perceived to carry "good tidings" to the superiors, tends to travel faster than bad news. Many subordinates believe that by suppressing unpleasant news, they are doing the boss a favor or keeping him in a good humor. They, in fact, are doing him a harmful disservice by shielding him from the truth, thus forcing him to make value judgments based upon partial information or information taken out of context.[32]

Organizational barriers to effective communication, on the other hand, include:

1   —**Organizational environment:** Bittner cited the "soldier-bureaucrat" nature of police organizations as a major obstacle to effective police communication. He explained that the proliferation of formal regulation and the single-minded care that is given to their enforcement has created a flow of communication that moves almost exclusively downward through the chain of command.[33] Bittner remarked that most of this downward flow of communication does not actually relate to the realities of police work or relates to it only in a superficial way. The result, Bittner pointed out, was twofold: (a) It causes a "flooding" of all communication channels to capacity. (b) It creates a virtual absence of feedback to the in-

30. N. F. Iannone, *op. cit.*, p. 56.   32. *Ibid.*

31. *Ibid.*, p. 57.   33. Egon Bittner, *op. cit.*, p. 67.

stitution beyond the kind of record keeping that barely serves statistical purposes.[34]

2 —**Organizational size:** The larger the size of a police department, the more complex its communication network tends to be. The complexity of so many multi-directional channels multiplied by so many hierarchical levels in a large police organization can seriously affect the speed and accuracy of messages flowing through the department. When channels are overly complex, messages will tend to be delayed at strategical bottlenecks. Also, the more persons involved in the interpretation of communications, the greater the possibility that the end product will be distorted or diluted.[35]

3 —**Overloading of channels:** It causes jamming, much as in the case of bottlenecks. Overloading results from lack of discrimination in separating relevant and irrelevant information by communicators. Joseph Massaie pointed out that more messages do not necessarily mean more information. Unless the amount and relevancy of police information are governed by a systematic set of priorities, the police department will be bogged down in paperwork and spend too much of its time listening to trivia rather than doing what really has to be done.[36]

4 —**Leadership:** The attitudes of leaders concerning information, classification, and capricious secrecy can have a sterilizing effect on the passing of necessary information to all concerned parties. The intentional suppression of communications by leaders and supervisors can also cause a serious breach in the flow of information. Since the survival and welfare of policemen depend heavily on the acquisition of accurate information on time, the chances are that in the case of gross suppression of information, officers would turn to operate a "black market" communication system based on the exchange of secrets for favors. Obviously the results would be most aggravating to the officers involved, to the leaders and supervisors in charge, and to the cohesion and morale of the department as a whole.

34. *Ibid.*, p. 68.

35. N. F. Iannone, *op. cit.*, p. 58.

36. Joseph L. Massaie, *Essentials of Management*, (Englewood Cliffs, New Jersey: Prentice-Hall, Inc.), 1964, pp. 71–73.

CHAPTER ELEVEN

MANAGEMENT OF POLICE LEADERSHIP

Overview

A philosopher once said that there are at least three subjects on which no wise man should ever attempt to write: *love, genius,* and *leadership.* Of the three, the last is probably the most mysterious, the most capricious, and the most unpredictable. No amount of training, no sedulous nurturing by the family or the social group, no long line of ancestry piously dedicated to the eventual flowering of a leader has proved a sure means of developing leaders.

Wherever one turns in history, the prime mover of civilizations was certainly leadership. Masses of people consistently followed leaders whether they were prophets, kings, astrologers, generals or scientists. People seem to have always needed that sense of direction offered by a few gifted persons. Throughout the centuries of history, however, leadership not only in abstract theory but also in the practical experience of everyday living has been one of the most controversial subjects. Students of sociology and political science have studied leadership, have speculated about it, and have proposed many theses for its success, but none of these theories has proved to be applicable to *all* groups at *all* times. It is still a most puzzling question to try to explain objectively how some individuals manage to influence others so strongly so as to change their attitudes toward life, work and play, while other individuals remain so stationary, unable to understand— let alone influence—their *own* approach to simple living.

In public service, and especially in public organizations, the role of leadership is not only vital but paramount. To determine how important leaders are, one has to try to consider the history of the United States without Abraham Lincoln, Franklin D. Roosevelt, or Harry Truman. At a lower level of government, one can easily perceive the dominant role of leadership in administration by studying the performance of leaders like Robert McNamara, J. Edgar Hoover, Henry Kissinger and many other public leaders. Reflecting on the influence of leaders like these, one can appreciate the accomplishments of these people in strengthening the Armed Forces, fighting law breakers, and achieving peace. Yet, none of these accomplishments could have been possible by the individual efforts of these men alone. They were made possible because these men succeeded in influencing the thoughts, decisions, and performances of others.

Leaders are crucial in government—from chief executives through department heads on down to the critically important level of front line supervisors.[1] When performing well, leaders give vision and tone to their agencies, influence the decision-making process, stimulate effective communication, build character, and transform pieces into programs. Only through effective government leadership was the Tennessee Valley reclaimed, the Great Depression reversed, Hitler defeated, Europe reconstructed, and several Americans launched off in a "great leap for mankind" on the cratered surface of the moon.

Leadership Defined

Despite its complexity, "leadership" has been defined as: [2]

.   .   .   the consistent ability to influence people in desired ways.—Robert Golembiewski

.   .   .   the ability to provide those functions required for successful group action.—Weldon Moffitt

.   .   .   the capacity and will to rally men and women to a common purpose.—Field Marshal Montgomery

.   .   .   a kind of work done to meet the needs of a social situation.—Philip Selznick

.   .   .   the exercise of authority in the making of decisions.—Robert Dubin

.   .   .   the process of influencing group activities toward goal setting and goal achievement.—Ralph Stogdill

.   .   .   [a leader is] one who can generate effective individual and group action to accomplish agency goals.—J.D. Williams.

Nature of Leadership

The word "leadership" can be traced at least as far back as early Greek and Latin, where it derived from an original term meaning "to act".[3] Hannah Arendt shows that the two Greek verbs *archein* which meant "to begin, lead, or act" and *gerere* which meant "to pass through, achieve, or finish", correspond with the two Latin verbs *agere:* to set into motion or lead, and *gerere:* to bear or carry out. It was believed that each act of leadership consisted of two parts: a beginning made by a single person, and an achievement performed by a number of others, who by "bearing" see it through. The leader begins a motion and expands it through the efforts of his followers,

1. J.D. Williams, *Management Begins with Man*, a forthcoming text in public administration from Little, Brown and Co., 1971, p. 105.

2. All these definitions are quoted from J.D. Williams' study of the nature of leadership, *Ibid.*, p. 106.

3. Hannah Arendt, *The Human Condition*, (Chicago: University of Chicago Press), 1958, p. 188.

who are dependent upon him for guidance in the execution of initiated move.   In other words, leadership consists of two functions: *origination* by the leader and *execution* by the followers.

Plato opened a gulf between the two parts of leadership by his theory of the leader as a "philosopher king" who need not act at all but simply think for those who are capable of starting and executing. The essence of leadership was viewed by Plato as chiefly the "wisdom" necessary to prevail over social moves and countermoves carried out by the loyal followers.   The role of leadership was mainly one of overseeing the behavior of others.

During the early Italian renaissance, Niccolo Machiavelli, in 1513, presented his pragmatic concept of leadership in *The Prince*. He argued that a powerful leader was needed in major instances—at the birth of an organization and at times of severe crises.   The Prince was to be known by his talent and his ability to shift quickly and gracefully from persuasion to cajolery, from flattery to intrigue, from diplomacy to violence and, when necessary, to concoct just any formula necessary to retain power and escape disaster.[4]   Among the notable political leaders who were charged with practicing the Machiavellian approach were Frederick the Great, Napolean Bonaparte, Benito Mussolini, Andrew Jackson, Franklin D. Roosevelt, and many others.

It was Thomas Carlyle (probably a forerunner of Max Weber) who developed a keen awareness of the historical impact of the *great man* concept.   Carlyle wrote that among the undistinguished masses are men of light and magnetism, mortals superior in power, courage, and understanding.   The history of mankind, noted Carlyle, is a biography of its great men—"although their moral character may be less than perfect, they have intuitive insight and great sincerity."[5]   In these respects, Carlyle considered them superior, and, therefore, should be followed and obeyed to the point of worship.   Carlyle's thesis of leadership focused on the role of these "great men" who are the most important to the functioning of a society.

While Carlyle loved regimentation of followers around the great man and conceived of the ideal society as a kind of feudal community bound together in hero worship, John Stuart Mill abhorred that approach to leadership.   He looked upon the great man as one who should restore independence and originality by enlightening his followers and giving them a robust aptitude for critical and independent thought.[6]

4. Niccolo Machiavelli, *The Prince and the Discourses*, (New York: Modern Library), 1950, p. xxxvii.

5. Thomas Carlyle, *On Heroes, Hero-Worshipping and the Heroic in History*, (New York: Crowell), 1840, p. 10.

6. Edwin A. Burnett, *The English Philosophers from Bacon to Mill*, (London: Modern Library), 1939, p. 99.

In Mill's theory of leadership, it is found that the ingredients of domination, which were amplified by Machiavelli's cunning and force, or Carlyle's "seeing-eye intuition", were no longer crucial. Instead, Mill emphasized collective efforts and noted that "we only appear capable of anything great by our habit of combining." [7] Mill later advocated that the best way to find the great leader was through the institution of democracy. In this way, if heroes turn out to be shams, they can easily be dethroned without causing disorder or war.

Friedrich Hegel championed the "fashion concept" or *zeitgeist* theory of leadership. He suggested the idea that leaders are the instrument of historic forces. Obsessed by the great German dream, he predicted a great military leader who would fulfill its destiny. In Hegel's thesis, a leader is great in the sense that he understands the invincible logic of events and cooperates with history. It is the occasion, in Hegel's philosophy, that makes the "great man" rather than the reverse.[8]

Another attempt to explain modern leadership was made by Karl Marx and Friedrich Engels who were students of Hegel. They introduced the theory that the main force that propels the individual into social relationships is his *need to work*. They argued the case of "socio-economic leadership" as a result of the rise of the laboring classes in capitalist systems. Marx and Engels believed that leaders are necessary yet insignificant in terms of the inevitable changes of the course of history. They rejected Hegel's appeal to national patriotism and emphasized the need for class loyalty based on new patterns in economic production and distribution of wealth.

Administrative leadership developed in the twentieth century with the proliferation in public agencies and the ever-increasing need for organization, direction, supervision and control. Different from all previous theories, administrative leadership was characterized by the ability to follow a blueprint of rules and regulations. Regardless of any particular traits, biological, sociological, psychological or otherwise, bureaucratic chieftains who exerted sufficient control over their agencies and maintained the *status quo* were recognized for meritorious service. Being innovative, progressive, motivational, or successful in increasing the productivity of the workers was only secondary. The chieftain's seniority in the agency and his ability to memorize and recite the rules and obligations of his department were valued much more highly than his concern for his workers or their

7. Eugene E. Jennings, *An Anatomy of Leadership*, (New York: Harper and Brothers), 1960, p. 6.

8. See the works of George Wilhelm Friedrich Hegel as introduced and edited by Carl Friedrich, *Lectures on the Philosophy of History*, (London: G. Bell and Sons), 1890; and *Philosophy of Right*, (Oxford: Clarendon Press), 1965.

welfare. In fact, an admitted concern for the latter was perhaps seen as an administrative weakness and a leadership liability.

TYPOLOGY OF LEADERSHIP APPROACHES

Notwithstanding the previous discussion of the nature of leadership, studies made and research conducted are still far from presenting an accurate account of what constitutes leadership. Students of leadership have produced a multitude of lists of "traits of leadership". Such lists are either posed with complete generality or are presented as "good" and "bad" leadership traits. While most of these lists can be discounted on the grounds that any experienced layman could sit down and make up equally valid lists, most of the available research seems to have emphasized the utility of one or more of these approaches to leadership:

1 —The genetic approach.

2 —The personality approach.

3 —The sociological approach.

4 —The situational approach.

5 —The charismatic approach.

6 —The systematic-management approach.

The first five approaches will be described briefly in order to provide an analytical background to the following discussion of management leadership. The sixth will be discussed in detail and presented as the leadership approach most applicable and serviceable in police administration.

1 —**The Genetic Approach.** This was first presented by Sir Francis Galton in the nineteenth century and pertained to the nature of genetics. The Galton thesis declared that genius is inborn and bound to assert itself despite adverse circumstances. Children born of "superior genes" (compared with "normal" or "defective" genes) are apt to be intelligent, energetic, and headed for leadership. Galton's theory emphasized the theme that "blood will tell": the son of a lord would become a lord, and the son of a layman would become a layman.

While the genetic approach can not be totally discredited, leadership students today raise serious doubts about the hegemonic role of genes. Also biologists acknowledge today the influence of environment on the gene structure and growth. Geniuses do not always produce geniuses and "inferior" parents may produce "superior" offspring. Even if some human characteristics are inherited, heredity is not all that important in human affairs. While it has to be taken in consideration, "it need not be worshiped in a democratic society".[9]

2 —**The Personality Approach.** By far the largest body of material on leadership is based on the theory that leadership is a result of the personal traits and characteristics of the leader. Leadership in this approach bears a vital relationship to individuality. By virtue of his individuality, a person is able to perform in ways different from, and superior to, his peers and thus qualifies for leadership.[10] The leader who pushes his way up does so through the combination of a "strong" personality, a vigorous ego, and a steady determination to accomplish superior goals. While historically such a leader has been labeled a "born leader", modern students of leadership make a clear distinction between the defunct genetic model and the personality egoistic model. The examples of Napoleon, Hitler, Andrew Jackson, DeGaulle, and Nasser, among others, are self-evident. None of these was born to superior parents. They, however, were dominant egoists who showed early characteristics of leadership.

James Martin divided personality into *habits, attitudes,* and *traits.* A dynamic combination of these three would form a personality pattern peculiar to the individual. Although no one personality is perfectly integrated, psychologists expect that there will be a unique functional interrelationship of these three components which will characterize a leader. For such leadership to materialize, these functional interrelationships must be so striking, so challenging, and so stimulating as to thrust that person into a superior position.

The personality approach emphasizes three common personality models of leadership: the *autocratic,* the *paternalistic,* and the *bossist.*

a —The *autocratic model* is authoritarian in nature. Leaders justify their domination on the grounds of superiority. They tend to be objective, overt, and positive. They proceed aggressively and obtrusively. They command, captivate, and move with precision. They exercise great freedom and act as a law unto themselves. They are proud, boastful, cocksure, or seemingly so. In the extreme, autocratic leadership is ruthless.[11]

9. For a critical analysis of hereditary leadership see, H.S. Jennings, *The Biological Basis of Human Nature,* (New York: W.W. Norton & Co.), 1930, p. 384.

10. Emory S. Bogardus, *Leaders and Leadership,* (New York: Appleton-Century, Inc.), 1934, p. 4. For more information on the personality approach, see Ordway Tead, *The Art of Leadership,* (New York: Whittlessey House), 1935; James Martin, *The Tolerant Personality,* (Detroit: Wayne State University Press), 1964; and Howard Wriggins, *The Ruler's Imperative,* (New York: Columbia University Press), 1969.

11. Ordway Tead, *op. cit.,* p. 20.

b —The *paternalistic model* is perhaps the most common. It is Washingtonian in nature, fatherlike and considerate of the welfare of the group members. Such a leader may overrule the wishes of the group if these seem ill-advised. If mistakes are made by the group, the paternalistic leader assumes responsibility. Hence, he does his best to safeguard his group from error by making the final choices himself.[12]

c —The *bossist model* emerged in the mid-twenties. It is a pseudo-political type of leadership which is found between autocracy and paternalism and is more common in local government than in state or federal government. The boss is an extroverted person, a dubious individual, a shrewd master who plays upon human feelings. He ranges from the coarse, crude, autocrat in a factory to the suave politician. The boss calls himself a "realist" and all others "dreamy theorists". He knows his business well, takes whatever he can get, keeps for himself as much as he dares, and divides the rest among his associates. He demonstrates superior individuality and climbs to leadership by a combination of skill, industry, perseverence, good judgment, brute force and good fortune. And he usually has nobody to thank but himself.[13]

3 —**The Sociological Approach.** According to this approach, leadership is an aspect of social movements. Sociologists see leadership as the activity of influencing people to work together for a common end. Leadership in this model is considered a product of group life. It involves a number of persons in mental contact; a person may assume dominance over the others *only* by their consent. The leader thus becomes their delegated representative, but only as long as a dialogue between the leader and the group lasts. If such a give-and-take relationship ceases to exist, the representative status of the leader usually is withdrawn.

The role of the leader in this model is often evident in democratic organizations where leaders are elected to position. The role of followers becomes equally important since they can refuse to obey or to take punishment rather than blindly follow. The leader, therefore, must continually consider the various reactions by his followers.

The leader in this model has to act when the group demands action. He has to be more resourceful than his fellowmen. He has to stimulate group members into making a decision. While the leader is fairly independent in his judgment, it is assumed that "right" simply means satisfactory to the members.

12. *Ibid.*, p. 22.

13. William Bennett Munro, *Personality in Politics*, (New York: Macmillan Company), 1925, p. 67.

The sociological approach of leadership most logically encompasses the image of the democratic leader. He grows out of the needs of the group, seeks to define these needs, and stimulates the members to secure adequate satisfaction. The democratic leader draws people up to their *best* level and does not push them in line with his own purposes. He suggests rather than orders, ministers to his group members, and trains them to become leaders and eventually replace him.[14]

4 —**The Situational Approach.** This suggests that leaders must have situations or moments that will bring their genius to the fore, and without such situations many great men would remain unknown. William James suggested that effective leadership occurs by a *proper marriage* between the personality of a leader and the presence of a particular situation.[15] James' thesis seems to confirm the older "time spirit" theory by Hegel and by Johann Fichte. The latter emphasized that situations call upon personalities to play required roles in fulfillment of destiny. Thus, situational leaders may be powerful not primarily because they are great, but because they skillfully exploited a "ripe situation".[16]

A most famous example of situational leadership is that of Theodore Roosevelt. The situation of the United States then was that of a nation which held in its hands the fate of other nations but was seriously menaced by exceptional dangers from its neighbor from the south. With the picture of the American dilemma he anticipated in mind, he proclaimed to the young nation, "Here is a task and I have got to do it".[17]

5 —**The Charismatic Approach.** A charismatic leader is distinguished from all other leaders by his capacity to inspire loyalty toward himself as the source of authority apart from an established status.

Max Weber adapted the term *charisma* from the vocabulary of early Christianity, where it meant a *god-given gift,* to denote one of three types of authority in his classic thesis on legitimate government. Weber made a distinction between traditional authority based on "immemorial tradition," rational-legal authority based on "legiti-

---

14. Gleaned from William Foote Whyte, "Leader-Follower Relations in Street-Corner Society", published in Harold Proshansky and Bernard Seidelberg, *Basic Studies in Social Psychology*, (New York: Holt, Rinehart and Winston), 1965.

15. William James, "The Dilemma of Determinism", in his book *The Will to*

Believe, (New York: Dover Publications), 1965, p. 26.

16. Eugene Jennings, *op. cit.*, p. 9.

17. *Ibid.*, p. 93.

macy of rules," and charismatic authority based on "devotion to an individual" endowed with supernatural or extraordinary powers.[18]

While elements of charismatic leadership may be present in all forms of leadership, the preeminently charismatic leader is distinguished from other leaders by his *superhuman* or exceptional qualities. It is not so much what the leader is, however, but how he is regarded by those subjected to his charisma.

A charismatic leader may be viewed by his followers as imbued with a sense of mission, religious zeal, military heroism, providence or other gifts which are ascribed to a few. He is often seen as the savior of the nation, the community, the organization, or the group. Ann Ruth Willner suggested that the charisma of a leader is bound to and may even depend on his assimilation in the thoughts and feelings of the populace, in their sacred figures, divine beings and heroes. Willner further explains that the charismatic leader communicates to his followers a *sense of continuity* between himself and his mission and their legendary heroes and heritage.

Charismatic leaders like Churchill, Hitler, Gandi, DeGaulle, Nasser, and on the American scene Jackson, Kennedy, and MacArthur, strongly influenced their followers. They managed, in different degrees, to elicit from their peoples devotion and awe unsurpassed by most leaders. Their main weapons were personal magnetism and charm, which dominated their charismatic approach to leadership. In the course of interaction with his followers, the charismatic leader transmits, and his followers accept, his presentation of himself as their predestined custodian, his conviction of his mission, and their privilege of accepting his role as an architect of their destiny.

Because it often exceeds the dominance of constitutional authority, charismatic leadership, except in cases of crises and emergencies, is rarely appreciated in developed societies. It is commonly refuted on the basis of its lack of realism and its involvement in hero-worshipping. In public service, especially at the lower levels, charismatic leadership has often proved to be short-lived, unstable, unpredictable, and its results, by and large, disastrous.

THE SYSTEMATIC–MANAGEMENT APPROACH

Rational administration must be predictable, fair, and stable. The affairs of rational administration, therefore, cannot be left to the genealogy, personality, or charisma of a "do-it-yourself" leader. Moreover, the general users of public services today are not interest-

---

18. Max Weber, *The Theory of Social and Economic Organization,* edited by Talcott Parsons, (New York: Oxford University Press), 1947, p. 328.

ed in the kind of leadership the *man behind the desk* has except in as much as that leadership would affect the efficiency and effectiveness of the public services they receive. This is furthermore supported by the fact that, bureaucracy today, "the headless, fourth branch of government" is led largely by a group of *anonymous* leaders, whose leadership the public can not recognize anyway, even if that public was interested in tracing it. All that the public seems to be concerned with in the present administrative society is to have chief technocrats with a specialized "ability to get the right things done." [19]

The systematic-management approach to leadership applies, by definition, to leadership of public and private agencies. Its success does not depend on "blue blood", looks or charm, or oratory and the use of rhetoric. It is temporary in nature and is usually limited to the length of tenure in office. While most leaders in this category are appointed to their positions of leadership as in the case of cabinet members, heads of bureaus, federal judges, police chiefs and corporate directors, management leaders could also reach their positions through the electoral process. Examples of the latter include state judges, county sheriffs, and chairpersons in many corporate and private enterprises.

As the title indicates, this approach to leadership is fundamentally systematic. It is organized along the lines of natural and behavioral sciences. Its primary purpose is the attainment of prescribed goals and objectives through methodical means. Agency staff may include professional planners, decision makers, communicators and researchers, but such an agency may still operate below its level of potential as long as it lacks that dynamic spark which could systematically convert ideas into results, policies into realities, and blueprints into tangible products. The management approach to leadership strongly emphasizes the need for brainy individuals who are educated and experienced in the use of behavioral methodology, economic theories, and managerial techniques. Thus, when public agencies today agonize over the shortage in management leadership talents, they certainly are not implying a shortage in administrators or bureau heads. What such agencies are looking for are qualified specialists who can assume management leadership and exercise it systematically, industriously and effectively.[20] As an example, Hersey and Blanchard cite recent statistics from the business world which indicate that "of every 100 new business establishments started, approximately 50, or one-half, go out of business within two years. By the end of five years, only one-third of the original 100 will still be in

19. Peter Drucker, *The Effective Executive*, (New York: Harper & Row Publishers), 1967, pp. 21–22.

20. Paul Hersey and Kenneth H. Blanchard, *Management of Organizational Behavior*, (Englewood Cliffs, New Jersey: Prentice-Hall, Inc.), 1972, p. 67.

business".[21] Hersey and Blanchard confirm that most of the failures
are attributed to "ineffective management leadership".[22]

Management leadership is the art of work motivation and productivity. It is basically a special relationship between the manager-
leader and his working groups and individuals. Its objective is primarily *twofold*: the development of job satisfaction due to the impact
of the "bright" leader on his staff, supervisers, and workers. The
other is the increase in agency productivity as a result of the leader's
motivational effort, coordinating ability, and dedication to goal
achievement.

George Terry defined management leadership as "the activity of
influencing people to strive willingly for group objectives".[23] Robert
Tannenbaum, Irving Weschler and Fred Massarik referred to this
type of systematic leadership as an "interpersonal influence exercised
in a situation and directed, through the communication process, toward the attainment of a specialized goal or goals".[24] A review of recent management literature also reveals that most managers today
consider leadership as the process *of influencing the activities of
workers in an effort to achieve agency goals under situational constraints*. From this consensus, it follows that the study of management leadership is primarily concerned with the talents of these managers as they interact with certain task situations.[25]

TRAITS AND TASKS OF LEADERSHIP

While management leadership does not specify a set of universal
traits that a leader must possess when he is appointed or elected to
his position, leaders of public agencies obviously do not come pack-
aged. To General Mark Clark, the necessary traits included confidence, energy, timing, tenacity, concern, morality and faith.[26] Presi-

21. Peter Drucker, *The Practice of Management*, (New York: Harper & Row Publishers), 1954.

22. Paul Hersey and Kenneth H. Blanchard, *op. cit.*, pp. 67–70.

23. George R. Terry, *Principles of Management*, 3rd ed., (Homewood, Illinois: Richard D. Irwing, Inc.), 1960, p. 5.

24. Robert Tannenbaum, Irving R. Weschler, and Fred Massarik, *Leadership and Organization: A Behavioral Science Approach*, (New York: Mc-Graw-Hill Book Company).

25. For more information on this subject, see Robert Kahn and Daniel Katz, *Leadership Practices in Relationship to Productivity and Morale*, (Ann Arbor: Institute for Social Research), 1952; Robert Zager, "Management and the Productivity of Labor", *Advanced Management*, (June, 1961), V. 26; Chris Argyris, *Integrating the Individual and the Organization*, (New York: Wiley), 1964; David T. Stanley, *Men Who Govern*, (Washington: Brookings), 1967.

26. General Mark W. Clark, "What it Takes to be a Leader", *Reader's Digest*, (July, 1967), V. 91, pp. 160–162.

dent Kennedy's list contained courage, judgment, integrity and dedication.[27] David Thompson, a notable management consultant, suggested that the ideal management leader ought to be other-people oriented, flexible in his approach as the situation may demand, strongly committed to work, and watchful for rewarding situations for his workers.[28]

While these traits are obviously so broad in nature and could be applicable to any leader, whether he is a politician, a bishop, a general, a county sheriff, a chief surgeon, or a garage superintendent, managers virtually *grow* in their abilities and mature in their leadership traits. The growth process is not taught by rote but learned by example, inspiration, and unremitting practice. New and refined managerial traits gradually develop by constant exposure to work complexities, by continuous exercise of choice among severe odds, by awesome endurance of social and political pressures, and, naturally, by the processes of training and education. Management leadership matures when the *young executives* learn and absorb their lesson, synchronize their skills, feel relaxed with their *feet in the fire,* and become open, knowledgeable, and optimistic "shapers of values".[29]

Rensis Likert, an ardent supporter of management leadership, therefore, extended his trait list considerably in his portrayal of the mature management leader. To Likert, a good manager: [30]

1 —has an unselfish, sympathetic, cooperative attitude toward workers;

2 —is interested in his workers' success;

3 —exhibits a democratic mentality;

4 —is enthusiastic about the attainment of agency goals;

5 —demonstrates intellectual thinking;

6 —has a planning capability;

7 —possesses a friendly personality;

8 —has a supportive attitude;

9 —sets high standards;

10 —coaches and trains his teams.

27. U.S. Civil Service Commission, *A Guide for Executive Selection,* (Washington: GPO, Personnel Methods Series #13), 1961, p. 1.

28. David W. Thompson, "Some Criteria for Selecting Managers", *Personnel Administration,* (January-February), 1968, V. 31, pp. 32–37.

29. Harlan Cleveland, *The Future Executive,* (New York: Harper and Row Publishers), 1972, pp. 120–121.

30. Rensis Likert, *New Patterns of Government,* (New York: McGraw-Hill), 1961, pp. 10, 101 and elsewhere.

J. D. Williams, among many other concerned writers on management traits, offered a list of seven managerial essentials: [31]

1 —Breadth of vision without which administrators would tend to look upon their powers in narrowly and isolated terms and fail to conceive of any higher public service than that of carrying out a static set of structured functions.

2 —Personal integrity which would not make *angels* out of *administrators,* which is impossible anyway in their present human form, but induce honesty, decency, and moral responsibility in the business of administration.

3 —The art of compromise by which administrators could know "when to give a little in order to get a lot in the name of public good".

4 —The ability to make appropriate decisions, especially on critical human questions, despite the fettering constraints of rules and regulations.

5 —The ability to delegate work assignments to selected subordinates and share responsibilities with the work force.

6 —Great language skills to articulate the polyglot of issues and simplify the expression of directions, ways, and means to the general publics concerned.

7 —A sense of humor, not because administration is a laughing matter but because a democratic society needs to be reminded of the humanness of its public servants. Also, because a rapier wit is a superb weapon for administrative self-defense.[32]

The other approach to the study of management leadership is the task approach. This approach, on the other hand, amplifies the situational aspect of leadership. It deemphasizes significance of leadership traits and limits the role of leaders to that of "executors" of administrative tasks, technocrats, and careful supervisors. Proponents of the task approach stress that tasks must be accurately specified and standards of performance exactly defined.

Proponents of the task approach are plentiful. Philip Selznick suggested these tasks as the most significant: [33]

1 —Giving tone and direction to the organization as a whole and leaving routine aspects to deputies.

31. J.D. Williams, *op. cit.*, p. 127.

32. There is something beautiful about the thought of Franklin D. Roosevelt in an annual address to the Daughters of the American Revolution greeting them as "My fellow immigrants". And somehow history and the moment both seemed to come together through President John F. Kennedy when he welcomed America's Nobel and Pulitzer laureates to a White House dinner, "the greatest assemblage of brains in this House since Jefferson had breakfast alone".

33. J.D. Williams, *op. cit.*, p. 18.

2 —Deciding critical issues.

3 —Defending institutional integrity.

4 —Mediating internal conflict.

5 —Guiding change and reconstruction.

Peter Drucker offered this list of manager task skills: [34]

1 —Knows where his time goes.

2 —Focuses on outward contributions.

3 —Builds on strength.

4 —Concentrates on a few areas most likely to yield high results.

5 —Makes effective decisions.

The controversy over trait-oriented leadership and task-oriented leadership has for long persisted with little hope for ever being resolved. While the lists offered by both sides seem to overlap considerably, neither side has been able to present empirical evidence to support its stand conclusively. Traditionalists who strongly supported the trait approach seen to be deeply involved in the situational analysis of leadership and vice versa. Leaders of the real world of management, as a result, seem to have developed a balanced combination of both approaches. For instance, Floyd Mann has proposed three kinds of leadership "skills" in which he combined both traits and tasks. He suggested competence in management, human relations, and technical know-how.[35] Corson and Paul, as another example, identified four skills: capacity for directing others, understanding of the agency's internal environment, understanding of the external environment, and a deep awareness of the substance of the programs being managed.[36]

In the final analysis, what this combinational compromise suggests is a) modern management has no use for leadership by "saints" or "heroes"; practicing *hero worshipping* by workers could be disastrous, b) traits are only personal and may offer little help to an agency unless its tasks are kept in order in the first place, c) leadership, in order to be effective, must be viewed as such through the eyes of the working groups who carry out management tasks, and d) even if the task approach may seem adequate, "well-traited" leaders would

34. Peter Drucker, *The Effective Executive*, (New York: Harper and Row, Inc.), 1967, pp. 21–22.

35. Floyd Mann, "Toward an Understanding of the Leadership Role in Formal Organization"; in Robert Dubin, *Leadership and Productivity*, (San Francisco: Chandler), 1965; J. D. Williams, *op. cit.*, p. 123.

36. J. D. Williams, *op. cit.*, p. 123.

be preferred since they can at least make workers more satisfied, secure and happy.

EFFECTIVE MANAGEMENT LEADERSHIP

The essence of management leadership is the ability to identify the needs of work groups and to meet these needs in ways conducive to optimal productivity. While such needs naturally vary from one organization to another and from time to time, they can only be seen in terms of two major categories: production-oriented needs and worker-oriented needs.

Production-oriented needs are work-centered. They relate to definition of goals, policy-making, program building, selection of means, effective communication, organizational development, evaluation of efficiency, effectiveness, and economy of the agency, etc. Such needs are usually met through task-oriented leaders like those suggested by Selznick, Drucker and others.

Worker-oriented needs, on the other hand, are personnel-oriented. They relate to improving interpersonal relations, enhancing informal organization, motivating subordinates, lending support, raising morale, and reducing friction among workers. Such needs are normally met through trait-oriented leaders like those suggested by Clark, Kennedy, Williams and others.

A series of studies were recently launched by Ohio State University and focused on these two categories of needs which leaders are supposed to provide. Along the same lines of production-oriented and worker-oriented analysis, the series broke down the functions of effective leadership into: [37]

(a) Initiating structure (IS), which covers leadership contribution to the designation of goals, selection of means, processing of work plans, and other routine management functions.

(b) Providing consideration for workers (PCW), which entails contributing to the motivation of personnel, removing "hygiene factors" causing frustration among workers, providing security and harmony among employees, and other necessary motivational functions.

Another model built along the same classification of the roles of management leadership was introduced by the Survey Research Center at the University of Michigan. In order to avoid redundance, it suffices to mention that the model followed the same Ohio classification under different names. The Michigan model simply referred to

37. The Ohio State studies mentioned here are summarized in Bowers and Seashore, "Predicting Effectiveness with a Four-Factor Theory of Leadership", *Administrative Science Quarterly*, (September, 1966), V. II, pp. 238–263.

IS as production-centered leadership and to PCW as employee-centered leadership.[38]

J. D. Williams, the notable management theorist from the University of Utah, added yet another version of effective management leadership configuration by discussing two major roles for leaders; (a) task roles, and (b) maintenance roles.

(a) *Task roles,* which are similar to IS and production-centered leadership, consist of two specific functions: (1) goal setting, and (2) selection of means.[39]

Goal setting is a basic concern of work groups in public agencies. Because goals are primarily determined by public policy, effective leadership has the obligation to help develop and articulate these goals and see to it that they are transmitted to all work units of the agency. Williams emphasized that the opportunity of leadership in this role lies *not* in simply being a *conveyer belt* between the legislative, the agency, and the public, but in positively initiating, and influencing, suitable public policies which can capture the imagination and energies of employees. By so doing, emphasized Williams, managers can help "the word become flesh and dwell among us".

Williams, moreover, emphasized that making goals come alive for workers is one of the great challenges of effective management leaders. He cited that "where there is no vision, the people perish", and it is the job of the effective leader to see to it that all his associates catch the vision of public policy by setting challenging—but reachable—goals for the agency. Through "shared goal setting", Williams explained, workers become "involved" and involvement "leads to commitment".

Selection of means is the second function of task roles to be performed by effective leaders. Williams asserts that while some goal setting may have to be handled by the leader on an authoritarian basis, a very substantial part of means selection ought to be left in the hands of work units themselves. Effective leaders should delegate the authority to work groups to develop workable procedures, identify practical methods, and determine the sequence and pace of work steps.

(b) *Maintenance roles* are similar to PCW and employee-centered leadership. In Williams' analysis, maintenance roles consist of three significant functions: (1) personal support of workers' needs, (2) representing them before political authorities, and (3) improving interpersonal relations.

38. J.D. Williams, *op. cit.*, p. 110.

39. Most of this discussion is gleaned from Williams views on management leadership as presented in his book, *op. cit.*, pp. 113–133.

Over and beyond the task roles which leaders have to play efficiently, the provision for workers' needs through maintenance roles is an absolute prerequisite for effective management over the long run. Providing the worker with occupational satisfaction and the preservation of a healthy group life among workers can not be ignored or put off. While it is the responsibility of the effective leader to meet his workers' maintenance needs, it is only realistic to assume that he would not be able to carry all these functions personally. Appropriate delegation would naturally be expected.

Through this first function, personal support of workers' needs, the effective leader ought to be able to help his workers overcome their personal problems, to appreciate their working conditions, to understand their supervisor's role, and to elevate the workers' perceptions of the "job" to a meaningful, worthwhile career. Such efforts by the leader may include helping the new employee to locate appropriate housing, helping the worker's spouse find an appropriate job, listening to the worker's complaints, sending him a get well card when he is sick or a congratulation card if he is promoted.

Through the second function, representing the workers before the political authorities, effective leaders are expected to be *able and willing* to fight the workers' battles with city hall. The effective leader must seriously and objectively represent his workers before the appropriate authority in charge of the agency. This includes the workers' petitions and requests regarding budget allocations, pay increases, fringe benefits, work hours and conditions. Naturally, without appearing like a *rebel leader* or championing illegal action by his workers, the effective leader should use his personal relations with the political authorities and support the legitimate claims of his workers. The leader should objectively relay the "mood of the agency" to the mayor, governor, or board of directors. Furthermore, he can offer his powers to reconcile differences and mediate reasonable solutions before relations are strained and responsible people *stop talking to each other.*

Through the third function, improving interpersonal relations among workers, effective leaders ought to improve the quality of group life and to build cohesiveness and resolve conflicts. This requires that the leader authorize training programs which will bring his agency levels together, develop an agency "mystique" (analogous to that of the Army Corps of Engineers, the Marine Corps and the FBI before Watergate), encourage and support informal groups within the agency (bowling club, fishing club, gourmet club, etc.) and preserve the agency's human fabric, especially through a group of dedicated front line supervisors.

By way of emphasis, let it be stressed again from the foregoing discussion that while all work groups universally have both task needs and maintenance needs, those needs do not constitute an agenda for leaders alone. Effective management leaders would be well advised to note an old maxim of John Stuart Mill that the whole purpose of government is to make men more self-governing, not to usurp the business of life from those who are perfectly capable of tending to that business themselves.[40] The portrait of the successful leader which begins to emerge, then, is that of one who can share his leadership responsibilities with his associates, teach his assistants the art of effective leadership and enable his men to perceive and appreciate its impact. "Enabling the organization" rather than unilaterally doing these himself is, indeed, the crux of management leadership.[41]

STYLES OF MANAGEMENT LEADERSHIP

Three basic styles of management leadership are usually identified as: *authoritarian, democratic,* and *laissez-faire.*

Because the value of democracy is so highly regarded in the American culture, a natural resentment to the notion of authoritarian leadership seems to be common. However, since most leadership positions in government service are not elective positions and since the processes of policy making and policy implementation are not—and cannot—be reached by employee vote, some element of bureaucratic authoritarianism must be accepted. Also since most management leadership positions are usually assigned to employees who have proven expertise gained through education, seniority, or both, it becomes only logical that these leaders be entrusted with the "final say" in decisions relating to the implementation of statutes, the choices among controversial alternatives, and the establishment of new administrative precedents in areas not before regulated by laws or court decisions. Aside from that, it must be stressed that management theories, which do not consistently support any one style of leadership, are not particularly enchanted with authoritative leadership either.[42] Except as a means of last resort, most contemporary research seems "to support the desirability of moving toward the democratic type" of leadership.[43]

40. John Stuart Mill, *Considerations on Representative Government,* (New York: Liberal Arts Press), 1958, p. 28.

41. This paragraph is taken almost literally from J.D. Williams, *op. cit.,* p. 115.

42. Robert T. Golembiewski, "Three Styles of Leadership and Their Uses", *Personnel,* XXXVIII, No. 4, (July-August), 1961, p. 35.

43. John M. Pfiffner and Frank P. Sherwood, *Administrative Organization,* (Englewood Cliffs, New Jersey: Prentice-Hall), 1960, p. 364.

Authoritarian leadership tends to dominate the organization. The manager's attitudes toward his employees has a Tennysonian sound: "You are not to make a reply; you are not to reason why; you are but to work and die". This kind of management leader assumes both the task roles and the maintenance roles, makes the work assignments, lays down the time schedules, encourages uniform procedures, blasts poor workmanship, and by tone of voice and by *iron pen* makes it unmistakably clear *who is boss.*[44]

The democratic style contemplates a leader who involves his workers significantly in means selection and in group maintenance activities where feasible and appropriate; consults with them in regard to objectives and long range plans; is a builder of men rather than *robots;* realizes that he does not know it all and that his employees know a great deal; and is strongly committed to the proposition that *management begins with people.* The democratic manager leads, but rarely dictates; consults, listens, and persuades, but rarely commands; sees to it that issues are faced up to and resolved, not dodged; and makes it perfectly clear that, along with his concern for human beings working with him, he also has work standards and production standards against which he will measure the whole organization's performance.[45]

The laissez-faire style leadership is essentially a no-leadership pattern. It is a kind of anarchistic pattern of administration where all of the task roles and all of the maintenance roles devolve upon the work groups themselves to be performed. The spirit of laissez-faire leadership seems to be *do your own thing and let us hope for the best.* Perhaps the most common locale of the laissez-faire style is the *country club* organization pattern common among friendship groups where the supervision of tasks and maintenance of roles are passed around on a highly informal basis.[46]

To explain the three styles of management leadership even further, White and Lippitt produced the following table: [47]

Authoritarian	Democratic	Laissez-faire
1. All determination of policy by the leader.	1. All policies a matter of group discussion and decision, encouraged and assisted by the leader.	1. Complete freedom for group or individual decision, with a minimum of leader participation.

44. J.D. Williams, *op. cit.*, p. 115.

45. *Ibid.*

46. *Ibid.*

47. Ralph White and Ronald Lippitt, "Leader Behavior and Member Reac-

Authoritarian	Democratic	Laissez-faire
2. Techniques and activity steps dictated by the authority, one at a time, so that future steps were always uncertain to a large degree.	2. Activity perspective gained during discussion period. General steps to group goal sketched, and when technical advice was needed, the leader suggested two or more alternative procedures from which choice could be made.	2. Various materials supplied by the leader who made it clear that he would supply information when asked. He took no other part in work discussion.
3. The leader usually dictated the particular work task and work companion of each member.	3. The members were free to work with whomever they chose, and the division of tasks was left to the group.	3. Complete non-participation of the leader.
4. The dominator tended to be "personal" in his praise and criticism of the work of each member; remained aloof from active group participation except when demonstrating.	4. The leader was "objective" or "fact-minded" in his praise and criticism, and tried to be a regular group member in spirit without doing too much work.	4. Infrequent spontaneous comments on member activities unless questioned, and no attempt to appraise or regulate the course of events.

Neither the task-oriented approach with absolute concern for production, nor the maintenance-oriented approach with absolute concern for employees, is, however, totally correct. The effective management leader must learn to mix them in an appropriate combination. A "magic formula" by which a universally-acceptable combination is set up, however, does not exist and most likely will never be found as long as administration is performed by neither angels or robots. The right combination will also vary from one organization to another, from one administrative environment to another, from one leader to another, and clearly from one time to another.

To provide some guidelines, however, by which the "right formula" is to be reached, Robert Blake and Jane Mouton devised their famous model by which managers could anticipate the likely results of the combinations they select. In their Managerial Grid model, Blake

tion in Three Social Climates", in D. Cartwright and A. Zander (eds.), *Group Dynamics, Research and Theo-* *ry*, (New York: Harper and Row), 1960, p. 528.

and Mouton presented five resulting situations which would most likely appear under possible combinations.[48] Figure 24 illustrates their model of the Managerial Grid.

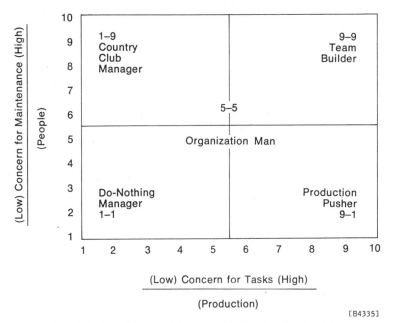

Fig. 24. The Managerial Grid of Effective Leadership

Concern for tasks (production) is illustrated on the horizontal axis. Production becomes more important to the leader as his rating advances on the horizontal scale. A leader with a rating of 9 on the horizontal axis has a maximum concern for production. The vertical axis indicates concern for maintenance (employees). People become more important to the leader as his rating progresses up the vertical axis. A leader with a rating of 9 on the vertical axis has maximum concern for employees.[49] The degree of concern one has for production and for people decides the way one acts. For example, a manager with a high degree of concern for production and a low one for people will push production without regard for people. The Grid permits 81 possible combinations of which five are considered major leadership styles; (a) the 1,1 do-nothing manager, (b) the 1,9 country club manager, (c) the 9,1 production pusher, (d) the 9,9 team builder, and (e) the 5,5 organization man. The resulting leadership situations are described as follows:

(a) Do-nothing manager (lower left): Exertion of minimum effort to get work tasks done or employee needs met. It is a form of a

48. Robert R. Blake and Jane S. Mouton, *The Managerial Grid*, (Houston, Texas: Gulf Publishers), 1964.

49. Paul Hersey and Kenneth H. Blanchard, *Management of Organizational Behavior*, (Englewood Cliffs, New Jersey: Prentice-Hall, Inc.), 1972, p. 72.

"cop-out", but does not necessarily mean inept manager. 1,1 is a survival strategy for retaining membership to enjoy the benefits of retirement without really making an involved or committed contribution to the success of the organization. Black and Mouton called this manager "visible without being seen".

(b) Country club manager (upper left): Exertion of minimum effort to get work tasks done and a maximum effort to get employee needs met. It is a form of a "big happy family", where employees have a strong voice in the making of policy especially with regard to what they would like to do or avoid doing. The role of the manager is therefore reduced to "first among equals".

(c) Production pusher (lower right): Exertion of maximum effort to get work tasks done and a minimum effort to get employee needs met. Notwithstanding lack of concern for people involved, the manager here is considered successful since he gets the job done most efficiently and effectively. Decisions are made by the manager alone and his policies are clearly dictatorial. The role of the manager here would be similar to that of a "slave driver".

(d) Team builder (upper right): Exertion of maximum effort to get work tasks done and a maximum effort to get employee needs met. It is the most favored style by managers based on their *feel* for what is right. The manager here is not only considered successful because he gets the job done efficiently and effectively, but also because he stimulates his workers to do it *with pleasure*. The manager in this style would be secure, intelligent, democratic, humanistic, and "great to work for".

(e) Organization man (center): Exertion of a moderate effort to get work tasks done and an equal effort to get employee needs met. The manager here would be mediocre only concerned about meeting "the requirements" as specified by work manuals. People would be viewed as "position holders" who should be treated by the "rights and privileges" of the job. The role of the manager would be limited to that of a "custodian in charge".

While Blake and Mouton thought so highly of the 9,1 manager who can accomplish definite work results, they worried about the side effects which this pattern may produce among workers. Being treated like "tools of production," they argued, soon would become a deterrent to effectiveness especially among conscientious workers. The ideal type of administrative leadership, they stressed, was naturally 9,9 management. Leveling and openness, the authors explained, can guarantee a better job and provide maximum satisfaction to most workers.

Blake and Mouton stress that their model is valuable in precipitating change in managerial thought and styles of leadership. The model makes it easier to identify negative and positive aspects and shows the managers what it is that they are doing and what they ought to replace it with. Moreover, the model can help managers sort out and evaluate their associates and colleagues who have been successful and understand how they differ from the others.

To further explain the gray areas between the "production pusher" 9,1 and the "team builder" 9,9 Tannenbaum and Schmidt offered an amplified view of the situation. They depicted a broad range of leadership behavior on a continuum moving from authoritarian to democratic extremes as follows.[50] Figure 25 illustrates the continuum:

(Authoritarian) .... (Democratic)

Task-Oriented   Maintenance-Oriented

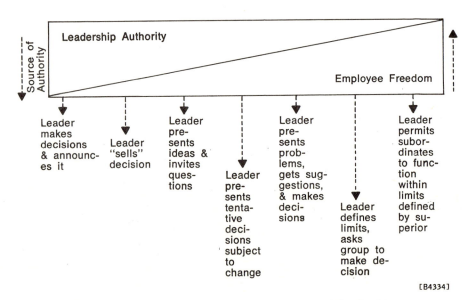

[B4334]

Fig. 25. Authoritarian-Democratic Continuum of Leadership

Leaders whose behavior is observed to be at the authoritarian end of the continuum tend to be task-oriented and care very little if any about the personal needs of their employees. On the other hand, leaders, whose behavior is observed to be at the democratic end of

50. *Ibid.*, p. 71.

the continuum, tend to be maintenance-oriented and care very highly for the satisfaction and happiness of their employees. The laissez-faire behavior, which apparently was not worth any due recognition by Tannenbaum and Schmidt, extends far beyond democratic leadership on an imaginary continuum. As mentioned earlier, laissez-faire has no established policies or procedures, attempts to influence no one, and is generally considered as totally ineffective in public service.

To conclude this discussion on effective management leadership, it must be stressed that in the real world of management, leaders do not, and probably cannot, calculate in advance what their leadership style will be like. If that were not the case, the chances are that the majority of managers in America would have selected to be democratic leaders, a situation far from being true in today's public and private agencies. Practical management is situational in nature, and effective management must be able to change its style not only in response to changing agency conditions but also in anticipation of these changes. In stressful conditions, for instance, Korlen states that authoritarian leadership would "be more satisfying and tension reducing".[51] In stable times, on the other hand, "one's *a priori* sentiments are all with the democratic style".[52]

The intelligent selection of the style of leadership to be applied, as well as the *graceful* shift from one style to another, is indeed the crux of the art of management leadership. Mainly situational in nature, the following leads may be worth special consideration:

(1) Relationship between leadership style and the intelligence level of workers: In a study by A. D. Calvin, it was found that authoritarian leadership effected a 100% improvement in the output of "dulls" in contrast to their output under democratic leadership.[53]

(2) Complexity of work situation: Golembiewski noted that where solutions to problems are very obvious, the authoritarian style may be more productive. Where, on the other hand, problems are complex and answers may be multiple, democratic leadership would be more productive.[54]

51. David C. Korlen, "Situational Determinants of Leadership Structure", *Journal of Conflict Resolution*, (September, 1962), pp. 222–235.

52. J.D. Williams, *op. cit.*, p. 116.

53. For more information about Calvin's study, read Robert Golembiewski, "Three Styles of Leadership and Their Uses", *Personnel*, (July-August), 1961, p. 37.

54. *Ibid.*, pp. 38–39.

(3) Extent of group cooperation needed for the job: Golembiewski also found in his study that when little cooperation is needed in task performance, the authoritarian style may function more effectively than its democratic counterpart.[55]

(4) Desired output: Rensis Likert reported in a study of leadership patterns in thirty-one production units that a high correlation existed between output and the freedom of workers to map out their own work processes (naturally a condition that would prevail under democratic leadership).[56]

(5) Identification of the leadership style applied: In a study by N. Z. Medalia, the leadership preferences of authoritarian and nonauthoritarian groups were measured. Medalia found that where only 36% of the nonauthoritarian group expressed hospitable attitudes towards their leaders, 59% of the authoritarian group accepted their leaders. Medalia assumed from his sample that the correct identification of the authoritarian personalities of a given set of workers coupled with strong leadership could result in a 23% improvement in group attitudes toward their chiefs.[57]

In summary, it is the work situation which is most significant in dictating the style of leadership at the time. While the right selection of the leadership style can make a substantial contribution to agency productivity and employee satisfaction, three basic conclusions must be realized: 1) the laissez-faire style flunks out as a possible leadership approach in government, 2) the authoritarian style is most effective in repetitive work tasks, especially among low-intelligence employees, and 3) the democratic style is preferable among above-average intelligence workers, especially those workers dealing with reasonably complex problems and multiple solutions.

EFFECTIVE POLICE LEADERSHIP

As a general rule, no system of effective police management can survive without effective leadership. Furthermore, any attempt to reform management in a police agency will be virtually futile if the incumbent chief elects to block it or negate its accomplishments. Effective police managers will produce effective police departments, and

55. *Ibid.*

56. Rensis Likert, *New Patterns of Management*, (New York: McGraw-Hill), 1961, p. 20.

57. As summarized by Robert Golembiewski, in J. D. Williams, *op. cit.*, p. 117.

ineffective police managers can not help but produce ineffective police departments.

Effective police leadership today has to be managerial in nature. All other approaches to leadership mentioned earlier, *genetic, personality, sociological, situational* or *charismatic,* would be too risky for the operation of a police agency. They tend to be too unpredictable, inconsistent, submissive, politically entangled, or strongly egotistical to provide a systematic, stable, and efficient flow of police services. Management in the public service, and particularly in the police, can not afford to take such a leadership risk. The purpose of management leadership, lest it is forgotten, is *not* to glorify the chiefs or perpetuate their heroic deeds. It is rather to provide an environment of rationality and dedication conducive to the achievement of goals effectively and fairly. The appointment of an unqualified police leader, therefore, could be the most damaging single mistake in the operation of a police department. Not only would such an appointment impair the flow and quality of services rendered to the public, it most likely would also decrease the productivity of the department, weaken the will and morale of officers, and expose the department to allegations of ineptness, rigidity, and corruption.

The reason why poor leadership is so detrimental to the progress of any police force is multifold: (1) In such a quasi-military structure all strategic decisions are made at the chief's level of hierarchy. (2) The chief personally selects all supervisors who can yield any real power within the organization. (3) The chief and his powerful supervisors set the department's philosophy regarding the selection of goals and means. (4) The chief, through his authority over his supervisors, enjoys complete control over all departmental operations and determines the quantity and quality of work tasks. (5) The chief, through his sanction powers, retains the ultimate power to punish and reward within the organization. (6) The chief, through his capacity as a chief executive, is the department's spokesman and defender before the local government, the public, and the mass media. (7) The chief has the ultimate veto power over all decisions, plans, communications—and most importantly—expenditures. It becomes obvious, therefore, that unless police leadership is well entrusted to someone with adequate education, expertise, judgement, and skills, not only would the police department suffer in its daily operations, but also the public it serves would become confused, frustrated, uncooperative, and, on many occasions, belligerent and maybe violent.

It is, however, gratifying to know that in light of the recent advancement in police science and technology, the increasing modernization in police organization, and the noticeable change in the police mentality, the old images of the "boss chief" and the "western sheriff" are fading away. Within the agency, for instance, the traditional reverence to the chief's authority based on his charisma, political connections, or conniving abilities, seems to be questioned and occasionally challenged by younger policemen. Outside the agency, on the other hand, the general view of the American public seems to have matured from a primary interest in the personality of the police chief, to one concerned with the efficient and responsive flow of services he can offer. With the nightmare of Watergate still fresh in the minds of many citizens and the increasing demand for more legalistic and specialized police services, the emerging image of the chief is a low-profile manager who is gifted with free thinking, concern for the people, self-confidence, demonstrated abilities, and obviously managerial skills.

The Task Force Report of 1967 persisted throughout its section on "developing police leadership" by saying that the future of police leadership *has to be managerial*. It strongly criticized and condemned traditional police leadership in which "sound management practices apparently are not understood nor used by administrative and command personnel .   .   .   planning and research are not utilized   .   .   .   staff inspection as a control device is not known".[58] Blaming this situation on poor police leadership, which "denied access to fresh outside executive talent of proven ability", the report proceeded to state that:

> The chief has had [no] training in police administration, command, or supervision   .   .   .   the chief's desk duties have created an unfavorable situation in which proper administrative and command precepts are not followed and in which field supervision and training is nonexistent.[59]

The report, in another reference, narrowed down the responsibility for this poor leadership to the lack of preparation of police chiefs and to the absence of standard qualifications for the position:

> Not infrequently the chief is wholly incompetent to discharge the onerous duties of his position. He may lack experience, executive ability, character, integrity, or the confidence of his force, or all of them put together.[60]

As a response, most likely to the report, the International Association of Chiefs of Police passed a resolution in 1968 emphasizing the need for *managerial* police leadership. The resolution said:

> .   .   .   the appropriateness and effectiveness of police service could best be assured through able direction and

58. *The Task Force Report* on the Police, 1967, p. 45.

59. *Ibid.*

60. *Ibid.*, p. 44.

leadership   .   .   .   the role and tasks of supervisory and command personnel are markedly different from operational duties, and the achievement of skill in supervisory and management functions depends upon adequate training.[61]

The state of police leadership, however, has not improved much since the "year of the report". No significant changes have been made with regard to the possible establishment of professional requirements beyond those necessary to becoming a police officer. Police chiefs still serve without a contract—at the *pleasure* of the mayor, city manager or a specified board. Police chiefs, except in rare cases, have *no tenure in office*. And no federal or state-mandated minimum standards for the selection and *training* of chiefs exist. Consequently, many police chiefs today remain primarily occupied with their survival on the job, their maintenance of peaceful relations with city hall, and their manipulation of the appearances of efficiency.

Although several authors and a few police practitioners have written and spoken up for leadership reform, no one has been as open, vigorous, and articulate as have Clarence Kelley, Robert DiGrazia, and Donald Shanahan.

Clarence Kelley, the FBI director, expressed his views before an association of police chiefs and urged the participants to be courageous and *innovative* thinkers. Kelley suggested that effective police leaders be *initiators* of change instead of being compulsed and coerced into it by external factors. Effective police chiefs, the director implied, ought to be in control of the policing profession, to guide its directions and scientifically change its properties toward the goal of full professionalization. Mr. Kelley told the assembled chiefs:

> Let us be honest with ourselves. Most of the substantial changes we have made as a profession in recent decades have been dictated by external pressures. Too often, we have instituted changes under compulsion and coercion. Too often, we have been hesitant and uncertain and by such delays we have made our decisions ineffective. Rather, we need to inculcate into our personnel, at all levels, an attitude which encourages creative and innovating thinking. We need to encourage a perception of change as part of the thinking process   .   .   .   The lack of innovation brings stagnation.[62]

61. From "Upgrading Police Leadership" an address by Boston Police Commissioner Robert J. DiGrazia before the Police Foundation's Executive Forum on Upgrading the Police, Washington, D.C., April 14, 1976, p. 7.

62. *Ibid.*, p. 4.

Robert Di Grazia, the former police commissioner of Boston, an educated, vigorous and outspoken practitioner, raised a major controversey among policemen and politicians alike when he coined the term "pet rocks" to describe traditional police chiefs who could not "move, grow, change, or innovate".[63] Di Grazia offered a profile for the current state of underdeveloped police leadership in America. His profile, cited here in his own words, stressed: [64]

—Mere survival, that is the goal of most of us . . . we police chiefs have no vision of ourselves beyond that of being survivors with gold braid.

—Most of us stand silent and let politicians get away with law and order rhetoric.

—Most of us are not telling the public that there is relatively little the police can do about crime.

—Few of our colleagues are questioning traditional practices and promoting innovation, demanding increased productivity, upgrading personnel and encouraging serious research.

—Most of us were good police officers who become chiefs because we were able to perform well on the three-hour, paper-and-pen test one Saturday morning.

—Do we take risks and truly lead? Seldom. Rather we seek to assure that our voyage on the departmental ship be a smooth one, at least until we reach our retirement port.

Beyond the basic goal of survival, Di Grazia asserted that most police chiefs remain immobile "in the often deadening insularity of the only police department [a chief] ever knew".[65]

In an attempt to offer a profile of the professional or the future "managerial-type" police leader, Di Grazia raised these questions: [66]

—Are we trying to expand our horizons and deepen our skills as leaders?

—Are we accepting greater challenges, satisfying our normal ambitions and enhancing our abilities?

—Are we demanding of ourselves and fellow police leaders in the department the unsettling experience of confronting new ideas . . . or do we relaxively settle back into the stereotypes and traditions we learned as rookies?

63. *Ibid.*, p. 3.

64. *Ibid.*, throughout the address.

65. From former Boston Police Commissioner Robert Di Grazia's address before the Annual Convention of the American Academy for Professional Law Enforcement, Hartford, Connecticut, May 27, 1976.

66. *Ibid.*

—Are we implementing through our leadership the new idea that, one way or another, affects our policing system?

—Do we welcome outside researches to test our traditional police strategies?

—Do we seek improved ways of delivering police services and enlisting better personnel?

Donald Shanahan, a veteran policeman who turned educator, emphasized the essential need for management techniques in police leadership. Shanahan explained that under traditional police management, most hierarchies are so encumbered with rules, traditions, and public laws, that even leaders can not truly point out the right direction or set the pace. Traditional leaders, he indicated, simply *follow precedents* and *obey regulations; none move at the head of the crowd.* Shanahan proceeded to say that such administrators lead only in the sense that the "carved wooden figurehead leads the ship." [67]

In drawing his profile of future police management leadership, Shanahan prescribed a model consisting of five basic management patterns: [68]

(a) **Management by Objectives** which emphasizes a goal-oriented philosophy and attitude. It focuses on results, with less concern for method as long as it is within acceptable legal and moral limits. It involves long-term planning and results in the directions that police leaders rationally need and wish to pursue.

(b) **Proactive Management** by which the police leader would consider the problem at hand unfettered by the risks (mainly political and social) involved in the decision. The main ingredients of proactive management are creativity and innovation. It is mostly carried out by *ad hoc* committees of police researchers and outside consultants.

(c) **Anticipatory Management** which is based on intellectual enrichment, selection of alternatives and a thorough evaluation of the consequences of the decision both internally and externally.

(d) **Adaptive Management** which is simply the possession of enough flexibility to adapt to the changing conditions in environment, community, judicial rulings, and organizational structure.

67. Donald T. Shanahan, "The Changing Police Leadership", a presentation made before the Tenth Interagency Workshop, Sam Houston State University, The Institute of Contemporary Corrections and the Behavioral Sciences, (Huntsville, Texas), 1975.

68. *Ibid.*

(e) **Reactive Management** and crisis management which intelligently and systematically respond to situations as they arise. Such responses naturally vary in accordance with the situation, the mental preparation of the leader, and the options available to the leader at the time of the crisis.

Shanahan suggested two major management strategies to be adopted by "police managers":

(a) **Collegiality of Command:** This strategy stems from the complexities associated with the functions of the police leader. Because of the enormous demands on his time, his physical abilities, and intellectual capacity, a police manager has to seek help from the staff. Under the concept of collegial command, the police manager must be willing to share his authority and power as well as his operational responsibility and accountability. A self-actualized chief must provide the opportunities for his qualified staff members to participate in the decision-making process and to grow through the challenges of their position on the police force.

(b) **Political Statesmanship:** The effective police leader should be able to use his management abilities to meet the test of the diplomat. He should be able to conform, confront, compromise, and collaborate in order to achieve his objectives without, however, getting involved in illegal, unethical, or immoral practices. While the concept may, admittedly, prove too risky, if applied by insecure leaders, Shanahan suggests that mature and effective managers should be able to practice political statesmanship in an intangible manner "almost to the point of being abstract".

The final part of this discussion of leadership will address three practical questions because of their particular association with effective police leadership:

1 —The insider versus the outsider police chief.

2 —The tenure of the police chief.

·3 —Preparation of the police chief.

1 —The Insider versus the Outsider Police Chief

A question most frequently debated in selecting a police chief is whether to look for a new chief inside or outside the local police department. The vehemence with which this argument is pursued is sometimes quite startling to students of police leadership. While the debate is not at all easy to follow, arguments have been advanced as if some special leadership quality attaches to being located within the department or outside it. Instead, the question should be seen as a factor that simply needs to be weighed along with other qualifications.[69]

The conventional argument against outsiders is that they either will be unable to undertake needed changes until they become familiar with local style, personnel, and policing techniques, or they will attempt to impose inappropriate, alien, and potentially explosive standards and ideas on the local force.[70]

The argument against insiders is that because of their parochialism and inbred professional background, they will severely limit development and innovative change in the department. They may also reinforce existing undesirable tendencies, factions, or complacency, the argument runs.

The case for outsiders usually emphasizes the value of new ideas, the prospect of hiring unusually high-quality talent, and the broad professional contacts and abilities that are not available within the department.

The case for insiders focuses on the advantages of stability within the department, the high morale such a selection would foster among personnel, and the continuity of the same political ties that existed before.

The arguments, abstract as they are, can go on endlessly, trying to determine which chief would be more effective. The "inside" advocates assert that the advantages of an "outsider chief" are not worth the risk of disturbing the department, demoralizing its men, and starting a lengthy period of reconciliation with the *imported* views, philosophies, and policies of an outside *intruder*. These advocates, furthermore, emphasize that however skillful the outsider chief may be, he would immediately face insuperable difficulties which may linger for quite some time, causing considerable disruption within the department and thus jeopardizing its efficiency and productivity.

The "outside" advocates, on the other hand, stress the fact that the advantages of an "outsider chief" outweigh the anticipated risk of temporary departmental adjustment. These advocates assert that "a search" for a new chief (except in cases of death, inability to perform, retirement or voluntary resignation) carries, by definition, the notion that the department is not well administered and may require fresh leadership. The role of the "outsider chief", therefore, with su-

69. Michael J. Kelly, *Police Chief Selection, A Handbook for Local Government*, (Police Foundation and International City Management Association), 1975, p. 15.

70. *Ibid.*

perior managerial skills, a technological perspective, and a fresh set of policies and plans, would be necessary and beneficial. With regard to the temporary unrest a department may experience during the transitional period, the "outside" advocates assert that it is only natural and may occur even with an "insider chief" assuming command. The effective "outsider chief", they note, would be more willing to learn about the department, could understand it better, and could build adequate loyalty for the institution and support for himself *in no time.*

In whichever direction the argument may proceed, from a managerial point of view the supreme goal is the selection of the most effective leader available. Whether he is an outsider or an insider, the effective leader is expected to be able to quickly overcome the transitional difficulties associated with *leadership displacement* and rapidly produce the necessary harmony and cohesion. It is, therefore, advisable, where local law permits, to include both inside and outside candidates in the search. There are several reasons for this combinational approach. Even when a selection authority is relatively certain it has a first rate prospective chief on the local force, it (and perhaps the inside candidate) will want to confirm that judgment by comparing the candidate with the best that can be found outside the department. The selection authority, whether it be by mayor or manager, public safety commissioner or civil service, can learn much more from both outsiders and insiders about the local department, procedures in other police departments and possibilities for directions the department can take. Decision-makers will not really be in a position to judge possible negative characteristics, such as parochialism of an insider or the political awkwardness of an outsider, without having some basis of comparison. The supply of effective management talent is obviously too limited to justify closing the search to insiders or outsiders on the basis of what may be premature judgments at the beginning of the process.[71]

2 —Tenure of the Police Chief

No psychological or behavioral theory can normatively support the suggestion that insecure superiors are comfortable in leadership positions or are capable of positively influencing work groups and individuals. Such individuals, as Abraham Maslow consistently theorized, and Robert Di Grazia strongly confirmed in the police world, would be more concerned with their survival needs than with those of the departments they lead, the men they direct, or the publics they serve. Insecurity in leadership may cause *fear, hesitation, suspicion, overreaction,* and *often paranoia.*

71. *Ibid.,* p. 17.

A few cities in America establish fixed terms of office for police commissioners and chiefs. These cities include Baltimore where the chief's tenure is six years and Boston where it is five years. The average tenure of the police chief in the rest of the nation, however, is slightly over four years in cities under 300,000 in population and is less than two and one-half years in cities over 500,000 in population.[72] In a recent study done by the Police Chief Executive Project, the tenure of top police leadership was found to be "alarmingly short". The results of a survey that was made of 1,401 police chiefs and 831 of their immediate superiors showed that 40% of the police chiefs had not remained with the same agency for at least three years. In addition, the study showed that the tenure of police chiefs in large agencies was shorter (2.8 years) than the tenure of those in small municipalities and counties (5.1 years).[73]

The reason for this short-tenure situation is that almost all police chiefs are appointed upon political considerations, and the length of their service is made coterminous with that of the political chief executive, an American political practice since the Jacksonian administration.

Under this arrangement, the terms of department heads end with that of the mayor or the appointing authority, and the new head of city government replaces them with new department executives. It is held by those who continue to support this procedure that a newly elected mayor should have the whole-hearted support of his principal subordinates at the outset, and that they should be individuals who are in sympathy with his outlook and aims.[74]

Aside from sheriffs who are elected for a fixed term of office, most American cities do not specify a tenure in office for the police chief. In the predominant majority of cities, chiefs serve *at the pleasure* of the mayor, city manager, police board, or council members. This "tenureless" situation could cause an agonizing feeling of insecurity and anxiety within the chief's personality and reflect negatively on his discharge of duties. He may become worried about his paycheck from one month to the other. He may become overconcerned about his future and the welfare of his family. Questions as to how long he can hold on to his position, or who is conspiring among his subordinate to get his position, may become quite real and cause the *insecure chief* a lot of sleepless, long nights. He, conse-

72. Allen P. Bristow and E.C. Gabard, *Decision Making in Police Administration*, (Springfield, Ill.: Charles C. Thomas, Publisher), 1961, p. 12.

73. International City Management Association, *Target*, August 1976, Vol. 5, Issue 6, p. 1.

74. John M. Pfiffner, *Municipal Administration*, (New York: Roland Press Company), 1940, p. 31.

quently, may turn too submissive and subservient to the politicians who run the city, and, in turn, they may take full control of the police department. Moreover, the *tenureless chief* may become inhibited in speaking his mind or taking an independent posture. Naturally, disagreeing with the mayor or the appointing authority could be fatal professionally, and attempting to change police policies and practices, to the disliking of any of *the mayor's men* would be extremely risky.

Furthermore, the vast majority of the beneficiaries of the police services may become too "insignificant" to the chief, as would the harmless rank and file at the police department. The *hand* of the police chief may become too heavy on them as a compensation for his insecurity and anxiety. Their safety and welfare may be used *and abused* by the paranoid chief as means for appeasing the power holders in the city, or, infrequently, in a desperate move to hit back at his opponents. Egon Bittner described this situation well by saying:

> One reason why the more serious aspects of police work suffer from low visibility is that they center around the lives of people [chiefs] whose voice is either not heard or does not count on the forum of public opinion. It is exceedingly rare that policemen [chiefs] make decisions that have a direct and lasting effect on the circumstances of the middle and upper classes. .   .   .   But for the poor, the ghetto, the slum dwellers, the devious, the deviant, and the criminals—the policeman is a figure of awesome power and importance.[75]

In election years *the tenureless* chiefs get especially edgy. Their fear of losing their job if the prevailing administration is defeated is compounded even more by their obsession with "trying to play the game right" while reflecting the image of being most supportive of the *committee to reelect the mayor*. After the election is over, the chief may either find himself replaced or pressured into a retaliation campaign against the political adversaries who almost "cost us the elections". The lack of a fixed tenure for the police chief, and the serious implications it fosters, can certainly make the chief "look small" in the eyes of his subordinates, "on trial" in the eyes of the politicians, and "partial", to say the least, in the eyes of the public.

This practice of "non-tenured" police chiefs, as mentioned earlier, has its firm roots in the theory of democracy and the accountability of appointed officials to the politicians elected to govern. The need for fixed tenures, on the other hand, is inherent in the theories of stability in office and efficient management. A short tenure poli-

75. Egon Bittner, *op. cit.*, p. 74.

cy coupled with a high turnover rate lowers the department's morale, affects its productivity, and incurs extravagant costs in the recruitment processes of advertising for, of selecting, and of hiring new chiefs.

Democracy and efficiency, in the American system of government, *are by no means incompatible.* Pfiffner believes that there is little reason why municipal department heads should not be chosen under merit system rules and hold their offices for renewable fixed terms. He came to this conclusion after observing the application of the merit system and fixed terms to department heads in Los Angeles County government over a period of years. Pfiffner pointed out that the applied system in Los Angeles County created a "high order of professional attainment, administrative competence and integrity without any noticeable decline in public accountability or in the quality of services rendered".[76] Along the same lines of Pfiffner, Raymond Fosdick, a notable police reformist, wrote:

> Continuity of service based on freedom of choice has a real meaning . . . We shall never solve the police problem in America until we give honest and effective leadership an opportunity to show what it can do. Some time or other, we have to make a beginning of trusting our public officials. [Political] checks and balances to curb and minimize possible abuses of power have gotten us nowhere . . . It is time to take off a few of the yokes that have made public administration an impossible task, and put new emphasis on positive qualities. The problem before us is not how to build up a structure that will circumvent dishonest and incompetent officials, but after finding a competent and honest official, to surround him with conditions in which he can make himself effective.[77]

While the protection of tenure is obviously necessary for the "competent and honest" police chiefs who otherwise would waste their time and energy heading off illegitimate political encroachment, such a tenure should not be used as a protection of the "incompetent and dishonest". While long term contracts should be used extensively to stabilize police leadership and enhance police productivity, "removal for cause" must always be incorporated and invoked. Only then will the democracy-efficiency matrix function harmoniously and the managerial potential of effective police leadership be emancipated to accomplish its challenging roles.

76. John M. Pfiffner, *op. cit.*, p. 31.

77. As cited by V.A. Leonard and Harry W. More, *Police Organization and* *Management,* (Mineola, New York: The Foundation Press, Inc.), 1971, p. 49.

3 —Preparation for Police Leadership

There appears to be a universal agreement that the functions of the police manager (decision-making, planning, communicating, coordinating, etc.), ought not to be performed by unqualified people. What the chief does or fails to do shapes the behavior and performance of a high-powered "coercive force" capable of literally enhancing or destroying the quality of life for so many for so long. The chief's role in this sense is thus just as important as that of the physician, the lawyer or the social worker, and preparing him for this critical function is correspondingly as important.

Effective police management must be viewed as a profession with managerial tasks markedly different from police operational duties. The management of such complex "coercive forces" can not be left to those Di Grazia described as managers whose "career balloons have been filled with time of service, luck on written tests, or political friendships".[78] Their management, on the contrary, has to be performed by "those who have acquired education and demonstrated skill".[79] Upgrading police leadership, declared Egon Bittner, is "a nondeferrable necessity and every alternative to it is nothing short of the betrayal of democratic ideals".[80]

To elevate police management leadership to the level of a professional vocation—indeed, to create a favorable condition for this development—it would appear absolutely unavoidable that those selected for these positions are educated in technical and scholarly knowledge. A modern profession, Bittner asserts, has to be "acquired in a protracted and assiduous study and validated by scientific criteria, rather than by standards of common sense accessible to all lay people".[81] For police management to receive professional recognition, it has to *earn* public respect and trust on the basis of its association with scientific scholarship and its ability to offer specialized solutions to complex problems.

The task of preparing police chiefs of the professional caliber described above is certainly a complex process which can not be the responsibility of one organization or group. The preparation process, it could be argued, must have its roots in the early childhood of the chosen individuals and its maturation gradually developed through the socialization they received by the family, school, church, peers, friends and employers. For the purposes of this discussion, however, only two areas will be examined and will apply to the later parts of the preparation process by the responsible government: a)

78. Robert Di Grazia, *op. cit.*, p. 6.   80. Egon Bittner, *op. cit.*, p. 75.

79. *Ibid.*   81. *Ibid.*, p. 77.

the selection of the right chief, and b) the education of the chief in the specialized tasks of management leadership.

(a) Selecting the Right Chief

From the previous discussion it becomes apparent that the selection of the right person for the chief position is of paramount importance. This necessitates the existence of standards determined in advance, publicized to all possible candidates, and seriously intended for use as an institutional policy for selection. Without such standards merits can not be equitably appraised and prejudicial selection can not be avoided.

Mimimum standards for selection are commonplace today. They are usually stipulated by state commissions on law enforcement officer standards and goals. However, while most of these standards seem to fall short of the basic management qualifications recommended by the President's Task Force Report of 1967, the application of these standards is too often bent to accommodate local political considerations. Also, while the consequences for violating these standards by appointing authorities may vary from one state to another, they are generally insignificant to the point of total ineffectiveness. Not only should these minimum standards be updated and raised from time to time, the appointing authorities must be persuaded into applying them voluntarily or compelled—by more serious penalties— into applying them. Selection considerations not based on absolute merits must be eliminated; political appointment must produce politically-oriented leadership, but meritorious selection produces meritorious leadership.

Without getting into greater detail on qualifications, some basic standards are usually required. They relate to citizenship, age, seniority, experience, educational level, personal character, and the like. Leadership qualifications, however, the basis of management effectiveness, are seldom stipulated or seriously considered as an important basis for preference among candidates.

As an example of the necessary leadership qualifications of a chief, Bert Johnson required these standards: [82]

1   —capabilities of building departmental morale;

2   —ability to contribute to the overall decision-making process in the county, *e.g.,* ordinance changes, organizational and personnel improvements;

3   —ability to communicate, *i.e.,* to listen, to speak, and to write without fear of misunderstanding;

4   —an interest in interdepartmental coordination;

---

82. Michael I. Kelley, *op. cit.,* p. 14.

5 —belief and experience in preparing a meaningful budget document;

6 —skills and interest in public communication from general reports to instilling employee consciousness of the public to follow-up of citizen complaints;

7 —ability to meet agreed-upon targets.

Another list of proposed managerial standards for police chiefs was proposed for the city of Seattle and consisted of: [83]

1 —ten to twenty years of law enforcement experience;

2 —proven ability and preferably a master's degree in personnel management and administration;

3 —a personal capability to deal frequently and effectively with the public;

4 —demonstration of an ability to work "under heavy fire": political, social, internal and external;

5 —a broad background in the technical and legal aspects of the criminal justice system;

6 —willingness to work the long hours of a top business executive for a fraction of the salary of those executives;

7 —openness to much-needed change and innovation in law enforcement;

8 —an ability to earn the respect and confidence of the rank-and-file policemen and the tax-paying public.

Yet another set of managerial standards developed by the IACP for their Assessment Center contained these qualities: [84]

Judgment	Creativity
Impact on others	Breadth of knowledge
Analytical abilities	Decision-making capabilities
Delegation readiness	Planning and organizational habits
Follow-up instincts	Sensitivity (tolerance, compassion)
Emotional maturity	Toleration of stress
Motivation	Realistic idealism
Administration courage	Sense of mission
Communication skills	Perseverance
Persuasiveness	Integrity

While these lists are obviously subjective and vague, some of the managerial qualifications mentioned can certainly be considered "positive" assets of the potential chief. Also, while no quantitative model has been devised to determine how much of each of these ingredients

---

83. *Seattle Times,* April 22, 1974, p. A. 24.   84. Michael I. Kelley, *op. cit.,* p. 12.

should be necessary and what substitutes could be used, an "enlightened" and "honest" appointing authority must be able to determine with some accuracy its order of priorities among these qualities. Some helpful qualifications are here cited merely as possible guidelines for the selection process:

1   —an understanding of human behavior;

2   —a decision-making competence;

3   —an experimental frame of mind;

4   —an analytical mind;

5   —a humanistic frame of reference;

6   —a concern for legitimacy and constitutionalism;

7   —a concern for efficiency and accountability;

8   —an appreciation of statistical analysis;

9   —a belief in planning and programming;

10   —a trust in scientific research;

11   —a concern for workers and an ability to motivate subordinates;

12   —a philosophy of crime prevention;

13   —an ability to communicate and express views.

Qualities of this nature would be most helpful and desirable for an effective police manager.   Abundance of policemen with these qualities is, however, unlikely, since the vast majority of senior-ranking policemen have not had the opportunity of attending college, let alone acquiring graduate training in these specialized disciplines. While a few candidates for the police chief position may be able to demonstrate ample expertise in managerial leadership without a college education, it can hardly follow that selection standards today can ignore college education as a logical requirement.

Collegiate education for police leaders is instrumental in reflecting appropriate leadership qualities. Sociologists point out that a liberal arts education has important functions far beyond the development of talented chiefs. It provides common social and moral restraints over the use of crude power arrangements, reinforces appropriate attitudes for the sustenance of democratic institutions, and maintains an open mind toward the existence of peaceful harmony among diverse population groups. In support of college education, the IACP has argued with increasing vigor in recent years that:

The campus must be looked to for the police officers of the future. It is nonsense to state or to assume that the enforcement of the law is so simple a task that it can be done best by those unencumbered by an inquiring mind nurtured by the study of the liberal arts . . . Their intellectual armament—so long restricted to a minimum—must be no less than their physical prowess and protection.[85]

Mindful of the recommendation by the Task Force Report of 1967 that "the ultimate aim of all police departments should be that all personnel with general enforcement powers have baccalaureate degrees",[86] and judging by the rapidly rising level of national education and by the increasing number and variety of college offerings in the areas of criminal justice and law enforcement which in turn are attracting an ever increasing number of in-service policemen, one may not be surprised if future police chiefs in metropolitan areas would be required to have a doctorate degree; in middlesized departments, a master's degree; and in all others, a baccalaureate degree.

In the preparation of effective police leaders, higher education would be instrumental in shaping their intellectual abilities and values. While occupational expertise is naturally necessary, a liberal arts education would certainly refine that expertise and elevate it to the level of an advanced, humanistic and scientific discipline.

(b) Educating the Police Chief

Competence is never born; it is *acquired* in a lengthy and painstaking process of growth and maturation. While the path of experience may be as risky as the succession of trial and error, experience in itself involves sporadic episodes of self-learning. Education, on the other hand, is programmed learning. It is short and condensed, and its results are fast and predictable. While unsupervised experience may reinforce bias, education reduces bias and suppresses its effects. Also while experience is tailor-made and may fit certain individuals in certain situations, education is standardized and provides uniform knowledge to all people. Moreover, while experience may provide some practical aspects of knowledge, education treats the conceptual basis for knowledge and offers the adequate tools by which diversified problems never experienced before, may be intelligently examined, systematically investigated, and—by the application of those tools—fairly resolved.

If police management leadership is to be professional, reliance on previous experience as a policeman will be insufficient. Police managers, besides experience, must master the application of managerial tools, methods, and techniques. Even among academically qualified chiefs, a constant reinforcement of knowledge is always necessary. New areas in behavioral sciences, motivation, personnel management, technological systems, empirical research, programming, budgeting,

---

85. Quinn Tamm, editorial in *Police*   86. *Task Force Report*, 1967, p. 127.
Chief, Vol. 32 (May 1965), p. 6.

human relations, etc., are discovered everyday and utilized by private and public agencies. The Task Force Report of 1967 mentioned areas of competence such as Management by Objectives, Planning, Programming and Budgeting Systems, Operations Research, and Information Systems, among others. It is as much the duty of the effective police managers to understand and familiarize themselves with these management innovations as it is the duty of the appointing governments to avail them of this knowledge. Undereducated chiefs, even if they are experienced, will most likely be reluctant to adopt, or adjust to, these innovations, and will most likely revert to old mechanisms. Under pressure they may even resent these innovations, denounce their use, and frustrate the managerial advantage expected by their application.

Not only will undereducated police leaders fail to produce effective management, they may also obstruct the development of future police managers. One such chief observed: "My men don't need no education. I've gotten along for forty years without an education, and I see no reason why they can't." Another remarked: "If they know more than me, the mayor may make them chief." [87] Such observations, needless to say, not only ruin the effectiveness of leadership in the police department, but also nullify the basic principles of leadership altogether.

Stressing this need for scientific competence, John Bonner, in a brilliant analysis of police leadership, indicated that performance, the end product of scientific competence, is the most significant element in effective leadership. In a study conducted by the College of Administrative Science, Bonner discovered that the difference between units with high morale and units with low morale was primarily the patrolman's belief that his commanding officer "knew his stuff". A police leader, proceeded Bonner, "must not only be competent in the physical and moral requirements of his profession, he must also renew his competence through various forms of continuing education". [88]

Clarence Kelley, Director of the FBI, addressing the graduating class of the 94th session in September of 1973, asserted that:

> Great demands are today being made on law enforcement
> people .   .   . if we are to be effective and attuned

87. John T. Bonner, Jr., "Leadership for Lawmen", *The FBI Law Enforcement Bulletin*, December, 1973, p. 7. Emphasizing the need for continued education even among scholars, the author mentioned the experience of retired Supreme Court Justice Oliver Wendell Holmes who was in his 90s when he was visited one day by President Franklin Roosevelt who found him reading Plato. When asked by the President, "Why Plato?," Mr. Holmes replied, "To improve my mind, Mr. President."

88. Vern L. Folley, "The Sphere of Police Education", *Law and Order*, Vol. 15 (February 1967), p. 21.

to times, we must constantly be learning and adapting in a constructive way.[89]

Emphasizing the value of educating high-ranking policemen of America, Kelley charged the graduating leaders by saying that the education they had received "has given them the tools to be competent officers". It is left to the police leader, "to find a new competence, a new zeal, a new strength to overcome the obstacles ahead and to go the *second mile* that often makes the vital difference between success and failure".[90] Toward the achievement of that *second mile,* police leaders must *keep marching on* the path of in-service education.

Thanks to the federal assistance offered by LEAA since 1968, most patrolmen in the nation today can receive in-service training in a variety of ways.[91] The President's Commission on Law Enforcement recommended that "every general enforcement officer should have at least one week of intensive training a year", and "specialized training should be a prerequisite for advancement".[92] Nevertheless, judged by the commission's standards, most police agencies are grossly deficient. Few departments anywhere provide systematic training for all personnel at all levels and in all areas of specialization. Except in the largest agencies, in-service training is "virtually negligible", the IACP reported to the Commission.[93]

At the leadership level, matters are even worse. Police chiefs and sheriffs, for all practical reasons, are not required to undergo any further training whatsoever. This seems to be so partly because they no longer have to compete for further promotions and partly because they believe they no longer need it. Aside from the very few who are motivated to pursue college education (at the undergraduate or the graduate level) on their own, the rest normally suffice with at-

89. Clarence Kelley, "A Call to Excellence", *The FBI Law Enforcement Bulletin, Ibid.,* p. 11.

90. *Ibid.,* pp. 11–12.

91. Charles B. Saunders, *Upgrading the American Police* (Washington, D.C.: The Brookings Institution), 1970, p. 134. The author reported that most departments of any size provide some training. Hundreds of agencies make use of the skilled instruction offered by visiting FBI instructors invite outside specialists to give occasional lectures, conduct periodic courses in specialized subjects, and send selected individuals to programs at state or regional police schools or universities. But only a minority of agency personnel are involved in these activities: although 81 percent of the departments in one survey reported some kind of specialized training, 51 percent said that less than one quarter of their entire force was involved, and only 13 percent reported involvement of over three quarters of their men.

92. *Task Force Report,* The Police, 1967, *op. cit.,* p. 113.

93. Charles B. Saunders, *op. cit.,* p. 133.

tending a criminal justice seminar or a law enforcement convention *whenever possible*, a situation which seems to occur more frequently if the location of the meeting agrees with their vacationing preferences.[94]

Other than attending such *business-vacation* conferences, which usually last between one and five days, the traditional and most widely attended training institution is the FBI National Academy in Quantico, Virginia. With 3,044 of its graduates still active in law enforcement, and over 27% of these occupying top executive positions in their agencies, the FBI National Academy has generally become known as the "West Point of Law Enforcement".[95]

Basically, however, the FBI academy is a training facility rather than an educational institution. It is staffed with expert FBI instructors qualified to lecture in several areas of law enforcement disciplines. The twelve week session the academy normally offers was not designed originally to prepare the officers for management leadership roles in their departments. The subject matter ranges from the proper method of keeping police records to the lifting of a fingerprint from the scene of a crime, from police photography to the calculation of an automobile's speed from skid marks.[96] Although the recently updated instruction offered at the academy makes a noticeable emphasis on the study of human relations in law enforcement, a natural ingredient of police leadership, advanced education in management techniques, operation research, quantitative analysis and behavioral sciences seems to be barely tapped. Moreover, an educational climate conducive of free and progressive thinking among the students seems still undeveloped in the present tradition of the academy. Appropriate leadership education must naturally originate in an environment pregnant with academic freedom, with the liberty to question established policies, and with ample exposure to novel views, opinions, and methods.

Another weakness with the training offered at the FBI academy is the fact that the program has little relevance to the problems of police leadership in municipal and rural areas. Current instruction offers limited insight into the roles of the police chief in dealing with external pressures from the polity, the mass media, and the public; in coordinating the department's activities with other departments; in procuring ample funds to sustain an efficient department; and in un-

---

94. A convention in Miami, Florida; Ocean City, Maryland; or Las Vegas, in summer would draw a crowd. On the other hand a meeting in Sacramento, California; New York; or Detroit may have to be called off for lack of participation.

95. Charles B. Saunders, *op. cit.*, p. 41.

96. Don Whitehead, *The FBI Story, A Report to the People*, (New York: Random House), 1956, p. 151.

derstanding the real dilemma of policing in crime-stricken metropolitan areas.

In the area of "management leadership", the program offered by the FBI academy was described by Saunders as "not so impressive as it appears in the annual report". He proceeded to state that:

> the 177,000 officers reportedly trained were in fact the total number of patrolmen assembled to hear the lectures. Although the agent's presentations are known to be of high quality, there is no way to judge the relevance of their material to the training needs of a particular audience.[97]

When Professor Jerry Dowling, an educator, an attorney and a former FBI agent himself, was asked about the viability of the FBI Academy as an institution for training police leaders, his reply was categorically "for police leadership . . . no; for teaching police practices and methods . . . yes." [98]

To alleviate this problem of inadequate in-service education for police leaders, many writers and police practitioners have lately called for an "American Bramshill", an equivalent of the British National Police College. Contrary to the common views by many exponents who like to call such an institution the "Police West Point", the analogy would seem more accurate if compared to the role of the "War College" in as much as it offers advanced training to senior officers in the Armed Forces.

Calling for the establishment of such a police college, Commissioner Di Grazia said:

> The nation needs a Bramshill. Just as Bramshill produces the future leaders of British policing, we should have a college for the education and development of police managers. None exists now, of course.[99]

Supporting Di Grazia is Donald Shanahan, professor of police administration, and a former policeman who wrote:

> One of the National Institute of Law Enforcement and Criminal Justice's new interests is undertaking a feasibility study of establishing a Bramshill-type capability or its equivalent for police leadership training. I support this unequivocally.[100]

97. Charles B. Saunders, *op. cit.*, p. 141.

98. Jerry Dowling, Associate Professor of Criminal Justice and Law Enforcement, Sam Houston State University, The Institute of Contemporary Corrections and the Behavioral Sciences, Huntsville, Texas, in an interview on July 6, 1976.

99. Robert Di Grazia, "Upgrading Police Leadership", *op. cit.*, p. 9.

100. Donald T. Shanahan, "The Changing Police Leadership", *op. cit.*, p. 20.

Aryeh Neier, executive director of the American Civil Liberties Union added by saying:

> Open a "West Point" of law enforcement to bring some men and women into police forces and prisons on the management level, [and it will] increase police self-respect, as well as citizens' respect for and cooperation with the police.[101]

Another writer, Stephen Wright, vice-president of the College Entrance Examination Board, also suggested Bramshill indirectly by promising to:

> institute an in-service program to train all of you to become the 'new' police . . . I intend to bring officers from the London police to demonstrate the firmness and courtesy for which they are famous.[102]

While there is certainly more excitement about Bramshill around the world than in Great Britain, the college, nevertheless, is perceived by the British Parliament, the police forces, and the British public as the ultimate solution to police professionalism. The motto of the college is *Studies Alitur Auctoritas:* "Authority is Strengthened by Learning". The underlying themes of the college are leadership, command and management. It provides higher training for present and future police leaders in the British Isles and the Commonwealth.

The college implements the belief that police forces have in their ranks sufficient leaders capable of managing their departments in a professional manner. Its basic aim is to equip present and future leaders with knowledge which could broaden their outlook, quicken their mental powers, increase their behavioral insights, and build their managerial skills. Thus equipped, the college administrators believe police leaders will be able to cope successfully with the obligations of progressive police leadership in the complex and rapidly changing society.[103]

The British Police College situated at *Bramshill House,* near Basingstoke, was founded in 1948 and was expanded in physical as well as educational capabilities in 1953, 1960, and 1969. The college is controlled by a Board of Governors under the chairmanship of the Permanent Under-Secretary of State for the Home Office (equivalent

101. Aryeh Neier, "If I Were Chief of Police of Gotham City", an accumulation of short articles, *The Civil Liberties Review*, (Vol. 2, No. 2), 1975, p. 6.

102. Stephen J. Wright, *Ibid.*, p. 22.

103. All the discussions cited here of the Bramshill College are taken from the manual, *The Police College Bramshill*, (London: Her Majesty's Stationary Office). The author who annually visits the police college has also collected some of his information through interviewing several of the college's instructors, administrators and students.

to the Department of Justice). The Board of Governors include senior civil servants, HM Chief Inspector of Constabulary, representatives of the County Councils Association, representatives of the Police Superintendents' Association (equivalent to IACP), educators, and other civilian and police members.

The college is headed by a Commandant who is assisted by three deans for Academic Studies, Police Studies, and Overseas Studies. The instructing faculty consists of civilian professors and police instructors who work harmoniously and present a balanced blend of academic-behavorial and police-technical courses. The college, which boards all its students during their training session, also houses a library with some 50,000 books capable of meeting the students' needs for extensive research projects.

The college uses a variety of instructional methods stressing individual and collective participation of student officers. The most common method is the "syndicate system". Each course is divided into syndicates of not more than twenty students; each syndicate is constituted to give a cross-section of the police experience of the whole course. The syndicate is supervised by a member of the faculty who gives regular, individual tutorial guidance as well as directing collective work. Lectures and presentations followed by questions and discussion are given by regular faculty members and frequently by visiting speakers. Students also lecture to their colleagues, thus sharing with them the results of their research and practicing their public speaking. A considerable amount of work is done in small group discussions, which stimulate participating students to identify their work problems, to express their candid views and to share the problem-solving process. Students often engage in role-playing, case-studies, and business games, and the opportunity for leadership is given throughout without constraints. Great emphasis is laid on the individual aspect of the student's work: discussion, lecture notes, writing of papers, research analysis. The cultivation of a philosophical, analytical, and behavioral approach is encouraged, and students are required to use initiative and imagination in carrying out their assignments and to make full use of audio visual aids and library facilities available.

The college offers five leadership courses. They are designed to stimulate and enhance leadership qualities and skills at five police levels. *First*, The Special Course trains young officers of outstanding promise. Successful completion of the course entitles these officers to be promoted to the level of first-line supervision (sergeant). The course, which lasts four months, provides instruction in academic and professional studies. The former area includes history, government, economics, sociology, psychology, international affairs and English. The latter includes police procedures, criminal law, court procedures, community relations, administration, organization, and management —all these with due emphasis on leadership.

Secondly, the Inspector's Course trains officers from the rank of inspector (lieutenant and captain) for the responsibilities of middle management administration. The course, which also lasts for four months, is preceded by one month of local training in force organization, and, like the Special Course, offers academic and professional studies with deeper penetration in the subject matter and greater emphasis on individual work.

Third, the Overseas Command Course, basically combines the previous two courses and is available to Commonwealth and overseas officers.

Fourth, The Intermediate Command Course is designed to further the development of selected inspectors who are considered by their chiefs to be fitted for the responsibilities of divisional heads (deputy chiefs). The course, which also lasts for four months, offers a syllabus that includes intensive work in police leadership, management science, behavioral studies and current police problems.

Fifth, The Senior Command Course is designed to equip the officers who attend for the highest posts in police service (chiefs). The course also lasts for four months and aims to prepare chiefs and their deputies for the responsibilities of a police chief executive. The course is highly sophisticated in the areas of future police trends, research projects, relationships between police organizations and government, internal management, and fiscal administration. At this level, leadership and management are studied in the widest police context, and work requires a weekly tutorial session under the supervision of a senior civilian professor.

Bramshill does not only teach leadership in a classroom setting, it also inspires and enhances the officer's sense of leadership through extra-curricular activities. Officers engage in sports, partake in college government, belong to the Police College Club, become members of the prestigious Henry Fielding Society, and the alumni meet each year in College Reunions. Bramshill, thus, has become *a unifying alma mater, a leadership concept, a state of mind,* and an institution that provides the British policemen with a sense of identification, pride, sophistication, belonging, and achievement.

In the United States, a specialized college of Bramshill's stature is necessary to promote police leadership by introducing and emphasizing "secular scientific scholarship". Egon Bittner strongly reiterated in his study of police roles that "the transformation of the conception of policing from the model of the man of arms to the model of the trained professional . . . naturally involves the mobilization of specifically delineated programs of study and instruction".

"The way", persisted Bittner, "is to form some institutions that can assume at least provisional jurisdiction over the solution of these problems". Drawing on analogies with the existing professions, Bittner suggested that such police institutions may have to perform similar services to those of graduate and post graduate professional schools.[104] Also, as if describing the alma mater spirit of Bramshill, without mentioning the name, Bittner concluded by saying that "the main reason for having professional schools of police work is to make a home for police work-study . . . It must be their own home", he said, "or the enterprise will be dispirited and doomed to failure." [105]

The implementation of the Bramshill concept in the United States, is certainly a difficult task to accomplish because of the uniqueness of the American police system; the tri-level structure; the local funding of police forces; the difference in pay among departments; and the difficulty of lateral movement for police leaders. Most of these difficulties, however, could be alleviated through the professional and financial contributions by LEAA in its *partnership role* designed particularly to upgrade local forces. Bramshill-type independent colleges can be established on a *regional basis* (to serve a few adjacent small states) or on a state basis (to serve large states like California and Texas or remote states like Hawaii and Alaska). Such colleges, serving as quasi-graduate police institutions, should be totally funded from LEAA allotments to that state or group of states. Funding should cover all aspects of operation: overhead, personnel, instruction, sustenance of students, travel, library needs and logistics. Each college should be governed by a board of directors selected by the governor, or governors, of that state or group of states from among prominent police leaders, academicians, and community leaders. Selection of instructors, curricula, and teaching methods may be approved by the governing body of directors in accordance with general guidelines and standards. The duration of college sessions and the frequency of their offerings may be determined in light of the regional or state needs. Quality of instruction must be continually controlled, evaluated and upgraded. Methods of instruction must be innovative and motivational, and adequate opportunities for faculty-student association beyond classroom meetings must be provided. Re-

---

104. Egon Bittner, *op. cit.*, p. 79. The author later clarified his proposal for a post-graduate police school by saying that it may seem preposterous to suggest the formation of post-graduate professional schools for police work at a time when most of those who practice the occupation have no more than a high school education. Worse yet, it may seem cynical to suggest that such schools be formed prior to the time the field of study can be defined or even adumbrated. But if these objections are taken at their face value, then none of the existing professional schools could have been founded in the first place, and some might have lost their right to exist even today.

105. *Ibid.*, p. 81.

search projects must be paramount. Competition among students should be enhanced and an atmosphere of "directed enlightenment" conducive to true education developed.[106]

Moreover, and in line with Bittner's serious call for a post-graduate police institution, a *super-Bramshill leadership college at the national level* may be equally necessary. Totally funded by the federal government, the institution would be controlled by an independent board of directors chosen from among the most qualified scholars, police practitioners, social philosophers and educators. The distinguished institution would serve as the ultimate "moulder" of police education, standards, and goals in America. Like the contributions by the War College, the National College of Surgeons, or the National Academy of Sciences, the prestigious institution would influence current police thought, contribute to the development of the criminal justice system, and enhance the quality of human life.

The national institution would accept police leaders from among the graduates of state and regional colleges. The duration and frequency of sessions would be determined by the board of directors. Curricula would emphasize the philosophies of leadership, management and police science. Participating leaders would be encouraged to engage in individual and collective research and to publish their work in national periodicals and books. The institution would consequently grow and extend its academic influence over state and regional colleges as well as over practicing forces throughout the police systems.

Naturally this proposal for improving management leadership in police agencies is presented in an abstract form. The idea may not be feasible at this time and may likely be resented by many police groups and associations. Many problems will still have to be researched and resolved. For instance, unlike Bramshill, there may not be a need for multiple-level leadership training (first-line supervision, middle management, and executive leadership); enrollment requirements would have to be devised; selection processes would have to be further defined; and minimum standards for employing police chiefs after they would have received this specialized training would certainly undergo serious changes.

The fruits of effective police leadership, especially if ample training is implemented, would be to impel the police occupation in the direction of becoming a highly efficient and effective mechanism functioning at the level of complexity, sophistication, and responsibility commensurate with the gravity of the problems it often meets today and certainly will meet in the future.

106. For more details on this proposal see Sam Souryal, "The Case for State Centralized Police Training", *Journal* *of Police Science and Administration,* (Vol. 3, No. 3), 1975, pp. 363–369.

PART FIVE

RESULTS OF EFFECTIVE POLICE MANAGEMENT

For a society to emerge and exist, a *simple* system of policing may be sufficient. For a traditional society to develop and prosper, an *organized* system of policing may be adequate. In a dynamic and a complex society like the United States, with its heterogeneous and mobile population, affluent groups and indigent minorities, overemphasis on individual rights and unmatched rate in rising crime, a *sophisticated* system of effective police management is essential.

The role of the police is not only to protect society but also to improve it. Only through a system of effective police management can police agencies project future conditions and determine the means and methods necessary to respond adequately to the changing needs and expectations of the community. Effective police management provides the flexible "business-like" environment necessary to adapt law enforcement practices to the changing social conditions, to strike a *harmonic mean* between the desire for aggressive police action and the requirements of law and propriety, and still to deliver the police service efficiently in a constitutional, legal, and ethical manner.

From an administrative point of view, there are only *two* alternatives by which police agencies can respond to the complex problems currently confronting them:

(1) The first is to continue, as has been true in the past, with police agencies functioning at the organization level and basic decisions reached in a traditional fashion with little regard to the requisites of organized planning, scientific research, and futuristic studies. This is obviously a comfortable police approach since it does not require substantial diversion from the conventional rules and practices and securely hides the police establishment behind a shield of bureaucracy, routine, and secrecy.

(2) The second alternative is to recognize police organizations as management agencies, capable of making independent, intelligent, and systematic decisions in response to the increasing demands and expectations of a democratic society. It is a difficult task since police administrators will have to join other groups of social managers, get involved in the future engineering of the society, and adapt their policies and performance to a set of unknown, or untested, conditions.

In contemporary America, the second alternative is *imperative*. Regardless of the shifting nature of society, people insist on the *best* police services possible regardless of their affluency or poverty, color or creed, or their particular location in the country. A system of enlightened and flexible police management is necessary not only to protect the *status quo* but also to match the rapidly changing conditions in our culture and help achieve the ideals of American civilization.

Reflecting on the American dream in terms of innovative police management, Chief James Parsons of Birmingham, Alabama, recently remarked in response to a reporter's question:

> I would like to see the police as community managers taking on much broader roles than just law enforcement. One role is an advocate for the poor and disadvantaged in America, one who is capable to recognize the causal factors in crime and help develop policy at the top level to eradicate those causal factors of crime and community disorganization.[1]

Stressing the importance of the managerial approach, the innovative police manager from Birmingham articulated the role of the future chief by saying:

> Of course he is the chief administrator for that department. He must see that the basic functions of management—the planning, the organizing—that there is proper direction . . . he has to be an astute manager and internal politician . . . he has to have proper timing. He has to take the temperature of the department to see just how far he can push it, and when is the proper time to push it.[2]

Leaving aside the "idealistic" dreams expressed by the Chief from Birmingham, and limiting our concern to the feasible and attainable improvements in the realm of police administration, this part will focus on some "realistic" results which effective police management can produce. These will include the following topics:

1 —Police Professionalism.

2 —Suppression of Police Corruption.

3 —Police Productivity.

1. James C. Parsons, "The Modern Police Administration in Dixie", an interview with Birmingham, Alabama, Chief James Parsons, *Law Enforcement News*, January-February, 1976.

2. *Ibid.*

CHAPTER TWELVE

POLICE PROFESSIONALISM

Overview

An assured result of effective police management is the springing of professionalism. It is the cumulative product of inspiring leadership, sound decision-making, appropriate planning, organizational development, motivation, and other management techniques. It is the ultimate growth and maturation of the police agency. It involves a *serious move toward excellence and a quest toward perfection in whatever the agency undertakes or its workers may do.* The continuous striving toward excellence and perfection is the *process of professionalization.* Achieving public recognition for such excellence and perfection is the *state of professionalism.*

Most directly stated, professionalism is the opposite of amateurism or individual enterpreneurship. Basically a professional abides by high standards of performance and needs minimal amount of supervision. He is an individual who can make sound decisions without having to be told what to do. Professional training is therefore geared as to develop the capacity to make judgments controlled by *internalized* values and habits. A professional group adheres to a special kind of integrity and independence, a genuine fidelity to ethical rules, and a distinguished standard of performance in the public service.[1] Living up to the group's ethical values and resisting corrupt temptation have always been the chief source of dignity that unites members of a profession into a cohesive group.

Professionalism begins with workers and then overflows to encompass organizations. To those workers it becomes a *concept of excellence,* a *state of proficiency,* and a *way of life.* A state of professionalism, it must be noted, is neither proclaimed by legislative enactment nor decried by an academic institution. It is fundamentally a product of public recognition of those associations which maintain special skills and reflect a deep sense of public dedication. Recognized professionals, such as doctors, lawyers, ministers, business managers, and professors, perform specialized services valuable to society. They are seen as having, beyond sheer expertise, commitment, responsibility, and devotion to alleviating human suffering. Such professionals operate under a set of norms which stipulate the primacy

1. Robert Shellow and Morton Bard, *Issues in Law Enforcement; Essays and Case Studies,* (Reston, Virginia: Reston Publishing Company, Inc.), 1976, p. 21.

of the client's *interest* and devotion to its cause. If conflict arises between that cause and the personal or commercial gain of the professional, allegiance would undoubtedly be to the former.

Professionalism obviously *can not exist without professionals.* While some of the latter do compromise public trust by unethical actions, it is equally true that the ultimate interest of the public still lie largely in the hands of the majority of those professionals distinguished by their willingness to abide by ethical standards. Individual and minor violations by professionals do not seem to shake the public trust. Gross and frequent violations, on the other hand, appear to substantially diminish the way in which the entire profession is regarded by the public.[2] The overall performance by a profession and public confidence are closely tied in a *symbiotic* relationship; performance induces confidence and enhances it, while erosion of public confidence, on the other hand, deteriorates performance.

The process of professionalization must, therefore, be viewed as a two way street: the occupation grows in its specialized competence and demonstrates its devotion to the quality of life; *then* the public reciprocates by supporting the occupation and endorsing its practices. As a result, a genuine recognition develops and the state of professionalism is acknowledged. Professionalism of occupations is obviously *earned,* not granted, and *deserved,* not bestowed.

All professions emphasize their service ideal through a code of ethics. Such a code provides a set of guidelines for conformity among the members of the profession. It directs the behavior of the members as to what is considered suitable, acceptable and moral by the occupation. It serves as a *covenant of dedication* and stipulates the behavioral norms of the members in their relations to the clients they serve. Violation of the code can result in censure, if not ostracism, by the professional organization. Although external sanctions such as disbarment, revocation of license or dismissal from a national association are rare occurrences in the learned professions, the possibility of rejection by one's peers for violation of professional norms as specified by the code of ethics provides a significant measure of control.[3]

While conformity to the code of ethics is a milestone in professional discipline, the right of "prudent discretion", on the other hand, is not only sanctioned but also encouraged. The freedom of the professional to make his own decisions, *based on a demonstrated ability to exercise sound judgment,* is never curtailed or collegially resented. This is true not only because there is seldom any absolute agreement on any one *right* answer to handle a situation, but also because the practice of prudent discretion is upheld on the basis of professional

2. *Ibid.,* p. 21.   3. *Ibid.*

commitment to intellectual freedom. Therefore, while professionalism espouses and advocates a given set of standards, it does not support regimentation or indoctrinated thinking. Recognized professions are usually so refined as to accommodate and gracefully resolve the controversy between standardization as group phenomenon and discretion as a learning experience toward group maturation.

The relationship between professionalism and education is worthy of a special note. A profession is commonly regarded as a special kind of occupation where technical knowledge is gained through long prescribed training. The knowledge itself is regarded as a systematic body of theory and practice. Within the medical profession, for example, the process of converting a layman into a disciplined, professionally-oriented person is very carefully planned. During those four years of medical schooling, the student works toward such excellence to the extent that professional behavior becomes part of him—*almost a reflex*. In other words, professionalism becomes internalized by the knowledge he receives, the experiences he gains, and the attitudes he learns from literature and research. By the time the student goes into a hospital as an intern, his professional behavior is almost second nature to him. Nobody has to tell him how to conduct himself, and appropriate behavior "is expected to follow as a matter of course from what he has learned and from his own sense of what is suitable and required by the particular situation".[4] Without an abstract body of knowledge continually upgraded by advanced research and directed toward the improvement of human life, an occupation may never be able to mature, and the attainment of a professional status may be impossible.

Professionalism Defined

Professionalism has been defined by experts in the field:

> [It is] a special kind of occupation where technical knowledge is gained through long prescribed training . . . the professional person adheres to a set of professional norms that stipulate the practitioner should do technically competent work in the 'client' interest.—Albert J. Reiss, Jr.[5]

> Any occupation wishing to exercise professional authority must find a technical basis for it, assert an exclusive jurisdiction, link both skill and jurisdiction to standards of training, and convince the public that its services are uniquely trustworthy.—Harold L. Wilensky[6]

---

4. *Ibid.*

5. Albert J. Reiss, Jr., *The Police and the Public* (New Haven, Conn., Yale University Press), 1971, pp. 121–122.

6. Harold L. Wilensky, "The Professionalization of Everyone", *American Journal of Sociology*, 70, 318, September, 1964.

A profession can be defined as a unique, essential service which places emphasis on intellectual techniques requiring specialized training.—Bertis H. Sellers [7]

Professions claim a body of theory and practice to justify their right to discover, define, and deal with problems.— Peter K. Manning [8]

A more detailed definition of professionalism was cited by the United States Bureau of Census primarily for application in the federal bureaucracy:

A professional worker is (a) one who performs advisory, administrative or research work which is based upon the established principles of a profession or science, and which required scientific or technical training equivalent to that presented by graduation from a college or university of recognized standing, or (b) one who performs work which is based upon science or art, and which work requires for its performance an acquaintance with the established facts, or principles, or methods gained through academic study or through extensive practical experience, one or both. [9]

For the purpose of this discussion, a profession will be defined as an *organized association in which specialized knowledge and learning is used for the welfare of a population in accordance with advanced standards of technical performance, ethics, and expertise.*

From the previous definitions it becomes apparent that the main elements of a profession are:

1   —A clearly defined body of knowledge, constantly augmented and refined through specialized literature and research.

2   —Facilities for ongoing education, rather than one-time training.

3   —Uniform minimum standards of excellence for selection, training, and performance.

4   —A realistic code of ethics that defines the relations of the members of the profession to the public.

5   —An unequivocal service orientation.

6   —A well developed sense of dignity sustained by a progressive culture and respected by the public.

7. Bertis H. Sellers, "Perspectives", *American Probation and Parole* (Vol. 1, No. 2), June, 1976.

8. Peter K. Manning, "The Police: Mandate, Strategies and Appearances", in Jack D. Douglas, *Crime and Justice in American Society* (Indian-apolis: The Bobbs-Merrill Company, Inc.), 1971, p. 149.

9. Harry W. More, Jr., *Critical Issues in Law Enforcement* (Cincinnati: The W.H. Anderson Company), 1972, p. 380.

7 —An organization which includes a governing body of members qualified to supervise the profession and to influence the maintenance of high quality standards.

Comparing these elements of professionalism to the present status of police organizations in America, one can easily infer that the wide majority of police agencies, especially at the local level, do not quite qualify as professional organizations. While some progressive departments are occasionally labeled "semi-professional", these departments may be considered *on the threshold of professionalism*. Also, while the ability to move beyond this threshold is certainly wide-open, without a concerted effort to improve the educational level of policemen, to upgrade their performance and to increase their dedication to public service, professionalism would be impossible.

In the following discussion a brief analysis of the present state of the police occupation will be made, and the role of effective management in professionalizing police agencies through the institutionalization of these elements will be examined. For the purpose of classification, however, the first three elements will be grouped under The Educational Facet of the analysis; the fourth, fifth, and sixth, under The Moral Facet; and the last, under The Structural Facet.

THE EDUCATIONAL FACET

Only in a progressive system of police management would the need for higher education among police become relevant and necessary. Only a professional manager would be seriously concerned with upgrading the present field of policing into one of a truly police science. Moreover, only under a system of professional police management can higher education for policemen be urged and required. Undereducated traditional chiefs would, for instance, still dismiss the commission's recommendation for a baccalaureate degree as unrealistic and probably as unnecessary. Ample evidence can be easily discerned from the fact that only federal police agencies today (FBI, DEA, Secret Service) along with a few state and metropolitan departments insist on the baccalaureate degree as a minimum requirement for their agencies.[10] Needless to say, any occupation which re-

10. For more information on this question, see Charles Saunders, *Upgrading the American Police* (Washington: D.C., The Brookings Institution), 1970, pp. 79–116. Also see George W. O'Connor, *Survey of Selection Methods* (Washington IACP), 1962, who indicated that in 1961, a survey conducted of over three hundred police departments showed that 24 per cent of those departments had no minimum educational prerequisite, while less than 1 percent required any level of college preparation. Moreover, in the New England states, over 72 percent of the departments surveyed did not even require their applicants to have a high school diploma. Also see Michigan State University, Institute for Community Development, *Police Training in the Metropolitan Region: Recommendations for a Regional Approach* (Detroit: The Metropolitan Fund), 1966, which indicated that in a survey

quires less than a college education will have difficulty projecting a professional image to an alert and degree-conscious populace.

While the complexity of the police task today is as great as that of any other profession, the need for scientific research seems obvious. Nevertheless, most police agencies in America today seem to pay only lip service to the cause of serious police research. The current claim to a discipline of police science, if scrupulously viewed, may indicate a gross overstatement, to say the least. Except for some technical practices in crime detection, communication systems, and information dissemination, the rest of police work remains simply vocational. While, for example, psychiatrists, lawyers and business managers, like policemen, engage most of the time in verbal conversations with their clients, police talk consists of little, or no, theory. Whether they are involved in a stoppage situation or an interviewing situation, policemen demonstrate limited knowledge of human relations and behavioral interaction and less than adequate familiarity with criminological theories, social theories, or even constitutional rights.

Effective police management, as a vehicle of professionalism, not only seeks higher education for policemen, it emphasizes a scientific approach to policing. In advanced research, as in police education, effective police management can stimulate experimentation, quantitative analysis, and the use of empirical inquiry. Under the auspices and funding of LEAA and its affiliated agencies, effective police management was partially able to identify some necessary research areas and stimulate national concern for major problems.

Not before the contributions of Quinn Tamm, former executive director of IACP, has police research truly been thought of as a vehicle for professionalizing police work. Tamm, in 1962, began a research and development division within IACP to collect statistical data for analysis by a professional staff of specialists. He also established a professional standards division to produce a variety of training materials which are now used in thousands of local agencies. The Center for Law Enforcement Research and a revamped monthly journal, *The Police Chief*, became vehicles for dissemination of new ideas and research findings to over six thousand members of IACP and scholars interested in the field.

A landmark in the development of management-oriented research on police problems was provided by the President's Commission on Law Enforcement and the Administration of Justice in 1967.

of over 5,700 police officers in the Metropolitan area of Detroit, over 75 percent had not attended college. In the Metropolitan Detroit survey, it was further shown that nearly 13 percent of the officers had not received high school diplomas.

Its two-year study was conducted by 19 commissioners and 63 staff members, including lawyers, sociologists, psychologists, system analysists and a variety of interdisciplinary specialists.   The Task Force Report, which is basically an intellectual thesis in police management, will be a valuable document for many years to come.   It provides professional guidance and direction in areas never tapped by many police agencies before.

As a result of the Task Force Report, many successful projects were developed by several management-oriented agencies.   Reference to a few of these projects was made in chapter 7.   By way of reminder, such projects include Lakewoodism, Team Policing, PPBS, Pilot Precinct, the Fourth Watch, Lateral Entry of Specialists, and the Police Legal Advisor.

Next to advanced educational requirements and scientific research, effective police management was partially successful through the Task Force study of 1967 in setting standards for entry in the police.   State commissions were established in all the states of the Union and were assigned the task of upgrading existing standards. While some of these commissions are more progressive than others, the later in quite a few states, still seem to be an extension of the traditional pre-management era.   Regardless of the warnings made by the President's commission of 1967 that the most important task in professionalizing the police is the improvement of the quality of police personnel, the report indicates that "existing selection requirements and procedures in the majority of departments aside from physical requirements do not screen out the unfit".[11]   Hence it is not surprising that "far too many of those charged with protecting life and property and rationally enforcing our laws are incompetent, corrupt, or abusive." [12]

Selection standards, which presently seldom meet the requirements of the President's Commission Task Force, can certainly be upgraded to a professional level.   Feasible improvements can reasonably include, besides education, the use of scientific indicators of aptitude or predictors of success in police work.   Systematic and accurate tests could measure intelligence, character, and emotional stability. Similar tests could be used to determine the length of probationary period, type of performance rating to be applied by the department, nature of promotion exams, and necessary training programs.

Unless the educational facet of present police agencies is upgraded through effective management, agencies will not only continue to be viewed as non-professional, they will become "a serious trouble in all major cities   .   .   .   unlikely to be solved without major

11.   *Task Force Report* on the police, p.   12.   *Ibid.*
125.

changes in the purpose, recruiting methods, training, organization and tactics".[13]

THE MORAL FACET

For policemen to earn a professional status, they must also reflect a genuine concern for the public they serve and a dedication to humanity through compassion and sacrifice. Public support of the police is perhaps never more vividly demonstrated than in times when a policeman is slain or injured in the line of duty. Pictures of the slain officer, of the mourning members of his family, and of the funeral given by his colleagues, as well as accounts of the heroic act of the policeman in defense of the victim, stimulate maximum sympathy and support for the police. While this phenomenon should not be interpreted as an invitation to trade-off invaluable lives of policemen for the attainment of a professional status, such situations clearly indicate the fact that the general public appreciates a *sense of true devotion* and is ready to reciprocate by acknowledging professionalism. As explained earlier, however, the process must start first by the workers themselves projecting a moral picture of their goals, practices and motives. Reciprocation in terms of public support and acknowledgment of professionalism may follow next.

The moral facet of police professionalism can be seen in terms of these components: 1) ethical codes, 2) deeds, and 3) attitudes. The first entails police *morals* and philosophies; the second, police *practices* and standards of performance; and the third, *beliefs* and opinions.

(1) The first component of the moral facet relates to the present code of ethics as a yardstick of police morals and philosophies. Apart from the general ethics stipulated in, or inferred from government laws and ordinances, professional ethics are proclaimed in a code of ethics.[14] While all such codes attempt, by and large, to

---

13. David Burnham, *New York Times,* July 7, 1968.

14. The code was first developed by the California Peace Officers' Association and the Peace Officers' Research Association of California in 1956. The International Association of Chiefs of Police adopted it in their 1957 Conference. Later it was adopted by the National Conference of Police Association, and by many other law enforcement organizations. A full copy of the text follows:

Law Enforcement Code of Ethics

As a law enforcement officer, my fundamental duty is to serve mankind; to safeguard lives and property; to protect the innocent against deception, the weak against oppression or intimidation, and the peaceful against violence or disorder; and to respect the constitutional rights of all men to liberty, equality, and justice.

I will keep my private life unsullied as an example to all; maintain courageous calm in the face of danger, scorn, or ridicule; develop self-restraint; and be constantly mindful of the welfare of others. Honest in thought and deed in both my personal and official life, I will be exemplary in obeying the laws of the land and the regulations of my department.

present a rather "emotional image" of what the organization and its workers embody in terms of ethics, standards, and motivation, the police code seems to have "overdone it" at a great risk to coherence and credibility.   If the average citizen is expected to believe what the police code of ethics states in its present version, such a citizen must be assumed either "an angel or a fool".   The "unrealistic" language of the code makes it more of a restraint on police professional behavior than a stimulant, and smacks with an air of artificiality, phoniness, and perhaps gives a "snow job" impression.   For example, the second paragraph reads:

> I will keep my private life unsullied as an example to all; maintain courageous calm in the face of danger, scorn, or ridicule; develop self-restraint; and be constantly mindful of the welfare of others.   Honest in thought and deed in both my personal and official life, I will be exemplary in obeying the laws of the land and the regulations of my department.[15]

The unbelievably altruistic note of the previous statement especially in terms of being "honest in thought and deed" certainly confuses the public as well as the policeman himself.   Needless to say it is rather naive to believe that a human being in contact with his social milieu today would be totally honest in deed, let alone in thought.   It certainly *takes a saint* to behave in this manner, and it naturally *takes another* to believe that the first was truly a *human*.

The lack of realism reflected by the present police code of ethics can certainly be viewed by the intelligent policeman as an obstacle on the road to professionalism.   Reaching such a level of performance, restraint, and self-discipline must be viewed as an "impossible dream" and the incoherent disparity between the reality of police life and the myth portrayed by the code, is shattering.   The code, consequently, is seen by many policemen as an inapplicable piece of literature designed primarily for "public relations" and not binding on their "real" behavior.

Whatever I see or hear of a confidential nature or that is confided to me in my official capacity will be kept ever secret unless revelation is necessary in the performance of my duty.

I will never act officiously or permit personal feelings, prejudices, animosities or friendships to influence my decisions.   With no compromise for crime and with relentless prosecution of criminals, I will enforce the law courteously and appropriately without fear or favor, malice or ill will, never employing unnecessary force or violence and never accepting gratuities.

I recognize the badge of my office as a symbol of public faith, and I accept it as a public trust to be held so long as I am true to the ethics of the police service.   I will constantly strive to achieve these objectives and ideals, dedicating myself before God to my chosen profession . . . law enforcement.

15.   The Code, *Ibid.*

From the public's point of view, the "unrealistic" code has caused a lot of misconception of the police and their role. Any performance lower than what the code states can be seen as betrayal of the mission or at least a gross dereliction of duty. Problems that arise between the police and the public are consequently blamed on the police, who do not "live up to what they profess." Furthermore, the public expectation of the role of the police in modern society may become too blurred, mixed with fantasy, and thus dysfunctional. As to illustrate this state of role confusion, August Vollmer commented:

> The citizen expects police officers to have the wisdom of Solomon, the courage of David, the strength of Samson, the patience of Job, the leadership of Moses, the kindness of the Good Samaritan, the strategical training of Alexander, the faith of Daniel, the diplomacy of Lincoln, the tolerance of the Carpenter of Nazareth, and, finally, an intimate knowledge of every branch of the natural, biological, and social sciences. If he had all these, he *might* be a good policeman.[16]

(2) The second component of the moral facet relates to police deeds as shown by the practices and performances of policemen.

The basic condition that characterizes the professional police officer is that he operates under the law. A professional law enforcement agency must be managed in a fashion by which all police functions are carried out humanely, legally, and compassionately. Police education, training and management must be constantly guided by the democratic principles of the American society and its system of government. While the basic concept of authority must be consistently supported, the excessive use of power must be correspondingly suppressed. Under effective management, the "rule of law" must be constantly upheld and "unjustified discretion" indiscriminately censured. Moreover, effective management in compliance with the spirit of the law emphasizes that policemen, like all public servants, are human first, American second, and policemen third. Effective management must have its main interest in bringing police practices and performance to the level of advanced intergroup relations; thus, maintenance of harmony and peace within the community would become its primary concern.

Until a comparatively short time ago, it was not considered important that police officers get along with people, command their respect, and secure their cooperation. They did not have to know what

---

16. August Vollmer, former police chief of Berkeley, California, as cited by Harry W. More, Jr., *Critical Issues in*   *Law Enforcement* (Cincinnati: The W.H. Anderson Company), 1972, p. 208.

motivated people to act nor how they were likely to react in various situations.[17]   As a result, an abrasive relationship between the police and the community has become a major and explosive source of grievance, tension, and disorder.   Police forces, faced with the frustration of increasing insecurity on the job, unreasonable department regulations, weak and ineffective leadership, and disputed prestige, have resorted to aggressive power in their patrol practices, in their handling of suspects, and in their treatment of minorities.   The resulting relationship has become one of reciprocal tension and hostility aggravated by the lack of an effective mechanism for the resolution of conflict.   Further aggravated by a highly-contaminating police subculture, young policemen have used violence illegally in many of their daily tasks "because such usage is seen as just, acceptable, and at times expected by [their] colleague group".[18]

Police brutality continues to exist in one form or another. While hard to research and quantify with a degree of accuracy, brutal police practices consist of physical, psychological, and verbal (subtle or overt) abuses of authority.   It ranges from an indifferent or contemptuous glance to a sadistic application of illegal violence, from a cold silence to obscene vituperation, from an unwillingness to take proper police action to a delight in taking unnecessary action.

Denials of police brutality are common and as expected are basically offered by policemen.   One such denial states:

> Police brutality is a nonexistent, vicious allegation without basis in observed or proved fact that has been brought to bear against the police as a pressure weapon on the part of known liberal—radical—homosexual—left-leaning—potsmoking—peace-demonstrator—hippie—niggerlover types as a part of their continuing massive program to discredit regular police agencies so they can take over and invite the Russians in to loot and burn our homes, violate our daughters, and desecrate our churches.[19]

Whatever the facts may be, negative sentiments by the public have caused serious implications for the police.   Lack of public support of the police has evidently retarded their professionalization.   It interferes with police recruitment since intelligent young men would rather seek occupations which are not inordinately dangerous and which have the respect and support of the general public.   Public hostility also affects morale and makes police officers less enthusias-

---

17. A.C. Germann, Frank D. Day, and Robert J. Gallati, *Introduction to Law Enforcement and Criminal Justice*, (Springfield, Ill.: Charles C. Thomas, Publisher), Sixteenth Printing, 1970, p. 230.

18. *Ibid.*, p. 239.

19. *Ibid.*, p. 239.

tic about doing an effective job. Furthermore, it may lead some officers to leave the force and accept more prestigious or less demanding employment.

Also, as expected a dissatisfied public will not support the police before legislative bodies when management requests an improvement in police salaries, an increase in the number of the men on the force, and modernization of buildings and equipments. Perhaps most significant of all, when the police and the public are at odds, the police force tends to insulate itself from the public and thus becomes less capable of understanding and communicating with the clientele which provides its legitimacy and reason for being.

True or alleged brutality by modern policemen must be viewed as primarily a product of ineffective management by police agencies. Regardless of the obvious behavioral deviance on the part of groups and individuals in the community, and notwithstanding the unfavorable socio-economic conditions which might breed hatred and hostility against the police, effective management is the only vehicle which can induce professional calm "in the face of danger, scorn, or ridicule, [and] develop self-restraint and respect [for] the constitutional rights of all men".[20]

Effective management—through proper selection of personnel, advanced education, constant training, progressive organization and stimulative leadership—can certainly fill the gap between a mythical code of ethics and the reality of a harsh police environment.

To explain these general areas ordinarily available to all police administrators some specific means are cited here as examples for innovative projects: [21]

1 —Develop and adopt policy guidelines to assist officers in making critical decisions in areas where police conduct can cause tension.

2 —Develop and use innovative programs to insure widespread community support for law enforcement.

3 —Review police operations in the ghetto and high-crime areas to ensure proper conduct by police officers and to eliminate abrasive practices.

4 —Provide more adequate police protection to ghetto residents to eliminate their high sense of insecurity and the belief in the existence of a dual standard of law enforcement.

5 —Establish fair and effective mechanisms for the redress of grievances against the police and other municipal employees.

20. *The Code of Ethics.*

21. *Report of the National Advisory Commission on Civil Disorders,* (Washington, D.C.), 1968, p. 301.

6 —Establish a "Community Service Officer" program to attract ghetto youths for police work.

7 —Recruit more minority officers into the regular police force and review promotion policies to insure fair promotion for minority officers.

(3) The third component of the moral facet relates to police attitudes as demonstrated in the beliefs and opinions of policemen.

While some doctors, lawyers and bankers may not necessarily have an amicable relationship with their clients because of the high fees they charge or because of the lengthy waiting periods which clients must endure, these professionals ordinarily perform within a relationship of mutual respect with their public. Policemen, if they are to become professionals, must likewise develop such a "special", *if not necessarily amicable,* relationship with the public they serve. The British police, for example, which is commonly referred to as the most professional police system in the world, has secured this special relationship with its public. Sir Robert Mark, Commissioner of the Police of the Metropolis, in a recent address stated that, "Three independent public opinions in the last 18 months suggest that the police enjoy more confidence and respect than any other British institution".[22]   The Commissioner proceeded to explain that the warmth of that relationship is due, in part, to:

> the fact that the police . . . seem able to control political demonstrations and industrial disputes without using any special weapons or equipment . . . and not least our constant and frequently seen readiness to help anyone in distress or to respond to public need in any kind of emergency. These factors undoubtedly make a deep impression on public opinion.[23]

To a large extent, the professional status of the police depends on the attitudinal relationship that exists between the police and the public. If the police has, or develops, a favorable attitude toward the public and if the latter responds favorably, a state of professionalism can be forthcoming. On the other hand, if such a relationship fails to materialize, the desired state would be impossible.

The present attitudinal relationship between the police in the United States and the public, by and large, remains strained, and an air of mutual suspicion seems constantly looming in the background. As far as minority groups are concerned, the relationship may be described as indeed a problem.

---

22. Sir Robert Mark in an address delivered on April 13, 1976, in Washington, D.C., before the Executive Forum on Upgrading the Police which was sponsored by the Police Foundation, *The FBI Bulletin*, July 1976, pp. 3–9.

23. *Ibid.*

The Task Force Report, 1967, described the attitude which existed between the police and the public by stating:

> Although support and respect for the police is increasing, the status accorded to the police is still far lower than that of other professions .   . .. In a 1961 survey of status given to occupations, the police ranked 54th out of 90 occupations which tied them with playground directors and railroad conductors.[24]

The survey referred to by the Task Force Report was perhaps done by Albert Reiss in 1961. The original finding quoted by Saunders in a later reference indicates that the police in fact ranked below machinists, undertakers, electricians, welfare workers, and agricultural agents as well.

While the public attitude of the police in America is certainly changing, the old image does not seem like fading away. While many citizens are realizing that crime cannot be understood as a narrow range of behavior by certain types of people, and that crime control cannot be accomplished by the police alone, the stereotype of the "dumb cop" unfortunately remains. The stereotype is confirmed by the memory of many adults who recall the days when any able bodied man with the proper political allegiance could find a place on the force. Moreover, the stereotype seems to be always reinforced by the continual revelations of police dishonesty, brutality and corruption. One observation which perhaps sums up this attitudinal question stated that "the American is not overly impressed by police authority, considering the police officer as a badly paid job holder, not above being fixed by a bribe".[25]

Among minority groups, public attitude is even worse. Members of the black community firmly believe that police brutality and harassment occur repeatedly in Negro neighborhoods. This belief, stated the National Advisory Commission on Civil Disturbance in 1968, "is unquestionably one of the major reasons for intense Negro resentment against the police".[26]

The extent of this belief is suggested by several attitude surveys. In 1964, a *New York Times* study of Harlem showed that 43 percent of those questioned believed in the existence of police "brutality". In 1965, a nationwide Gallop Poll found that 34 percent of Negro men

24. *Task Force Report on the Police,* 1967, p. 134.

25. Max Lerner, *America as a Civilization,* (New York: Simon and Schuster), 1957, p. 433.

26. *Report of the National Advisory Commission on Civil Disorders, op. cit.,* p. 302.

believed there was police brutality in their areas. In 1966, a survey conducted by the Senate Subcommittee on Executive Reorganization found that 60 percent of Watts Negroes aged 15 to 19 believed there was some police brutality. Half said they had witnessed such conduct. A study by U.C.L.A. of the Watts area found that 79 percent of the Negro males believed police lack respect for, or use insulting language to, Negroes, and 74 percent believed police use unnecessary force in making arrests. In 1967, an Urban League study of the Detroit area found that 82 percent believed there was some form of police brutality.[27]

Moreover, the President's Commission on Law Enforcement and Administration of Justice in 1967 stated that studies of police-community relations in eleven localities throughout the country indicated serious problems of Negro hostility to the police in virtually all medium and large cities. The commission concluded that "many Negroes see the police as their enemies; and they see them as protectors of white people, not as protectors of Negroes, as well".[28]

While the true extent of police brutality and unjustified practices may never be accurately determined, the existence of an attitudinal problem between the police and the black segment of the society can neither be denied nor ignored. It is not the physical existence of polic brutality and malpractice that degrades the moral facet of the police and frustrates their attempts to professionalize; it is, rather, the prevalence of an attitude that it exists.

Attitudes of policemen, on the other hand, are as crucial as those of the public. The existence of a negative police attitude further complicates the attitudinal problem and frustrates the possibility for professionalism even more. Recent studies sponsored by the President's Commission on Law Enforcement and Administration of Justice confirm the existence of a strong feeling of antagonism among policemen in response to what they viewed as public hostility. William Westley observed that because the public views the police with suspicion and distrust, "the police in turn see the public as their enemy".[29]

Westley, describing the attitude of some policemen in his famous study, quoted one rookie policeman:

> One of the older men advised me that if the courts didn't punish a man we should. He told me about a sex

27. *Ibid.*, p. 302.

28. *Task Force Report on the Police*, 1967, p. 148.

29. William Westley, "The Police: A Sociological Study of Law, Custom, and Morality", in Ernest W. Burgess and Donald J. Bogue (eds.), *Urban Sociology*, (Chicago: University of Chicago Press), 1964, p. 169.

crime and said the policeman has the right to use the necessary force to make an arrest and that in that kind of crime you can use just a little more force.[30]

James Baldwin, in his study of police attitudes in Westville, found that the patrolmen in that community, and probably in many other communities, had their own paranoid thoughts about the public. Describing some of these attitudes, Baldwin narrated the feelings of those officers:

> He has never himself done anything for which to be hated . . . and yet he is facing, daily and nightly, people who would gladly see him dead, and he knows it.[31]

A particular attitude dominates the minds of most policemen. That is the unwritten rule that a copfighter must be dealt with harshly and often violently. One city detective remarked:

> An attack on a cop is viewed by the police as the most serious thing in the world. When there is a 1013 call (the New York signal for a policeman in trouble) all hell breaks loose and patrol cars from all over the city respond . . . . The rightful worry about our own safety leads to the belief that any kind of physical response—or sometimes even an angry word—is a cause for a wack across the head or a few punches. I have seen an old drunk being creamed for having taken a harmless swing.[32]

Describing the attitude of some policemen about students, Dr. Watson, a researcher of police attitudes stated:

> You must remember that most policemen because of their training and background believe that civil disobedience is completely wrong . . .. They [the policemen] really become outraged and confused when they hear some kid question the guts of those fighting in Vietnam or hear some Barnard girl shouting a dirty word.[33]

Colin McInnes, a policeman, added more insight to the attitudinal problem of the police:

> Some civilians fear us and play up to us, some dislike us and keep out of our way but no one—well very few indeed —accepts us as just ordinary like them. In one sense

---

30. *Ibid.*

31. James Baldwin, *Nobody Knows My Name*, (New York: Bell Publishing Company), 1962, pp. 65–67.

32. *The New York Times*, July 7, 1968.

33. *Ibid.*

. . . we're just like hostile troops occupying an enemy country.[34]

Describing the policeman's feeling of isolation and alienation, a policeman revealed his true feeling by saying that, "I try to put my police work into the background, and try not to let people know I am a policeman. Once you do, you can't have normal relations with them".[35]

Emphasizing the notion of police isolation and alienation, Niederhoffer attributed the poor attitudinal relationship the police have with the public to their cynicism and anomie. He declared that, in the police world, "cynicism is discernible at all levels, in every branch of law enforcement".[36] Niederhoffer reiterated Read Bains' assesment that policemen are committed to the belief that "the citizen is always trying to get away with something" and that "all men would commit crimes except for the fear of the police".[37]

The main type of police cynicism, declared Niederhoffer, is one directed against life, the world, and people in general. It is endemic to policemen of all ranks and persuasions. Professional policemen, explained Niederhoffer, must be concerned about transforming and eventually controlling "the system"; otherwise, they will join the rest into the trap of cynicism.

Niederhoffer added that when the cynic policeman becomes increasingly pessimistic and misanthropic, he finds it easier to reduce his commitment to the social system and to its values. If the patrolman remains a "loner", his isolation may lead to psychological anomie and, infrequently, to suicide.[38]

To sum up this discussion on the moral facet of police professionalism, it must be stated that the social prestige of the police has been slowly on the rise, especially since the end of the Vietnam War. Through improved management, police have been receiving "higher" education and "better" training, and police-community attitudes have improved. Backed by sound planning, intelligent decisions, and a higher morale, policemen in the future may be able to resolve their attitudinal "hang ups" and respond humanly to the needs of the public. This would close the present chasm between a would-be profes-

34. Colin McInnes, *Mr. Love and Justice*, (London: New English Library), 1962, p. 20.

35. Jerome Skolnick, "A Sketch of the Policeman's Working Personality", as cited in Arthur Niederhoffer and Abraham Blumberg, *The Ambivalent Force*, (Waltham, Mass.: Ginn and Company), 1970, p. 138.

36. Arthur Niederhoffer, "Police Cynicism", as cited in Arthur Niederhoffer and Abraham Blumberg, *The Ambivalent Force, Ibid.*, p. 179.

37. Read Bain, "The Policeman on the Beat", *Scientific Monthly*, 48, (1939), p. 451.

38. Arthur Niederhoffer, "Police Cynicism", *op. cit.*, p. 180.

sional police force and their primary clientele. One warning, however, is offered by Germann, the veteran policman and educator: "There are a lot of deadhead and not-too-bright people in police management positions, and substantial change will only come over the dead bodies of some current Neanderthal incumbents".[39]

THE STRUCTURAL FACET

Besides the strong emphasis on education and morals, professions are characterized by a system of internal discipline. Such a system is maintained by a governing body of members assigned to oversee adherence to the educational and moral standards and to censure deviant behavior. These governing bodies also serve other functions. Not only do they perform as a quality-control mechanism, they serve as a symbol of the prestigious status of the profession and as a unifier of its subgroups. Stands taken by such bodies are accepted as a part of the profession's "ideology", a violation of which constitutes a serious matter that warrants investigation and possible censure.

To exercise this supervisory responsibility, physicians, for instance, have the American Medical Association, lawyers have the American Bar Association, and accountants have the Association of Certified Public Accountants. By way of comparison, the police occupation, for all practical purposes, has no counterpart for these. While doctors may get licenses revoked, lawyers may be disbarred and CPA's suspended, policemen—though they might be punished for malfeasance—usually continue an uninterrupted career with their departments, and, if they are fired, ordinarily have no difficulty joining another police agency or a sheriff's department.

The police governing body presently in charge of the question of professionalization is underdeveloped and ineffective. At the national level there is the International Association of Chiefs of Police which "serves the law enforcement profession and the public interest by advancing the art of police science".[40] It has a staff of police management consultants, educators and trainers, research analysts, and specialists who develop and disseminate improved police practices and promote police understanding. Since its inception in 1897, IACP has traditionally attempted to improve and professionalize police service through the provision of assistance and advice. Although the attempts have been well-motivated, the impact of IACP has been superficial. The mere fact that police agencies have failed to professionalize indicates the failure of IACP as an influential governing body capable of affecting serious change.

39. A. C. Germann, "Community Policing: An Assessment", 60, *Journal of Criminal Law, Criminology, and Police Science*, 90, (1969).

40. International Association of Chiefs of Police, 1975–76, *International Training Calendar*, Maryland, 1975, p. 7.

The apparent inadequacy of the IACP may be attributed to the following factors:

1   —It has no jurisdiction over police agencies at any level of government.

2   —Its membership is strictly voluntary.

3   —It has no authority to intervene and investigate alleged police malfeasance.

4   —It is primarily viewed as an organization of chiefs, serving only their interests.

5   —Its leadership is generally perceived as politically-oriented.

Charged with being basically ceremonial in nature, IACP has had particularly little influence on local police agencies.[41]   Consequently police standards at the street level have failed to develop, and illegal actions by delinquent members of the police have not received uniform sanctions, if at all.   Moreover, police agencies have remained in disunity, corruption has continued unabashed, and the police reputation, regardless of all noble intentions to upgrade it, has not been much enhanced.

At the state level there are several police and sheriff associations which, also in a ceremonial manner, are emulating the role of IACP with perhaps even less effectiveness.   Mainly occupied with internal feuds and power struggles among the participating agencies, state associations are distracted from the original function of a governing body.   This obviously has left local agencies in a state of "professional disarray".   Without an effective and a trustworthy forum capable of instituting discipline in police agencies and offsetting malicious criticism of policemen, public disrespect may continue to mount and remaining public support may quickly erode.

The failure of IACP and other state associations to provide an effective forum for police, though saddening, should not leave the occupation in a hopeless situation if attention is focused on the recommendations of the Task Force Report.   The report, in a serious attempt to establish such forums, turned to State Commissions on Law Enforcement Officer Standards and Goals.

As the Judicial Qualification Commissions, which in each state supervise the judicial profession, set standards for judges, and review

41. As a result of dissatisfaction with IACP, ten major urban police leaders selected to "dump" the organization as the spokesman for local agencies and founded a new organization of police chiefs, saying they hope it becomes an influential national voice on police issues.   These leaders formed instead the Police Executive Research Forum to promote research and work toward improving police practices nationally. The leaders stated that they "refuse to accept archaic styles of leadership, to rely on untested traditional police leaders [within IACP], to speak out openly on the complexity of crime and on other police issues". *Houston Post*, July 29, 1976.

inappropriate conduct by delinquent judges, the new role of state commissions can be expanded and strengthened. Without removing control of law enforcement from local agencies, such commissions could help professionalize police departments in each state. By providing effective leadership, setting and maintaining high standards for policemen, and purging the profession of its unethical elements, State Commissions on Standards and Goals could be the long-awaited-for effective governing body.

In establishing these Commissions, the Task Force Report suggested they be empowered to: [42]

1 —Evaluate the current situation through studies and hearings.

2 —Set basic minimum selection standards applicable to all departments.

3 —Encourage civil service reforms and promote programs that can help departments adjust to the new standards.

4 —Suggest ways of assessing attitudes of applicants in order to keep prejudiced persons out of police service.

5 —Suggest ways of removing impediments to lateral entry in the police.

6 —Help greatly to improve police organization, management and operations.

This type of state commissions is by no means novel. They were first initiated in New York and California in 1959 before they were ordered in all states by the President's Commisson on Law Enforcement and Administration of Justice in 1967.[43] Some of them are more effective than others; all, however, could and should be significantly improved. In most states today commissions still have no power to establish mandatory standards, nor do they have the jurisdiction to look into cases of police malpractice. Furthermore, many commissions do not have the right to revoke or suspend the certification policemen receive either automatically upon graduating from a police academy or upon merit after some advanced training. This lack of power on the part of the commission seriously handicaps their impact. If properly constituted and empowered, State Commissions on Standards and Goals could play a significant role in the professionalization process of police agencies. In addition to their su-

42. *Task Force Report*, 1967, p. 218.

43. As early as 1952, the American Bar Association, in conjunction with the National Conference of Commissioners on Uniform State Laws, recognized the need to develop a State Council to serve as a catalyst in improving law enforcement. Together they published a Model Police Council Act. This act, with significant revisions, served as a model for the states of New York and California which established State Police Standards Commissions in 1959.

pervisory and investigatory roles, they can provide the "legitimate" missing link between the police and the state and local legislatures, harmonize relations between police agencies within the state, conduct necessary research on complex police issues, offer advisory opinions, and become the professional spokesmen for police agencies in their disputes with public and private organizations and groups.

Substantial resentment exists, it must be stressed, to the growth and effectiveness of these state governing bodies. This primarily stems from the sentiments of quite a few police chiefs, mostly in small police agencies, who are not professionally-oriented. Their attitudes vary from stubborn opposition to change to honest doubt in the wisdom of standardization. Most of these chiefs are not willing to accept restrictions on their authority to set their own standards regarding selections, training, education, or ethics. Their favorite argument is that of local autonomy and the need to maintain local authority since policing in America is basically a local responsibility.

Effective management does not dispute the concept of local autonomy. What it disputes, however, is the overemphasis on autonomy at the sacrifice of professional standards. The only effective way of combining autonomy and standardization is through the concept of "professional accountability". The application of the concept provides for a fine mix of "local control" by police departments and "reasonable supervision" by State Commissions on Standards and Goals. The right of the latter to inquire, investigate, and inspect, however, must be recognized. While many policemen and managers may still resent the concept of "professional accountability", the principle, it must be stressed, has always been a major part of democratic systems and a pivotal ingredient of the American system of checks and balances especially between the federal and state levels of government.

Defining the extent of "professional accountability" and determining the limits of "local control" and "reasonable supervision" is naturally a legislative question to be determined by each state. Precautions to prevent undue power by the commissions conducting "fishing expeditions" and "illegal snooping" must be taken in accordance with legal guidelines. Common provisions of public law in terms of the need for public hearing and solicitation of views must be used. Acceptance by policemen, and particularly by chiefs and sheriffs, is certainly crucial. Through their *enlightened concern* for the police as a profession and insistence to improve the police image, policemen can influence the legislative process in the direction of expanding the role and scope of Commissions as professional governing bodies. The risks of possible undue intervention by the Commissions in the private affairs of local departments should not become a local *obsession* which might block the road to professionalism. If such risks, which obviously are taken by all government agencies at all times, had created such an obsession to doctors, lawyers, accountants or professors, none of these groups would have become professional today.

It is crucial, therefore, that legislation expanding the powers of these commission be broad enough to authorize them to take the following actions:

1 —To adopt regulations establishing mandatory minimum standards relating to educational, moral, and mental fitness which shall govern the selection of police officers.

2 —To establish mandatory minimum training standards with the authority to determine and approve curricula, to identify required preparation for instructors, and to approve facilities acceptable for police training.

3 —To certify police officers who have acquired various levels of education, training, and experience to perform adequately the duties of the police service.

4 —To conduct surveys of the administration and operation of police departments or aid in providing for surveys to be conducted by other agencies or consulting firms, and to assist in the analysis and interpretation of their recommendations.

5 —To conduct and stimulate research by public and private agencies designed to improve police organization and management.

6 —To make such inquiries and inspections as may be necessary to determine whether or not the standards established in the regulations are in fact adhered to.

7 —To intervene and investigate allegations of serious abuse of police power by any department or any of its members and recommend appropriate disciplinary action to be taken against the perpetrators.

8 —To revoke or suspend certification of delinquent policemen in accordance with public hearing regulations and the right to appeal.

9 —To report regularly to the state legislature on the state of police affairs and the progress of reform.

While the impact of such commissions on police professionalism may seem vague at this time, effective police managers must be willing to at least try the concept of "professional accountability" and evaluate its results. Without giving it a chance to be tested in the real police world, the chances are that the present state of police professionalism will not improve much in the future.

CHAPTER THIRTEEN

SUPPRESSION OF POLICE CORRUPTION

Overview

While professionalism is still viewed as a cherished police ideal, corruption is, perhaps, commonly seen as a widely accepted reality. Professionalism and corruption lie at the opposite ends of the performance spectrum. The former attracts and upgrades average workers toward a level of excellence; the latter causes their deterioration and apostasy. The only controlling force along this spectrum of police performance is effective management. As it moves determinately toward upgrading police professionalism, it simultaneously suppresses corruption by neutralizing its attraction and blocking its chances to mature.

Suppression of police corruption through effective management is not only possible but is the natural product of its application. By removing, or minimizing the effects of, the department's "hygiene factors" such as insecurity, implausible working conditions, and ineffective policies and procedures, the agency's environment would become less conducive to corruption. Also, by enhancing the "motivators" within the department, such as increased responsibility, recognition, sense of achievement and actualization, the internal immunity of individual policemen would be reinforced.[1] If the environmental pressures of corruption are neutralized or considerably reduced and the immunity level of individual policemen maximized, the chances for corruption to occur would be minimal. While whole or "total" elimination of corruption may sound as idealistic as "absolute" professionalim, the effectiveness of police management in curbing corruption can only reflect the ability, determination and professionalism of the managers in charge.

Government corruption obviously refers to corruption by workers within government organizations. Government, which is traditionally expected not to *cheat, lie, or steal,* does not, in fact, cheat, lie, or steal. Only "corrupt" workers within the government do. Ethical government, it must be emphasized at the outset, is in the minds of the people who work it: *their virtues make it virtuous and their sins make it sinful.*

Police corruption is certainly not the most harmful sort of corruption in America today, although the general public seems inclined

---

1. Readers are urged to recall Frederick Herzberg's Motivation-Hygiene theory previously discussed in Chapter Six.

to view it as probably the ugliest.   There seems to be more public criticism of police corruption than of any other kind of government corruption, whether it be in legislation, adjudication, or the mighty labyrinth of bureaucracy.

Exacting ethical standards and maintaining an honest police organization, however, is essential.   Because the police are entrusted with the enforcement of the fundamental rules that guide the conduct of society, a policeman's violation of the law or his *malicious* failure to enforce it doubly dishonors the law and the authority he represents.   Emphasizing the need for ethical police conduct, the Task Force Report stated:

> Dishonesty within a police agency can, almost overnight, destroy respect and trust that has been built up over a period of years   .   .   .   nothing undermines public confidence in the police and the process of criminal justice more than the illegal acts of officers.[2]

Also as to dramatize the adverse effect of police corruption, the report stated in the same reference that "when the dishonest cop headline appears, honest police officers throughout the country are adversely affected, the feeling of pride slips and a hint of shame takes hold".[3]

The violations in which policemen are involved vary widely in character.   The most common are: improper political influence and favoritism, acceptance of gratuities or bribes in exchange for nonenforcement of laws, particularly those relating to gambling, prostitution, and liquor offenses, which are often extensively interconnected with organized crime; the fixing of traffic tickets; minor thefts; and occasional burglaries.[4]   The Task Force Report also reveals the commonality of instances of police officers in high-crime neighborhoods engaging "in such practices as rolling drunks and shake-downs of money and merchandise in the very places where respect for law is so badly needed".[5]

Contrary to the idealistic notion of government, police organizations are not *pure* organizations.   They are *human* associations operated by *real people* in the midst of a complex social, political and economic "environment".   Police chiefs are appointed by political authorities which may be corrupt, sheriffs are elected by popular votes which may be influenced, police officers are selected by fallible systems of hiring, and supervision of policemen, especially those on the beat, can not be constantly precise.   Furthermore, police conduct on the job is basically a "personal style" which is the product of unique

2.   *Task Force Report*, 1967, p. 208.   4.   *Ibid.*

3.   *Ibid.*   5.   *Ibid.*

cultural, social, psychological and economic backgrounds. Therefore, curbing corruption and, hopefully, eliminating it must be perceived as a sensitive multi-dimensional operation based on behavioral research, proper evaluation techniques, and a patient and open-minded appraisal of human motivation and work pressure. Effective management is the only "school" which provides this composite.

Corruption Defined

From the legal point of view, definitions of corruption can be found in every criminal code applied in the nation. Violations of those codes by policemen constitute police corruption.

From a sociological point of view, corruption can be placed in the category of *arbitrary power,* since it always presupposes the use of power to achieve a purpose other than that for which this power was granted. Not all arbitrary power, however, can be called corruption, since arbitrary power may also proceed from fancied patriotism or simply from a confused state of mind. While arbitrary power, *i.e.,* illegal arrest or harrassment of suspects, may sometimes result from corruption, lack of appropriate standards or training may also produce the same result.

Corruption could also be viewed in moralistic terms as the *failure to demonstrate compassion or to keep a promise.* This approach, however, creates plenty of doubts arising from the value criterion involved and the temporal nature of judgments. What is moral to a particular individual may not be to another, and the change of times and situations may strongly influence such judgments.

From a political point of view, moreover, corruption has developed a *connotation of oppression,* or an extra-legal instrument used by political groups or individuals to gain influence by suppressing the public will. In strictly political terms, corruption in politics has, at times, even been viewed as functional to the maintenance of a political ideology in the same way that reform is.[6]

The most common use of the term corruption, today, essentially relates to the *concept of the public office and to deviations from norms binding upon its incumbents.* This use of the term seems to relate more closely to most contemporary concerns for police corruption. The following definitions will attempt to explain it further:

> [Corruption] is a general term covering misuse of authority
> as a result of considerations of personal gain, which need not
> be monetary.—David Bayley [7]

6. Samuel P. Huntington, "Modernization and Corruption", *Political Order in Changing Societies,* (New Haven, Conn.: Yale University Press), 1968, pp. 59–71.

7. Arnold J. Heidenheimer, *Political Corruption,* (New York: Holt, Rinehart and Winston, Inc.), 1970, p. 5.

[Corruption is] behavior which deviates from the normal duties of a public role because of private-regarding (family, close private clique), pecuniary or status gains; or violates rules against the exercise of certain types of private-regarding influence. It includes such behavior as bribery, nepotism, and misappropriation.—J. S. Nye [8]

A public official is corrupt if he accepts money or money's worth for doing something that he is under duty to do anyway, that he is under duty not to do, or to exercise a legitimate discretion for improper reasons.—M. McMullen [9]

A more functional definition of corruption was introduced by Arnold Rogow and Harold Lasswell who defined it as "deviations from the norms of public or civic order".[10] The authors noted that a system of public or civic order must, by definition, "exalt common interest over special interest".[11] A corrupt act must, therefore, be recognized as *any violation of the common interest for a personal advantage.*

CHARACTERISTICS OF POLICE CORRUPTION

A basic characteristic of corruption in general, and police corruption in particular, is the fact that it is *intentional.* The public duty involved must be perceived but is neglected or misperformed. Unintentional failure to meet a recognized duty does not necessarily constitute an act of corruption; it may be due to lack of communication, understanding, or mere inefficiency. The corrupt policeman "must know the better and choose the worse; the inefficient officer does not know any better".[12]

Another characteristic of corruption is the fact that it is a *learned behavior* which develops in a group setting.[13] Since nobody is born corrupt and policemen are so well-screened prior to employment at a fairly young age, one may legitimately conclude that the phenomenon of corruption must have developed through exposure to job-related situations, association with criminal elements, affiliation with corrupt peers and supervisors, or frustration with work conditions and policies. Removing, therefore, the "hygiene factors" which cause work dissatisfaction and upgrading the attitudinal levels of workers within the police agency should prevent the spreading of corruption.

8. *Ibid.*

9. *Ibid.*

10. *Ibid.*, p. 54.

11. *Ibid.*

12. Sam S. Souryal, "Stages of Police Corruption", *Police Chief,* Vol. XLII, No. 2, February 1975, pp. 63–65.

13. *Ibid.*

A third characteristic is that corruption entails a *maturation process*.[14] Young rookies are seldom "hooked" on "auto corruption" or embarked on grave violations. The corruption process ordinarily *grows on* the practicing officer. The new officer slowly and gradually discovers the advantages which other officers and public officials are deriving from their jobs and then starts to learn, experiment with, conceptualize, and improvise the techniques of corrupt practices. As the individual policeman's lust for power and prosperity increases, his self-resistance and adherence to departmental regulations erodes correspondingly. An effective manager who occasionally "takes the temperature of his workers" would be able to spot this deterioration and work on blocking it and reversing its direction.

Yet another characteristic of police corruption is the fact that it is basically a *response to external propositions, pressures, and expectations*. Policemen do not bribe or brutalize each other. Their acceptance of a gratuity or a bribe is overwhelmingly in response to offers made to them by citizens and their brutality is usually in response to real, or imaginary, passes made at them. Operating in such a highly-gestural environment is a part of the police function. For example, they are required to enforce parking and gambling laws, though most of the community might prefer them not to. Expression of public resentment to the enforcement of such laws greatly increases the temptation to go along and accept favors, gratuities or bribes, or to simply ignore violations. Political corruption is another example of the gestural environment of the police. Because of subtle hints by *higher-ups*, organized crime and vice operations have continued to plague so many cities today. Effective management, through its positive approach, efficiency measures, and *courage*, can define the boundaries of the police environment, reduce gestural transactions, and limit illegitimate political penetration.

CATEGORIES OF POLICE CORRUPTION

Within the general definition of corruption as a violation of public office for personal gain, three basic categories are identified:

(a) Nonfeasance which is failure to perform a prescribed duty.

(b) Malfeasance which is the commission of an act which is positively unlawful.

(c) Misfeasance which is the improper performance of an act which may be properly executed.

Examples of nonfeasance are plenty. The most common example is the practice of nonenforcement of the law in the areas of prostitution, gambling, liquor, and traffic. Whether the officer would expect

14. *Ibid.*

to receive payoffs for his failure to enforce such laws, or merely enjoy the satisfaction of *beating* an "inappropriate law", the officer would be guilty of nonfeasance.   Examples of malfeasance include the common practices of *swiping* a valuable item from the scene of a crime, raping or molesting a jailed suspect, or extorting small store keepers whose businesses he is assigned to safeguard.   Examples of misfeasance include illegal arrests, search without a probable cause, or an unjustified stop-and-frisk.

PATTERNS OF POLICE CORRUPTION

The President's Commission on Law Enforcement and Administration of Justice in its Report on the Police, 1967, identified four patterns of police corruption.   They included: (a) political corruption, (b) nonenforcement of the law, (c) theft, and (d) kickbacks.

(A) Political Corruption

Government corruption in America, stated the Task Force Report, has always troubled historians, political reformers, and the general public especially since the middle of the 19th century.   The police, especially the metropolitan forces, were often the tool through which political corruption was discharged.   While police forces themselves are targets for political patronage, favoritism, and other kinds of illegal influence, such forces are frequently directed so as to expedite corrupt political ventures.   Police chiefs and sheriffs, for instance, are *not to bother* organized crime activities, vice operations, and gambling rings condoned by, if not allied with, corrupt political machines.

The report stated that even in some cities where reforms have ended open political control, policemen who make trouble for businessmen with strong political influence may still be transferred to punishment beats, and traffic tickets may still be fixed in some places through political connections.   "Honest and conscientious police chiefs", noted the report, "often have an extremely difficult time eliminating these practices   .   . .. Appeals to a mayor, city council, or prosecutor may, of course, be fruitless, since they themselves may be involved in or condone such practices".[15]   Credit was also duly given to effective police management by the report, when it cited a case of political corruption foiled by an effective police manager: "the appointment of an honest chief of police ended a regime that was so closely controlled by organized crime that the community seemed helpless in its grip".[16]

15. *Task Force Report*, 1967, p. 209.   16. *Ibid.*

(B) Nonenforcement of the Law

Besides the illegitimate influence of political corruption, *selective nonenforcement of the law* by policemen persists because, in many areas, neither the police nor the rest of the criminal justice system have the resources or ability to attempt full enforcement. This creates a situation most conducive to corruption whereby gestural temptation increases and internal immunity diminishes.

While the wholesale corruption of prohibition days has passed, selective enforcement still exists and leaves the door wide open for bribery, favors, gratuities and other illegal activities. Examples include areas of traffic and accident investigation, criminal charges, health requirements for public places, regulation of wrecker services, in addition, of course, to related areas of organized crime. The Task Force Report cited many examples including this interesting one told by a patrol division commander:

> This fellow was president of the local service club and he was always shoving something into the officer's hand saying, 'here's a little trinket for the wife!' He did the same thing with delivery men and others in return for small favors. In our case it was in appreciation for the officer not tagging overparked or double-parked customers' vehicles in front of the shop.[17]

In another example the report cited a common practice by detectives to provide a list of names of selected officers to leading law firms and large hotels for distribution of liquor at Christmas time. In yet another example the report mentioned "contractors who wished to unload materials at curbside had to pay a given per diem to the precinct captain".[18]

(C) Theft

The problem of theft by police officers sometimes takes a form less blatant than the occasional, well-publicized burglary such as the Summerdale incident, which resulted in the reorganization of the entire Chicago police department in 1960, and the 1961 apprehension in Denver of a ring of police burglars which resulted in the dismissal of 52 men.[19] In some cities, the report stated, some officers kept stolen property recovered by investigation, stole small items from stores when a patrol inspection discovered an unlocked door, or emptied the pockets of drunks before they were taken to the stationhouse. Some officers have also been known to take building material and actually

17. *Ibid.*   19. *Ibid.*

18. *Ibid.*, p. 210.

transport it in police cars. In one city officers picked up nails, tools, bundles of shingles, roofing paper and other items from the "midnight supply company" while working their shift. They were remodeling their houses and rationalized their acts on the basis of numerous reports of stolen property from building contractors, presumably much of it taken by workers on the job. One of the officers was a former building trade worker and looked upon this form of "toting" as an accepted practice.[20]

A new category of police thefts has been added lately which combined burglary with political corruption. It involves "break-in jobs" into offices of suspected political groups, foreign embassies, and offices of professional individuals for the purpose of obtaining secrets or evidence. Fred Cook asserts that what is known in the Bureau (FBI) as a "bag job" are often resorted to and are "done every day in the Bureau".[21] Such "bag jobs", reported Cook, are "nothing less than the entering of a person's home in his absence without a search warrant, in direct violation of the Fourth Amendment of the Constitution".[22] When Director Kelley was asked most recently whether such "bag jobs" committed by his agents or informers have ended, he refused to confirm they have. The director stated, "I wish I could say categorically, unquestionably, that this is not going on".[23] While this type of theft may be still confined to agencies serving at the federal level (CIA and FBI) and justified primarily on basis of national security and dedication to the democratic system of government in the United States, the heart of the matter still remains that it constitutes illegal criminal acts punishable by the laws of the democratic system of government they are trying to serve. Emulation of this type of theft by state or local agencies could be extremely harmful to the concepts of rule of law, due process of law, and professional policing.

(D) Kickbacks

Particularly in the case of traffic offenses there is also an opportunity, which has sometimes resulted in publicized incidents for policemen to receive payments for business referrals such as towing companies, ambulance companies, garages, and lawyers who specialize in traffic accident damage suits. In one large city, the Task Force Report stated that lawyers' *runners* with radio-equipped cars sometimes showed up at accidents. "The result was an automatic $25 for the police officer handling it if the victim would be influenced to ac-

20. *Ibid.*

21. Fred J. Cook, *The FBI Nobody Knows*, (New York: Macmillan Company), 1964, pp. 24–27.

22. *Ibid.*

23. *The Houston Post*, August 12, 1976.

cept the attorney".[24] Licensing, inspection, and truck weighing duties also have afforded opportunities for this sort of unethical conduct.

ETIOLOGY OF POLICE CORRUPTION

What causes corruption among policemen and deteriorates their performance is naturally hard to determine accurately. Theories, however, revolve around the notions of human weakness, departmental environment, and external pressure.

The first theory which relates corruption to human weakness was presented by James Madison in the 51st Federalist Paper. Madison wrote that "if men were angels or angels were to govern men we would have no need for government and no worries about the conduct of government".[25] But since neither condition prevails, there is a need, Madison acknowledged, for auxiliary precautions against government employees getting out of hand. The Madison theory, when applied to the police situation, naturally explains corruption in terms of the human weakness of some individual officers and their lack of integrity. The theory strongly supports the natural immorality of some people who attach a relatively low value on probity and public interest and a high value on the exchange of favors and private gain.

The second theory which relates corruption to departmental environment and peer pressure was labeled after Abraham Lincoln. Also called the *war theory,* it stemmed from Lincoln's determination to win the Civil War at any cost. Toward that goal "anything goes that may be required for victory", Lincoln was quoted.[26] This theory assumes that policemen turn corrupt because of their attempts to cope with departmental pressure and to earn collegial acceptance. Portrayed as a group of zealots who aim at maintaining a tough image for their department, these zealots turn corrupt as a result of their overzealousness which often exceeds the limits of rationality and order. Mort Sterns expanded on this theory when he described the impact of the police subculture on the new rookie:

> He knows he is being watched by all the older hands around. He senses that an unfavorable report handed in by a senior man could blackball him. He watches closely what the others do. He is eager to be accepted. He does what he can to show his guts. He backs up his partner in any way

24. *Task Force Report*, 1967, p. 210.

25. The 51st Federalist Paper as cited in J. D. Williams, *Management Begins with Man*, a forthcoming text in Public Administration, Little, Brown and Co., p. 292.

26. J. D. Williams, *Management Begins with Man*, A forthcoming book in Public Administration from Little, Brown and Company, p. 292.

he can. He accepts advice gracefully. Then he gets little signs that he is making a good impression . . . it may happen like this. The older man stops at a bar, comes out with some packages of cigarettes, he does this several times. He explains that this is part of the job . . . and it is his turn to make the butt—one thing leading to another . . . after six months they have become conditioned to accept free meals, free packs of cigarettes, turkeys at Thanksgiving, and liquor at Christmas from respectable people in their district. The rule book forbids all this, but it isn't enforced. It is winked at at all levels.[27]

Sterns adds by saying that the rookie thus eager to get accepted by his colleagues and supervisors submits to the department's "lifestyle". He gradually becomes accepted as a reliable officer. In time he learns all the bad habits of his senior officers. Being in this environment for at least eight hours a day, six days a week, the officer gets indoctrinated into believing that the majority of people he comes in contact with are "thieves, con men, dope addicts, and out and out nuts . . .. Americans are not funny, they have a resentment for authority and the policeman is authority in person".[28]

The third theory which relates corruption to external pressure explains corrupt behavior of policemen in terms of the so-called *eleventh commandment;* "thou shalt not tempt". Also called the *Apple Theory,* it was attributed to Lincoln Steffens who in reply to some ministers of the gospel who asked him about the origin of sin said:

You blame it on Adam, he blamed it on Eve, and she blamed it on the serpent. But I am here to tell you that the origin of sin was the apple, the reward for doing evil.[29]

According to Steffens public officials and policemen are ordinary men facing extraordinary temptations. He contended that corruption is *not* necessarily the result of failing character but rather the inevitable consequence of a social system which holds out to men great prizes in terms of power, wealth and status—if only they are bold enough to seize them. Corrupt politicians, policemen, and public officials in fact behave in a corrupt manner because corrupt businessmen and influential men tempt them and generously bribe them. According to Steffens, the socio-economic system must be changed and the recognition of the value of money as a status of individuals must be altered. Only then, added Steffens, will corrupt businessmen, and influential men find no utility in practicing corruption.

27. Mort Sterns, *Journal of Criminal Law, Criminology, and Police Science,* November 1962, Vol. 53.

28. *Ibid.*

29. J. D. Williams, *op. cit.,* p. 292.

Naturally, attempts to explain police corruption in terms of one theory or the other would be most difficult to do since corruption "grows on" individual policemen in a long maturation process which combines all three theories and perhaps several undiscovered ones. Also researchers (assumingly uncorrupt individuals) may never be able to figure out the exact ingredients of corruption by examining individual cases since "ethics are a lot like shoes—you don't know how they fit until you wear them".[30] Studies in the collective behavior of corrupt policemen, however, were able to identify several stages of corruption which may match one or more of these theories.

THE STAGES OF POLICE CORRUPTION

In their attempt to "fit their shoes on", corrupt police officers go through six successive stages: (1) precorruption stage, (2) experimentation stage, (3) accustomation stage, (4) conceptualization stage, (5) improvisation stage, and (6) benediction stage.[31]

1. Precorruption Stage

It usually begins after the probationary period when the officer can enjoy a fair amount of job security. He starts to cool down, regulate his pace, and realize the tremendous burden of the job compared to the low pay it offers. In natural disappointment, he looks around for possible job gratification. In his enthusiastic effort to learn the ropes of the department, the new officer may accidentally come across stories and rumors involving members of the force. He may observe peculiar indications of sudden affluency or abnormal power of some colleagues. He may have to drive his sergeant to a suspicious location or overhear an extramarital telephone call coming in for an idolized supervisor. In an attempt to further explore and discover, the intelligent rookie quietly indulges in a private endeavor to collect information, reconstruct events, and reevaluate the performance of his peers. His mind at this stage is confused and his desire to find out for himself becomes irresistible. If not too professionally oriented, the officer at this stage will select a wait-and-see stand usually highly susceptible to the slightest external stimulus.

2. Experimentation Stage

In this stage, the policeman seems to be moving around with a lot of unanswered questions. His eagerness to try for himself polarizes him toward the experimentation approach. Within the department as well as on the street, the ambitious policeman seems to be looking for an experience with corruption. He may justify a corrupt

---

30. *Ibid.*

31. The following stages are taken from Sam Souryal, "Stages of Police Corruption", *op. cit.*

contact as a testing ground for his morals and willpower. Another policeman may view such a contact as a break from the ordinary. Still a third policeman may welcome such a contact as a necessary teaching experience. The impact of the policeman's first experience with corruption is hard to determine. It varies as much as individual policemen and the kinds of contact vary. Though a few policemen may be horrified by what they have done, the average policeman will view the experience as harmless, gratifying, and probably attractive. The duration of the experimentation stage may be relatively long or short, but generally speaking, the longer it lasts the more likely it is that the policeman will firmly progress into the accustomation stage.

3. Accustomation Stage

Unless the policeman is too stupid or too unlucky, petty corruption (*i.e.,* free meals, haircuts, clothes, and a steady additional income) will fit fairly well into the lifestyle of the middle-aged policeman. It compensates for the smallness of his pay and thus exalts his economic welfare, as well as that of his wife and children. In time, the policeman becomes happier with himself, physically heavier, his children healthier, and his wife's wardrobe more stylish. The accustomation stage can last as long as the private life of the officer is turning brighter and nobody in the department is caring to raise questions. Two main factors may suddenly disturb the accustomation process: a religious revival in the heart of the officer or his wife, or a well-documented complaint filed against the officer by an unsatisfied customer. In most cases, individual officers at this stage would have developed enough power within the department so as to be able to circumvent the effect of the latter factor.

4. Conceptualization Stage

In this stage the officer realizes and accepts corrupt practices as a way of police life. The more he knows of others' sharing his extraoccupational privileges, the more he rationalizes their occupational legitimacy. The officer at this stage becomes more attuned to incidents of corruption in other departments and occupations and thus appreciates the modesty and harmlessness of his. Common reference is usually made to corrupt politicians and businessmen who indulge in massive, nationwide corruption. In time, the conceptualization stage gradually progresses into a firm belief that limited extraoccupational help for the *poor overburdened* policeman is truly justifiable. Some officers at this stage may even recognize some corrupt practices as a convenient compromise between the police and petty criminals on the grounds of saving court time, jail expenses, and salvaging of the public images of individuals who otherwise would be socially stigmatized as criminals.

5. Improvisation Stage

This stage usually develops among a few older policemen. They are mostly more experienced, more shrewd, and more ambitious than the rest of the force. They operate on the basis of the Arab proverb, "Since you are going to steal anyway, you ought to grab a camel rather than a cat". Experienced officers at this stage tend to practice small group corruption. They apply more or less organized crime methods with the exception of resorting to killing each other. They organize themselves in syndicates and divide labor among themselves equitably. Profits, however, are distributed by rank. Improvised corruption may involve gambling, prostitution, extortion, and drugs. It is performed in well-planned operations rather than sporadic practices. Connections with corrupt politicians and businessmen (and naturally with criminals) are the rule rather than the exception; and police rhetoric, as a cover-up becomes enormous. Tactics of improvised corruption are usually as limitless and shapeless as human intelligence and sin can be.

6. Benediction Stage

This stage involves some rare high-ranking police *godfathers,* who run a network of "auto-corruption", mostly by proxy. Metaphorically speaking, the godfathers have reached Abraham Maslow's state of *self-actualization* in corruption. They feel comfortable only in corrupt departments and implicitly, but vehemently, seek to chastise honest departments. They pity the helplessness of police legal practices and advocate their versions of "Machiavellian policing". They publicly associate with a conservative political machine, a suspicious business cartel, or a reactionary social minority. Benedictors of police corruption are fortunately a very small group entrenched in strategically viable locations. Internally, they control their forces by repressive methods and select their lieutenants from among notoriously corrupt policemen. Promotion to key administrative positions is determined by ability and experience in maintaining such a policy and purging of dissenters. The benedictor policeman usually has no profound interest in law, and certainly not in criminal law. He is far more concerned with building a vile, political and/or economic base. His tenure as a benedictor will be short-lived as he will soon move to other political or business offices.

Needless to say, these stages should, by no means, be viewed as a set of absolute facts. They are postulates collected from observation and experience. Some of them necessarily overlap and others may even be viewed as unnecessary and can be skipped. Furthermore, characteristics of each stage may not necessarily fit all individuals at that stage. While corruption is as individual as finger prints, the postulates only try to provide a chronological classification which may help the effective manager conduct more meaningful research by selecting more representative samples.

EFFECTIVE MANAGEMENT AS SUPPRESSOR OF CORRUPTION

As the writers of the Old Testament observed, "When the righteous are in authority, the people rejoice, but when the wicked beareth rule, the people mourn".[32]   The effective police manager need not worry too much about corruption.   By virtue of running an effective system of management, corruption will have neither reason to exist nor hospitable grounds to survive.   The *godfathers* will eventually wither away through resignation, reformation, or accepting the awesome consequence through the "chopping axe".   Young rookies will have little motivation to get involved in corruption and too much loyalty to sacrifice their careers.   Effective management, in its own rights, contains the antidotes to police corruption.

Effective management constantly aims at increasing the immunity of workers within the organization while simultaneously reducing the external pressures directed at their corruption from without. Through the application of its basic features, such as stimulative leadership, widely-shared decision making, effective communication, decentralization of responsibility, generation of agency loyalty, enhancement of units interdependence, and promotion of workers toward actualization, corruption should subside and may disappear. This should not imply that effective police managers may sit back and ignore the possibility of men *little lower than angels* flirting with a variety of well polished *juicy apples* offered to them.   Effective managers must periodically "take the temperature" of their workers to help prognosticate creeping corruption and provide management with ample warning to act.

The practice of taking the temperature of the department warrants a special note.   Even effective managers running a perfectly "clean" and integrated administration ought to stop at certain intervals and evaluate the performance of their workers.   This would assess agency productivity and spot symptoms of existing or creeping corruption.   Toward this goal, effective management utilizes a set of measuring devices to keep watch on the progression or regression of performance in their agencies.   These devices, often referred to as "intervening variables", include testing the following: [33]

   (a) continuity of work in the absence of a supervisor;

   (b) number and substance of complaints filed against workers;

32. Proverbs 29:2.

33. Rensis Likert, *New Patterns of Management*, (New York: McGraw-Hill), 1961, p. 196.

(c) quality of services performed;

(d) absenteeism;

(e) turnover (the quit-rate among employees);

(f) employee attitudes toward the agency, its policies, and its system of administration;

(g) interpersonal, intragroup, and intergroup feelings;

(h) incidents subject to disciplinary actions;

(i) strikes, slowdowns, and acts of sabotage.

Through the use of carefully designed attitude tests and improved techniques, data and trends on all these variables can be secured for the edification of management. Testing these intervening variables periodically can help predict falling outputs and spot areas where corruption might be developing. Indications of a worker's frustration, alienation, poor workmanship, interpersonal hostilities or insubordination can point to the existence of a corruption trend.

Some of the basic tools by which effective management can prevent, stop, and reduce corruption in police agencies, include:

1 —The Recruitment-Selective Sieve: The most appropriate place to head off corruption in a police organization is at the port of entry in the personnel office. Recruitment for a police service "open to the talents" should look for more than talent. Effective management must keep its concern for attracting persons who have integrity and reliability as well. All of the selection techniques available today must be used, including comprehensive background investigations and reliable tests to determine aptitude and emotional stability. The Task Force Report, in this reference, added that "State Commissions could suggest ways of assessing applicants attitudes in order to keep prejudiced persons *out* of police service and to aid in assigning men to duties for which they are best fitted by temperament and background".[34]

2 —Articulation of Policy: Effective management establishes policies that outline in detail proper and improper police practices. Such policies are stressed in training, reviewed fully with officers at all levels, and publicized in the community at large. Effective management defines the limits of accepting gifts, gratuities and favors by policemen and stresses that prompt action would be taken against persons who participate in violations. Definition must also be made of the common situations in which temptations to engage in dishonest conduct may arise.

34. *Task Force Report*, 1967, p. 217.

As an example of these situations, the Douglas Subcommittee of the U.S. Senate suggested these guidelines for public officials: [35]

(a) No personal profiteering from inside knowledge or position.

(b) No accepting of gift or promise of employment from anyone with whom you conduct the public business.

(c) No divulging confidential information which would give outside parties any monetary advantages.

(d) No undue personal involvement with those with whom you conduct the public business.

Another set of guidelines were presented by Congress in 1958 and labeled "Code of Ethics for Government Service". The government employee should: [36]

(a) Put loyalty to the highest moral principles and to country above loyalty to persons, party, or government departments.

(b) Uphold the Constitution, laws and legal regulations of the United States and of all governments therein and never be a party to their invasion.

(c) Give a full day's labor for a full day's pay; giving to the performance of his duties his earnest effort and best thought.

(d) Seek to find and employ more efficient and economical ways of getting tasks accomplished.

(e) Never discriminate unfairly by the dispensing of special favors or privileges to anyone, whether for remuneration or not; and never accept, for himself or his family, favors or benefits under circumstances which might be construed by reasonable persons as influencing the performance of his governmental duties.

(f) Make no private promises of any kind binding upon the duties of office, since a government employee has no private work which can be binding on public policy.

(g) Engage in no business with the government, either directly or indirectly, which is inconsistent with the conscientious performance of his governmental duties.

(h) Never use any information coming to him confidentially in the performance of governmental duties as a means for making private profit.

35. U.S. Senate, Committee on Labor and Public Welfare, Ethical Standards in Government (Committee print, 82nd Congress, 1st Session), 1951.

36. House Concurrent Resolution 175, 85th Congress, 2nd Session, 1958.

Also see Executive Order 10939 by President Kennedy, "To Provide a Guide on Ethical Standards to Government Officials", *Federal Register*, (May 5, 1961).

(i) Expose corruption whenever discovered.

(j) Uphold these principles, ever conscious that public office is a public trust.

The Task Force Report cited the rules and regulations developed by the Oakland Police Department as a model for other departments. Samples of these rules are: [37]

Section 310.70. Members and employees shall not under any circumstances solicit any gift, gratuity, loan, or fee where there is any direct or indirect connection between the solicitation and their departmental membership and employment.

Section 310.71. Members and employees shall not accept either directly or indirectly any gift, gratuity, loan, fee, or any other thing of value arising from or offered because of police employment and any activity connected with said employment.

Section 310.80. Members and employees shall not solicit or accept free admission or passes to theatres and other places of amusement for themselves or others except in the line of duty.

3   —Political Accountability: The police manager should be responsible to only one executive and not to minor city officials. The relationship between the police manager and the political chief executive must be clear and open. The areas and extent of political intervention into the affairs of the department must be defined and limited to the constitutional overseeing power. Other political officials may bring their suggestions to the police manager through the political chief executive. Meddling in the department's internal affairs by these officials is prohibited. Political pressures must be discontinued and legitimate requests may be processed in accordance with administrative laws and procedures. The role of the chief as a mature and conscientious executive, however, should ordinarily allow a close working relationship with the political authority.

4   —Internal Investigation Units: Effective management is by no means *naive* management. While it advocates unity, rationality and reason, it, on the other hand, does not operate in a *laissez-faire* fashion. Punishment, as a last resort, is an inherent element of effective management and must be viewed as necessary especially with the *birds which can sing*

37. *Task Force Report*, 1967, p. 213.

but would not.[38] Internal investigation units play a dual role: general intelligence and investigation of misconduct. In their role pertaining to intelligence collection, these units may not only gather data on police behavior and assess the police image among the public, but they also give attention to the study of causes and manifestations of misconduct and suggest to the police manager appropriate ways to prevent corruption. In their roles as investigative bodies, these units must fairly but firmly look into specific complaints by the citizenry, by suspects, and by *all* those who come across the police subsystem. The purpose of investigation must be to dig up legitimate evidence, question the suspected policeman, build a meritorious case and present it to the leadership in charge of the department to make a decision whether to prosecute the officer, take disciplinary action against him, or deal with it as the policy dictates.

5 —Training: Effective management emphasizes the in-service training of officers regarding the importance of ethics in law enforcement. Modern techniques include stress training sessions and role playing seminars. They educate the officers as to the types of action to be taken under strenuous conditions including, for instance, how an officer should proceed when he witnesses or learns of dishonest acts on the part of another officer or is physically or verbally abused by a suspect in a back alley situation. Such training sessions must accurately simulate real street situations and be opened for discussion by observing officers who would learn the meahanics of behavioral interaction.

6 —Guarding the Public Purse: Handling of public funds has long been a source of great temptation. An old saying rightfully stated that "an unattended purse teaches saints to steal". Regardless of how honest and trustworthy public officials or policemen are, the public purse has to be constantly guarded and expenditures accounted for under effective management; therefore, an advanced system of fiscal audit must exist. Whether the budget used is itemized, performance computed, or incorporated in a Planning and Programming System, it must constantly be under the scrutiny of a qualified controller who works in association with a network of city, state, and auditors of affiliated programs. Expenditures must be authorized by the department's chief executive and

---

38. A famous saying by Frederick W. Taylor with regard to able-bodied workers who would ostensibly refuse to abide with management policies. The full text by Taylor reads "scientific management has no use for a bird that can sing but won't sing".

spent for the designated purposes for which allotments are appropriated. Delegation of this authority must be kept within an adequate span and an effective system of accountability devised. A word of warning, however, is necessary. In effective management, too close a system of "insulating supervision" may boomerang. Keeping a needlessly strict watch over the shoulders of deputies would destroy their self-confidence, degrade their morale and frustrate their attempts to professionalize. In this reference, J. D. Williams remarked that "a hapless agency may be a good deal more helpless than a corrupt one".[39]

7 —External Checks: While effective management must be viewed as a self-sufficient system of administration, management "snobbishness" must not result. Moreover, however effective the police manager may be, he ought to recognize the need for, and appreciate, outside forces which represent additional checks on corruption. Whether these forces stem from the Police and Fire Board, City Council, Congressional investigating committee, the district attorney or county court, police managers must cooperate with these forces and assist in their investigation. Only when such forces exert illigitimate influence, when their proceedings disturb the normal operation of the department, or when their intervention impairs the morale of the organization, may the police manager defend his agency and solicit protection by the higher authority. In cases of this nature, an effective manager may be able to win and maintain the integrity of his department or he may lose and redeem the morale of his workers by rendering his resignation.

In conclusion, effective police managers, in their attempts to suppress corruption, would seem well advised not to rely exclusively upon a "Thou shall not" approach. Leadership, the power of example, building within the staff a dedication to the public interest, and advancing education in behavioral sciences, all represent vital defenses against profiteering at the public interest.

39. J. D. Williams, *op. cit.*, p. 299.

CHAPTER FOURTEEN

INCREASING PRODUCTIVITY THROUGH ORGANIZATIONAL DEVELOPMENT

Overview

The purpose of management is to attain progress. Effective management accomplishes progress through *improvement* where and when it is needed. What improvement is, however, is neither universal nor easy to identify. It varies from one administrator to another: one police manager, for instance, may emphasize improving police-community relations while another emphasizes apprehension and conviction rates. Improvement also varies by subject of interest, as in the case of the police chief who champions the cause of salary improvement for himself and his men but shuns the collateral need for improving his department's performance. Moreover, improvement may also vary from time to another. For instance, with the escalation in civil unrest and student riots in the late 60's, improvement in police performance was primarily geared toward riot control measures, equipments, and training. In the 70's, the picture has changed and improvement is now seen in terms of suppression of terrorist activities, taking of hostages, and other extortionist schemes.

In effective management, *improvement is predominantly seen in terms of increasing productivity.* Like improvement, productivity can be also confusing for it can mean different things in different situations. However, phrases like "doing the right thing the right way"; "working smarter, not harder"; "getting more bang from the buck"; and other similar terms can describe roughly how productivity is generally viewed.

Students of Public Administration use productivity to mean more specific concepts. To some it is efficiency, to others effectiveness and to still another group it is a combination of both. The concept of productivity also raises several questions as to its frame of reference, whether it relates to improvement of individuals, of units, of systems or to an amalgamation of these. Similar questions are also raised regarding the implementation of productivity and the nature of productivity programs. Some of the common definitions of productivity may, therefore, be useful to cite.

Productivity Defined

Productivity means the return received for a given unit of input. To improve productivity means to get a greater return for a given investment.—National Commission of Productivity [1]

Any activity that uses resources of one kind to produce a result of another kind can be said to be productive.—George H. Kuper [2]

Productivity is concerned with quality as well as quantity.—John A. Grimes [3]

Productivity=Acceptable Product/Man-Hour. If productivity increases, then: *either* the amount of product increases *or* the number of men decreases *or* the number of hours decreases *or* combinations of changes in the three variables will balance things out.—Harold W. Adams [4]

Accepting these definitions at their face value, they all basically refer to productivity as a combination of efficiency and effectiveness. Productivity, however, has a deeper meaning than a simple combination of these two components. To reiterate what was previously said in Chapter Six about efficiency and effectiveness, the former is an economic question, *a cost-benefit equation*, which seeks the achievement of goals at minimum cost (money, time, effort, etc.). The latter refers to the full achievement of goals by all means, *regardless of cost*. Productivity, nevertheless, is concerned, *above and beyond* efficiency and effectiveness, with other questions: a) the amount of resources available, b) the method of utilization of these resources, c) the quality of the service produced and its responsiveness to consumers' needs, and d) the type of organization used and its impact on the producers themselves in terms of gratification and job satisfaction.

For instance, while the bureaucratic-militaristic model of policing still applied by most police departments today is often cited as an example of both efficiency and effectiveness, it obviously does not rank high on the scale of productivity. Most of the time it resulted in a dissatisfied public and a frustrated group of policemen, regardless of whether crime rates increased or decreased. A well-managed productivity program would attempt to *modify its model of organization* so as to satisfy the needs and expectations of the public, to keep the policemen motivated and to reduce the rate of crime, all through the "economical" utilization of available resources. *The new dimension*

1. Harry W. More, Jr., *Effective Police Administration*, (San Jose, California: Justice Systems Development, Inc.), 1975, p. 401.

2. George H. Kuper, in *Reading on Productivity in Policing*, (Washington, D.C., Police Foundation), 1975, p. 2.

3. John A. Grimes, in *Reading on Productivity in Policing, Ibid.*, p. 47.

4. Harold W. Adams, "Solutions as Problems: The Case of Productivity", *Public Productivity Review*, Vol. 1, No. 1, September, 1975.

of maintaining the satisfaction of the producers and the consumers is crucial.

Most administrators tend to believe that productivity can go up or down like a barometer as an automatic response to change in management leadership. While this may seem true at first glance or for a short time (until the initial reaction to management change wears out), long-range productivity follows indeed the pattern of organizational development and the new state of mind of workers which the new management can introduce. A more functional definition of productivity, therefore, must take the factor of organizational development in consideration. A tri-dimensional definition of productivity may then be stated as "the attainment of prescribed goals at the highest quality and the lowest cost possible through the modification of the organization and its mentality in a manner conducive to the satisfaction of both producers and consumers within the constraints of available resources."

NATURE OF PRODUCTIVITY

Although it may sound more idealistic in the administration of public agencies, increasing productivity is the challenge and measure of effective management. Achieving it, at least in comparative terms, it must be stressed, is a long-term, tedious, and complex task. Traditional administrators are by definition not concerned with, and perhaps not aware of, the advantages of productivity improvement. Managers, who for all practical purposes must be aware of the advantages, sometimes get frustrated and give up. Only effective managers can marshall the commitment, capability, know-how, and courage necessary to embark on productivity improvement programs. If they don't, however, nobody else will do it for them and the administration of the agency will continue to function at the organizational level.

The National Commission on Productivity in its 1973 Report on *Opportunities for Improving Productivity in Police Services* emphasized four qualities which police managers must have to improve productivity: [5]

(1) *Commitment:* Elected and appointed managers must be ready and willing to work for productivity. Productivity improvement will not get far, the report indicated, "without real and visible political and organizational support from the top administrators".[6] Productivity improvement may require expenditure of dollars, time, energy, and a certain amount of risk-taking. These four commit-

---

5. These four characteristics were gleaned from a discussion by George H. Kuper, in *Reading on Productivity in Policing, op. cit.,* p. 8.

6. *Ibid.*

ments are not easy to make, especially since the payoffs from productivity improvements usually appear in the long term. However, the return on this kind of investment can be in the form of noticeable savings, improved service delivery, markedly enhanced relations with the public, and inflated department morale coupled with a genuine eagerness to serve.

(2) *Analytical capability:* Not all productivity opportunities are visible to the manager. It is necessary, therefore, to have an effective manager who can ask the right questions, enjoy controversy, stir up debate, determine whether an opportunity for productivity exists, and decide what is to be done next.

"Good" analysis can not be a "hit or miss shot". It must follow recognized systematic procedures and research that takes into consideration all relevant factors. It defines objectives, carefully reviews costs and outputs, weighs alternatives, establishes criteria, etc. Sometimes "good" analysis will require the technical expertise of a statistician or industrial engineer. It must always, however, entail the systematic application of common sense and logic.

(3) *Know-how:* Compared with commitment and analytical capability, this may be the easiest requirement to fulfill. It basically relates to the understanding of police functions, roles and procedures which in turn are the product of adequate education and training. In terms of necessary information, the effective manager can use the host of data collected by his research division. Such data can be derived from federal, state and local statutes, publications of national associations and other government agencies, and information continually collected on *best practices* adopted nationwide. The effective police manager would naturally modify the data in order to successfully apply it to his particular organization.

(4) *Development of new ideas:* Hundreds of minor adjustments in police operations can lead to small productivity gains. For instance reducing the area of painted markings on squad cars by several inches each, or using a more durable engine oil, could account for modest gains. But the major breakthroughs in productivity come from new ideas, different—*often radically different*—ways of thinking about old problems.

The development of new ideas is the crux of productivity since ordinarily there is no kind of education or training which can teach the manager and his staff how to think of "something" they never experienced before. Some of the excellent ideas lately experimented with were mentioned in Chapter Seven and included team policing, consolidation of communication services, PPBS, the fourth watch, and others.

THE PRODUCTIVE MENTALITY

If productivity improvement is to be more than a matter of reorganizational facade, a leadership maneuver, or a response to a crisis situation, managers must seriously organize their efforts and develop new *meaningful* programs. Effective managers, planners, researchers, and middle managers must be the pioneers of these programs and pool their analytical talents and idea-generating faculties into a "productive mentality." A productive mentality in this reference may be defined *as a state of mind in which decisions are made in accordance with the rules of science, methodology, economics and logic, hampered by a minimum of uncontrolled personal or group bias.* Contrary to popular thought, indoctrination, or rigid mental conditioning is counterproductive to the development of a productive mentality. This type of methodical mentality requires the greatest amount of free and imaginative thinking and the least amount of dogmatic constraints. Unscrupulous thinking nurtured under traditional training is highly repressive as well as contagious. It hampers the scope of intellectual vision, reduces the conception of reality and limits the free relay of feedback information. The appropriate application of the productive mentality presupposes the neutralization of all such constraints; otherwise a productivity improvement program would revert to another public relations project replete with *briefcase-toting, double-talking,* and *paper pushing.*

The development of a productive mentality can naturally be enhanced through the processes of education and training. Mastery of the areas of constitutional law, due process, civil rights and civil liberties, as well as the areas of behavioral research, methodology, social sciences, accounting and economics, can be of particular help in the development of a productive mentality. Such education, constantly emphasized by effective management, contributes to the open-mindedness of staff members and to their ability to suppress the effects of traditional attitudes and personal bias. By the same token, such education can also help staff members resist the accretion of new prejudicial attitudes in their productive minds.

Education, however, is only a beginning in the development of a productive mentality. The growth and maturity of such mentality ultimately rests with the department's orientation and leadership. Effective police managers are the only group of police leaders capable of liberating the organization and creating a climate of openness, scholarship, and professionalism. Only these managers can stimulate free communication within the organization, easy exchange of views, and a jovial and optimistic atmosphere conducive of productivity. Only these managers can create an organizational environment pregnant with opportunities for intellectual discussions, relaxed debates and constructive disagreements.[7]

Three basic concepts constitute the productive mentality which effective management must help install in its members:

(a) *A critical mind:* It is the best protection against misconception of facts. It provides the manager and his staff with a screening ability capable of scrupulously avoiding wild generalities. In this respect, the common organizational myths of strict supervision, unity of command, and obedience cannot be passed over lightly into a productivity improvement program. Another significant characteristic of the critical mind is that it scans a wide range of interests and experience. This breadth of view helps the management staff to spot incongruities in the general picture of the program rather than being bogged down in minute, insignificant details. Three more requisites may also be cited for the development of the critical mind: 1) avoidance of dogmatism, 2) appreciation of management tools and skills, and 3) experience in the police field.

(b) *Suppression of bias:* Bias may be defined as the genetic fallacy that a proposition is accepted or rejected, not on the basis of its value, but on the basis of its outcome. What constitutes bias is the will to believe a proposition is motivated by interests external to the context of the inquiry itself. A hypothesis is, therefore, accepted or questioned according to whether one's values would be better served if it were true than if it were false. Although bias may be conscious or unconscious, yielding to bias is characteristically *unconscious*.[8] At the head of every bias is a prejudgment—*a conclusion arrived at prior to the evidence and maintained independent of the evidence.* A productivity staff must be committed to resisting bias. By effective training, communication, leadership, and a healthy organizational environment, staff members can offset the impact of bias. Fortunately, productivity improvement programs do not require that bias be eliminated since it is virtually impossible. What is necessary is to be aware of it and suppress it when decisions are made.

(c) *The "why not attitude":* In concluding the eulogy of his brother Robert, Senator Edward Kennedy called the public's attention to still another quality of the late senator by saying: "Some men see things as they are and say 'why', others dream of things that never were and say 'why not'."[9] Effective managers and their staff cannot fail to realize the meanings inbedded in the senator's speech: (1) imagination may be customary, but *bold* imagination may be neces-

7. Sam S. Souryal, "The SCART of Criminal Investigation", *Journal of Police Science and Administration*, Vol. 2, No. 4, December, 1974, p. 456.

8. *Ibid.*

9. *Ibid.*

sary; (2) seeing may be adequate, but "seeing through" is productive; (3) man's powers are sufficient, but man's potentials are limitless.[10]

THE PROBLEM OF POLICE PRODUCTIVITY

In the past, police administrators were held primarily responsible for the occurrence of crime and violence; productivity was not an issue. Patrick V. Murphy notes that for long police departments were content to operate on the basis of history and tradition.[11] It consequently appears that this lack of uniformly acceptable standards and a clear understanding of the nature of police work have hampered the public, and often the police themselves, from developing a clear perception of the parameters of a professional policeman's job.

Productivity today is a major issue in local government and consequently poses serious questions to the police chiefs. The public, the politicians, as well as policemen themselves, expect "better" police services in more diversified areas with minimum duplication and waste, especially under the current conditions of spiraling inflation, recession, high rate of unemployment, and cutbacks in federal grants and aids to state and local forces. Questions of police productivity have become more and more persistent, and methodical solutions have to be seriously devised by police managers. The outputs, however, which can most clearly reflect police productivity, both in reality and in the public eye, defy quantitative expression and measurement. The problem is compounded by the fact that the value at stake is *public safety*. Moreover, even if it were possible to assess the police officer's productivity in the performance of his assigned duties, the relation of that performance (arrest, patrol, surveillance, etc.) to the final outputs associated with policing (e.g. reduction in crime rate and violence) is highly obscure. It remains, therefore, largely hypothetical to establish a reliable link between what might be termed "real productivity" (optimal deployment of resources with respect to a stated list of police activities) and the productivity which President Nixon apparently had in mind when he issued his inane—and potentially dangerous—summonses of the chief of the Washington police to engage in Oval office reviews of the previous month crime reports as an index of police performance.[12] Finally, policing is still so integral to the political and emotional climate of a city that it is often subjected to large and sudden changes in the priorities which condition judgments of productivity. Sensible assessment of police productivity, therefore, requires highly sensitive attention to a volatile array of purposes and values being served.[13]

10. *Ibid.*

11. Martin Singer, *Public Productivity Review*, Vol. 1, No. 2, December, 1975.

12. Edward K. Hamilton, *Readings on Productivity in Policing, op. cit.*, p. 11.

13. *Ibid.*, p. 13.

AREAS OF POLICE PRODUCTIVITY

Productivity improvement in industry is quite well understood. Its application to municipal services, and in particular to policing, is just beginning to be explored. The present dialogue and debate over police productivity are still concerned with how to identify police productivity in a meaningful formula, let alone the more difficult task of measuring it. Several areas, however, where productivity identification seems feasible will be discussed below: [14]

a —*Operations that involve large numbers of employees who perform routine and repetitive tasks.* These include such operations as parking regulation enforcement, traffic direction at school crossings, house checks, and report typing. For operations like these, James Morgan, former safety director of St. Petersburg, Florida, suggests that consideration should be given to hiring civilians to take the place of uniformed personnel. The chief factors are net cost and efficiency. If a $6,000-a-year-civilian replaces a uniformed desk officer who earns $12,000 a year, there would be no savings if the substitution is not really one for one; that is, if it actually takes two civilians earning a combined $12,000 a year to replace the one uniformed officer. If, however, these two civilians can increase output by more than 25 percent over that of the officer, there is an overall net increase in productivity, assuming the quality of work is the same. By the same token, if the police manager would hire a civilian programmer, planner, or analyst who is well qualified and capable for $18,000 a year to replace two sergeants in charge of development and research at the salary of $14,000 each, productivity would increase by about 36 percent. In addition, a well selected programmer, planner, or analyst might be able, through his advanced education and specialization, to increase the quality of the office output considerably.

b —*Functions that consume large numbers of manhours.* The most obvious of these, of course, is patrol. But patrol, in all probability, will not be scrutinized to see if the number of manhours devoted to it can be reduced since the visibility of the patrol force often draws more public attention than the quality of its performance. When, for instance, it was reported that only 1,000 of New York City's 31,000 police officers were on street patrol at any one time, the fact was widely criticized; the quality of the patrol function in NYPD, on the other hand, was not seriously examined and attempts to improve the situation were not consequently made.

---

14. This discussion was adapted from an article by James P. Morgan, former public safety director of St. Petersburg, Florida, *Ibid.*, pp. 129–149.

But the effective manager may first have to determine what proportion of his sworn officers are assigned to street patrol and how much of their street time is actually spent on the street. Morgan asserts that an abnormally high percentage of patrol time is spent in disorganized court sessions, traditional roll-call requirements, and other routine functions not associated with actually "traversing the beat" on the outlook for law breakers. Another major question to be solved by the effective manager streamlining the patrol function in most cities today is the one-man vs. two-man patrol controversy. The first practice, if seen by itself, naturally emphasizes efficiency in terms of patrolling the streets at a lower cost. The second emphasizes effectiveness in terms of what the patrol can effectively accomplish. If this controversy is examined in terms of productivity, questions of available manpower resources, classification of high-crime districts vs. low-crime areas, night shifts vs. day shifts, sentiments of officers assigned to the patrol division, and the effects of change on the general morale of the department must be taken into consideration. A productive solution may be the development of a two-man system in particular areas or at particular times. While such a combination may not uplift or lower morale, reforms in this direction would necessarily lead to substantial productivity savings.

c   —*Functions that normally result in backlogs of work.* A typical case here is the filling out of reports. By investigating the purpose of each type of traditionally required report, an effective police manager may find, for example, that:

1   —Some reports are not necessary and can be discontinued.

2   —Several reports serve the same purpose and therefore could be consolidated into one.

3   —Some reports are unnecessarily lengthy and can be shortened to save money, time, and effort.

4   —Some reports are filled out to serve non-police purposes, e. g. insurance companies or social welfare agencies. Such companies and agencies may have to be required to hire their own clerks to take care of these reports.

Many reports, states Morgan, may pile up needlessly because no one ever made a decision to discontinue them.

The procedure by which officers may fill out the necessary reports may also be altered to increase police productivity. Some ideas emerging in police departments today include:

1   —Patrolmen and detectives are issued typewriters to speed up the process once they return to their stations after patrol duty.

2   —Specialized stenographers are assigned to meet returning patrolmen and take their reports in shorthand dictation.

3   —Regular stenographers are assigned to take the officers' reports while on patrol through the medium of the two-way radio. Such reports are then prepared for the officers to review and sign upon arriving at the stationhouse after the patrol duty.

4   —Some departments issue pocket tape recorders for officers to tape their reports while on duty. Tapes are later transcribed, reviewed and signed.

d   —*Areas where unit costs are high.* Sometimes such costs can be justified in productivity terms. But if they cannot be justified, consideration should obviously be given to their reduction or elimination. There is little productivity logic, for instance, in providing every officer with a fully equipped pursuit vehicle, regardless of his assignment. A fully staffed and equipped photography lab may be a prestige item to a police department regardless of whether it is used to full capacity. Naturally it would be more in line with productivity, if such a lab is shared on a regional basis or authorized to serve other departments on a contractual basis.[15] Training is another area which involves relatively high cost. Spending $2,000 to send an officer to a training program offered by a prestigious institution when approximately the same program is offered locally for $200 is certainly a high price to pay for a fancy lapel pin. What is even worse is that the $2,000-officer often becomes the sole custodian of the knowledge offered at the training program. A formal system for diffusing the knowledge acquired at the training program, argues Morgan, "can greatly increase the output produced from the time and money invested."[16] If, however, the availability or quality of training offered at the local level would deprive officers from acquiring adequate and necessary training, sending officers to central or specialized training programs would not only be justified but recommended.

---

15. The author taught a class of policemen in a middle-sized city in Texas and noticed that all squad cars were equipped with digicomb systems operated by little computers in addition to regular two-way radios functioning in perfect conditions. Most officers however, were using the two-way radio system, and digicombs, which reportedly cost over half a million dollars, were left idle. Upon inquiring, the common answer indicated that while digicombs added to the prestige of the department, they were indeed unnecessary, and police operations were well served by the radio system. Further inquiry showed that the digicombs were installed primarily because of the availability of a federal grant which "had" to be used or otherwise returned to its original source.

16. See James P. Morgan, *Readings on Productivity in Policing, op. cit.,* p. 137.

OBJECTIVES OF POLICE PRODUCTIVITY

As mentioned earlier, the purpose of productivity is to enhance efficiency and effectiveness in such a manner that also "satisfies" both the producers and the consumers. In general, higher police productivity means keeping the police department's budget constant and improving performance, or keeping performance constant and reducing the size of the budget. But since budgets, in the practical reality of government bureaucracy, tend to continually increase annually, the objective of productivity must be seen in terms of improving performance at a higher rate than that of the budget. But since the concept of productivity cannot simply be transferred from the statistical field of economics to the field of social control and social services, increasing police productivity might be considered as basically seeking these objectives: [17]

(a) Upgrading current police practices to the highest level of performance.

(b) Allocating resources to activities which give the highest return for each additional dollar.

(c) Increasing the probability that a given result will be achieved.

(d) Making the most of the talents of police personnel.

Ideally each police department establishes its order of programs in concert with its political environment, public expectations, and, of course, its own management sophistication. Departments then proceed to identify intermediate objectives, the achievement of which will result in the attainment of the total program.

In practice, however, the process of setting objectives is often reversed. Instead of determining the mission (a set of programs) of the department, and then organizing to accomplish them, more often the apparent aims of ongoing activities are described and then built into departmental objectives. What is important, however, is that the different levels of objectives be clearly related and understood and that rank-and-file personnel meaningfully contribute to upgrading their departmental output.[18]

MEASUREMENT OF POLICE PRODUCTIVITY

A former Secretary of Commerce, Peter G. Peterson, said in 1972 that "productivity improvement without productivity measure-

17. See Harry W. More, Jr., *Effective Police Administration*, (San Jose, California: Justice Systems Development, Inc.), 1975, pp. 402–403.

18. *Ibid.*, p. 405.

ment is not possible".[19] Measurement is essential to indicate whether any improvement has indeed been achieved. Without productivity measurement, the manager would remain "in the dark" and unable to direct his organization, and the whole question of productivity would revert to a number of sporadic changes which in the final analysis might be more harmful than beneficial.

Major uses of productivity measurement include: [20]

1 —By identifying current levels of productivity, measurement can indicate the existence of particular problems.

2 —When productivity is measured over time, measurement can indicate the progress or lack of progress in improving productivity.

3 —When collected by geographical areas within a jurisdiction, productivity data can help identify areas in particular need of attention.

4 —Measurement can serve as a basis for evaluating specific activities. Measurement may indicate activities that need to be modified, organizational structures that need to be straightened out, or personnel who need to be reassigned.

5 —Measurement of existing productivity can provide police agencies with the information necessary to set productivity targets. Actual performance can subsequently be compared to the targets to indicate the degree of accomplishment.

6 —Productivity measurement information can be a major way of accounting for police operations to the public.

7 —Productivity measurements suggest performance incentives for both managerial and non-managerial police personnel.

8 —Measurement of data can be used for in-depth productivity studies of ways to improve other aspects of productivity.

Every productivity improvement program, therefore, will need a productivity measurement component both to help guide where productivity improvement is needed and to evaluate how successful the improvements have been.

While productivity measurement is evidently crucial to program evaluation, it must be recognized that it is not an end in itself. Measurement, by itself, will not tell a police agency what is wrong or what should be done to improve the situation. It is only an indicator to guide the agency in its productivity efforts.[21]

19. Harry P. Hatry, "Wrestling with Police Crime Control Productivity Measurement", *Readings on Productivity in Policing, op. cit.*, p. 86.

20. *Ibid.*

21. *Ibid.*, p. 88.

In all police productivity programs, nevertheless, measurement guidelines have to be developed to determine efficiency, effectiveness, and the amount of satisfaction of consumers and producers. These guidelines are usually developed in three basic steps.[22]

The first step is to develop a *structural-functional scheme* for classifying output. In the general area of policing, one would presumably categorize the number of sworn officers on the force, the amount of the budget, the territory of coverage, and the facilities. Manpower would further include, for instance, the number of patrolmen, detectives, staff personnel, etc. The budget would include amounts appropriated to specific activities like community-development, information, and training, while facilities would include substations, crime labs, vehicles, equipments, etc.

The second step relates to *operational outputs* which would need to be defined in terms representative of the various functions the police performs. Thus, measurements would relate to the operations of patrol, detection, community counselling, training, etc.

The third step is to determine quantitatively how much output each unit of structure produces, mainly in terms of percentages, ratios, scales, and mathematical relations. Such figures, for instance, indicate rates of apprehension, clearance, conviction, performance, responsiveness and complaints. Output measurements of this nature can be compiled and expressed in terms of the effectiveness of the output (e.g. clearance rate), or in terms of the speed of the output production (e.g. patrol response time or frequency of repair and maintenance), or the satisfaction of the service user and producer with the output (e.g. responsiveness rate, complaint rates, or turnover rate, disciplinary action rate).

LEVELS OF PRODUCTIVITY TO BE MEASURED

The picture of police productivity cannot be fully discerned by measuring the three beforementioned steps: structural, operational, and statistical. Measuring these steps must be further applied to the different levels of the policing capability. The following levels can be distinguished: [23]

1 —The individual officer level (sworn, civilian, auxiliary, etc.)

2 —The particular subgroup within the unit, such as foot patrol, motorized patrol, tactical force, canine corps, etc.

3 —The police unit, such as team, shift, precinct, district, or neighborhood

22. Charles R. Wise, "Government Productivity and Program Evaluation Issues", *Public Productivity Review*, Vol. 1, No. 3, March, 1976, p. 8.

23. Adopted from Harry P. Hatry, *op. cit.*, p. 90.

4 —The department as a whole

5 —The local criminal justice system including the police, prosecution, courts, corrections, and social services

The following diagram explains the interaction of measurement steps and levels within a police productivity program.

Measurement Steps	Police Officer	Police Subgroup	Police Unit	Police Department	C.J. System
Structural-Functional		X	X	X	X
Operational	X	X	X	X	X
Statistical					
Magnitude	X	X	X	X	X
Duration	X	X	X	X	X
Satisfaction	X	X	X	X	X

Suggested Levels for Police Productivity Measurement

[B4341]

Figure 26

MISCONCEPTIONS ABOUT POLICE PRODUCTIVITY PROGRAMS

The first misconception is that police departments do not need productivity improvement programs because improvements will occur automatically through the existing management process. This is not the case except with the very few effective managers who would be constantly concerned about productivity and would be continually building productivity programs. The rest have *to do something about it, initiate it, follow it up, and see it through.* For example, for many years police administrators and officers complained about the amount of time wasted by policemen waiting in courtrooms for their cases to be called. Most police administrators kept "griping" but did nothing to alleviate the productivity problem at hand. New York City Police Department, however, decided to do something about it. Studies were made of the situation which revealed that approximately 45 percent of the officers scheduled to appear in court were not actually needed. The department then worked out a plan with the district attorneys and court officials which eliminated some 28,000 police appearances in one year. The productivity improvement plan saved the department close to $4 million in one year. This change, which *did not just happen,* was initiated by some police managers who effectively applied the purposes and methods of productivity improvement programs.[24] Along the same lines, the police in Nashville devised a Police-Court Cooperation program to solve the problem many prosecutors have in obtaining a complete case report from arresting officers. A police liaison officer was assigned to the county district attorney general's office to insure that a completed copy of every arrest report was received by the prosecutor for case preparation. Previously, the district attorney's office often had to call in the arresting officers to review the facts of the arrest in detail. Because of this productivity improvement program, almost "50 percent of the cases are completed for grand jury presentation, while the remaining cases are either completed on the day set aside for grand jury handling or assigned a fixed future date".[25]

Another misconception is that productivity improvement and measurement are limited to industries which manufacture a product where output is easily measured. While it is naturally easier to measure output of cars and refrigerators than of intangible services, government agencies have started to apply effective measures to gauge productivity improvement in non-industrial areas. The National Commission on Productivity reports for example that the Detroit Police Department now uses a closed-circuit television system monitored by police trainees for stationhouse security. It cost $1.1 million to install and staff the system. Prior to that, Detroit was using 130 officers to protect stationhouses at a cost of $2.6 million. The new system has not only saved $1.5 million but also has meant better surveillance. Television cameras, the National Commission of Productivity stated "don't feel the cold the way human beings do".[26]

A third misconception is the belief that smaller police agencies do not lend themselves to productivity improvements. While it is true that smaller departments may not be able to achieve the substantial savings cited in the New York example, the value of productivity programs must be seen in relative terms. Morgan cites the example of the St. Petersburg, Florida, Police Department which put approximately five percent more sworn officers on the street in 1972 after establishing programs that eliminated one-third of all paperwork and allowed officers to dictate the rest over the phone into special equipment. Morgan also cited another small department with less than 50 officers which reduced sick leave resulting from traffic accidents by 15 percent in one year. The department did this by in-

24. James P. Morgan, *op. cit.,* p. 130.   26. James P. Morgan, *op. cit.,* p. 131.

25. *Target,* a newsletter published by International City Management Association, Vol. 5, Issue 5, July 1976.

troducing a defensive driving course for its officers; that made more workdays available, reduced injuries, and gave the community an example to follow.[27]

THE ROLE OF ORGANIZATIONAL DEVELOPMENT IN POLICE PRODUCTIVITY PROGRAMS

Decisions involving the resources, structure, methods, and contents of a productivity improvement program are made by the police manager and his staff. The latter, especially in metropolitan areas, usually consists of a small army of personnel occupying what is known as the Administration Division. The division in turn incorporates such bureaus as Research and Planning, Personnel and Budget, Program Evaluation, Statistical Analysis, Training, Inspection, Internal Affairs, Legal Advisor and probably several others. In middle-size departments, these bureaus may be represented by a much smaller staff, and in small departments it is fair to expect these functions to be scrambled in the chief's office one way or another. While these bureaus may appear in police departments under different titles or combinations of titles, the *people* in these bureaus are the raw material basic for any productivity program. Through these people and their harmonious relations all such programs are researched, planned, monitored, reviewed, and their productivity is measured and evaluated.

Productivity improvement programs, in an operational sense, are basically problem-solving processes. They deal with economic, environmental, and administrative problems as they appear in the organizational reality of the agency. To reach realistic solutions, therefore, *agency divisions and units must work closely and synchronize their capabilities so as to be able to communicate effectively and coordinate their efforts. This synchronization process is mainly what organizational development is about.* It is the function of the "brainy, low keyed, and imaginative" staff members to plan and devise an integrated structure before each productivity program is launched. It is hard, in fact, if at all possible, to envision a program which does not require some sort of organizational development through an act of creation, consolidation, or separation. Toward the implementation of any productivity program, effective management must do some readjustment of the existing organization.

The concept of organizational development is by no means new. It dates back to the development of administration itself. Through its continual occurrence, organization grew from primitive "make shift" arrangements of crude men and methods to the most specialized models of systems today. Furthermore, the process of organiza-

27. *Ibid.*

tional development will have to continue as long as present systems are unable to solve all man's problems in an "acceptable" manner. It will continue, in other words, as long as man and his need for improvement continue.

A forerunner of the organizational development concept was introduced by Gordon Lippitt, who used the term *organizational renewal* without directly linking it to productivity improvement. According to Lippitt, organizational renewal is:

> the process of initiating, creating and confronting needed changes so as to make it possible for organizations to become or remain viable, to adapt to new conditions, to solve problems, to learn from experiences.[28]

Chris Argyris later stressed *organizational revitalization* in his discussion of organizational development:

> At the heart of organizational development is the concern for the vitalizing, energizing, actualizing, activating and renewing of organizations through technical and human resources.[29]

In the same manner, John Gardner used the term *self-renewal* to refer to the avoidance of "organizational decay and senility". The purpose of self-renewal, he stated, is to regain vitality, and to enhance creativity and innovation. Furthermore, self-renewal would promote flexibility and adaptability through the establishment of conditions that encourage individual motivation, development and fulfillment.[30] Thus, along with the ideas of improved problem-solving and adaptability with change, the important notions of purpose and direction are central to organizational development activities.[31] Without them, organizational development would become a management liability, a waste in time, effort, and money.

Organizational Development Defined

Organizational development:

> is a long-range effort to improve an organization's problem-solving and renewal processes, particularly through a more effective and collaborative management . . . with the assistance of a change agent or catalyst and the use of the

28. Gordon L. Lippitt, *Organization Renewal*, New York: Appleton Century-Crofts), 1969, p. 1.

29. Chris Argyris, *Management and Organizational Development: the Path from XA to YB*, (New York: McGraw-Hill Book Company), 1971, p. ix.

30. John W. Gardner, *Self-Renewal: The Individual and the Innovative Society*, (New York: Harper & Row, Publishers), 1965, pp. 1–7.

31. Harry W. More, Jr., *Effective Police Administration, op. cit.*, p. 226.

theory and technology of applied behavioral science.—Harry W. More, Jr.[32]

is a planned organization-wide managed process to improve organization effectively by either coping with or controlling change with behavioral science knowledge.—Whisenand and Ferguson [33]

[is] an effort to manage all of the company's resources including its management style and behavior in relationship to each other.—Marvin R. Weisbord [34]

Organizational development, in light of its relation to productivity improvement, may be defined as the *readjustment in organizational structure, policies, and relationships as well as in attitudes, beliefs, and views of workers in charge, so as to adapt the organization to the purposes and shapes of productivity improvement programs.*

NATURE OF ORGANIZATIONAL DEVELOPMENT

As mentioned earlier, a change in organization for no purpose or for the purpose of change alone is not only meaningless but harmful. Continuity and stability of administration naturally outweigh any urge to change except for purposeful and directed improvement.

Changing organizations for the purpose of improvement, however, must adhere to specific guidelines and move toward prescribed goals. Such guidelines must be well researched and planned, and decisions authorizing their implementation soundly made. Harry More emphasizes that management intervention in organization must follow an action pattern.[35] Such a pattern must consist of, (a) preliminary diagnosis, (b) data gathering from the client group, (c) data feedback to the client group, (d) data exploration, (e) action planning, and (f) implementation. Because of this required action, More states that organizational development is frequently described as "organizational development through action research".

Organizational development, especially as presented by More, emphasizes collaborative management. In his analysis he stressed that management must be collaborative in the sense of not being hierarchically imposed from above but "owned as much by the subordinate as it is by the leader".[36] The key unit in organization development activities, More further emphasized, is the ongoing *work team,*

32. *Ibid.*, p. 225.

33. Paul M. Whisenand and R. Fred Ferguson, *The Managing of Police Organizations,* (Englewood Cliffs, New Jersey: Prentice-Hall, Inc.), 1973, pp. 415–416.

34. Marvin R. Weisbord, "What, Not Again! Manage People Better", *Think,* p. 2.

35. Harry W. More, Jr., *op. cit.*, p. 228.

36. *Ibid.*

which includes both superior and subordinates. They may be colleague or peer teams, such as found in the middle managers level. They may be technical teams such as the personnel group or a data processing team. They may be task forces consisting of members from a variety of functions (e.g. traffic enforcement, data processing, and planning). One major characteristic, however, must be emphasized: the temporal nature of these teams functioning in *ad hoc* groups. Such groups are temporary forums comprised of organic rather than the usual formal units. They grow out of need to collaboratively manage the productivity improvement program and its component problem-solving processes, rather than from static situations which always prevail.

The role of leadership in organizational development is not only unique but also most influential. While it is considered more of a "first among equals" in the *ad hoc* forum, leadership inspires these teams and constantly furnishes them with direction, sense of purpose, vision, and—above all—dedication. Effective leadership can maintain focus on the issues involved in the problem at hand and prevent its dilution into self-serving discussions or damaging criticism.

While organizational development does not have to begin at the top of the management ladder, administrative realities indicate they usually do. A recent survey by the National Industrial Conference Board found that approximately half of the OD efforts studied had been initiated by corporate presidents or board chairmen. In other organizations, "early OD experimenting and risk-taking was done by managers not much further down the hierarchy".[37]
While, idealistically, every member of an organization can and must participate in organizational development, the fact of the matter remains that workers are unique individuals, and their level of motivation, performance, and dedication vary from one to another and from one period of time to the other. Effective managers, on the other hand, who are responsible for the whole project cannot afford to sit by and relax. The success of the program relies on their constant watchfulness and readiness to intervene.

DYNAMICS OF ORGANIZATIONAL DEVELOPMENT

For any productivity improvement program to be successful, an effective organizational development plan must precede. Agency machinery, must be fully mobilized, its mentality "psyched up", and teams synchronized. The following concepts explain the basic dynamics by which this can be done effectively:

1 —Systems interaction. Through interaction, systems and subsystems of the organization can be fully activated. All units of

37. *Ibid.*, p. 238.

the police departments are interrelated and form a solid whole. When one part of the department is indifferent, disinterested, or antagonistic to the productivity plan, the capability of the whole department is seriously affected and reduced.

2 —Problem-solving interdependence. Members of the police department must be concerned and willing to join forces to fend off problems which face their department regardless of whether they personally or as groups win or lose. In this situation policemen and groups have a common stake in the productivity outcome, the achievement of which will have a gratifying effect on all of them. Treating interdependent problems as if they are independent usually leads to resistance to change, intradepartmental competition, jealousy, conflicting action, and possibly sabotage.

3 —Teamwork. Unless an attitude of teamwork develops and prevails, organizational development—and therefore productivity— will not work effectively. A team may be defined *as a group of individuals who hold a common purpose and who communicate effectively and share their knowledge and experience to achieve that purpose.*

As such, common purpose is the glue that holds the team together and provides the focus and direction to its function. Effective communication, collaboration, and pooling of knowledge and experience produce the transactional process out of which evolves a totality that is greater than the output by any individual working alone.

4 —Force interaction. The old Greek logic emphasized that each and every topic has a thesis and an antithesis (an opposite thesis). The result of openly debating these would result in a synthesis (a compromising thesis), which, in turn, would become a thesis by itself and trigger an antithesis and further develop another synthesis. Applying this logic to productivity improvement is not only helpful but necessary. It keeps elevating the level of conceptual thinking and promotes articulation of views to perfection. The effective manager must, therefore, keep presenting subjects for open debate, promote controversy, and synthesize ideas. By so doing, negative forces would not be neutralized or suppressed but exposed to the other dimensions involved and the limitations on the options proposed. One warning, however, has to be mentioned: unless the leadership in charge is "secure and mature", the Greek logic would fail, and the concept of force interaction would boil down to a power struggle fueled with factionalism, and selfishness. The first victim of such a situation will naturally be the leadership group. A not-too-distant second would be the department itself. The invisible victim, of course, is the public interest.

5 —Optimism. Research indicates that work climate affects the kind of results that individuals, groups, and organizations pro-

duce. An optimistic climate fostered by a productive mentality and a collaborative leadership can turn doubt into confidence, negative attitudes into support, and skepticism into a willingness to try. Optimism reflects cheerfulness, reinforces personnel motivation and eases the tension of risk-taking.

Possibilities of productivity improvement in the police are virtually unlimited. Areas of improvement encompass every aspect of police activity: patrol, criminal investigation, community relations, public security, traffic, training, budgeting, and planning. Improvement, however, must rely on a dynamic organizational development capability which can turn ideas into plans and plans into action. Without such a capability, police managers might have a lot of mute ideas which they are unable to translate into tangible action. Only effective managers can combine improvement ideas and organizational action and produce meaningful results.

*

INDEX